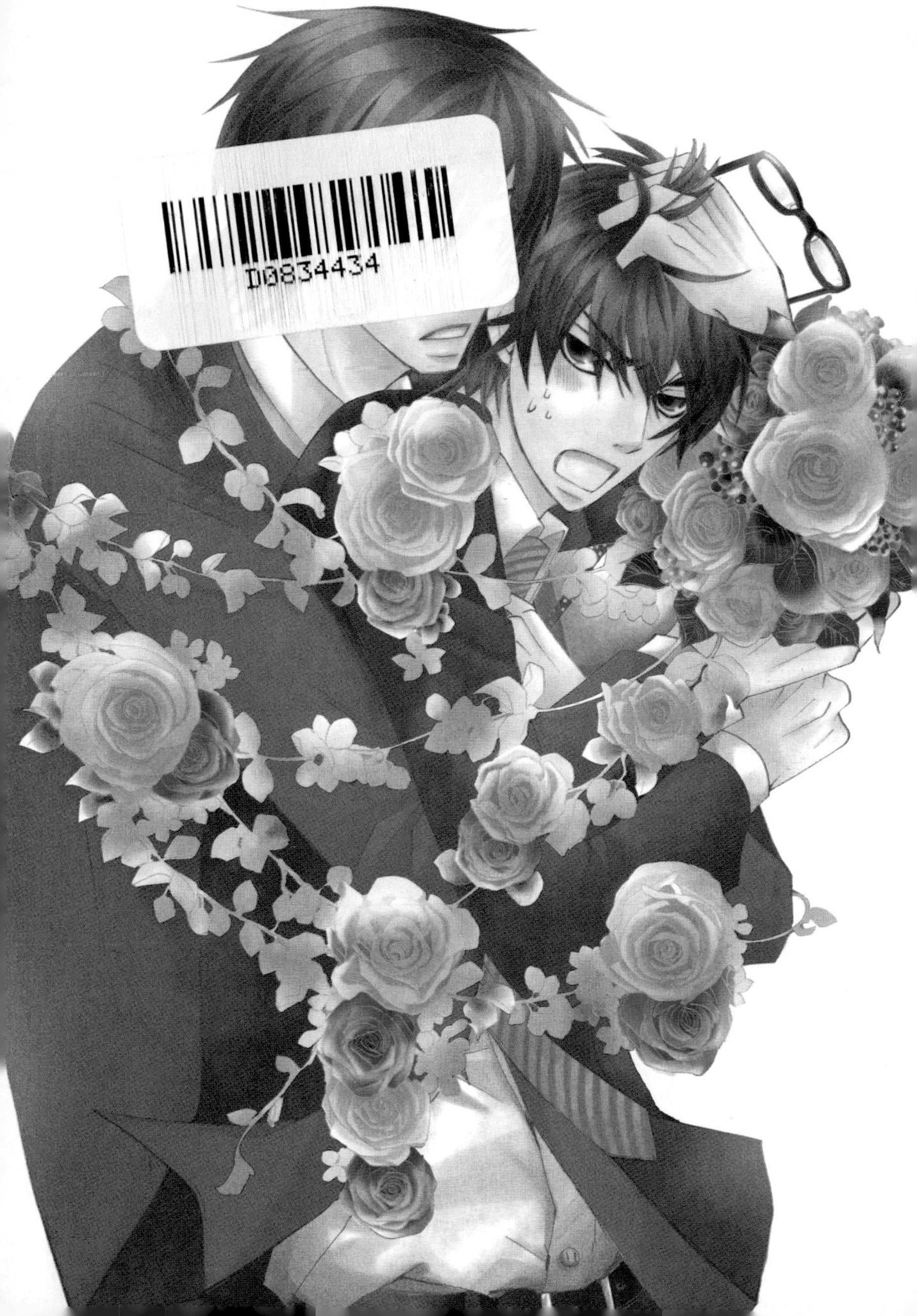

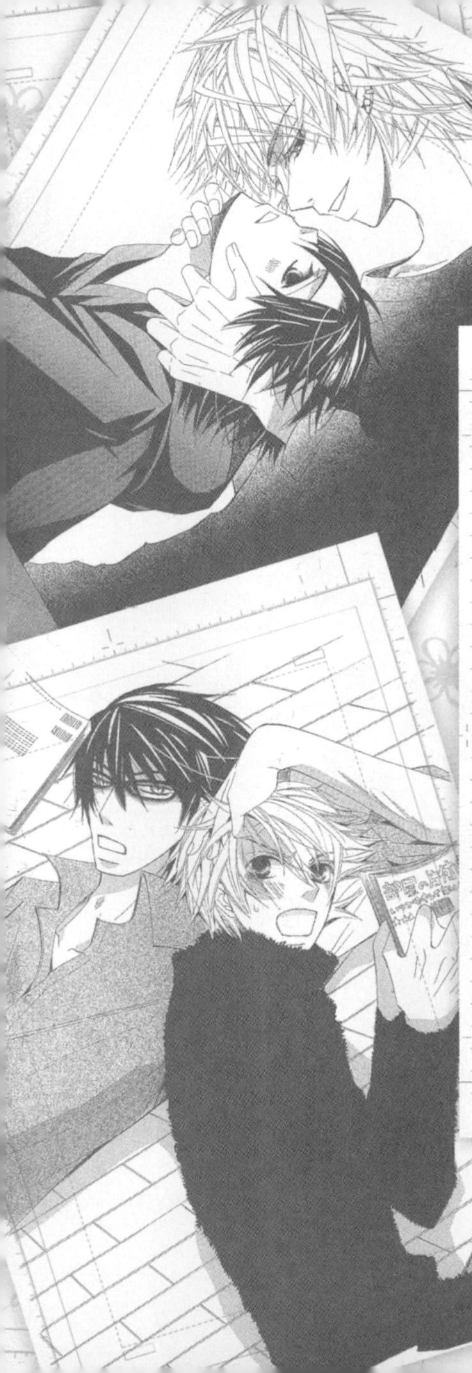

The World's Greatest First Love

The Case of Ritsu Onodera 4

Contents

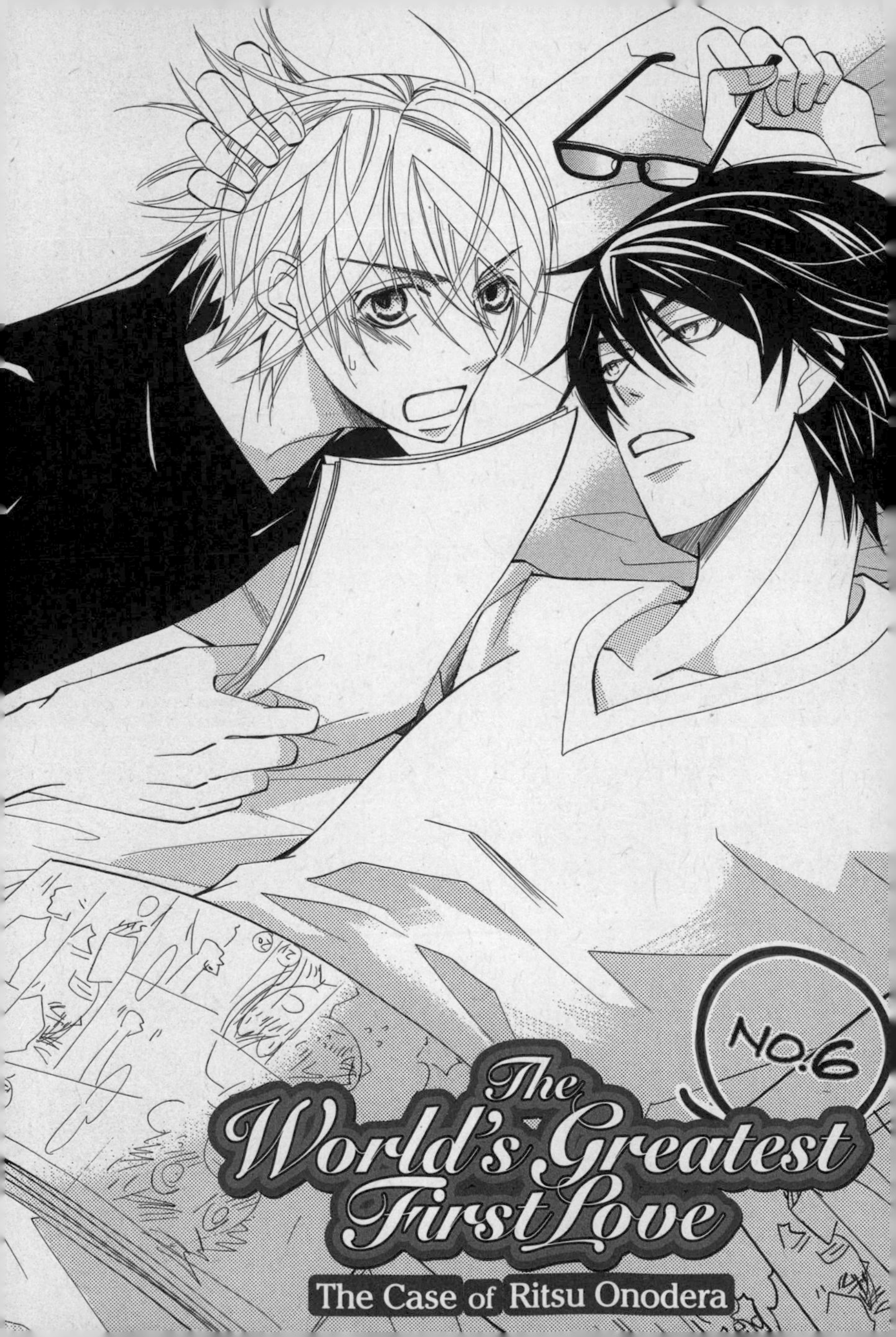
NO.6
The World's Greatest First Love
The Case of Ritsu Onodera

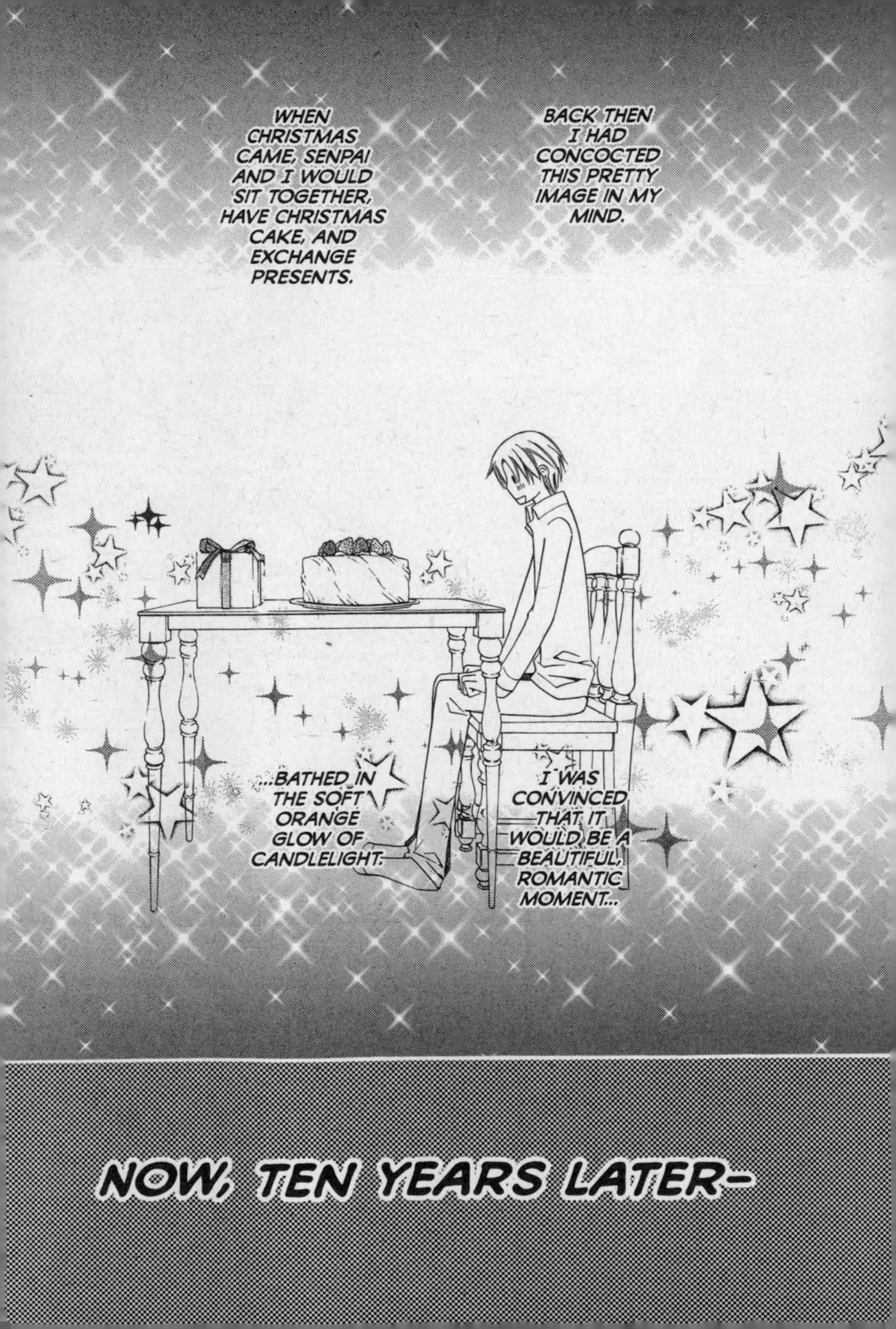
BACK THEN I HAD CONCOCTED THIS PRETTY IMAGE IN MY MIND.
WHEN CHRISTMAS CAME, SENPAI AND I WOULD SIT TOGETHER, HAVE CHRISTMAS CAKE, AND EXCHANGE PRESENTS.
I WAS CONVINCED THAT IT WOULD BE A BEAUTIFUL, ROMANTIC MOMENT...
...BATHED IN THE SOFT ORANGE GLOW OF CANDLELIGHT.
NOW, TEN YEARS LATER-

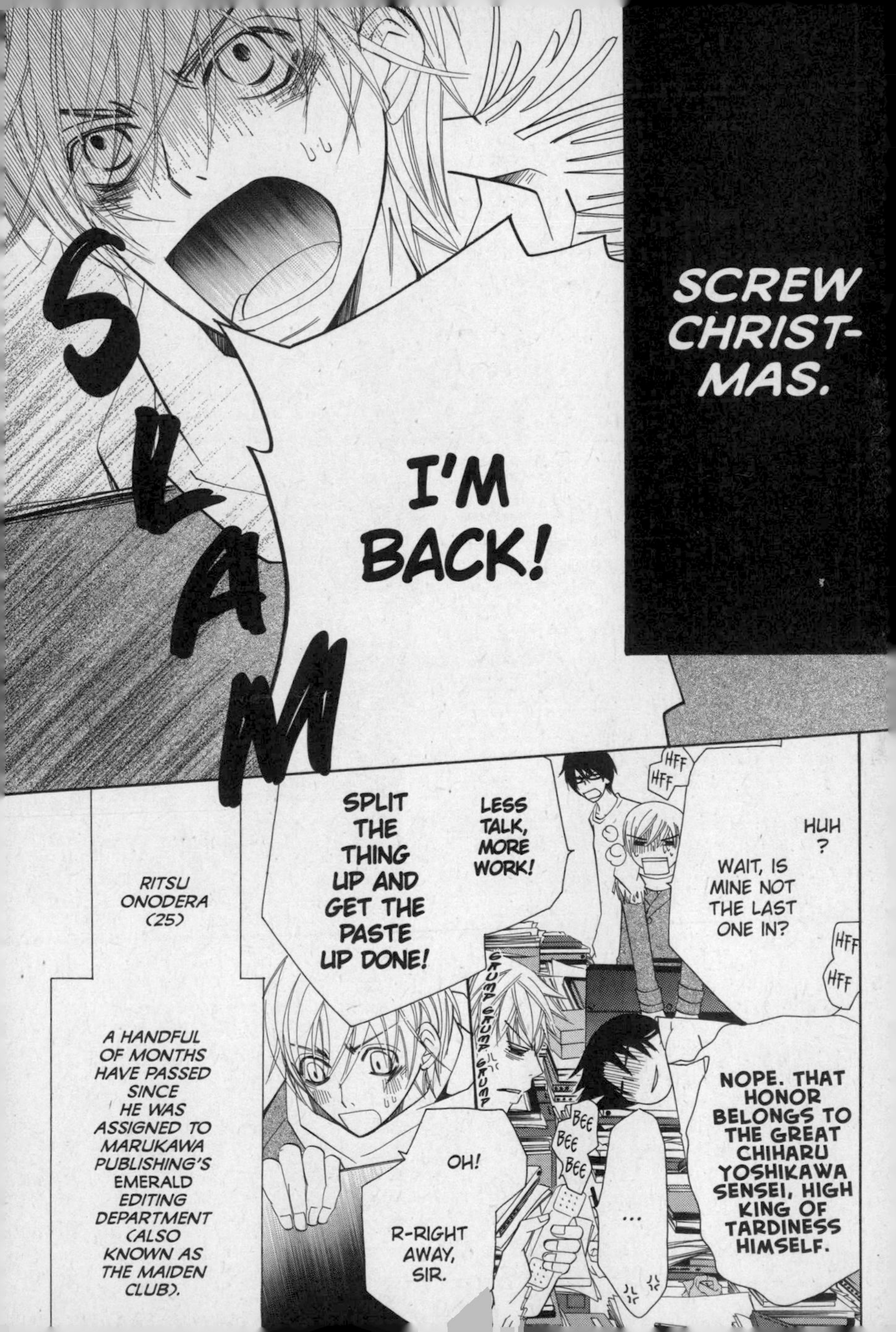
SCREW CHRIST-MAS.
I'M BACK!
SLAM
HFF HFF
HUH?
WAIT, IS MINE NOT THE LAST ONE IN?
HFF HFF
LESS TALK, MORE WORK!
SPLIT THE THING UP AND GET THE PASTE UP DONE!
GRUMP GRUMP GRUMP GRUMP
NOPE. THAT HONOR BELONGS TO THE GREAT CHIHARU YOSHIKAWA SENSEI, HIGH KING OF TARDINESS HIMSELF.
BEE BEE BEE
...
OH!
R-RIGHT AWAY, SIR.
RITSU ONODERA (25)
A HANDFUL OF MONTHS HAVE PASSED SINCE HE WAS ASSIGNED TO MARUKAWA PUBLISHING'S EMERALD EDITING DEPARTMENT (ALSO KNOWN AS THE MAIDEN CLUB).

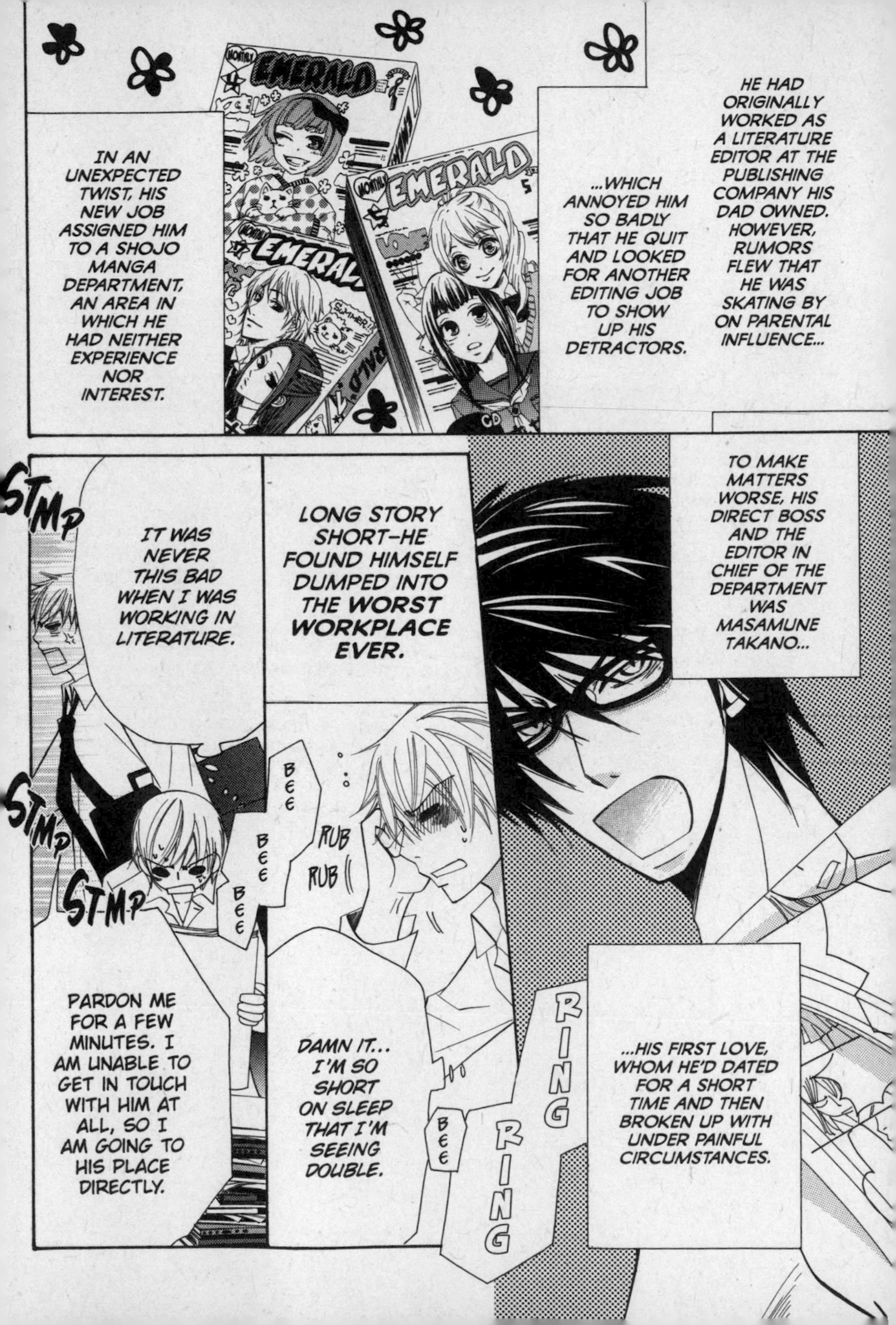
HE HAD ORIGINALLY WORKED AS A LITERATURE EDITOR AT THE PUBLISHING COMPANY HIS DAD OWNED. HOWEVER, RUMORS FLEW THAT HE WAS SKATING BY ON PARENTAL INFLUENCE...
...WHICH ANNOYED HIM SO BADLY THAT HE QUIT AND LOOKED FOR ANOTHER EDITING JOB TO SHOW UP HIS DETRACTORS.
EMERALD
EMERALD
EMERALD
IN AN UNEXPECTED TWIST, HIS NEW JOB ASSIGNED HIM TO A SHOJO MANGA DEPARTMENT, AN AREA IN WHICH HE HAD NEITHER EXPERIENCE NOR INTEREST.
TO MAKE MATTERS WORSE, HIS DIRECT BOSS AND THE EDITOR IN CHIEF OF THE DEPARTMENT WAS MASAMUNE TAKANO...
RING
RING
...HIS FIRST LOVE, WHOM HE'D DATED FOR A SHORT TIME AND THEN BROKEN UP WITH UNDER PAINFUL CIRCUMSTANCES.
LONG STORY SHORT—HE FOUND HIMSELF DUMPED INTO THE **WORST WORKPLACE EVER.**
BEE
BEE
BEE
RUB
RUB
DAMN IT... I'M SO SHORT ON SLEEP THAT I'M SEEING DOUBLE.
BEE
STMP
IT WAS NEVER THIS BAD WHEN I WAS WORKING IN LITERATURE.
STMP
ST-M-P
PARDON ME FOR A FEW MINUTES. I AM UNABLE TO GET IN TOUCH WITH HIM AT ALL, SO I AM GOING TO HIS PLACE DIRECTLY.

DECEMBER

			26	29
28	29	30	31	

↓

JANUARY

1	2	3	4
5			

BASICALLY, MANY PRINTERS CLOSE DOWN FOR A FEW WEEKS RIGHT AROUND THE NEW YEAR.

THUS, THE STANDARD MONTHLY DEADLINES NEED TO BE PUSHED UP TO ACCOMMODATE.

...WORKS OUT LIKE SO.

THE YEAR-END SCHEDULE...

SCREW YOU, YEAR-END!

AAAUGH!

MAYBE THEY'RE PERFORMING?

TO BE HONEST, I HEARD FROM OTHER CREATORS THAT THEY WERE HAVING TROUBLE PINNING DOWN THEIR ASSISTANTS TOO.

FOR SIMILAR REASONS...

NOT ONLY THAT...

WHAT?

YOU CAN'T GET AHOLD OF YOUR ASSISTANTS?

ARE THEY ALL SICK?

NO? THEY'RE TAKING PART IN A WINTER FESTIVAL?

REALLY?

RIP RIP RIP

UM, I'LL ASK AROUND AND SEE WHAT I CAN DO.

WHY? THAT'S EASY.

WHY DO WE HAVE TO GO THROUGH THIS EVERY YEAR?!

AUGH! I CAN'T TAKE IT ANYMORE!

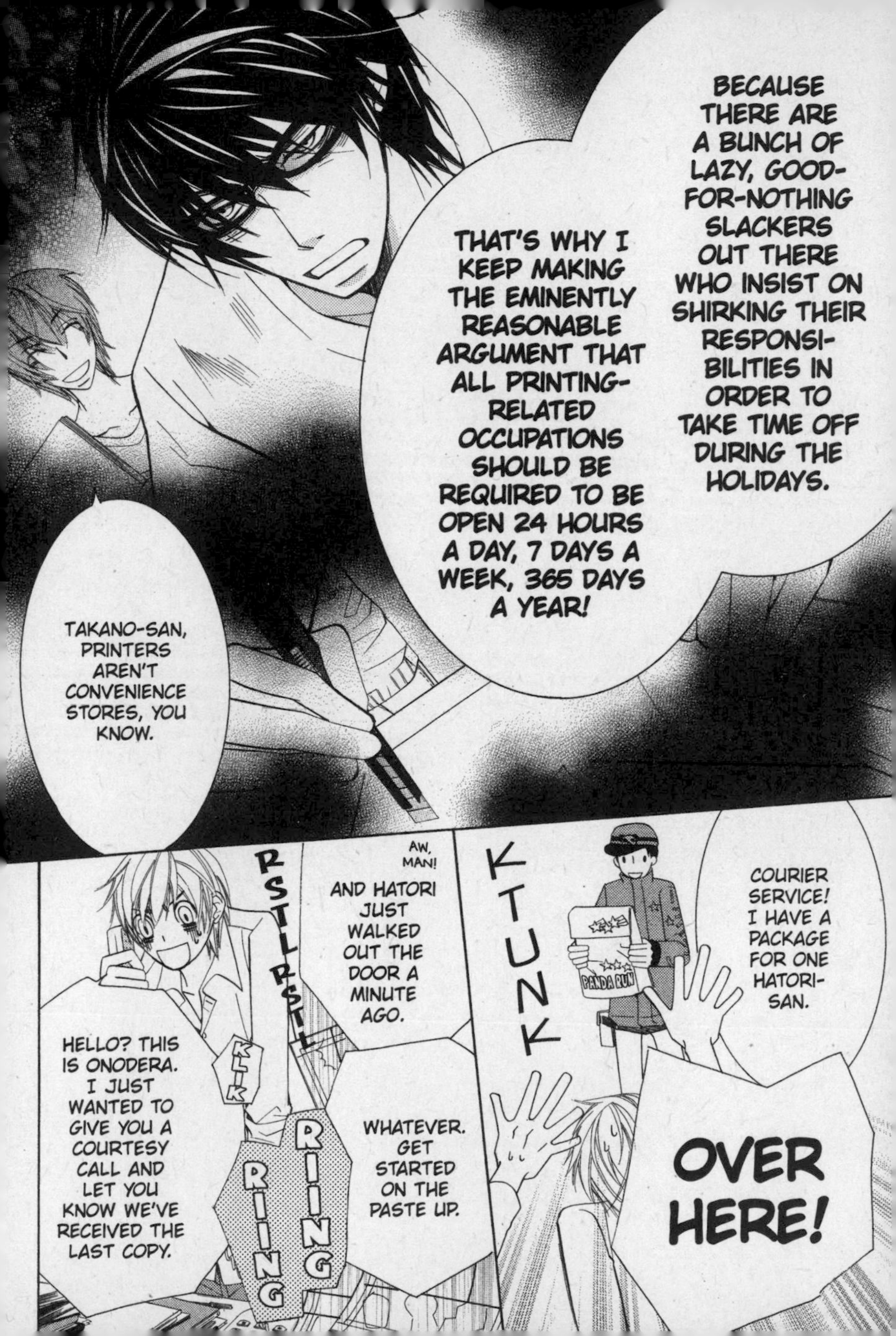
BECAUSE THERE ARE A BUNCH OF LAZY, GOOD-FOR-NOTHING SLACKERS OUT THERE WHO INSIST ON SHIRKING THEIR RESPONSI-BILITIES IN ORDER TO TAKE TIME OFF DURING THE HOLIDAYS.
THAT'S WHY I KEEP MAKING THE EMINENTLY REASONABLE ARGUMENT THAT ALL PRINTING-RELATED OCCUPATIONS SHOULD BE REQUIRED TO BE OPEN 24 HOURS A DAY, 7 DAYS A WEEK, 365 DAYS A YEAR!
TAKANO-SAN, PRINTERS AREN'T CONVENIENCE STORES, YOU KNOW.
COURIER SERVICE! I HAVE A PACKAGE FOR ONE HATORI-SAN.
PANDA RUN
OVER HERE!
KTUNK
AW, MAN!
AND HATORI JUST WALKED OUT THE DOOR A MINUTE AGO.
RSTL RSTL
WHATEVER. GET STARTED ON THE PASTE UP.
HELLO? THIS IS ONODERA. I JUST WANTED TO GIVE YOU A COURTESY CALL AND LET YOU KNOW WE'VE RECEIVED THE LAST COPY.
KLIK
RIIING
RIIING

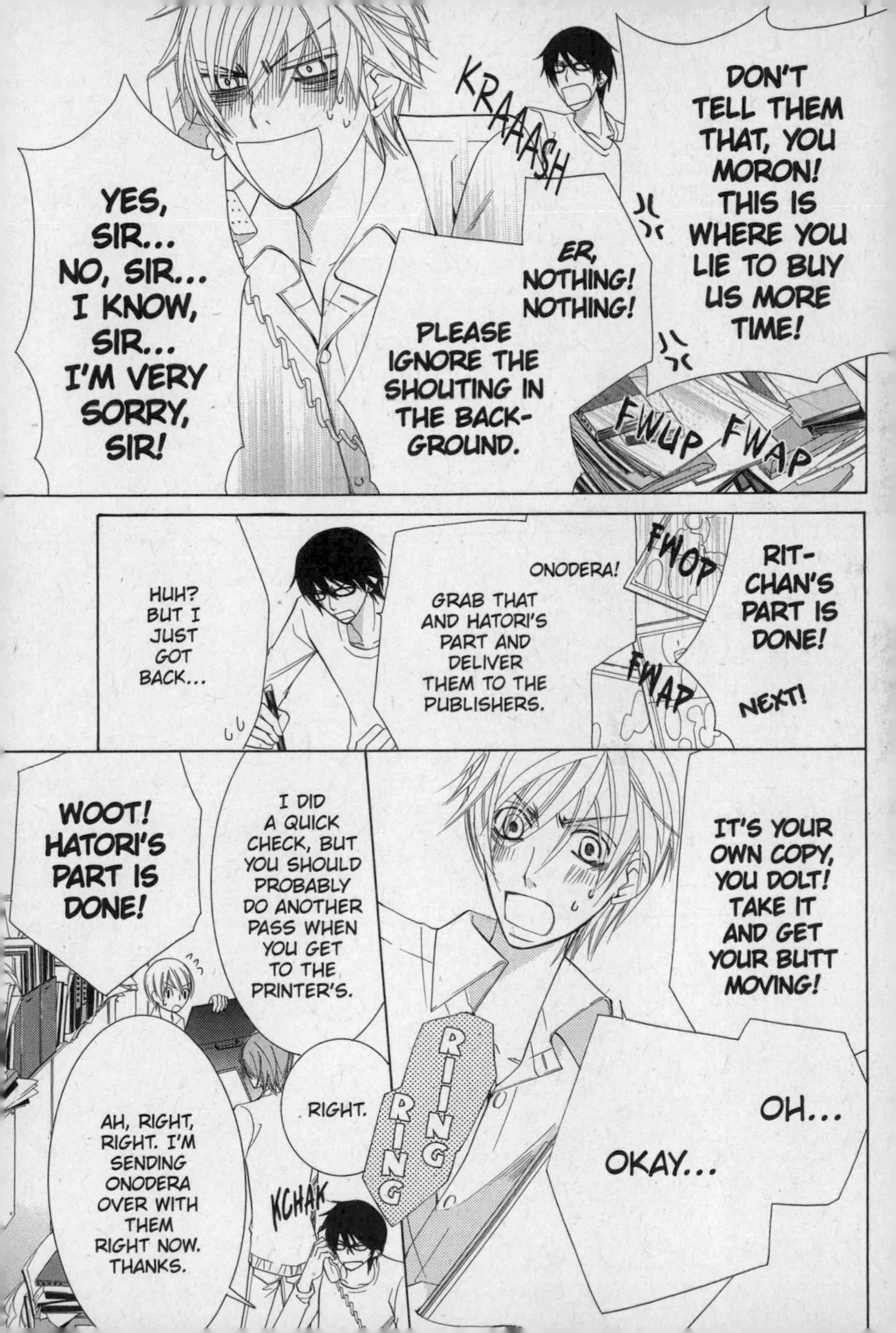
DON'T TELL THEM THAT, YOU MORON! THIS IS WHERE YOU LIE TO BUY US MORE TIME!
KRAAASH
ER, NOTHING! NOTHING!
PLEASE IGNORE THE SHOUTING IN THE BACK-GROUND.
YES, SIR... NO, SIR... I KNOW, SIR... I'M VERY SORRY, SIR!
FWUP FWAP
RIT-CHAN'S PART IS DONE!
NEXT!
FWOP
FWAP
ONODERA!
GRAB THAT AND HATORI'S PART AND DELIVER THEM TO THE PUBLISHERS.
HUH? BUT I JUST GOT BACK...
IT'S YOUR OWN COPY, YOU DOLT! TAKE IT AND GET YOUR BUTT MOVING!
OH...
OKAY...
I DID A QUICK CHECK, BUT YOU SHOULD PROBABLY DO ANOTHER PASS WHEN YOU GET TO THE PRINTER'S.
RIING RING
RIGHT.
WOOT! HATORI'S PART IS DONE!
KCHAK
AH, RIGHT, RIGHT. I'M SENDING ONODERA OVER WITH THEM RIGHT NOW. THANKS.

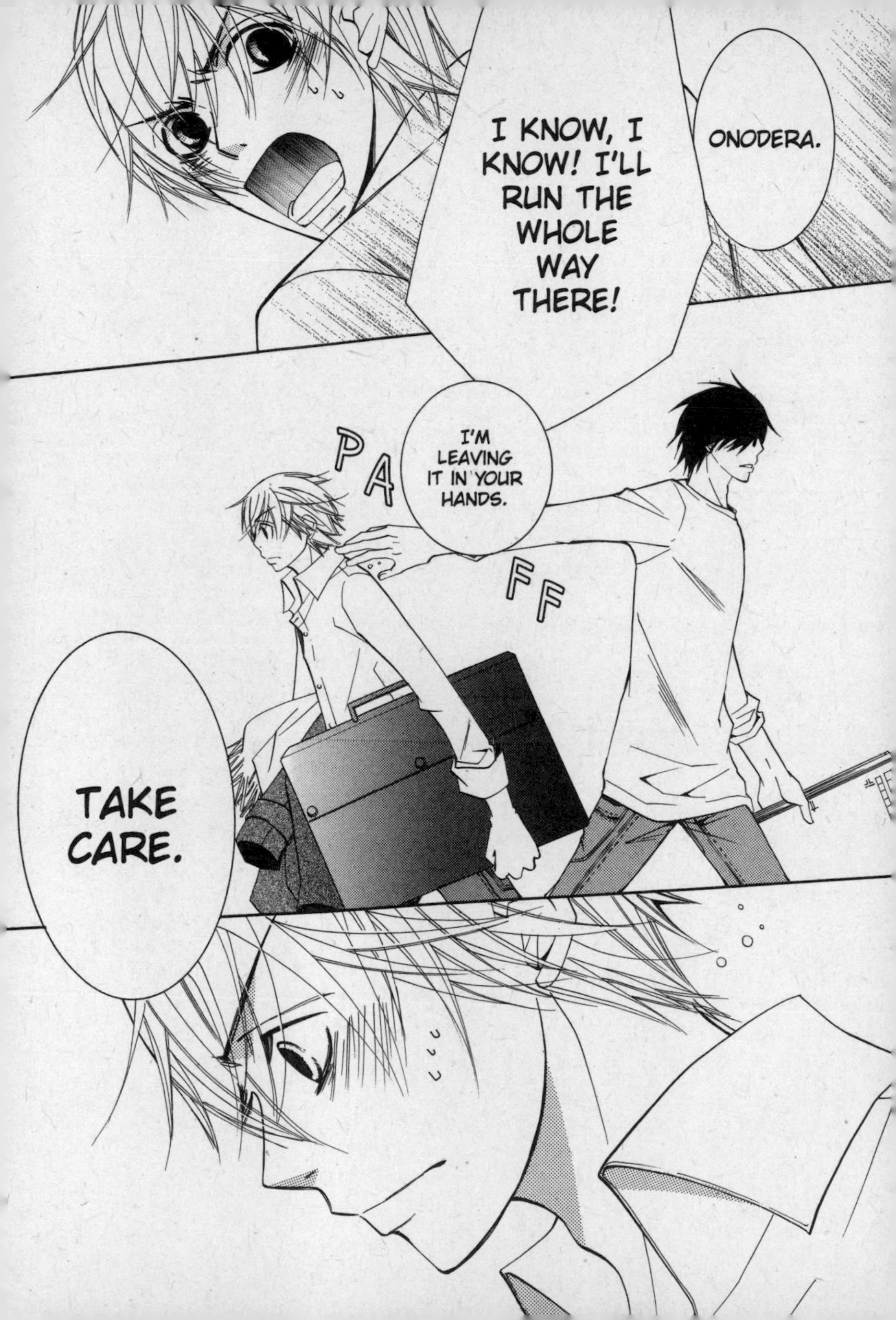
ONODERA.
I KNOW, I KNOW! I'LL RUN THE WHOLE WAY THERE!
I'M LEAVING IT IN YOUR HANDS.
PAFF
TAKE CARE.

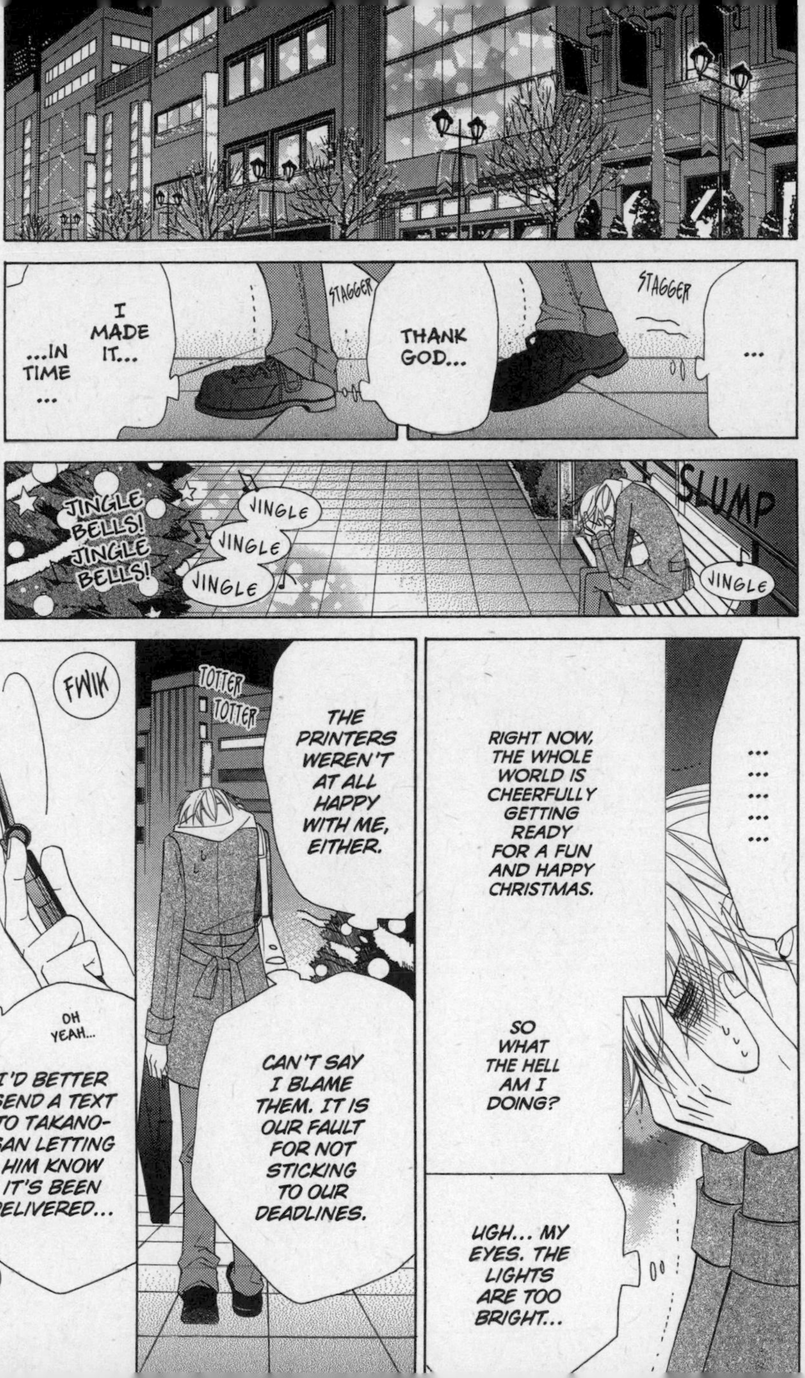
...
STAGGER
THANK GOD...
STAGGER
I MADE IT...
...IN TIME...
SLUMP
JINGLE
JINGLE
JINGLE
JINGLE
JINGLE BELLS! JINGLE BELLS!
.....
RIGHT NOW, THE WHOLE WORLD IS CHEERFULLY GETTING READY FOR A FUN AND HAPPY CHRISTMAS.
SO WHAT THE HELL AM I DOING?
UGH... MY EYES. THE LIGHTS ARE TOO BRIGHT...
TOTTER TOTTER
THE PRINTERS WEREN'T AT ALL HAPPY WITH ME, EITHER.
CAN'T SAY I BLAME THEM. IT IS OUR FAULT FOR NOT STICKING TO OUR DEADLINES.
FWIK
OH YEAH...
I'D BETTER SEND A TEXT TO TAKANO-SAN LETTING HIM KNOW IT'S BEEN DELIVERED...
BIP
BIP

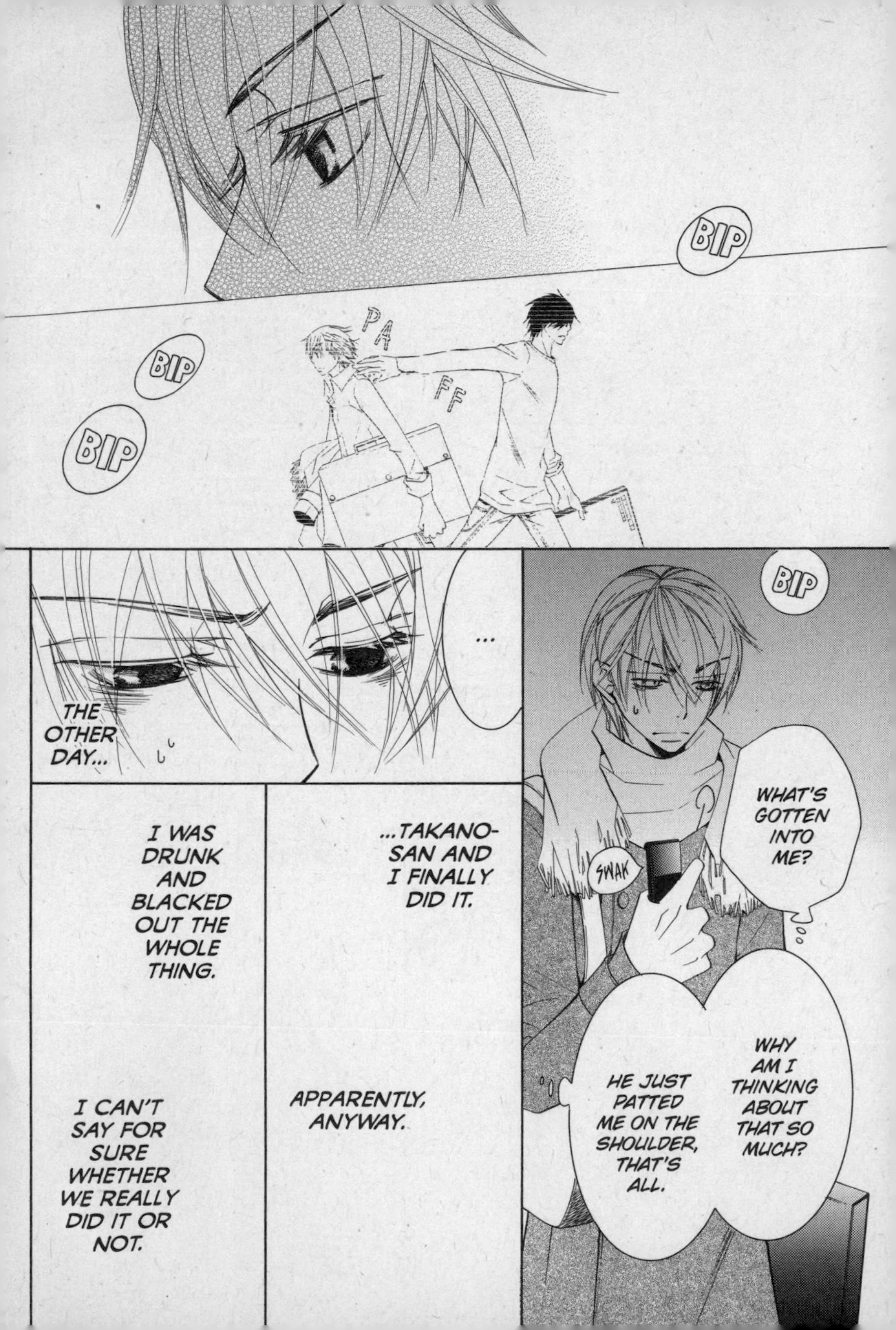
BIP
PAFF
BIP
BIP
BIP
SWAK
WHAT'S GOTTEN INTO ME?
WHY AM I THINKING ABOUT THAT SO MUCH?
HE JUST PATTED ME ON THE SHOULDER, THAT'S ALL.
...
THE OTHER DAY...
...TAKANO-SAN AND I FINALLY DID IT.
APPARENTLY, ANYWAY.
I WAS DRUNK AND BLACKED OUT THE WHOLE THING.
I CAN'T SAY FOR SURE WHETHER WE REALLY DID IT OR NOT.

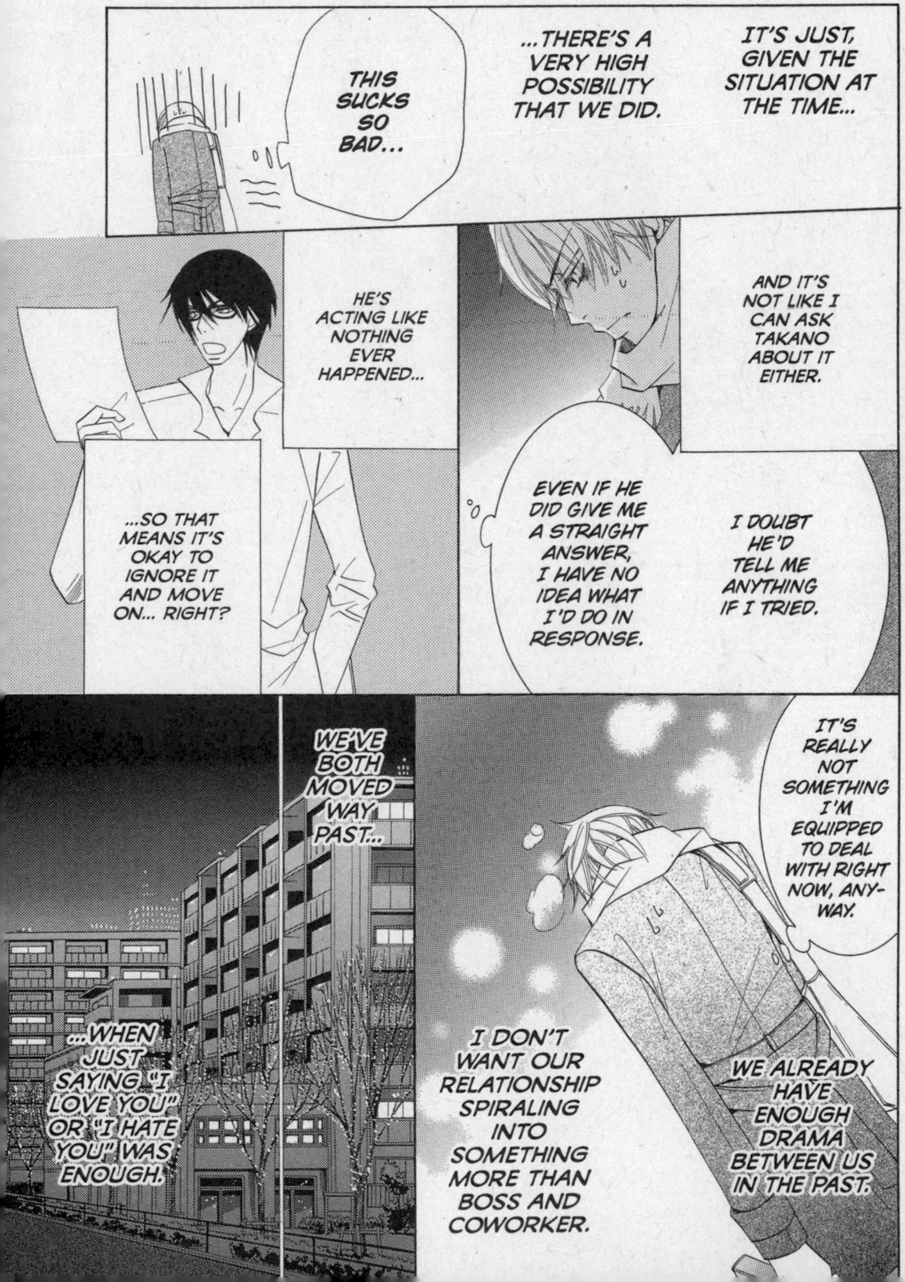
IT'S JUST, GIVEN THE SITUATION AT THE TIME...
...THERE'S A VERY HIGH POSSIBILITY THAT WE DID.
THIS SUCKS SO BAD...
AND IT'S NOT LIKE I CAN ASK TAKANO ABOUT IT EITHER.
I DOUBT HE'D TELL ME ANYTHING IF I TRIED.
EVEN IF HE DID GIVE ME A STRAIGHT ANSWER, I HAVE NO IDEA WHAT I'D DO IN RESPONSE.
HE'S ACTING LIKE NOTHING EVER HAPPENED...
...SO THAT MEANS IT'S OKAY TO IGNORE IT AND MOVE ON... RIGHT?
IT'S REALLY NOT SOMETHING I'M EQUIPPED TO DEAL WITH RIGHT NOW, ANYWAY.
WE ALREADY HAVE ENOUGH DRAMA BETWEEN US IN THE PAST.
I DON'T WANT OUR RELATIONSHIP SPIRALING INTO SOMETHING MORE THAN BOSS AND COWORKER.
WE'VE BOTH MOVED WAY PAST...
...WHEN JUST SAYING "I LOVE YOU" OR "I HATE YOU" WAS ENOUGH.

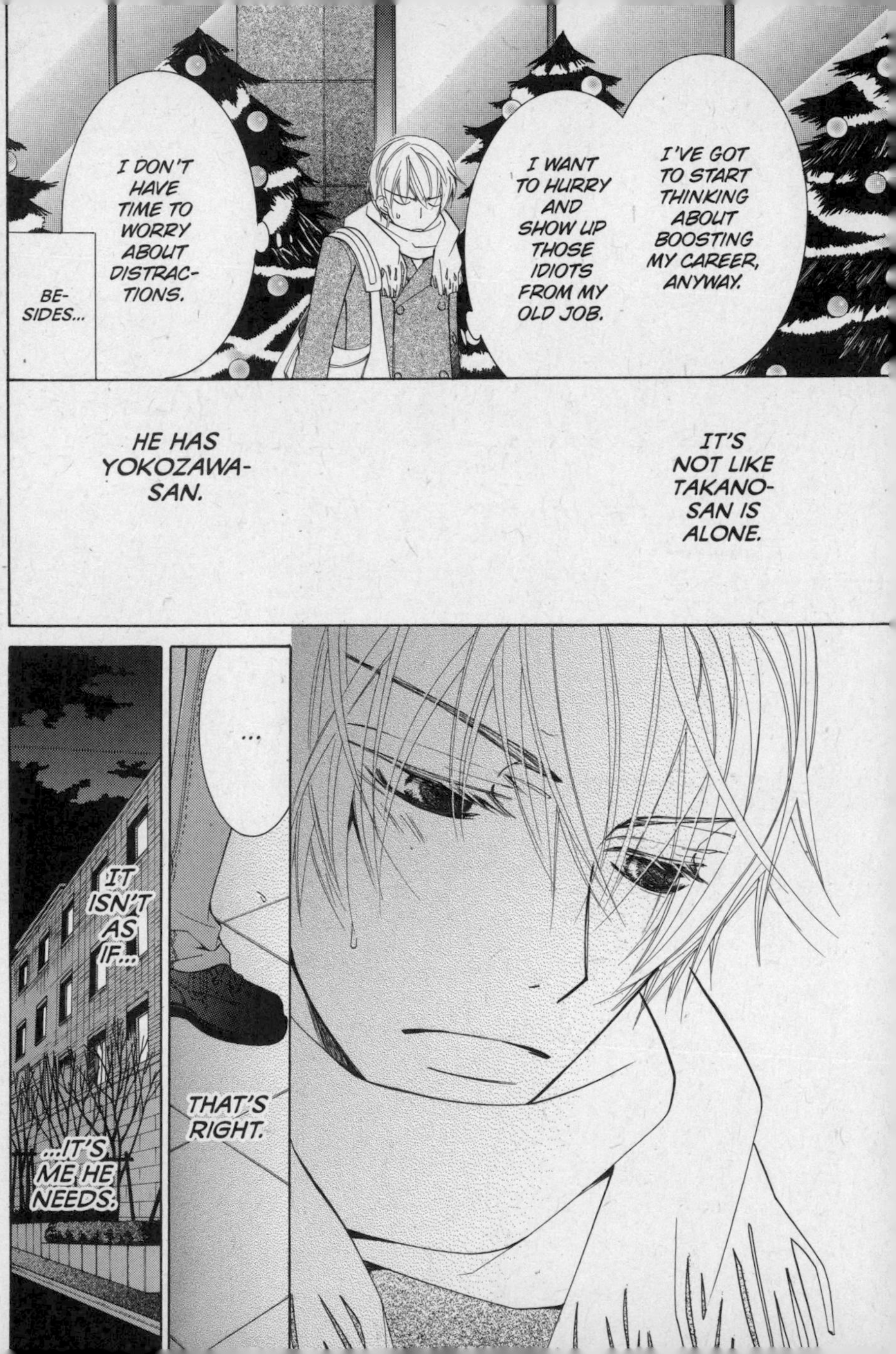
I'VE GOT TO START THINKING ABOUT BOOSTING MY CAREER, ANYWAY.
I WANT TO HURRY AND SHOW UP THOSE IDIOTS FROM MY OLD JOB.
I DON'T HAVE TIME TO WORRY ABOUT DISTRACTIONS.
BE-SIDES...
IT'S NOT LIKE TAKANO-SAN IS ALONE.
HE HAS YOKOZAWA-SAN.
...
THAT'S RIGHT.
IT ISN'T AS IF...
...IT'S ME HE NEEDS.

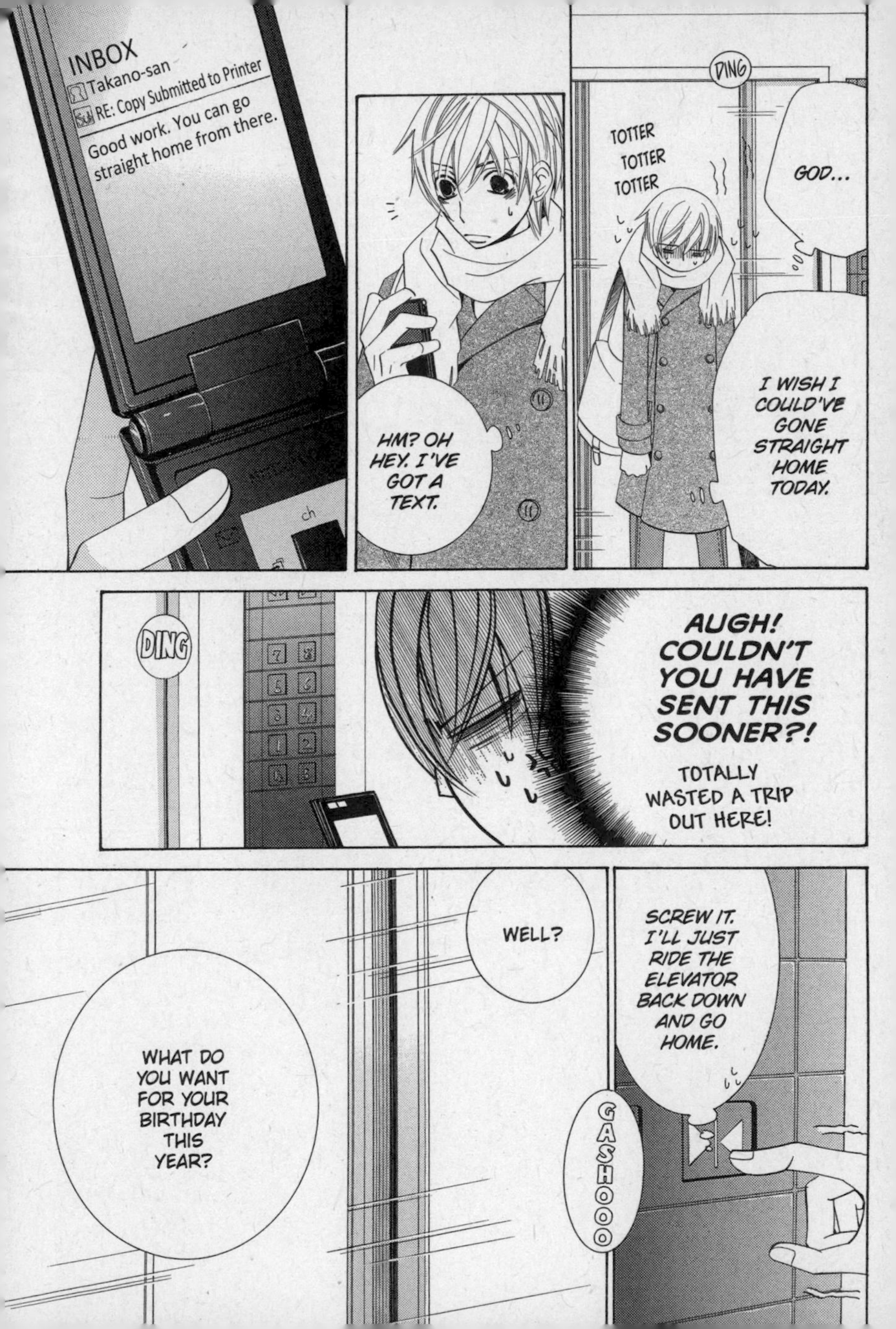
DING
TOTTER
TOTTER
TOTTER
GOD...
I WISH I COULD'VE GONE STRAIGHT HOME TODAY.
HM? OH HEY. I'VE GOT A TEXT.
INBOX
Takano-san
RE: Copy Submitted to Printer
Good work. You can go straight home from there.
DING
AUGH! COULDN'T YOU HAVE SENT THIS SOONER?!
TOTALLY WASTED A TRIP OUT HERE!
SCREW IT. I'LL JUST RIDE THE ELEVATOR BACK DOWN AND GO HOME.
GASHOOO
WELL?
WHAT DO YOU WANT FOR YOUR BIRTHDAY THIS YEAR?

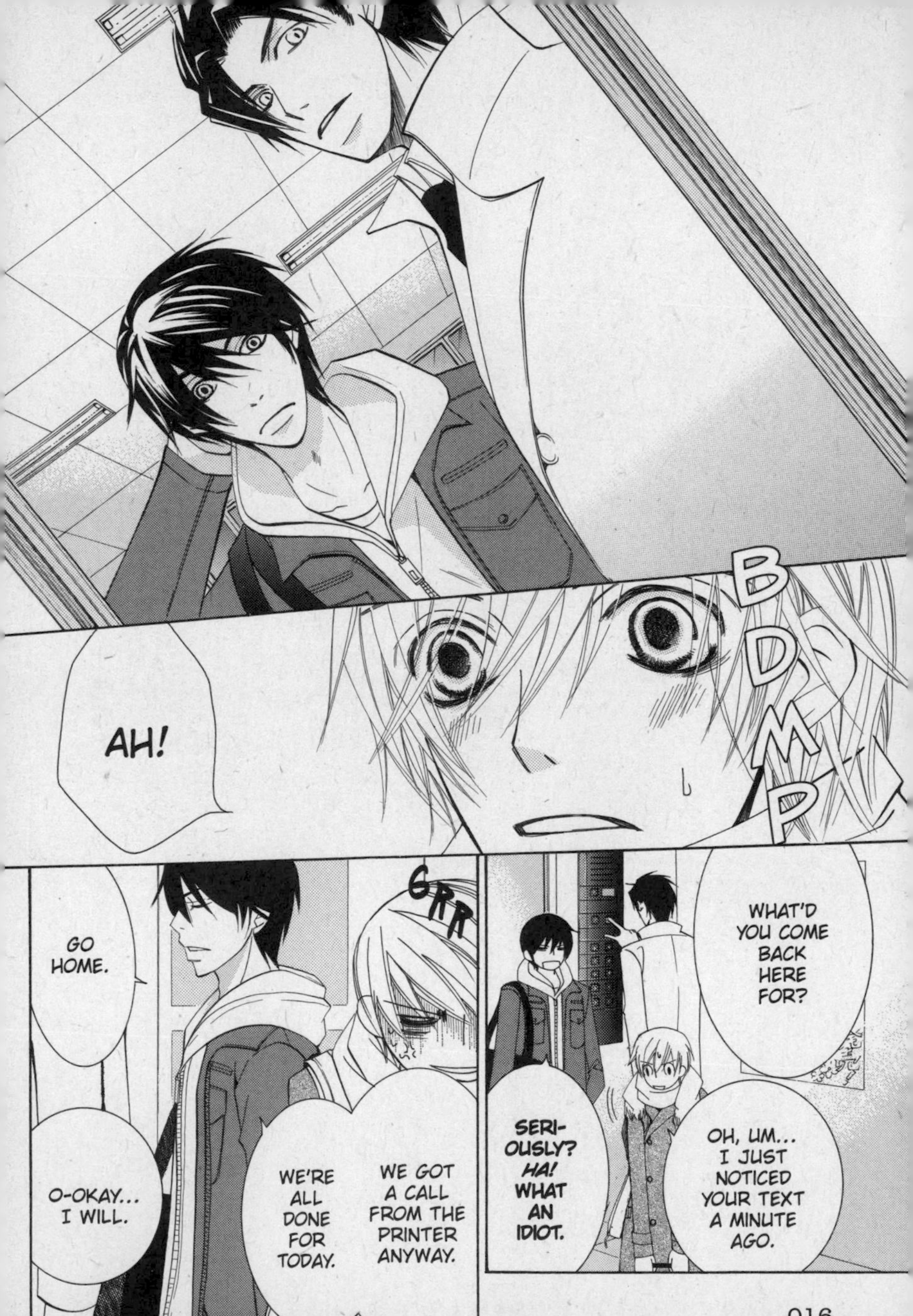
BDMP
AH!
WHAT'D YOU COME BACK HERE FOR?
OH, UM... I JUST NOTICED YOUR TEXT A MINUTE AGO.
SERI-OUSLY? *HA!* WHAT AN IDIOT.
GRR
GO HOME.
WE GOT A CALL FROM THE PRINTER ANYWAY.
WE'RE ALL DONE FOR TODAY.
O-OKAY... I WILL.

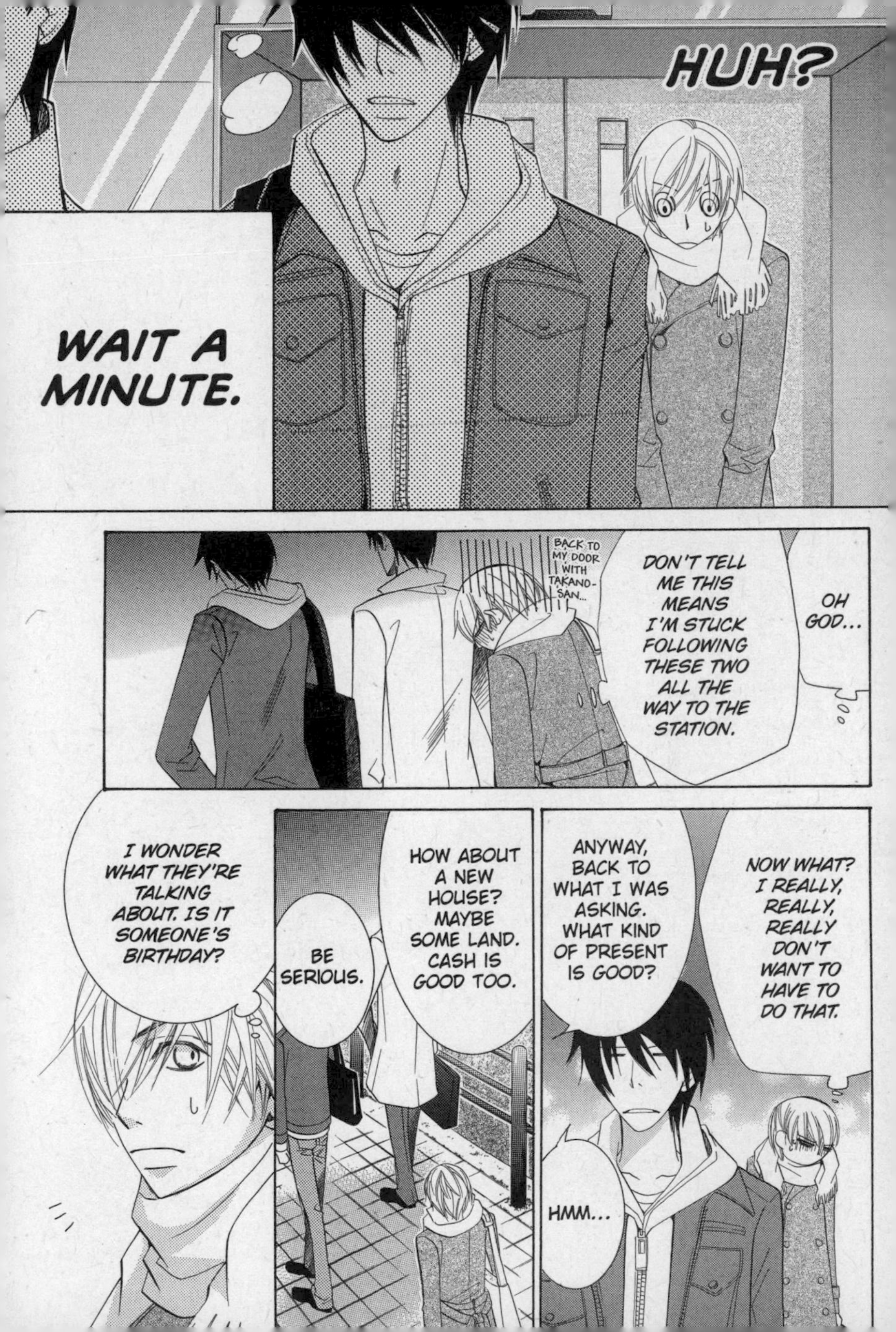
HUH?
WAIT A MINUTE.
OH GOD...
DON'T TELL ME THIS MEANS I'M STUCK FOLLOWING THESE TWO ALL THE WAY TO THE STATION.
BACK TO MY DOOR WITH TAKANO-SAN...
NOW WHAT? I REALLY, REALLY, REALLY DON'T WANT TO HAVE TO DO THAT.
ANYWAY, BACK TO WHAT I WAS ASKING. WHAT KIND OF PRESENT IS GOOD?
HMM...
HOW ABOUT A NEW HOUSE? MAYBE SOME LAND. CASH IS GOOD TOO.
BE SERIOUS.
I WONDER WHAT THEY'RE TALKING ABOUT. IS IT SOMEONE'S BIRTHDAY?

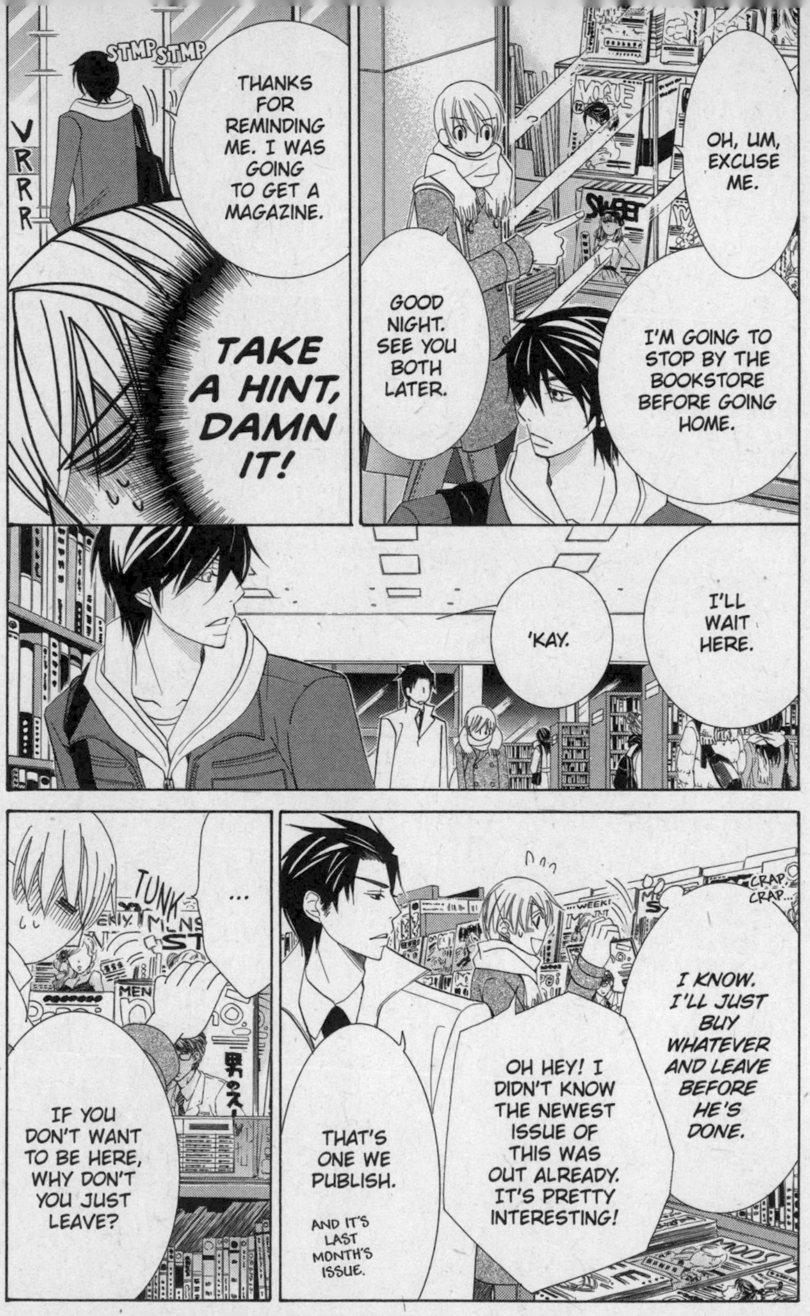
OH, UM, EXCUSE ME.
I'M GOING TO STOP BY THE BOOKSTORE BEFORE GOING HOME.
GOOD NIGHT. SEE YOU BOTH LATER.
STMP STMP
VRRR
THANKS FOR REMINDING ME. I WAS GOING TO GET A MAGAZINE.
TAKE A HINT, DAMN IT!
I'LL WAIT HERE.
'KAY.
CRAP, CRAP...
I KNOW. I'LL JUST BUY WHATEVER AND LEAVE BEFORE HE'S DONE.
OH HEY! I DIDN'T KNOW THE NEWEST ISSUE OF THIS WAS OUT ALREADY. IT'S PRETTY INTERESTING!
THAT'S ONE WE PUBLISH.
AND IT'S LAST MONTH'S ISSUE.
TUNK
...
IF YOU DON'T WANT TO BE HERE, WHY DON'T YOU JUST LEAVE?

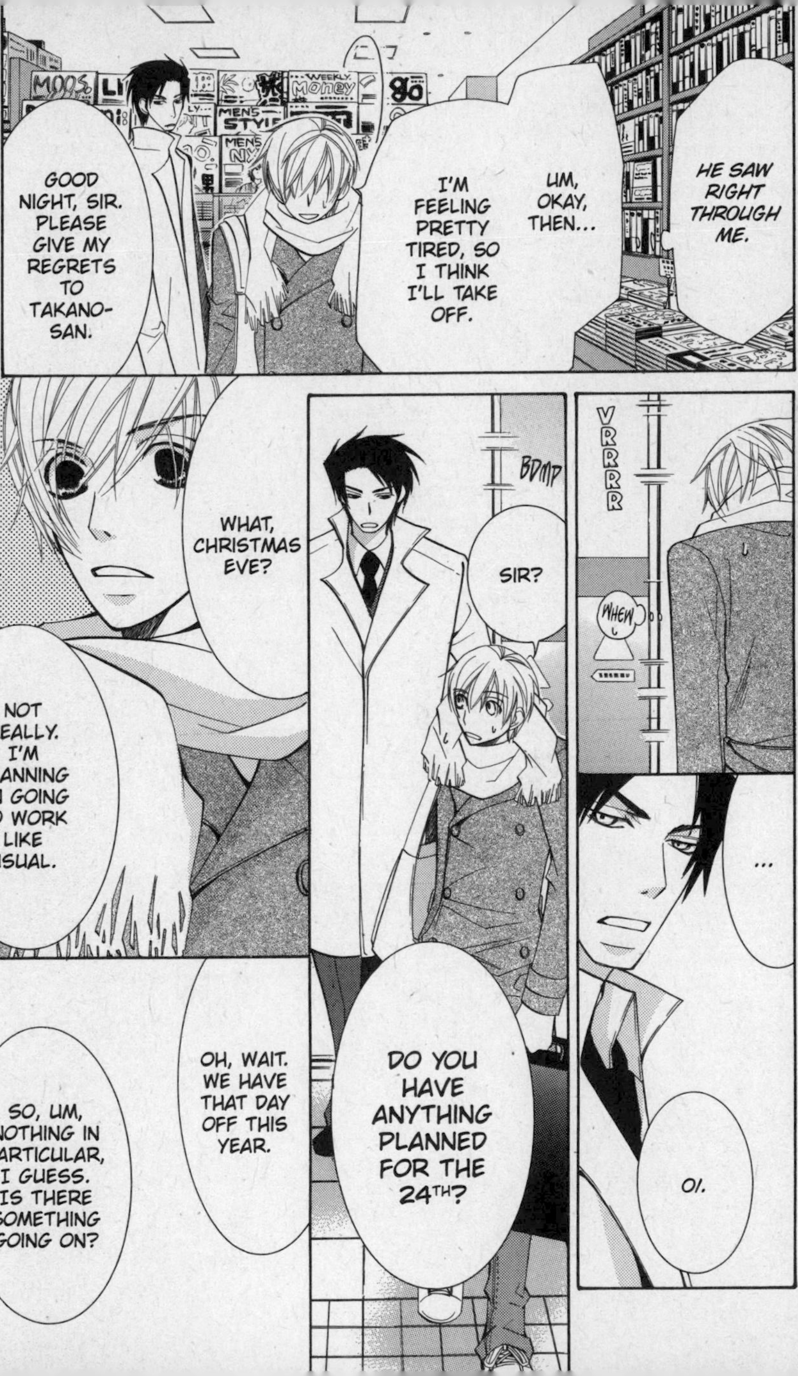

HE SAW RIGHT THROUGH ME.
UM, OKAY, THEN...
I'M FEELING PRETTY TIRED, SO I THINK I'LL TAKE OFF.
GOOD NIGHT, SIR. PLEASE GIVE MY REGRETS TO TAKANO-SAN.
VRRRR
WHEW
...
OI.
BDMP
SIR?
DO YOU HAVE ANYTHING PLANNED FOR THE 24TH?
WHAT, CHRISTMAS EVE?
NOT REALLY. I'M PLANNING ON GOING TO WORK LIKE USUAL.
OH, WAIT. WE HAVE THAT DAY OFF THIS YEAR.
SO, UM, NOTHING IN PARTICULAR, I GUESS. IS THERE SOMETHING GOING ON?

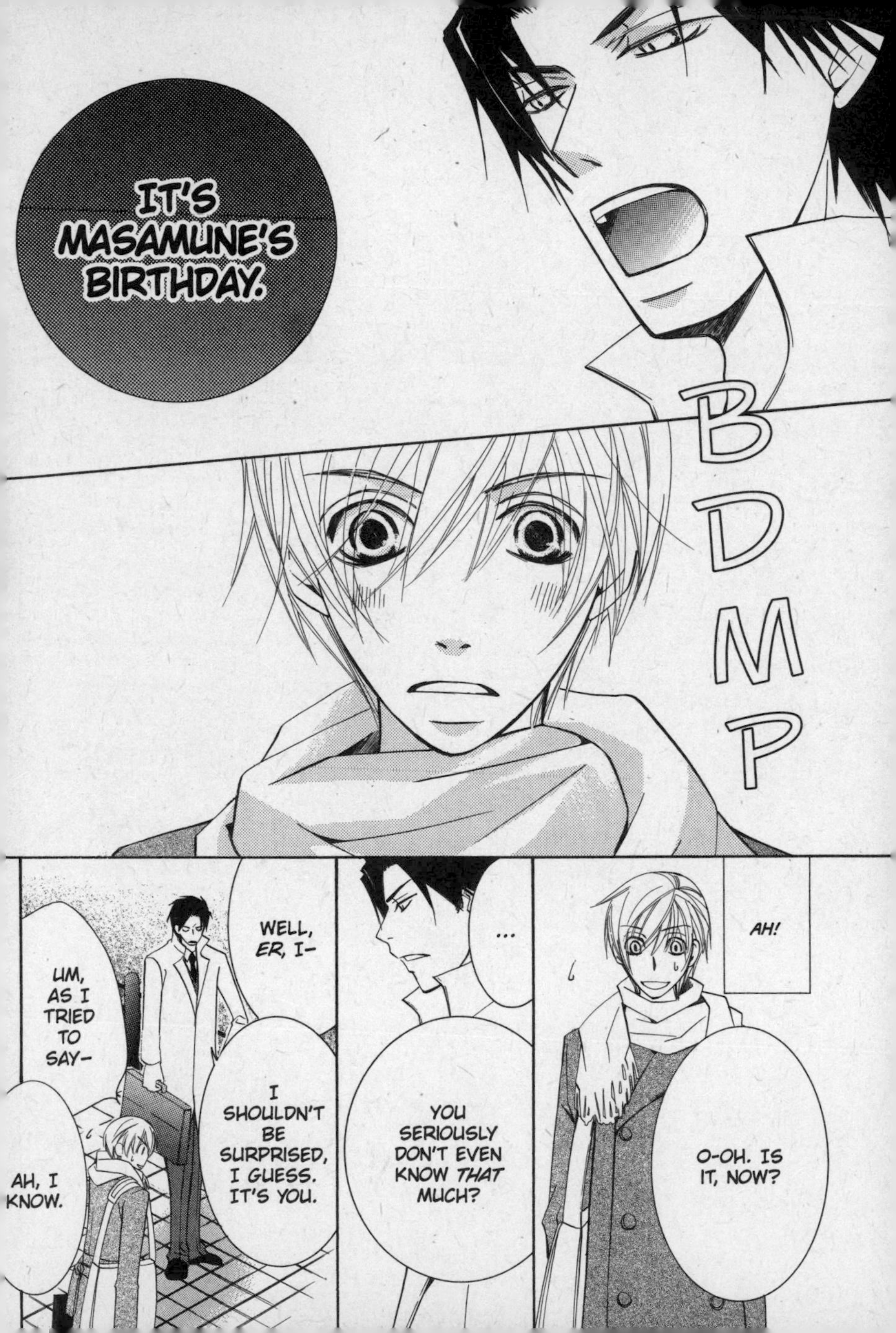
IT'S MASAMUNE'S BIRTHDAY.
BDMP
AH!
O-OH. IS IT, NOW?
...
YOU SERIOUSLY DON'T EVEN KNOW *THAT* MUCH?
WELL, *ER*, I-
I SHOULDN'T BE SURPRISED, I GUESS. IT'S YOU.
UM, AS I TRIED TO SAY-
AH, I KNOW.

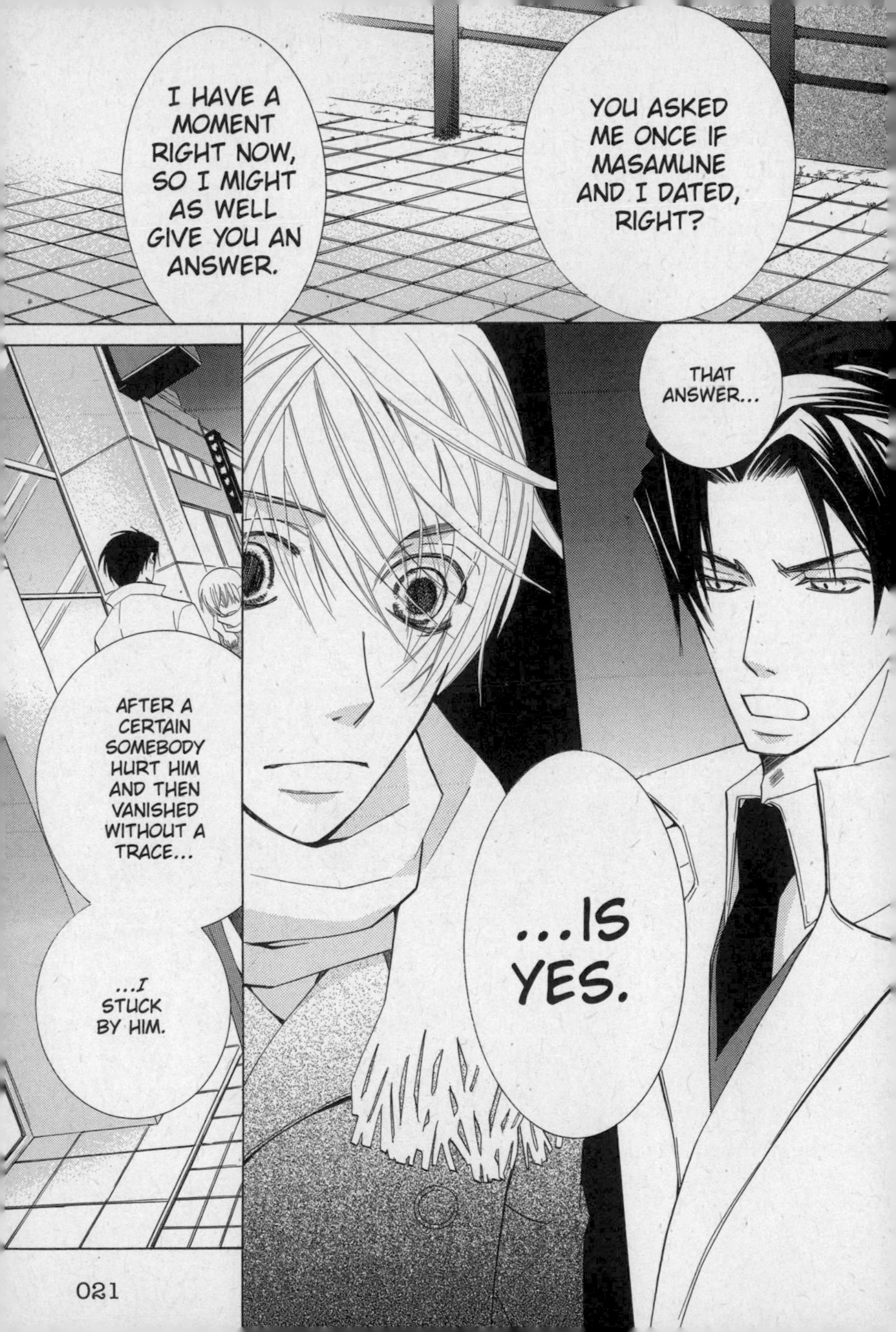

YOU ASKED ME ONCE IF MASAMUNE AND I DATED, RIGHT?
I HAVE A MOMENT RIGHT NOW, SO I MIGHT AS WELL GIVE YOU AN ANSWER.
THAT ANSWER...
...IS YES.
AFTER A CERTAIN SOMEBODY HURT HIM AND THEN VANISHED WITHOUT A TRACE...
...I STUCK BY HIM.

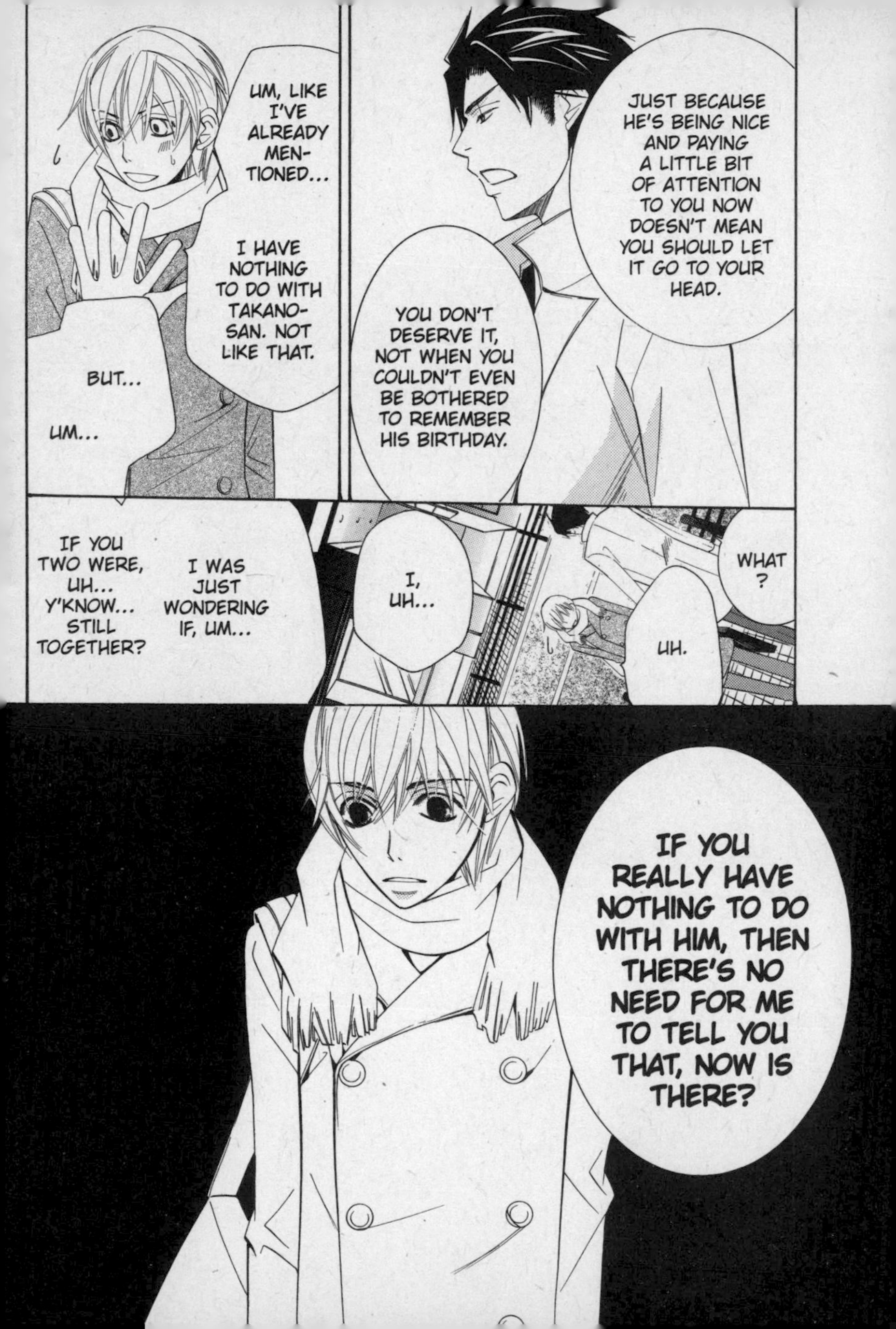
JUST BECAUSE HE'S BEING NICE AND PAYING A LITTLE BIT OF ATTENTION TO YOU NOW DOESN'T MEAN YOU SHOULD LET IT GO TO YOUR HEAD.
YOU DON'T DESERVE IT, NOT WHEN YOU COULDN'T EVEN BE BOTHERED TO REMEMBER HIS BIRTHDAY.
UM, LIKE I'VE ALREADY MEN-TIONED...
I HAVE NOTHING TO DO WITH TAKANO-SAN. NOT LIKE THAT.
BUT...
UM...
WHAT?
UH.
I, UH...
I WAS JUST WONDERING IF, UM...
IF YOU TWO WERE, UH... Y'KNOW... STILL TOGETHER?
IF YOU REALLY HAVE NOTHING TO DO WITH HIM, THEN THERE'S NO NEED FOR ME TO TELL YOU THAT, NOW IS THERE?

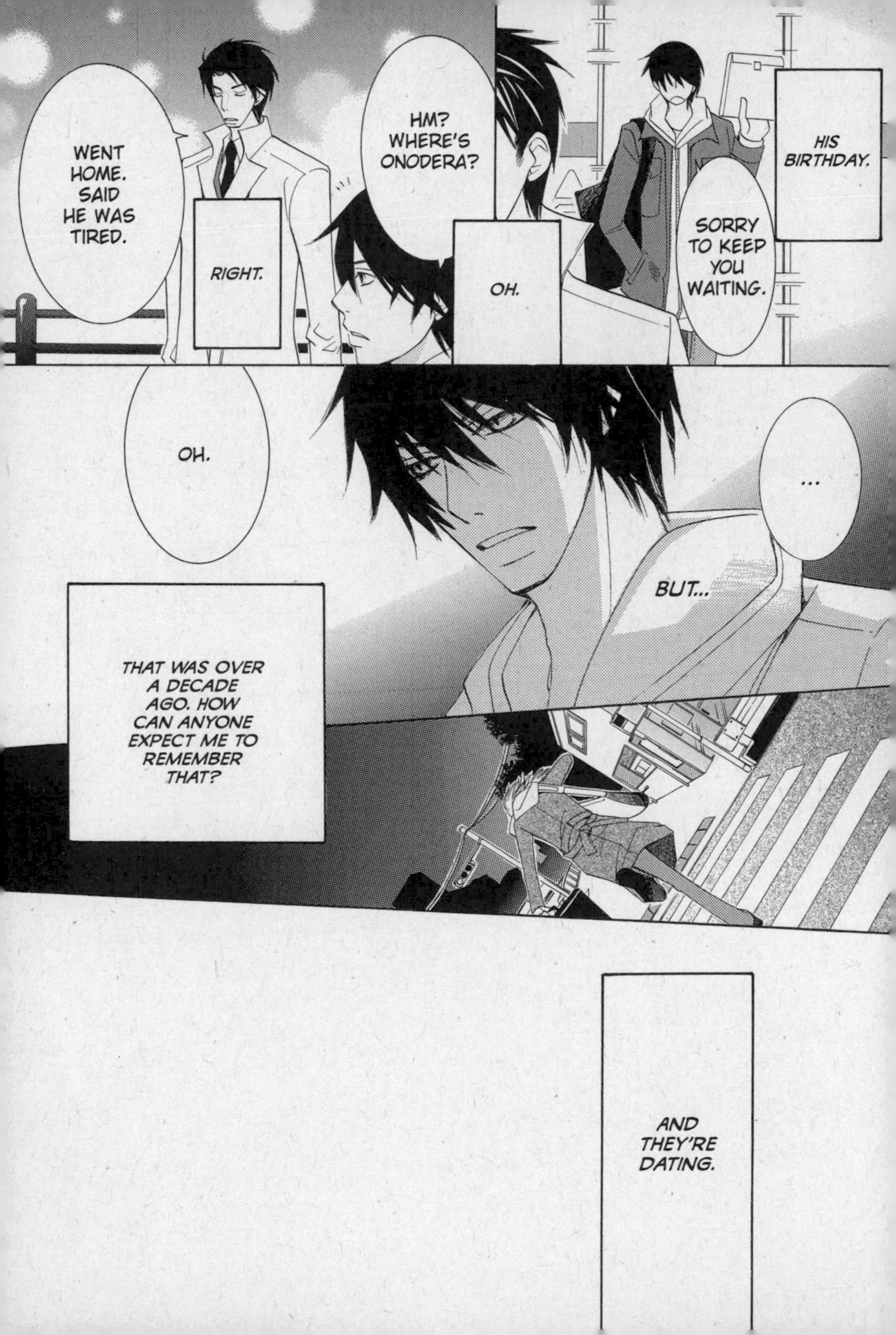
HIS BIRTHDAY.
SORRY TO KEEP YOU WAITING.
OH.
HM? WHERE'S ONODERA?
WENT HOME. SAID HE WAS TIRED.
RIGHT.
...
OH.
BUT...
THAT WAS OVER A DECADE AGO. HOW CAN ANYONE EXPECT ME TO REMEMBER THAT?
AND THEY'RE DATING.

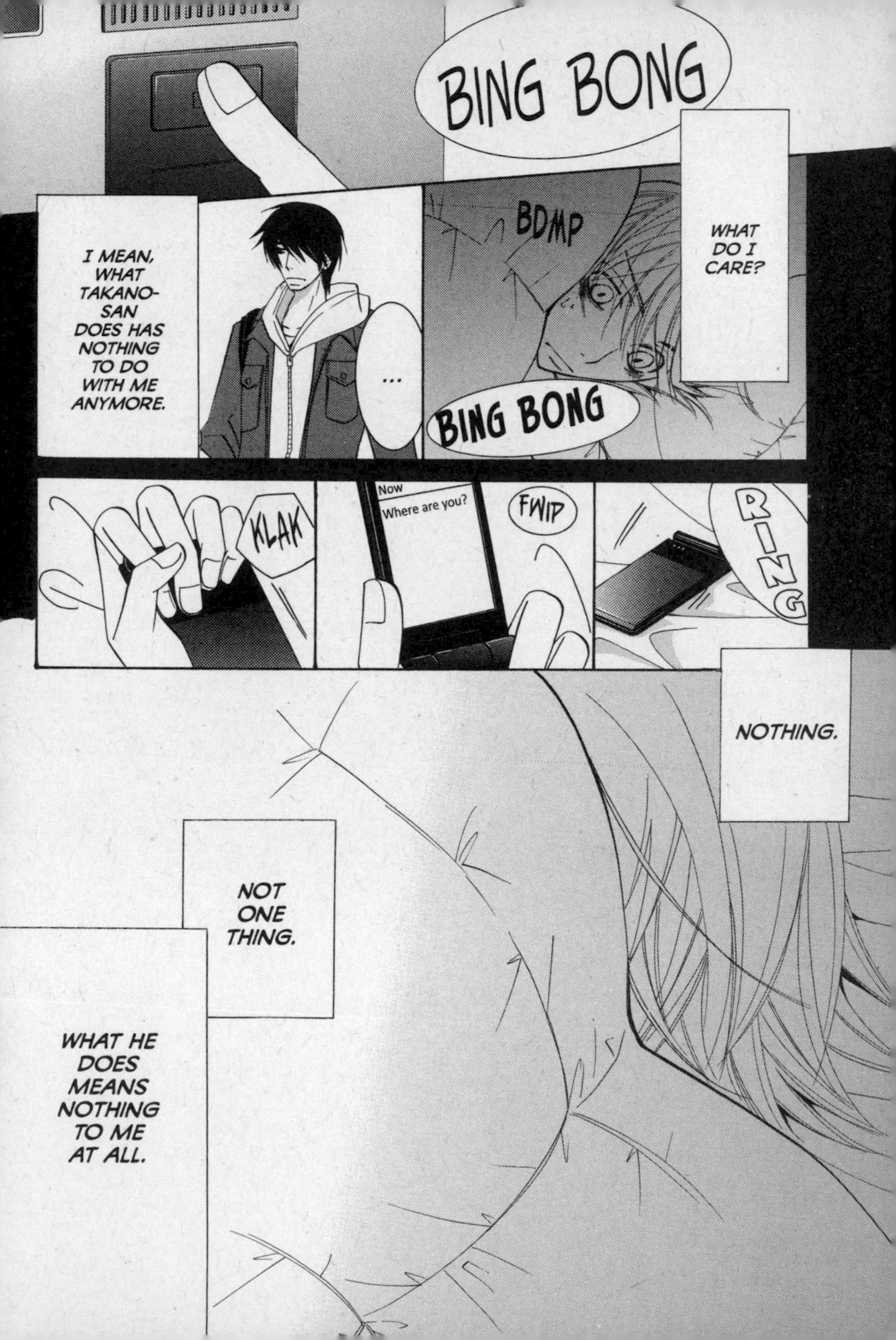
BING BONG
WHAT DO I CARE?
BDMP
BING BONG
...
I MEAN, WHAT TAKANO-SAN DOES HAS NOTHING TO DO WITH ME ANYMORE.
RING
FWIP
Now
Where are you?
KLAK
NOTHING.
NOT ONE THING.
WHAT HE DOES MEANS NOTHING TO ME AT ALL.

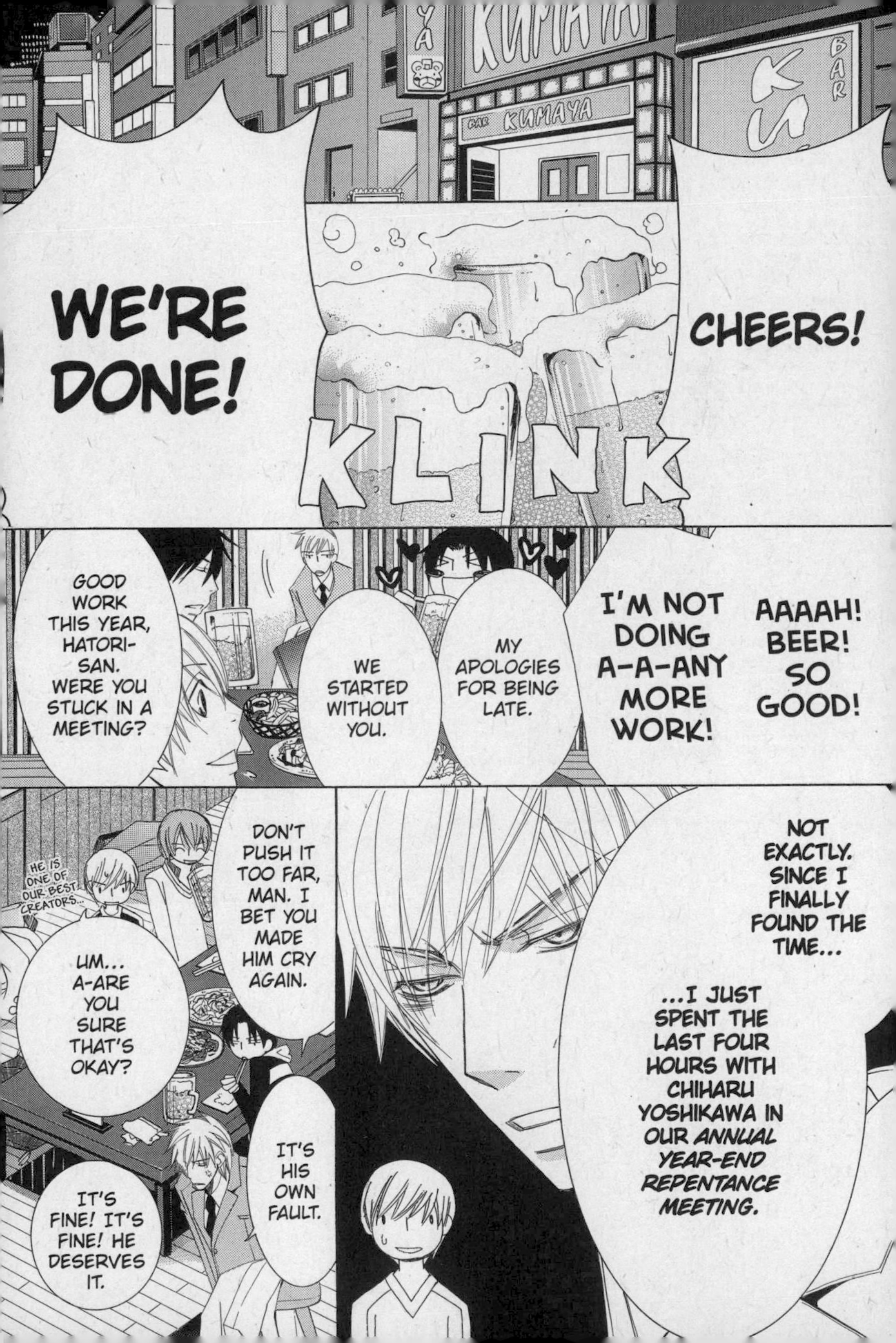

BAR KUMAYA
CHEERS!
WE'RE DONE!
KLINK
AAAAH! BEER! SO GOOD!
I'M NOT DOING A-A-ANY MORE WORK!
MY APOLOGIES FOR BEING LATE.
WE STARTED WITHOUT YOU.
GOOD WORK THIS YEAR, HATORI-SAN. WERE YOU STUCK IN A MEETING?
NOT EXACTLY. SINCE I FINALLY FOUND THE TIME...
...I JUST SPENT THE LAST FOUR HOURS WITH CHIHARU YOSHIKAWA IN OUR *ANNUAL YEAR-END REPENTANCE MEETING*.
DON'T PUSH IT TOO FAR, MAN. I BET YOU MADE HIM CRY AGAIN.
HE IS ONE OF OUR BEST CREATORS...
UM... A-ARE YOU SURE THAT'S OKAY?
IT'S HIS OWN FAULT.
IT'S FINE! IT'S FINE! HE DESERVES IT.

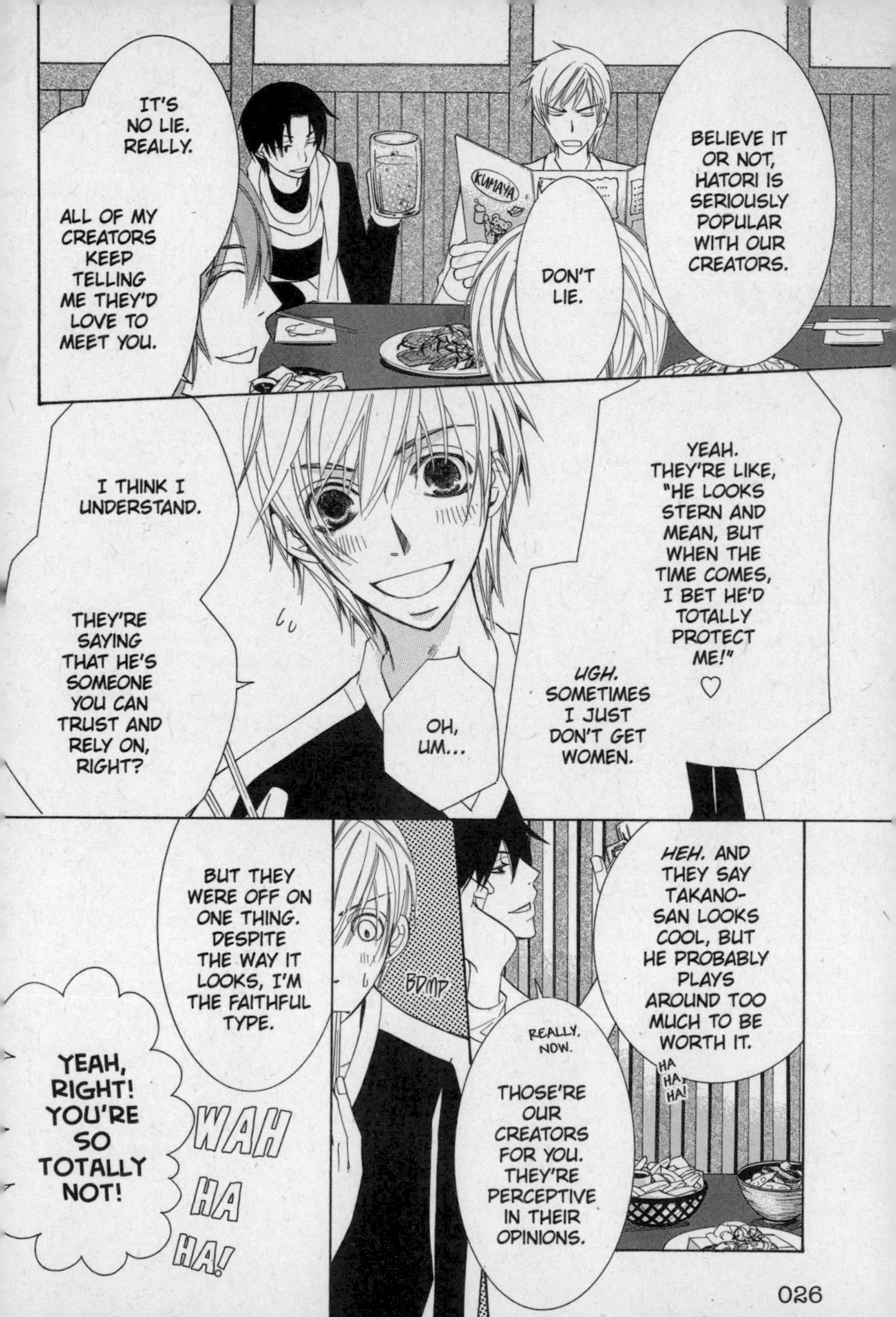
BELIEVE IT OR NOT, HATORI IS SERIOUSLY POPULAR WITH OUR CREATORS.
DON'T LIE.
IT'S NO LIE. REALLY.
ALL OF MY CREATORS KEEP TELLING ME THEY'D LOVE TO MEET YOU.
KUMAYA
YEAH. THEY'RE LIKE, "HE LOOKS STERN AND MEAN, BUT WHEN THE TIME COMES, I BET HE'D TOTALLY PROTECT ME!" ♡
UGH. SOMETIMES I JUST DON'T GET WOMEN.
OH, UM...
I THINK I UNDERSTAND.
THEY'RE SAYING THAT HE'S SOMEONE YOU CAN TRUST AND RELY ON, RIGHT?
HEH. AND THEY SAY TAKANO-SAN LOOKS COOL, BUT HE PROBABLY PLAYS AROUND TOO MUCH TO BE WORTH IT.
HA HA HA!
REALLY, NOW.
THOSE'RE OUR CREATORS FOR YOU. THEY'RE PERCEPTIVE IN THEIR OPINIONS.
BDMP
BUT THEY WERE OFF ON ONE THING. DESPITE THE WAY IT LOOKS, I'M THE FAITHFUL TYPE.
WAH HA HA!
YEAH, RIGHT! YOU'RE SO TOTALLY NOT!

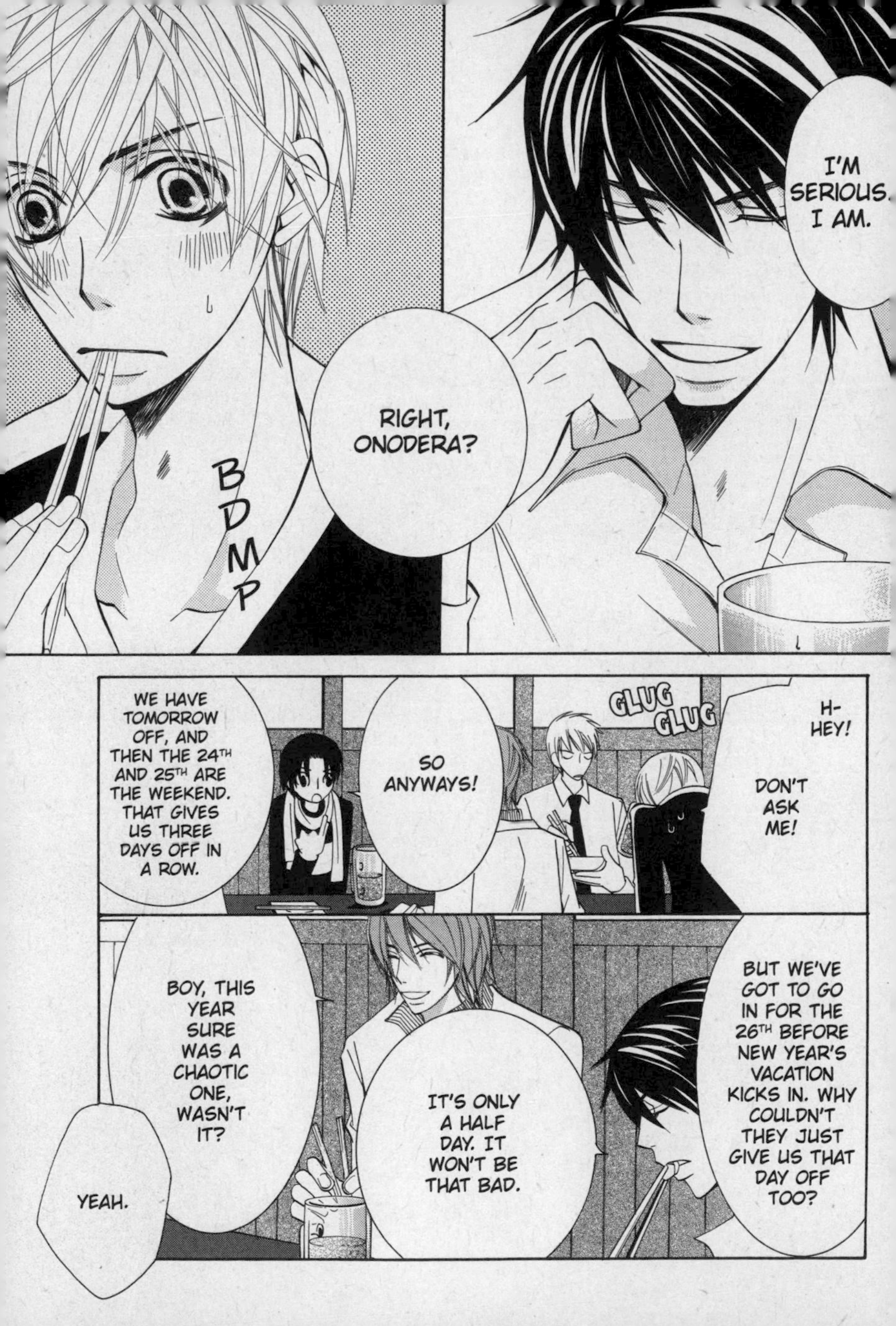
I'M SERIOUS. I AM.
RIGHT, ONODERA?
BDMP
H- HEY!
DON'T ASK ME!
GLUG GLUG
SO ANYWAYS!
WE HAVE TOMORROW OFF, AND THEN THE 24TH AND 25TH ARE THE WEEKEND. THAT GIVES US THREE DAYS OFF IN A ROW.
BUT WE'VE GOT TO GO IN FOR THE 26TH BEFORE NEW YEAR'S VACATION KICKS IN. WHY COULDN'T THEY JUST GIVE US THAT DAY OFF TOO?
IT'S ONLY A HALF DAY. IT WON'T BE THAT BAD.
BOY, THIS YEAR SURE WAS A CHAOTIC ONE, WASN'T IT?
YEAH.

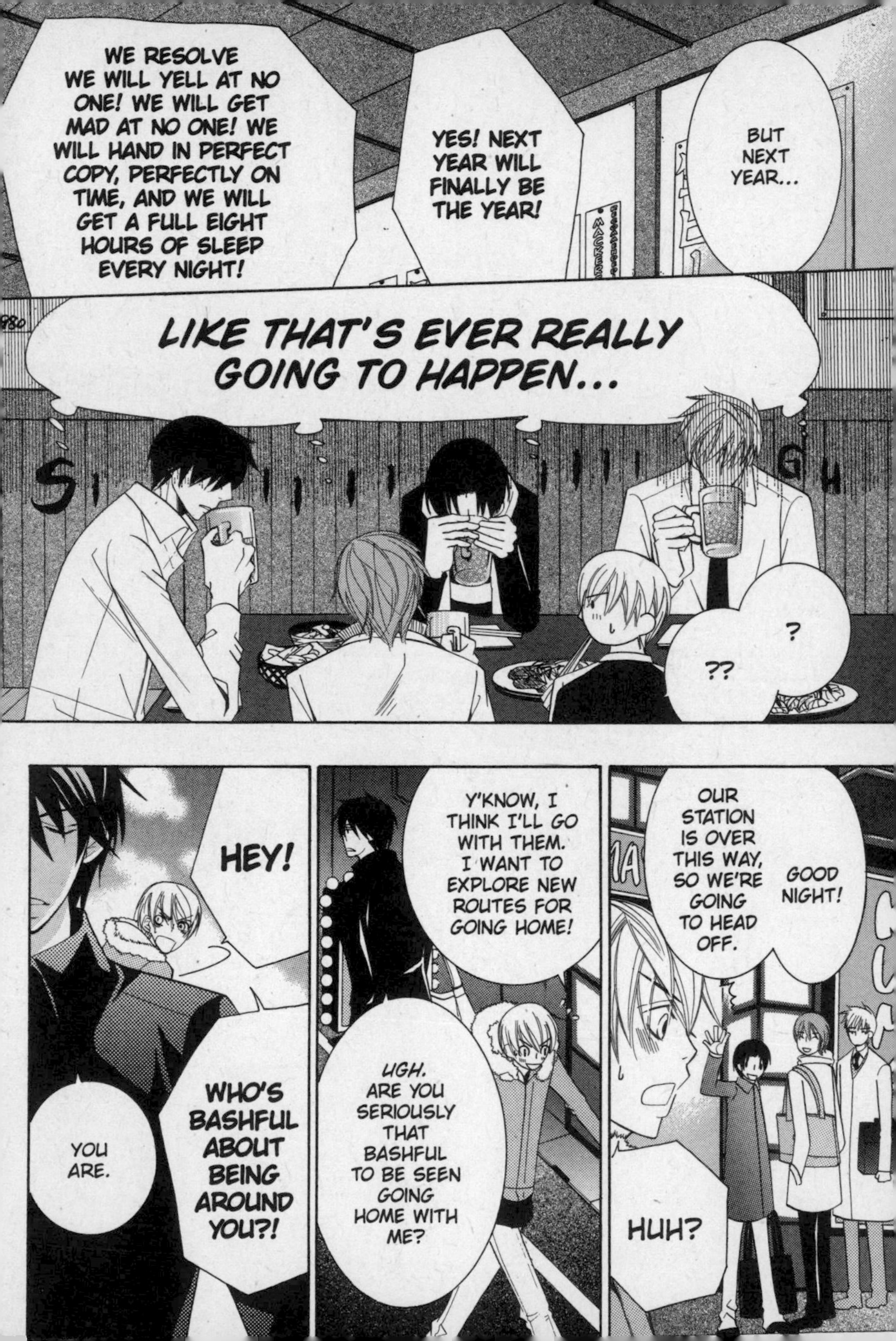
BUT NEXT YEAR...
YES! NEXT YEAR WILL FINALLY BE THE YEAR!
WE RESOLVE WE WILL YELL AT NO ONE! WE WILL GET MAD AT NO ONE! WE WILL HAND IN PERFECT COPY, PERFECTLY ON TIME, AND WE WILL GET A FULL EIGHT HOURS OF SLEEP EVERY NIGHT!
LIKE THAT'S EVER REALLY GOING TO HAPPEN...
SIIIIIIIIIIGH
?
??
OUR STATION IS OVER THIS WAY, SO WE'RE GOING TO HEAD OFF.
GOOD NIGHT!
HUH?
Y'KNOW, I THINK I'LL GO WITH THEM. I WANT TO EXPLORE NEW ROUTES FOR GOING HOME!
UGH. ARE YOU SERIOUSLY THAT BASHFUL TO BE SEEN GOING HOME WITH ME?
HEY!
WHO'S BASHFUL ABOUT BEING AROUND YOU?!
YOU ARE.

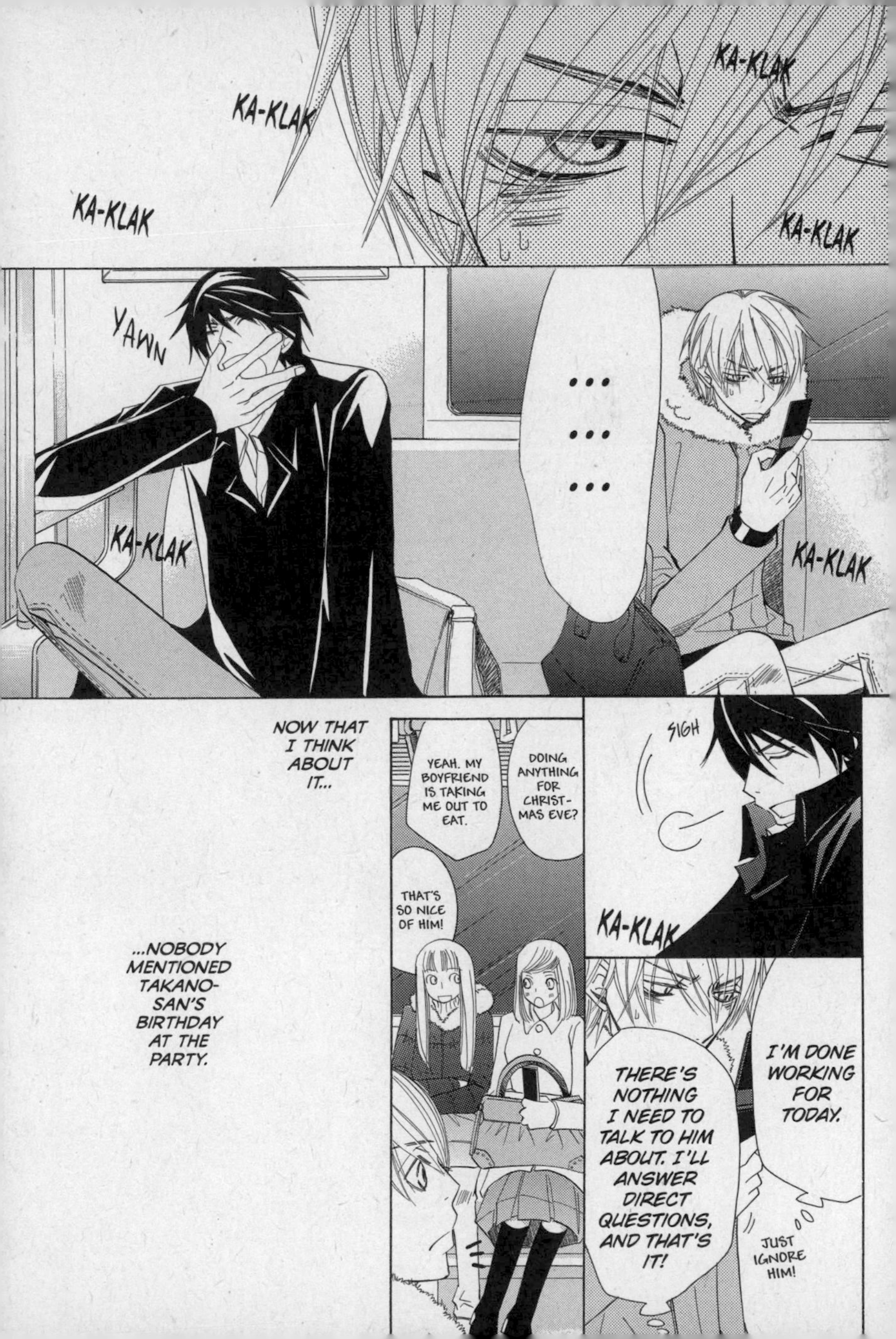
KA-KLAK
KA-KLAK
KA-KLAK
KA-KLAK
KA-KLAK
...
...
...
YAWN
KA-KLAK
SIGH
KA-KLAK
I'M DONE WORKING FOR TODAY.
THERE'S NOTHING I NEED TO TALK TO HIM ABOUT. I'LL ANSWER DIRECT QUESTIONS, AND THAT'S IT!
JUST IGNORE HIM!
DOING ANYTHING FOR CHRIST-MAS EVE?
YEAH. MY BOYFRIEND IS TAKING ME OUT TO EAT.
THAT'S SO NICE OF HIM!
NOW THAT I THINK ABOUT IT...
...NOBODY MENTIONED TAKANO-SAN'S BIRTHDAY AT THE PARTY.

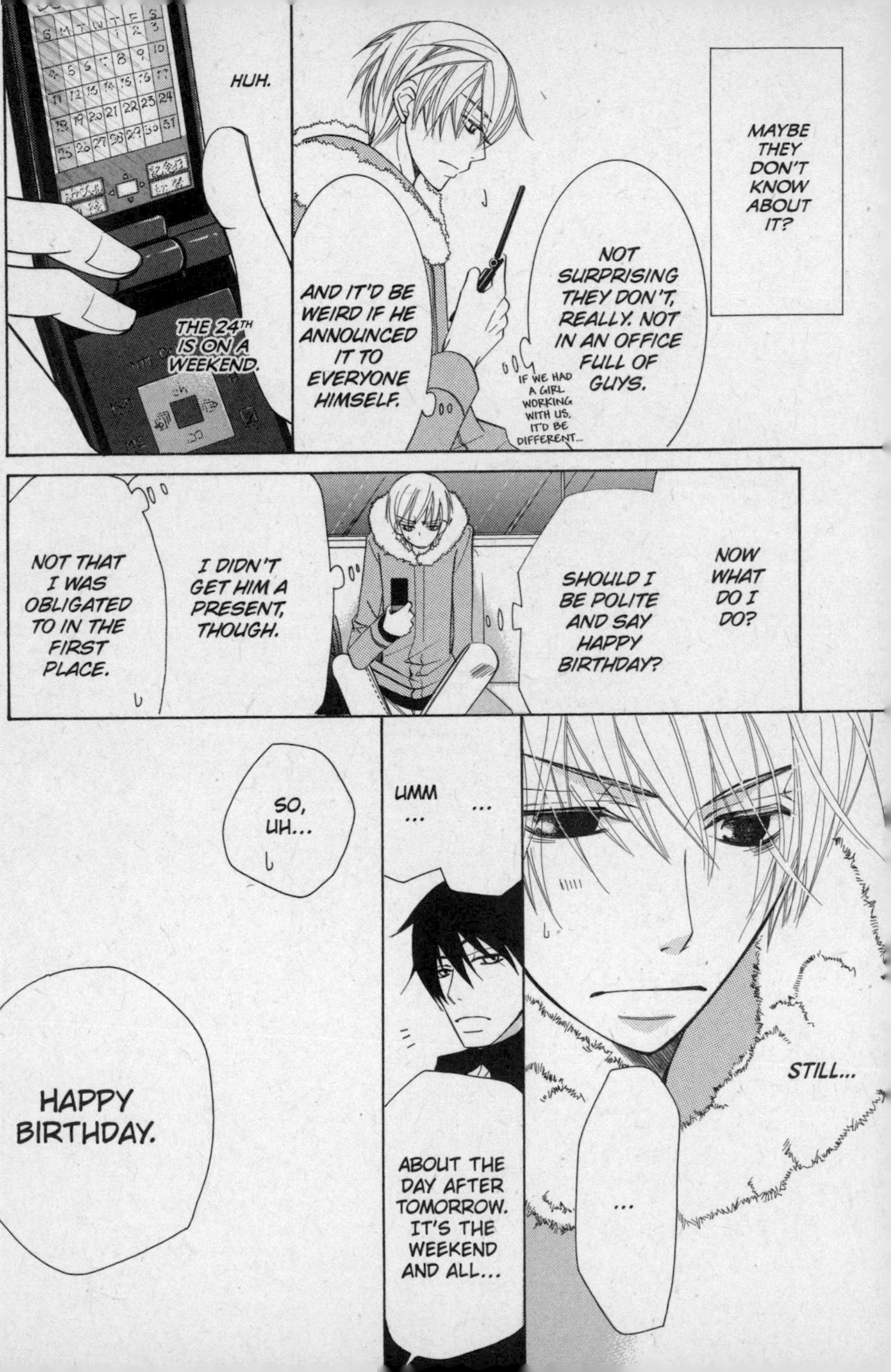
MAYBE THEY DON'T KNOW ABOUT IT?
NOT SURPRISING THEY DON'T, REALLY. NOT IN AN OFFICE FULL OF GUYS.
IF WE HAD A GIRL WORKING WITH US, IT'D BE DIFFERENT...
AND IT'D BE WEIRD IF HE ANNOUNCED IT TO EVERYONE HIMSELF.
HUH.
THE 24TH IS ON A WEEKEND.
NOW WHAT DO I DO?
SHOULD I BE POLITE AND SAY HAPPY BIRTHDAY?
I DIDN'T GET HIM A PRESENT, THOUGH.
NOT THAT I WAS OBLIGATED TO IN THE FIRST PLACE.
STILL...
...
...
UMM...
ABOUT THE DAY AFTER TOMORROW. IT'S THE WEEKEND AND ALL...
SO, UH...
HAPPY BIRTHDAY.

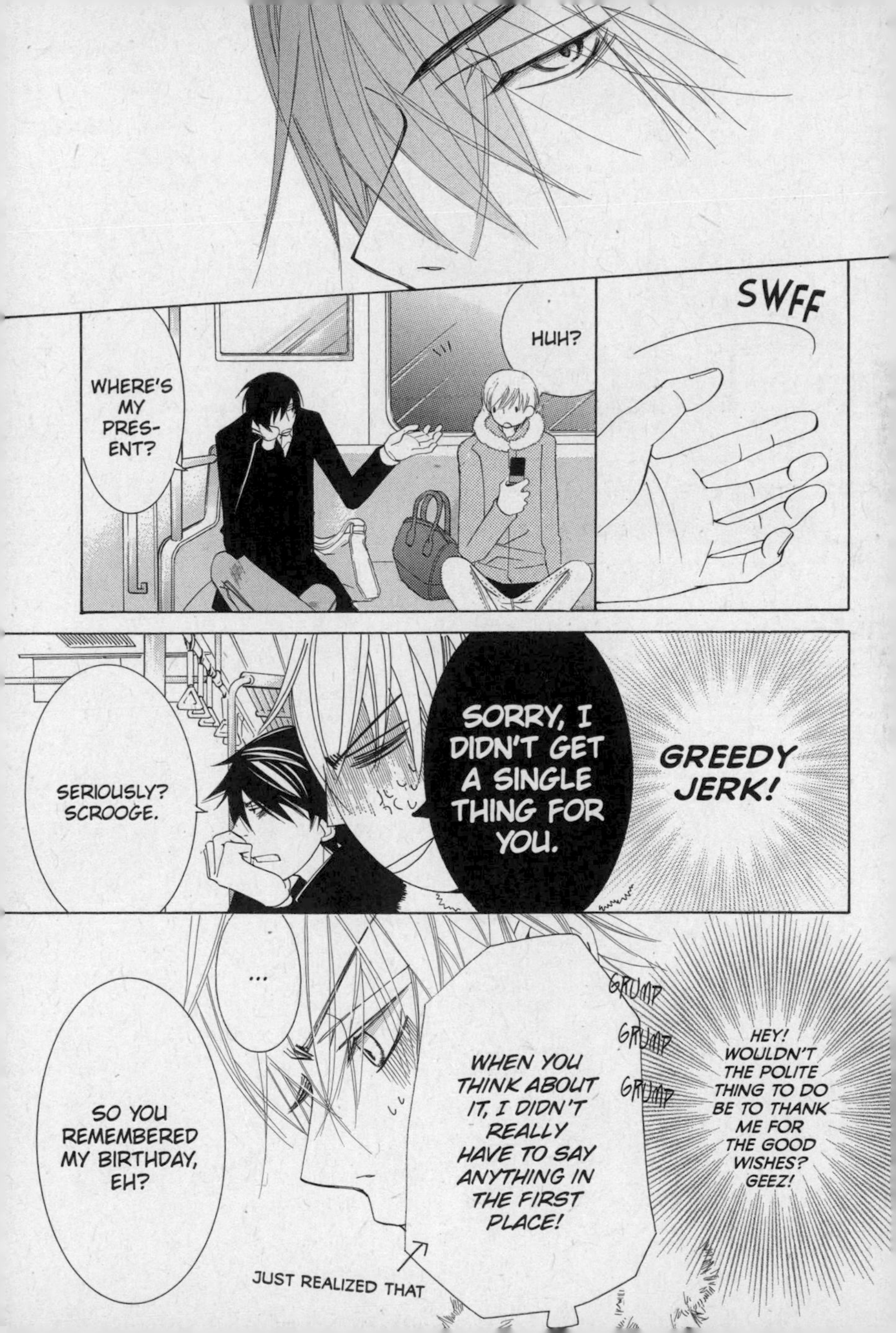
SWFF
HUH?
WHERE'S MY PRES-ENT?
GREEDY JERK!
SORRY, I DIDN'T GET A SINGLE THING FOR YOU.
SERIOUSLY? SCROOGE.
HEY! WOULDN'T THE POLITE THING TO DO BE TO THANK ME FOR THE GOOD WISHES? GEEZ!
GRUMP
GRUMP
GRUMP
WHEN YOU THINK ABOUT IT, I DIDN'T REALLY HAVE TO SAY ANYTHING IN THE FIRST PLACE!
...
SO YOU REMEMBERED MY BIRTHDAY, EH?
JUST REALIZED THAT

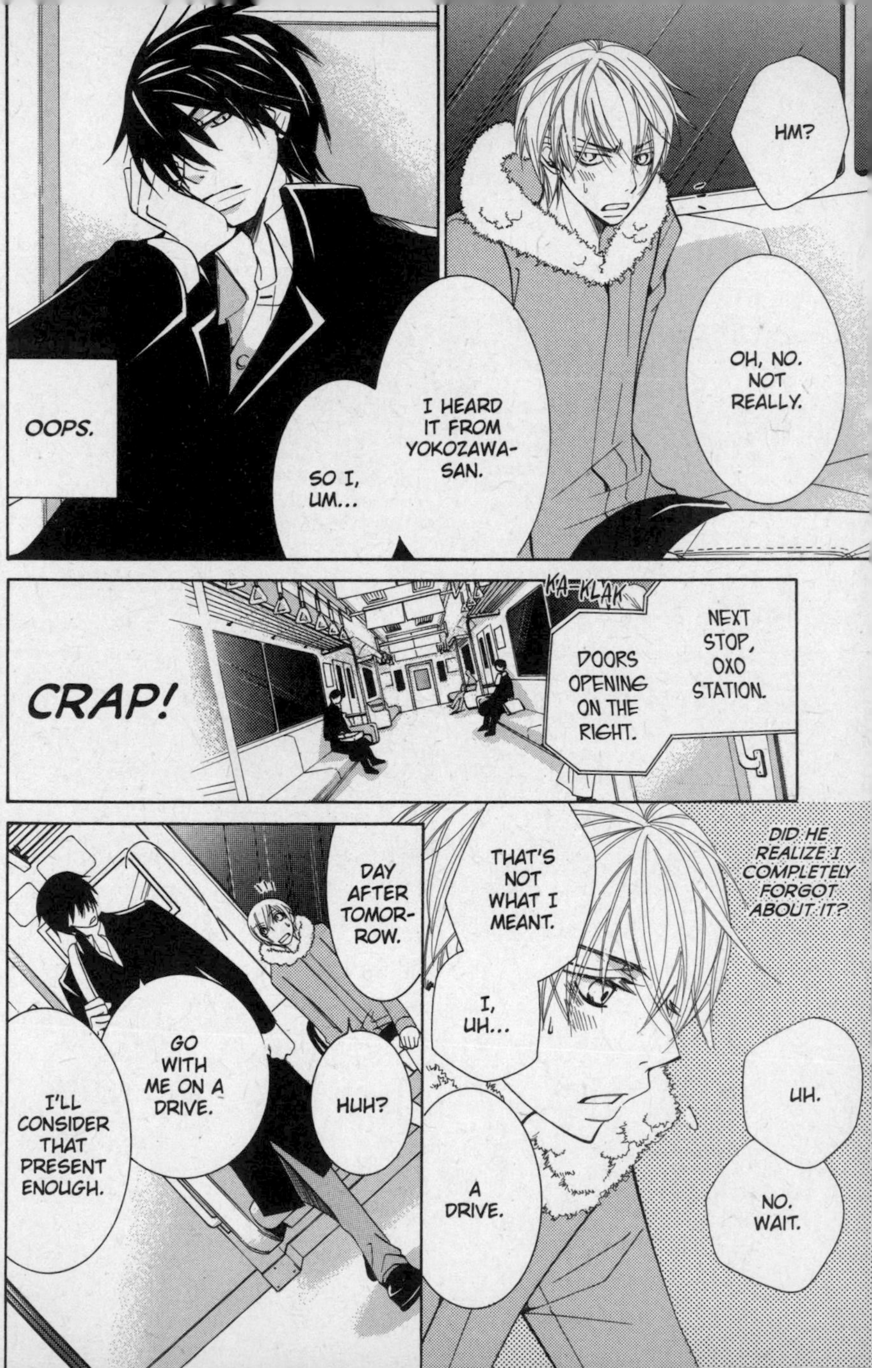
HM?
OH, NO. NOT REALLY.
I HEARD IT FROM YOKOZAWA-SAN.
SO I, UM...
OOPS.
KA-KLAK
NEXT STOP, OXO STATION.
DOORS OPENING ON THE RIGHT.
CRAP!
DID HE REALIZE I COMPLETELY FORGOT ABOUT IT?
THAT'S NOT WHAT I MEANT.
I, UH...
DAY AFTER TOMORROW.
HUH?
GO WITH ME ON A DRIVE.
I'LL CONSIDER THAT PRESENT ENOUGH.
A DRIVE.
UH.
NO. WAIT.

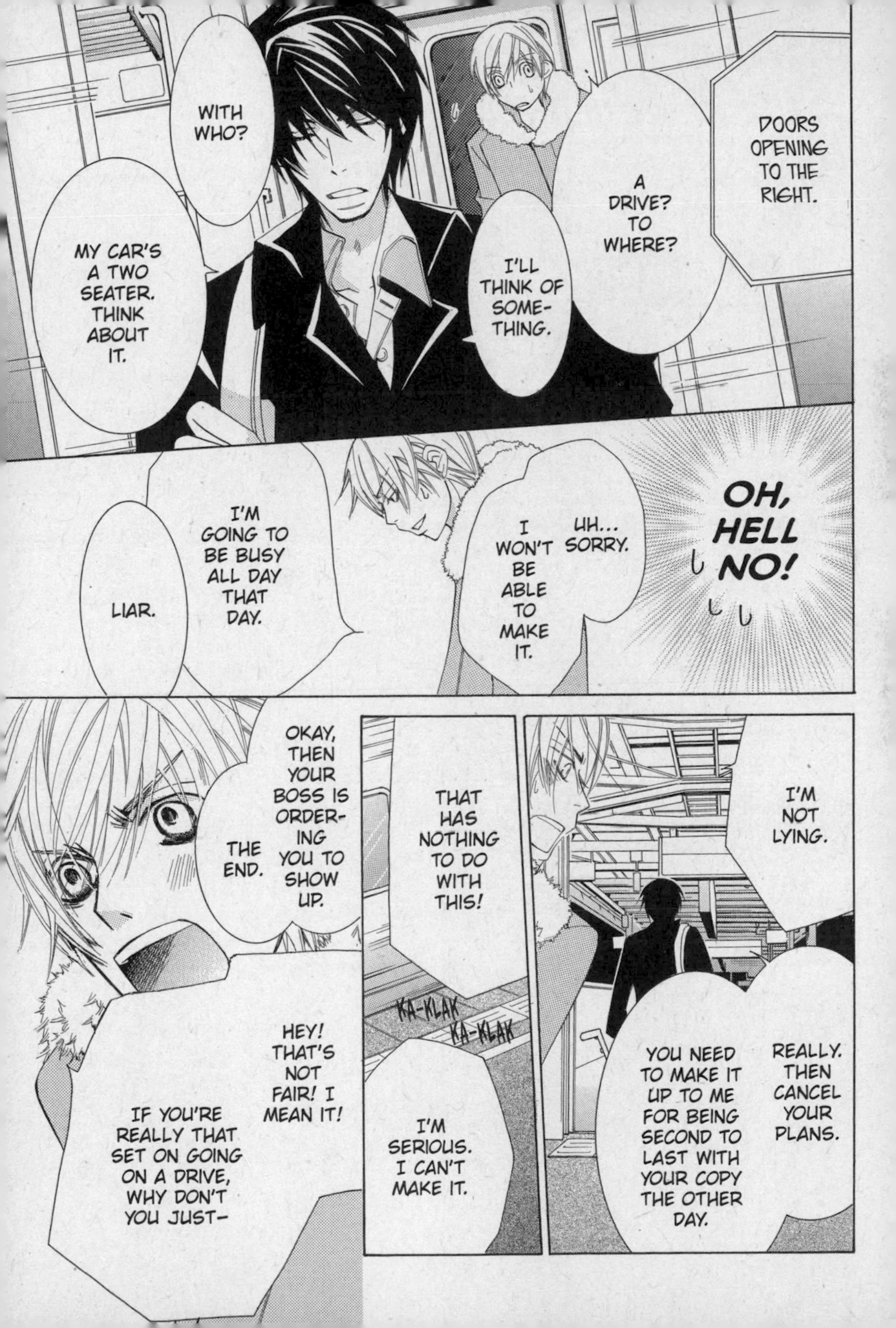
DOORS OPENING TO THE RIGHT.
A DRIVE? TO WHERE?
I'LL THINK OF SOME-THING.
WITH WHO?
MY CAR'S A TWO SEATER. THINK ABOUT IT.
OH, HELL NO!
UH... SORRY.
I WON'T BE ABLE TO MAKE IT.
I'M GOING TO BE BUSY ALL DAY THAT DAY.
LIAR.
I'M NOT LYING.
REALLY. THEN CANCEL YOUR PLANS.
YOU NEED TO MAKE IT UP TO ME FOR BEING SECOND TO LAST WITH YOUR COPY THE OTHER DAY.
THAT HAS NOTHING TO DO WITH THIS!
KA-KLAK KA-KLAK
I'M SERIOUS. I CAN'T MAKE IT.
OKAY, THEN YOUR BOSS IS ORDER-ING YOU TO SHOW UP.
THE END.
HEY! THAT'S NOT FAIR! I MEAN IT!
IF YOU'RE REALLY THAT SET ON GOING ON A DRIVE, WHY DON'T YOU JUST-

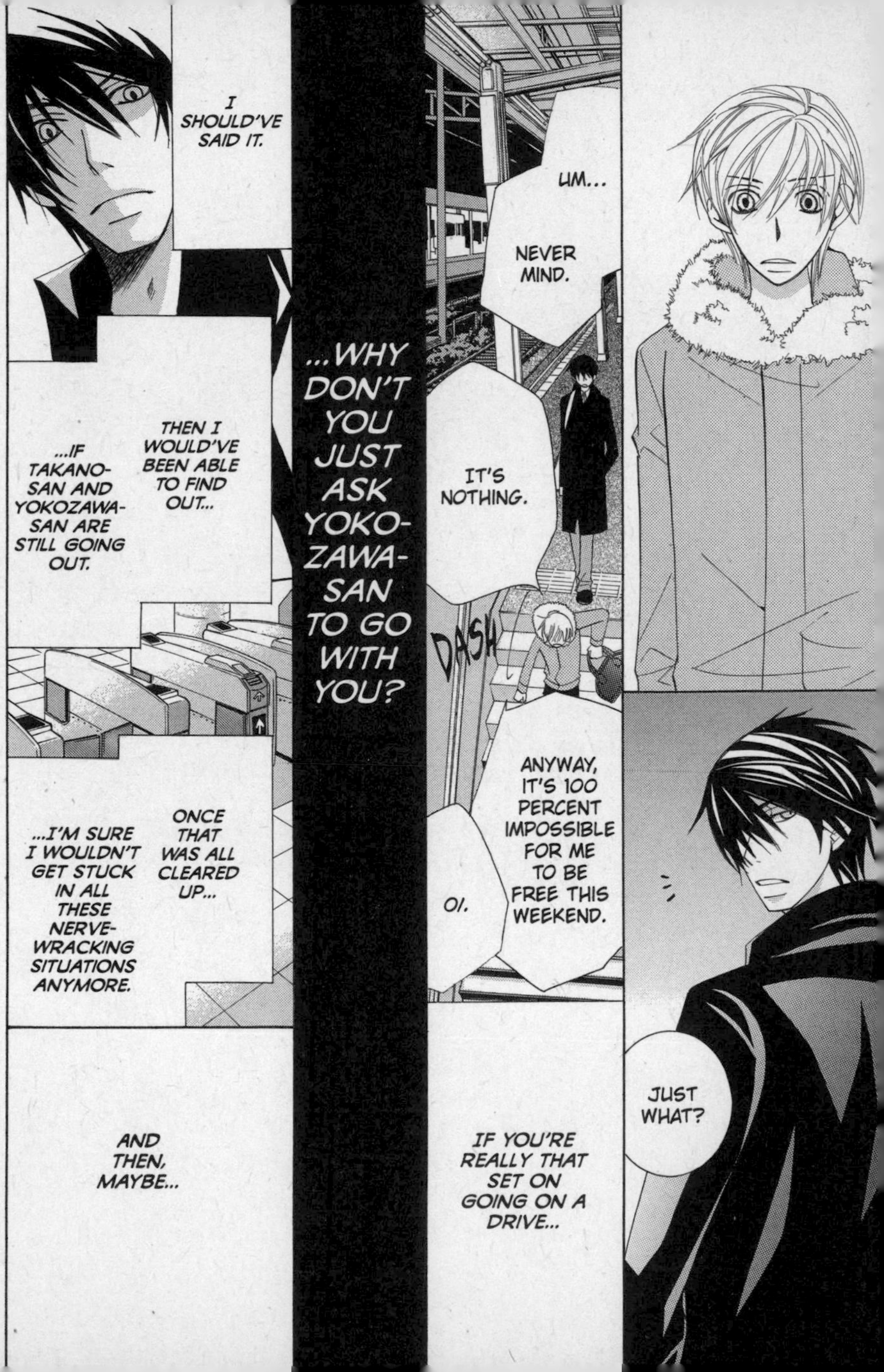
UM...
NEVER MIND.
IT'S NOTHING.
DASH
ANYWAY, IT'S 100 PERCENT IMPOSSIBLE FOR ME TO BE FREE THIS WEEKEND.
OI.
JUST WHAT?
IF YOU'RE REALLY THAT SET ON GOING ON A DRIVE...
...WHY DON'T YOU JUST ASK YOKO-ZAWA-SAN TO GO WITH YOU?
I SHOULD'VE SAID IT.
THEN I WOULD'VE BEEN ABLE TO FIND OUT...
...IF TAKANO-SAN AND YOKOZAWA-SAN ARE STILL GOING OUT.
ONCE THAT WAS ALL CLEARED UP...
...I'M SURE I WOULDN'T GET STUCK IN ALL THESE NERVE-WRACKING SITUATIONS ANYMORE.
AND THEN, MAYBE...

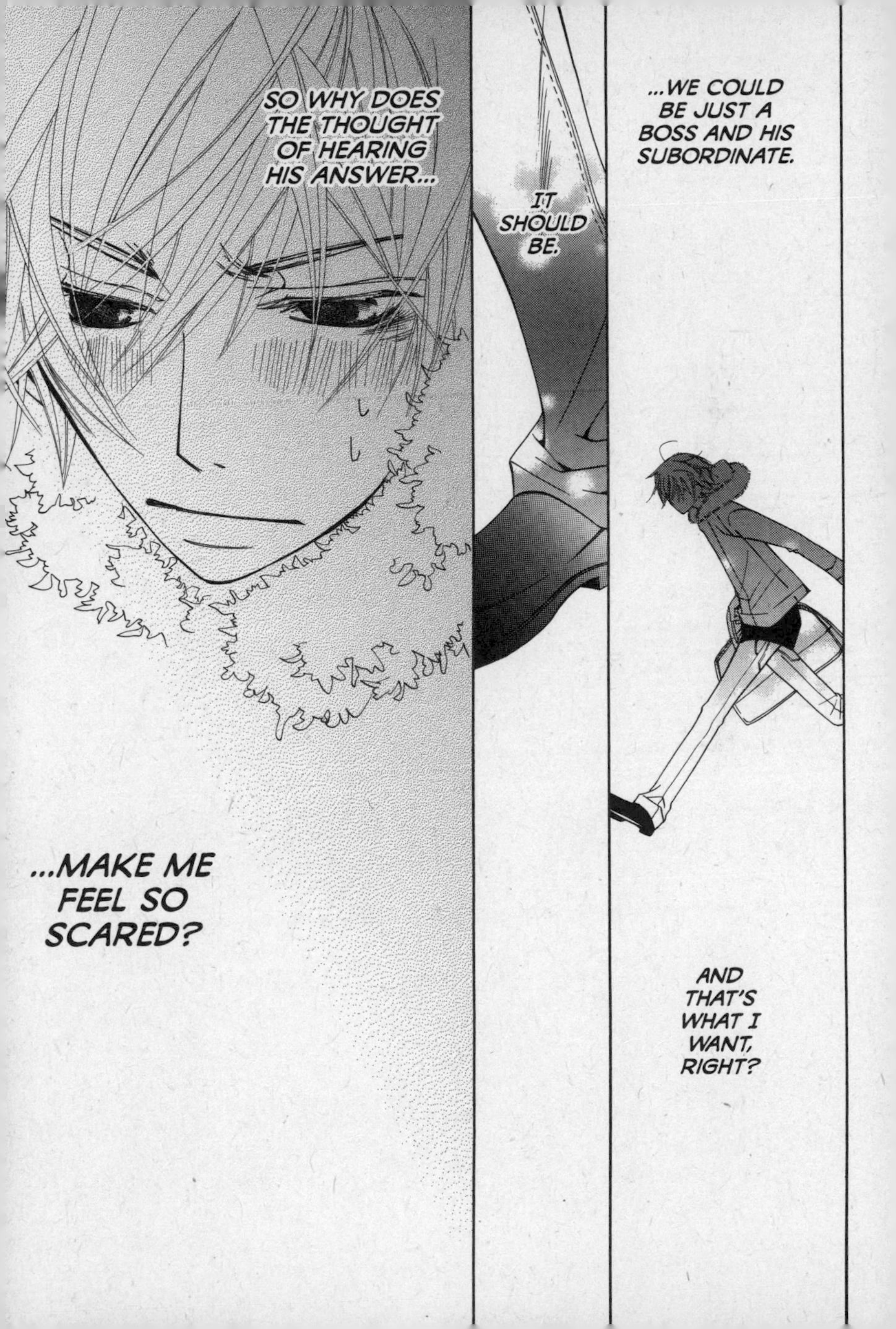
...WE COULD BE JUST A BOSS AND HIS SUBORDINATE.
AND THAT'S WHAT I WANT, RIGHT?
IT SHOULD BE.
SO WHY DOES THE THOUGHT OF HEARING HIS ANSWER...
...MAKE ME FEEL SO SCARED?

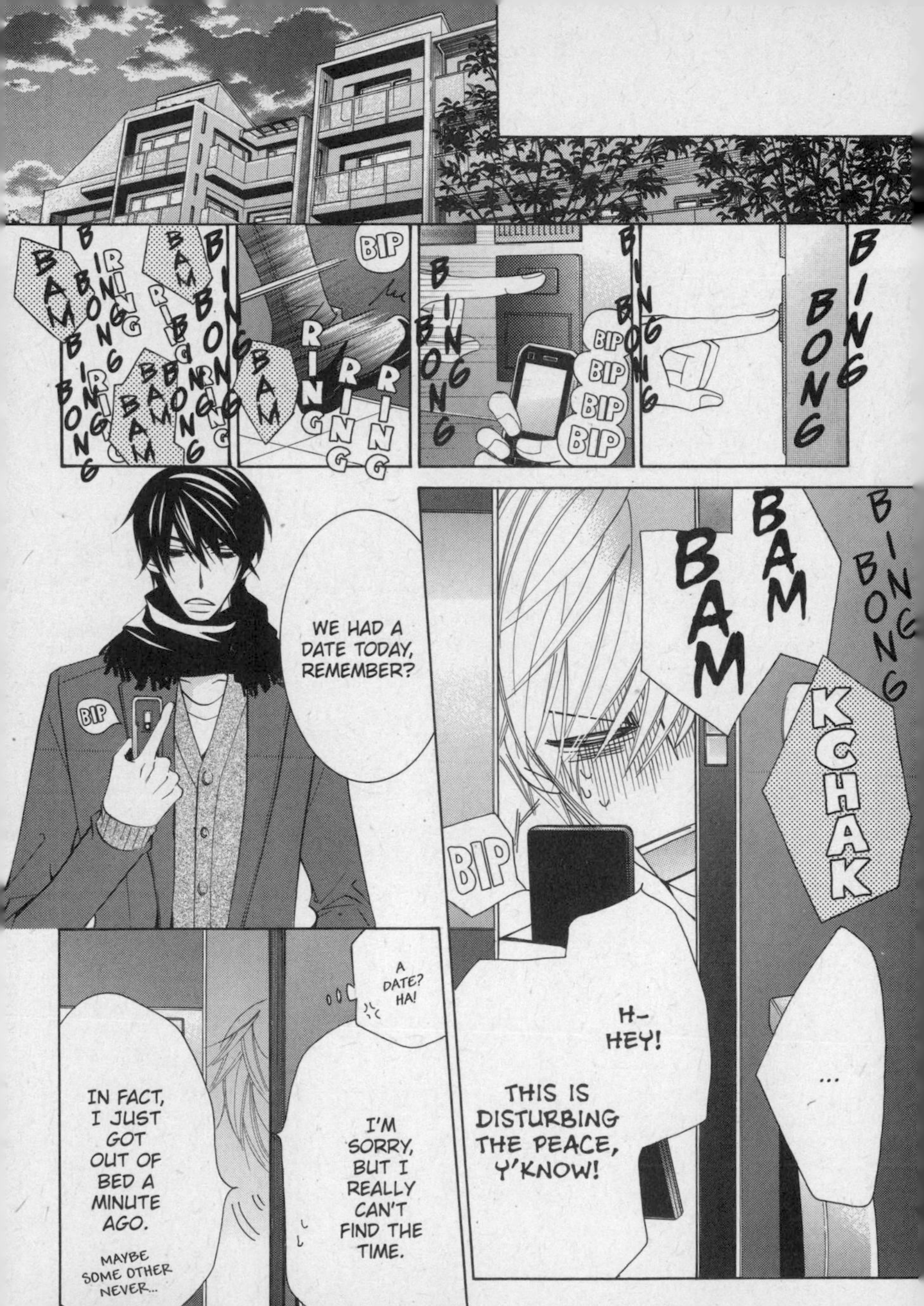
BING BONG
BING BONG
BIP BIP BIP BIP
BING BONG
BIP
RING RING RING
BAM
BAM BAM BAM
RING RING RING
BING BONG BING BONG BING BONG
BAM BAM
BING BONG
KCHAK
BIP
...
H- HEY!
THIS IS DISTURBING THE PEACE, Y'KNOW!
WE HAD A DATE TODAY, REMEMBER?
BIP
A DATE? HA!
I'M SORRY, BUT I REALLY CAN'T FIND THE TIME.
IN FACT, I JUST GOT OUT OF BED A MINUTE AGO.
MAYBE SOME OTHER NEVER...

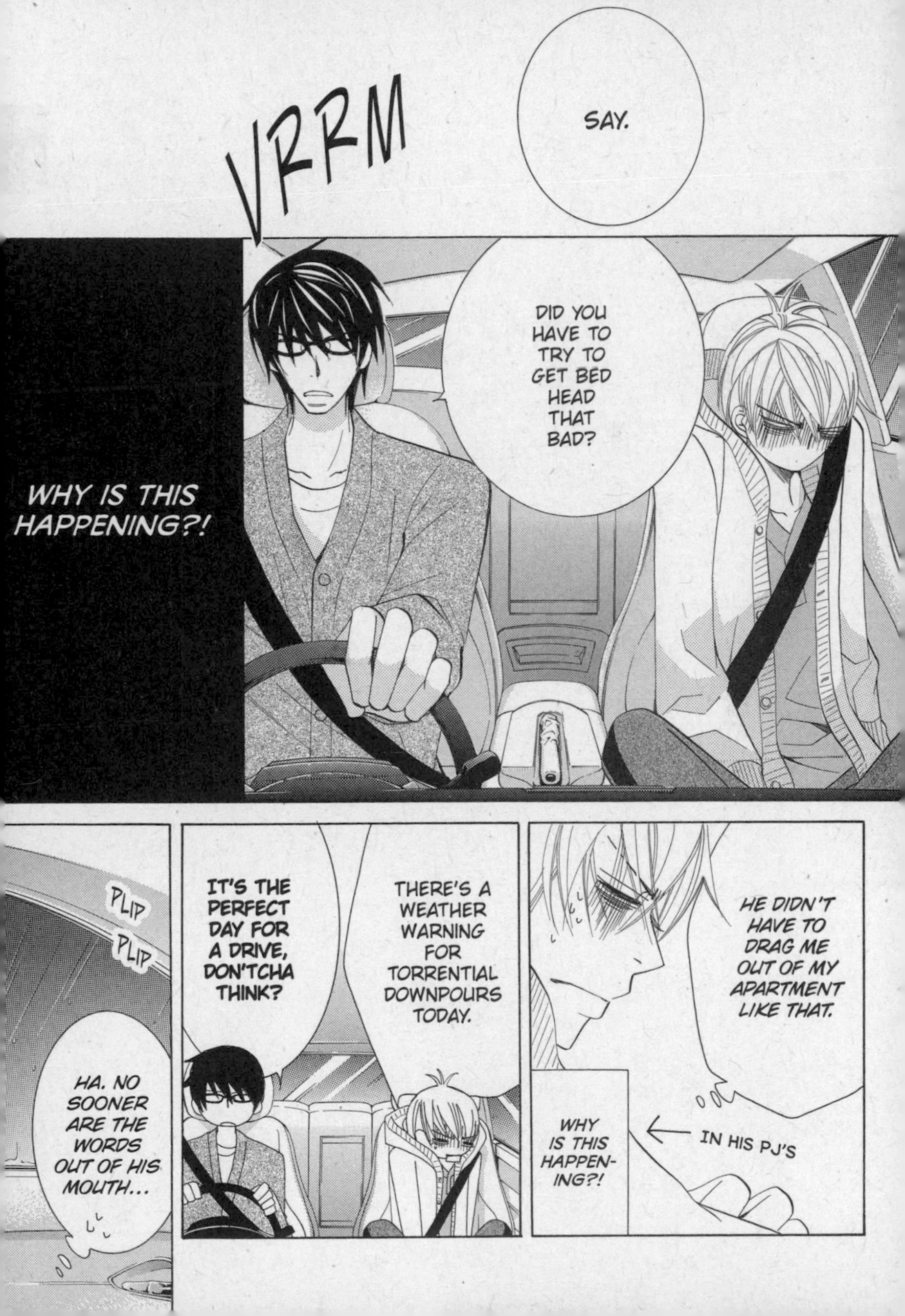
SAY.
VRRM
DID YOU HAVE TO TRY TO GET BED HEAD THAT BAD?
WHY IS THIS HAPPENING?!
HE DIDN'T HAVE TO DRAG ME OUT OF MY APARTMENT LIKE THAT.
IN HIS PJ'S
WHY IS THIS HAPPEN-ING?!
THERE'S A WEATHER WARNING FOR TORRENTIAL DOWNPOURS TODAY.
IT'S THE PERFECT DAY FOR A DRIVE, DON'TCHA THINK?
PLIP
PLIP
HA. NO SOONER ARE THE WORDS OUT OF HIS MOUTH...

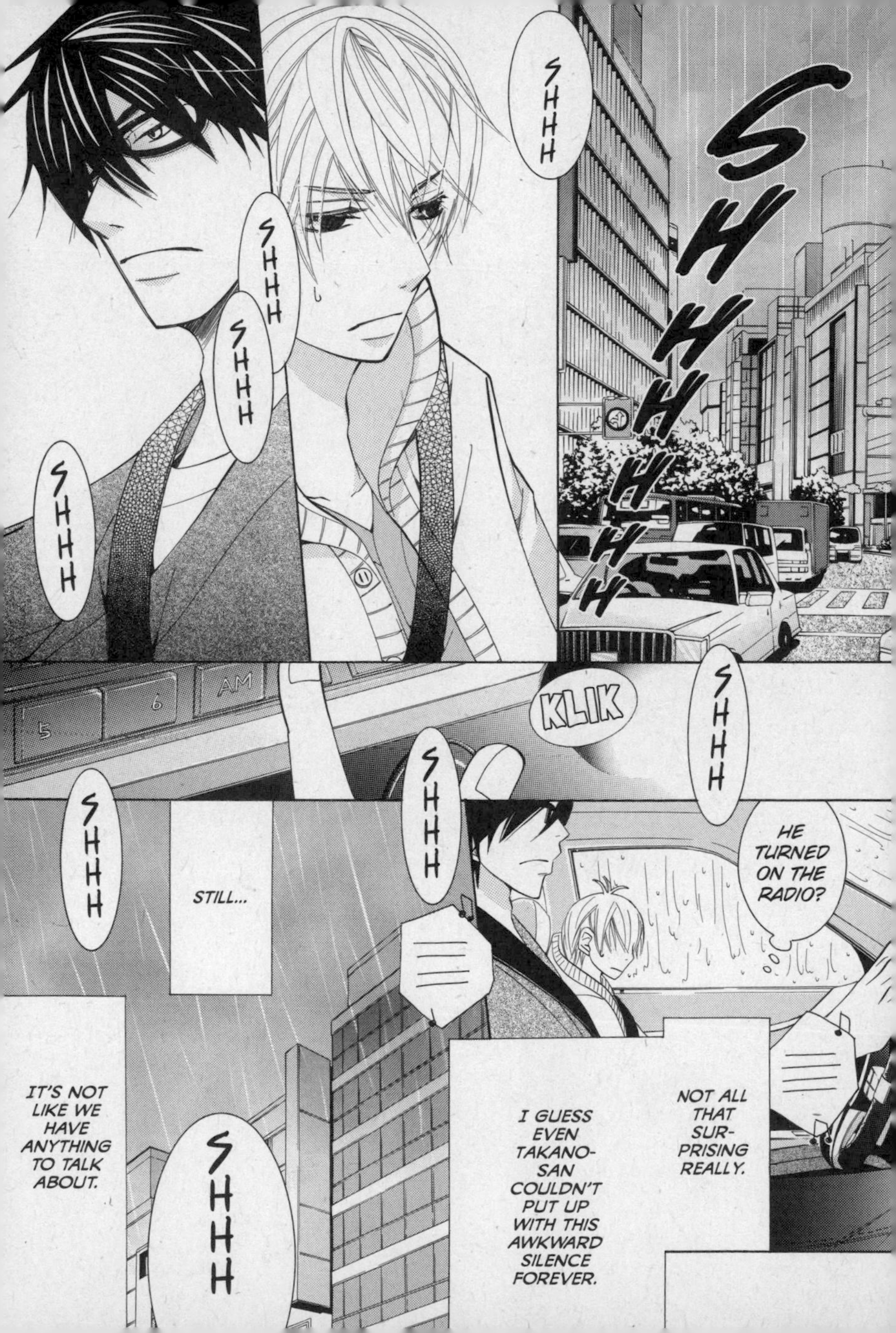

SHHHHHHHH
SHHH
SHHH
SHHH
SHHH
SHHH
KLIK
SHHH
HE TURNED ON THE RADIO?
NOT ALL THAT SURPRISING REALLY.
I GUESS EVEN TAKANO-SAN COULDN'T PUT UP WITH THIS AWKWARD SILENCE FOREVER.
STILL...
SHHH
IT'S NOT LIKE WE HAVE ANYTHING TO TALK ABOUT.
SHHH

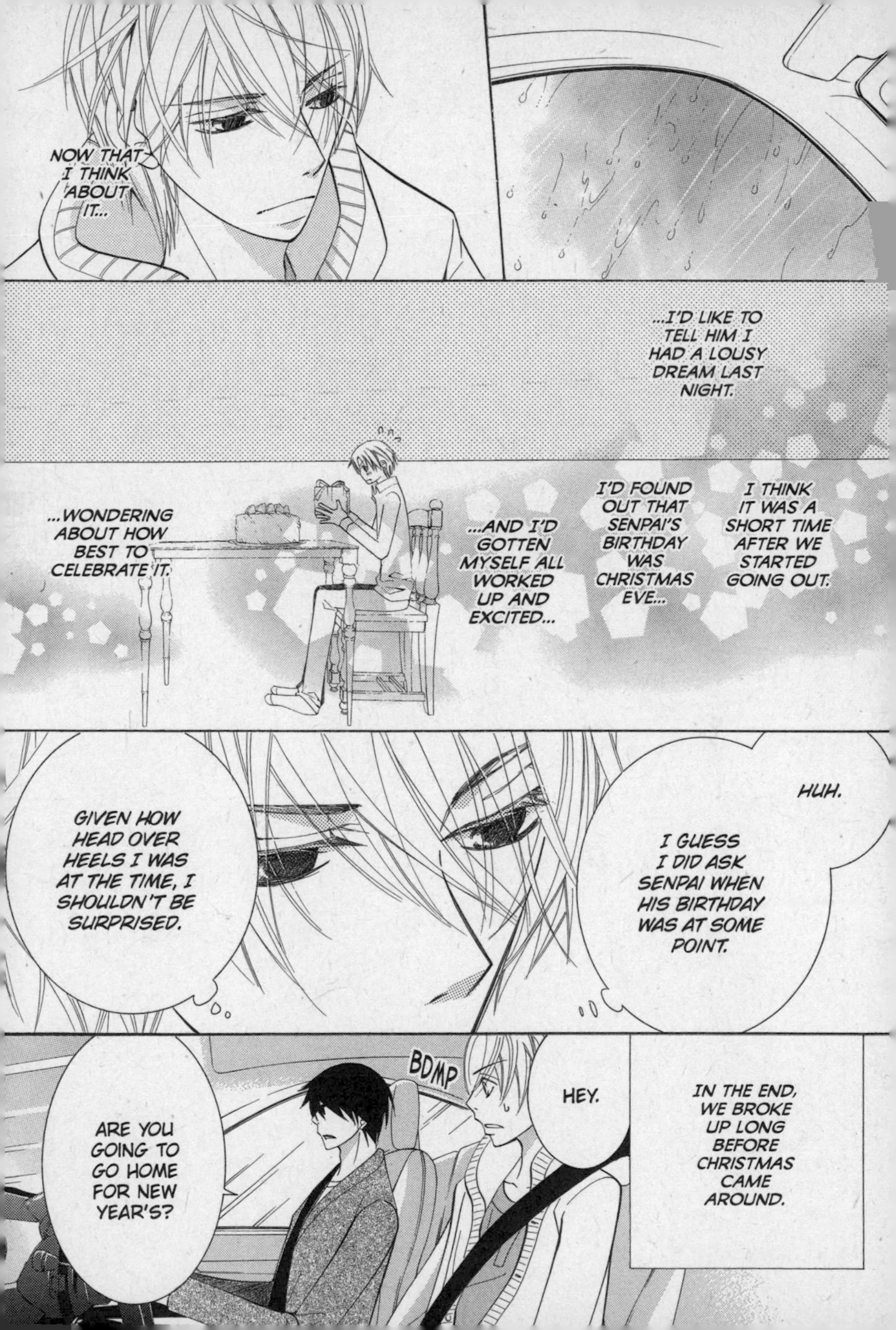
NOW THAT I THINK ABOUT IT...
...I'D LIKE TO TELL HIM I HAD A LOUSY DREAM LAST NIGHT.
I THINK IT WAS A SHORT TIME AFTER WE STARTED GOING OUT.
I'D FOUND OUT THAT SENPAI'S BIRTHDAY WAS CHRISTMAS EVE...
...AND I'D GOTTEN MYSELF ALL WORKED UP AND EXCITED...
...WONDERING ABOUT HOW BEST TO CELEBRATE IT.
HUH.
I GUESS I DID ASK SENPAI WHEN HIS BIRTHDAY WAS AT SOME POINT.
GIVEN HOW HEAD OVER HEELS I WAS AT THE TIME, I SHOULDN'T BE SURPRISED.
IN THE END, WE BROKE UP LONG BEFORE CHRISTMAS CAME AROUND.
HEY.
BDMP
ARE YOU GOING TO GO HOME FOR NEW YEAR'S?

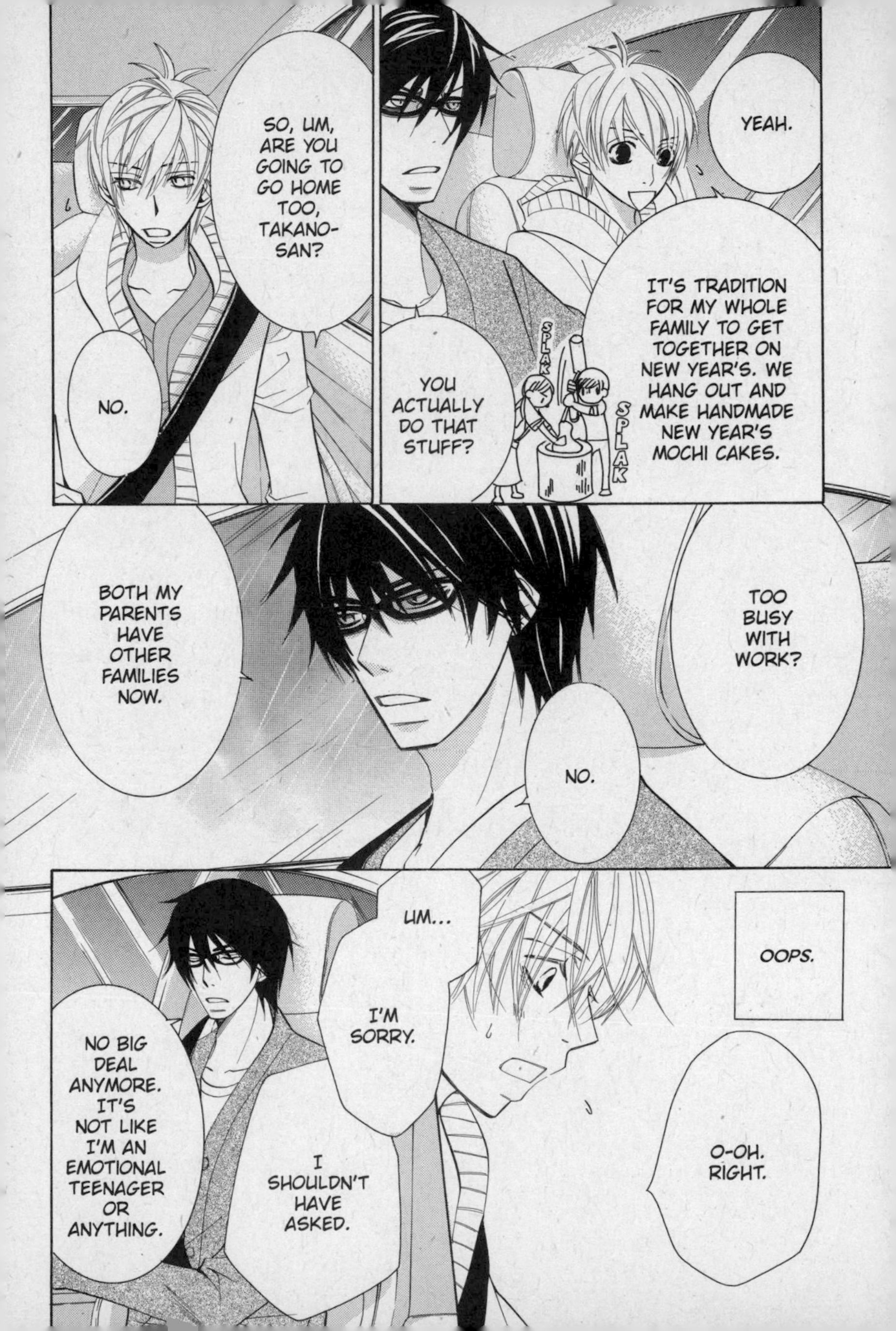
YEAH.
IT'S TRADITION FOR MY WHOLE FAMILY TO GET TOGETHER ON NEW YEAR'S. WE HANG OUT AND MAKE HANDMADE NEW YEAR'S MOCHI CAKES.
SPLAK
SPLAK
YOU ACTUALLY DO THAT STUFF?
SO, UM, ARE YOU GOING TO GO HOME TOO, TAKANO-SAN?
NO.
TOO BUSY WITH WORK?
NO.
BOTH MY PARENTS HAVE OTHER FAMILIES NOW.
OOPS.
O-OH. RIGHT.
UM...
I'M SORRY.
I SHOULDN'T HAVE ASKED.
NO BIG DEAL ANYMORE. IT'S NOT LIKE I'M AN EMOTIONAL TEENAGER OR ANYTHING.

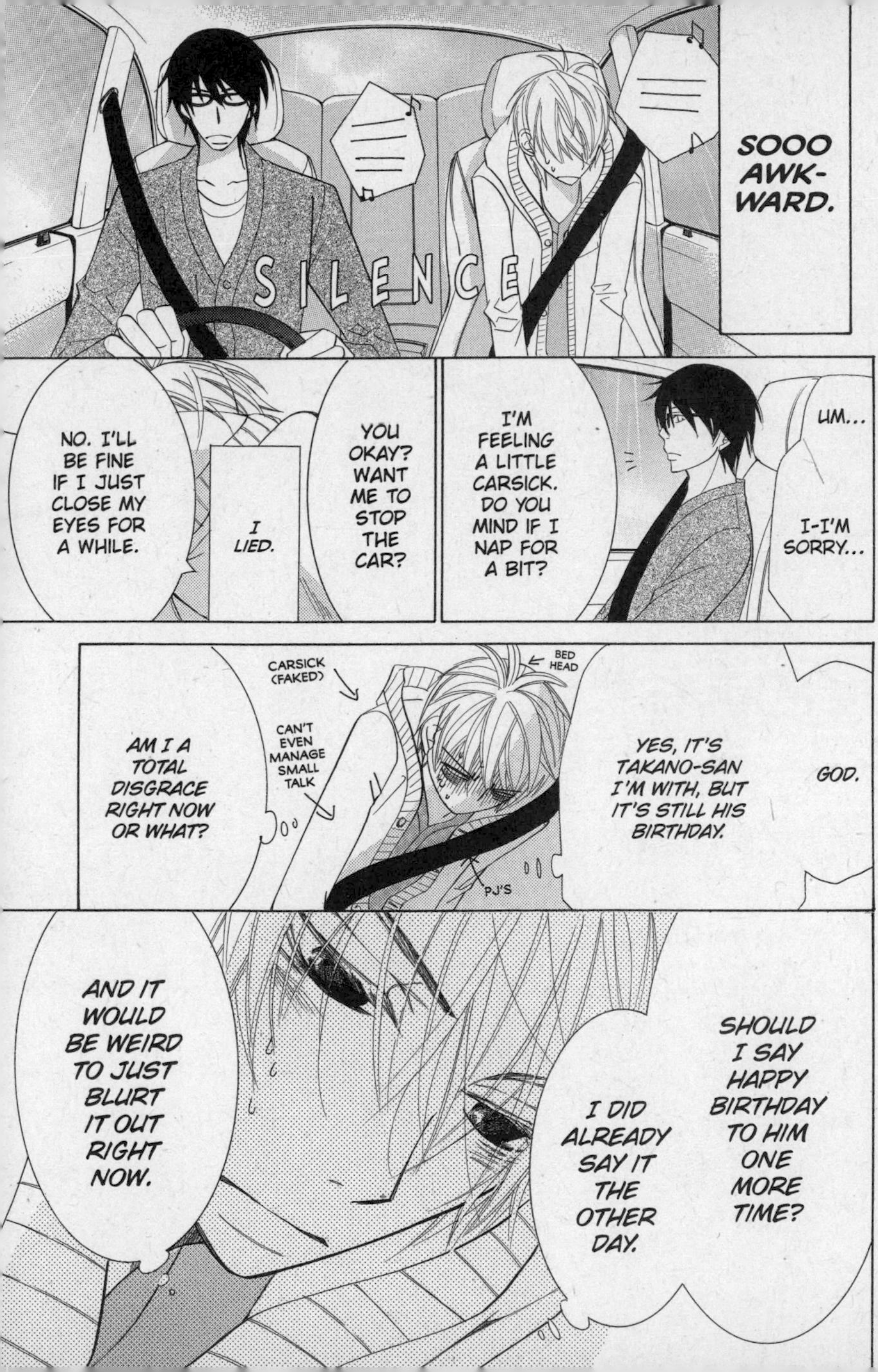
SOOO AWK-WARD.
SILENCE
UM...
I-I'M SORRY...
I'M FEELING A LITTLE CARSICK. DO YOU MIND IF I NAP FOR A BIT?
YOU OKAY? WANT ME TO STOP THE CAR?
I LIED.
NO. I'LL BE FINE IF I JUST CLOSE MY EYES FOR A WHILE.
GOD.
YES, IT'S TAKANO-SAN I'M WITH, BUT IT'S STILL HIS BIRTHDAY.
BED HEAD
CARSICK (FAKED)
CAN'T EVEN MANAGE SMALL TALK
PJ'S
AM I A TOTAL DISGRACE RIGHT NOW OR WHAT?
SHOULD I SAY HAPPY BIRTHDAY TO HIM ONE MORE TIME?
I DID ALREADY SAY IT THE OTHER DAY.
AND IT WOULD BE WEIRD TO JUST BLURT IT OUT RIGHT NOW.

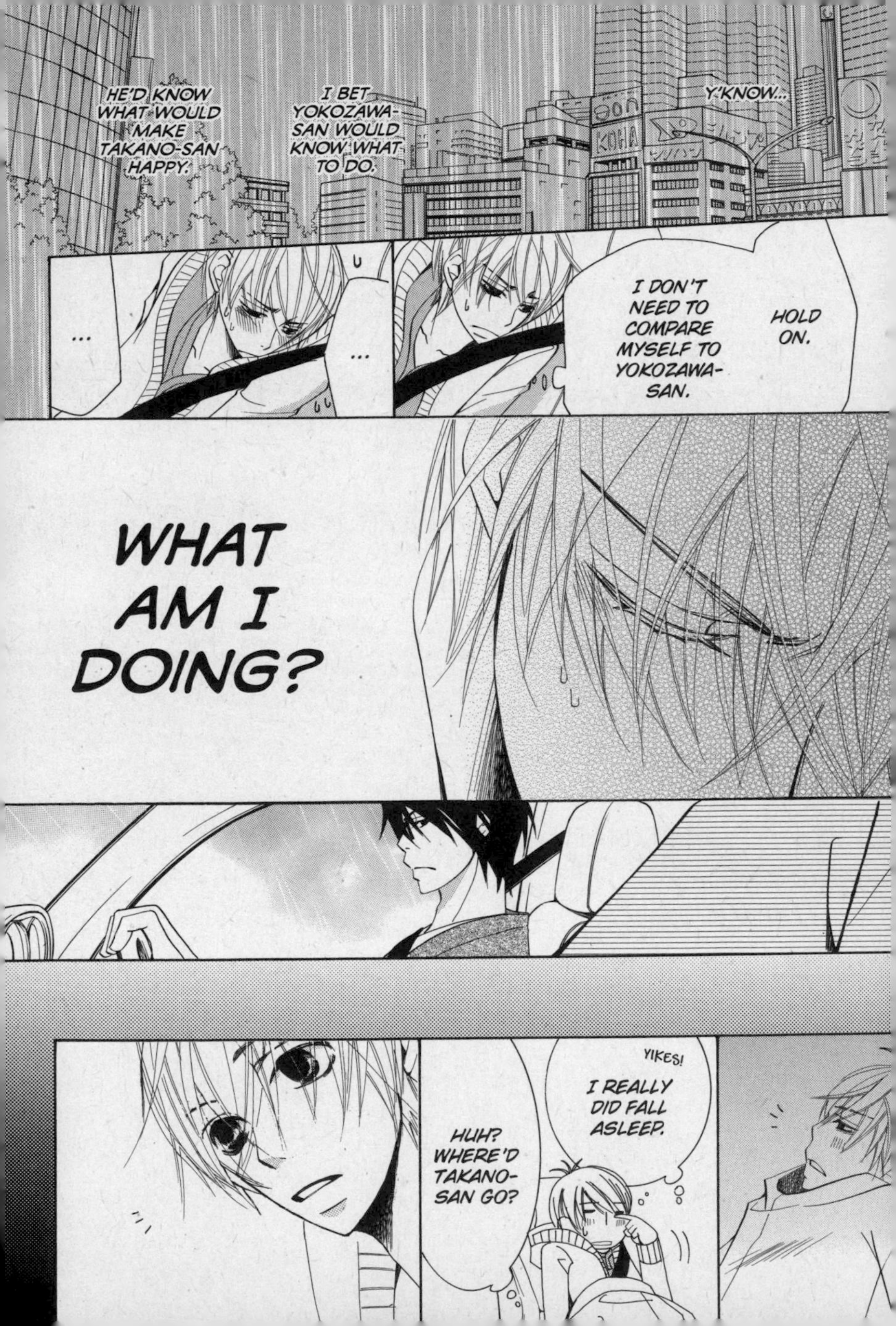
Y'KNOW...
I BET YOKOZAWA-SAN WOULD KNOW WHAT TO DO.
HE'D KNOW WHAT WOULD MAKE TAKANO-SAN HAPPY.
HOLD ON.
I DON'T NEED TO COMPARE MYSELF TO YOKOZAWA-SAN.
...
...
WHAT AM I DOING?
YIKES!
I REALLY DID FALL ASLEEP.
HUH? WHERE'D TAKANO-SAN GO?

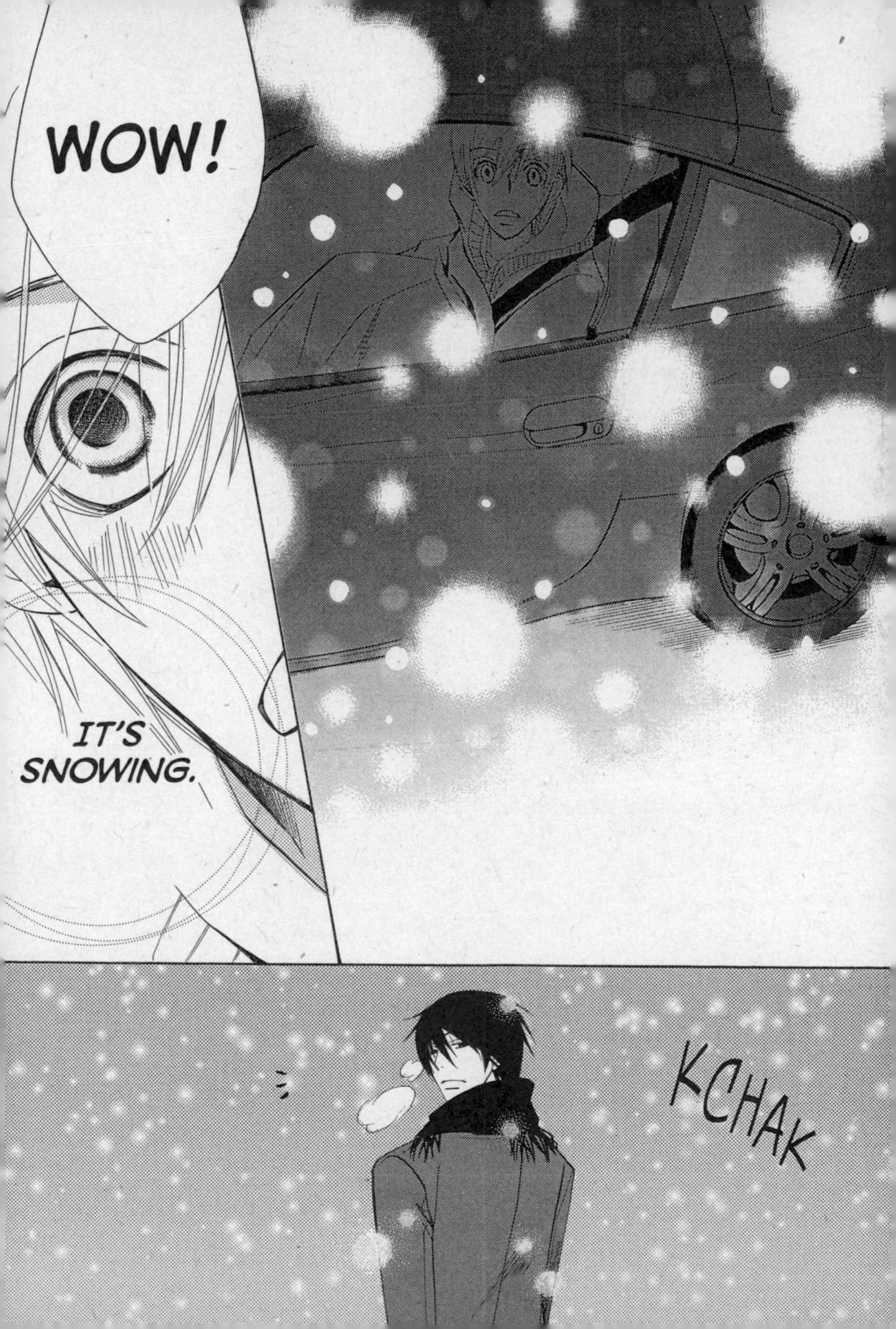
WOW!
IT'S SNOWING.
KCHAK

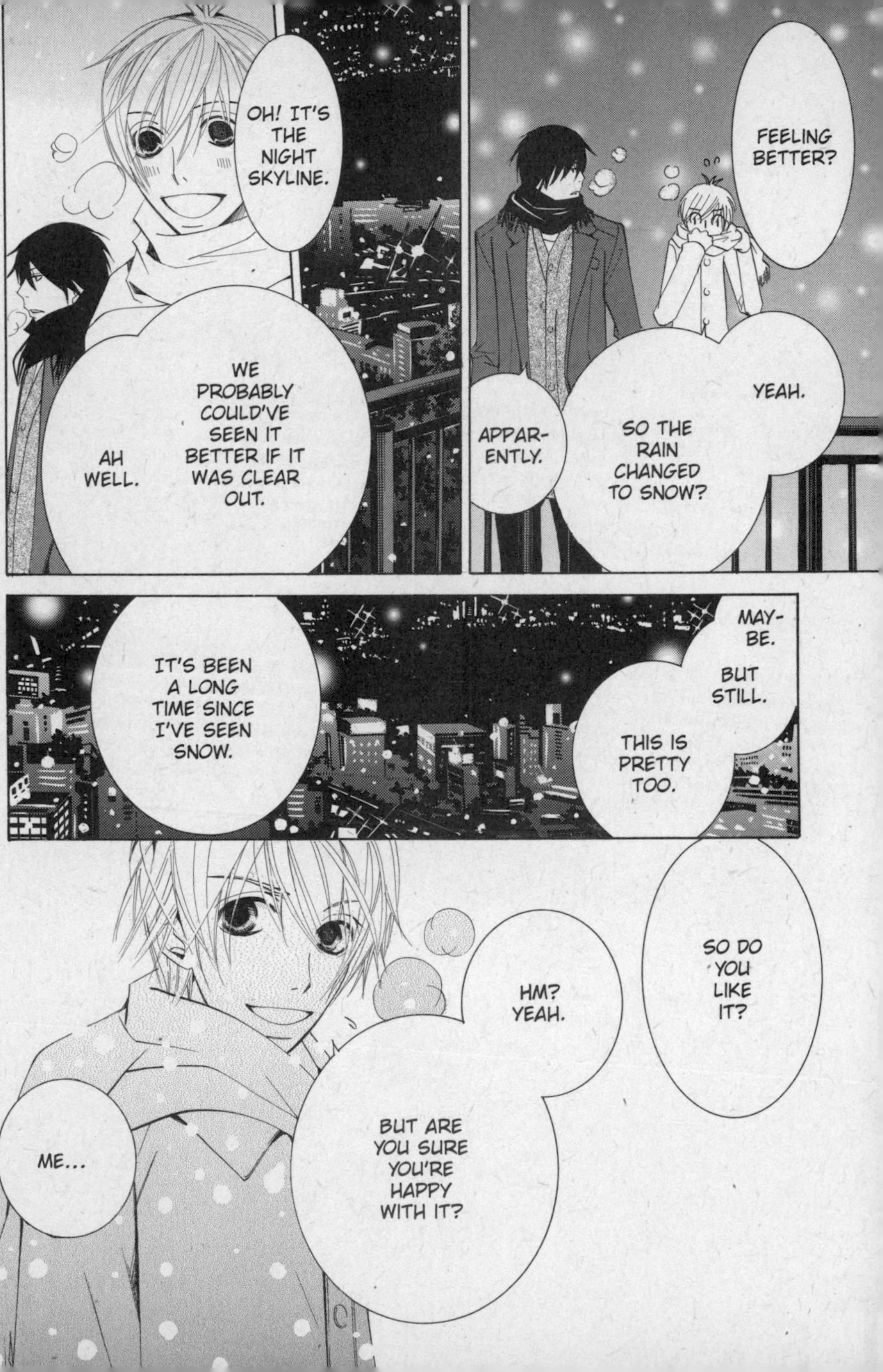
FEELING BETTER?
YEAH.
SO THE RAIN CHANGED TO SNOW?
APPAR-ENTLY.
OH! IT'S THE NIGHT SKYLINE.
WE PROBABLY COULD'VE SEEN IT BETTER IF IT WAS CLEAR OUT.
AH WELL.
MAY-BE.
BUT STILL.
THIS IS PRETTY TOO.
IT'S BEEN A LONG TIME SINCE I'VE SEEN SNOW.
SO DO YOU LIKE IT?
HM? YEAH.
BUT ARE YOU SURE YOU'RE HAPPY WITH IT?
ME...

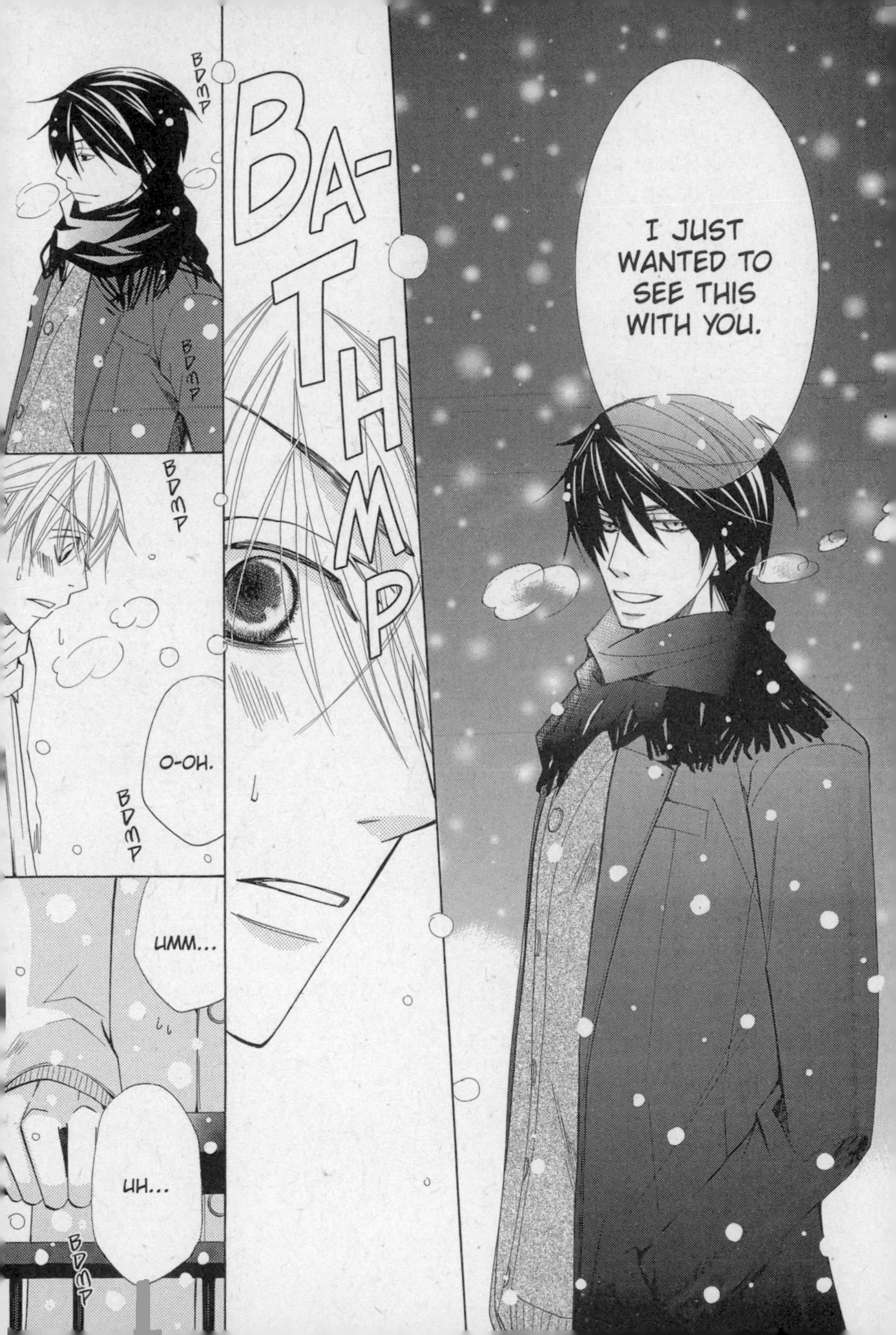
I JUST WANTED TO SEE THIS WITH YOU.
BA-THMP
BDMP
BDMP
BDMP
O-OH.
BDMP
UMM...
UH...
BDMP

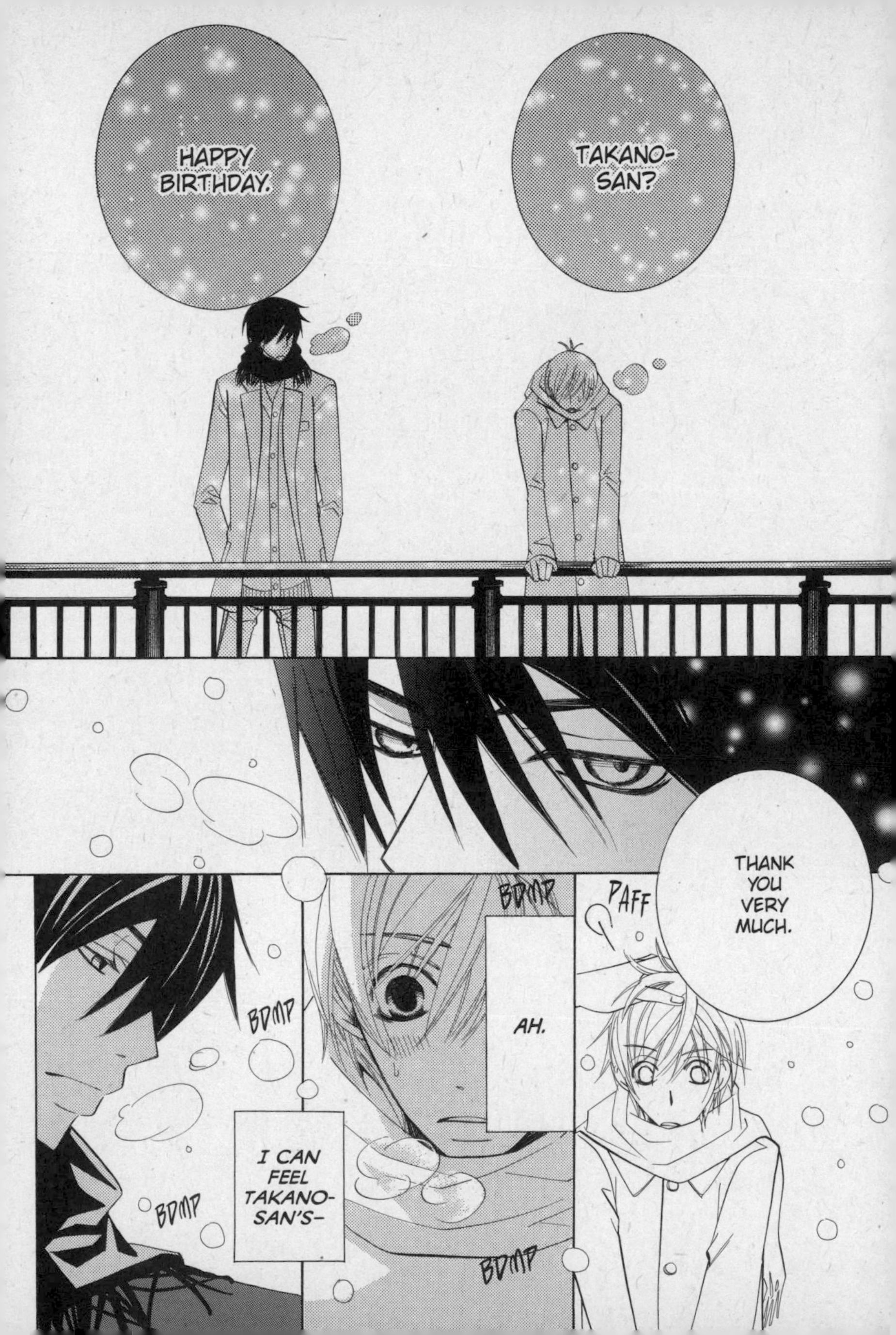

TAKANO-SAN?
HAPPY BIRTHDAY.
THANK YOU VERY MUCH.
PAFF
AH.
BDMP
BDMP
I CAN FEEL TAKANO-SAN'S-
BDMP
BDMP

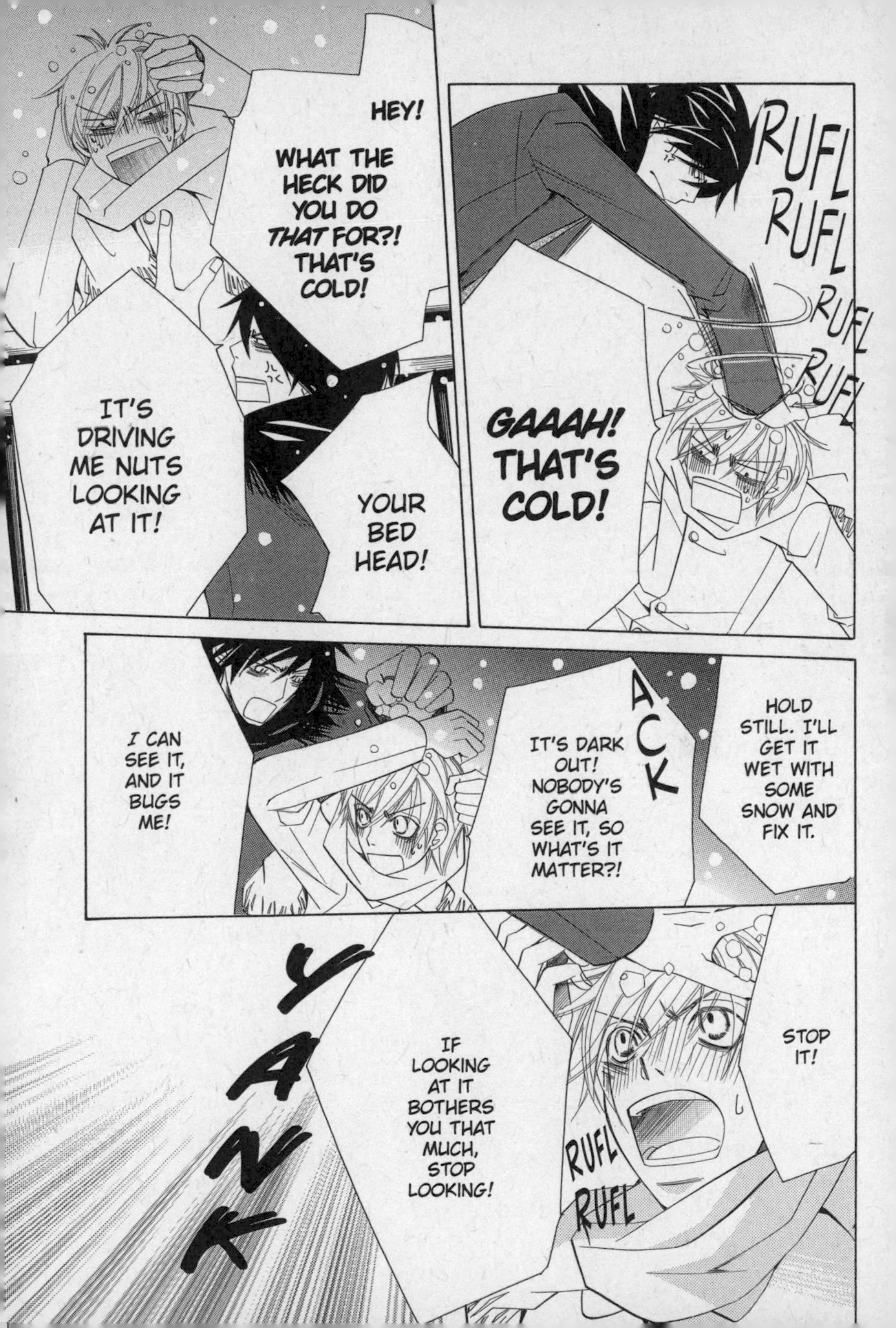
RUFL RUFL RUFL RUFL
GAAAH! THAT'S COLD!
HEY!
WHAT THE HECK DID YOU DO *THAT* FOR?! THAT'S COLD!
YOUR BED HEAD!
IT'S DRIVING ME NUTS LOOKING AT IT!
HOLD STILL. I'LL GET IT WET WITH SOME SNOW AND FIX IT.
ACK
IT'S DARK OUT! NOBODY'S GONNA SEE IT, SO WHAT'S IT MATTER?!
I CAN SEE IT, AND IT BUGS ME!
STOP IT!
RUFL RUFL
IF LOOKING AT IT BOTHERS YOU THAT MUCH, STOP LOOKING!
YANK

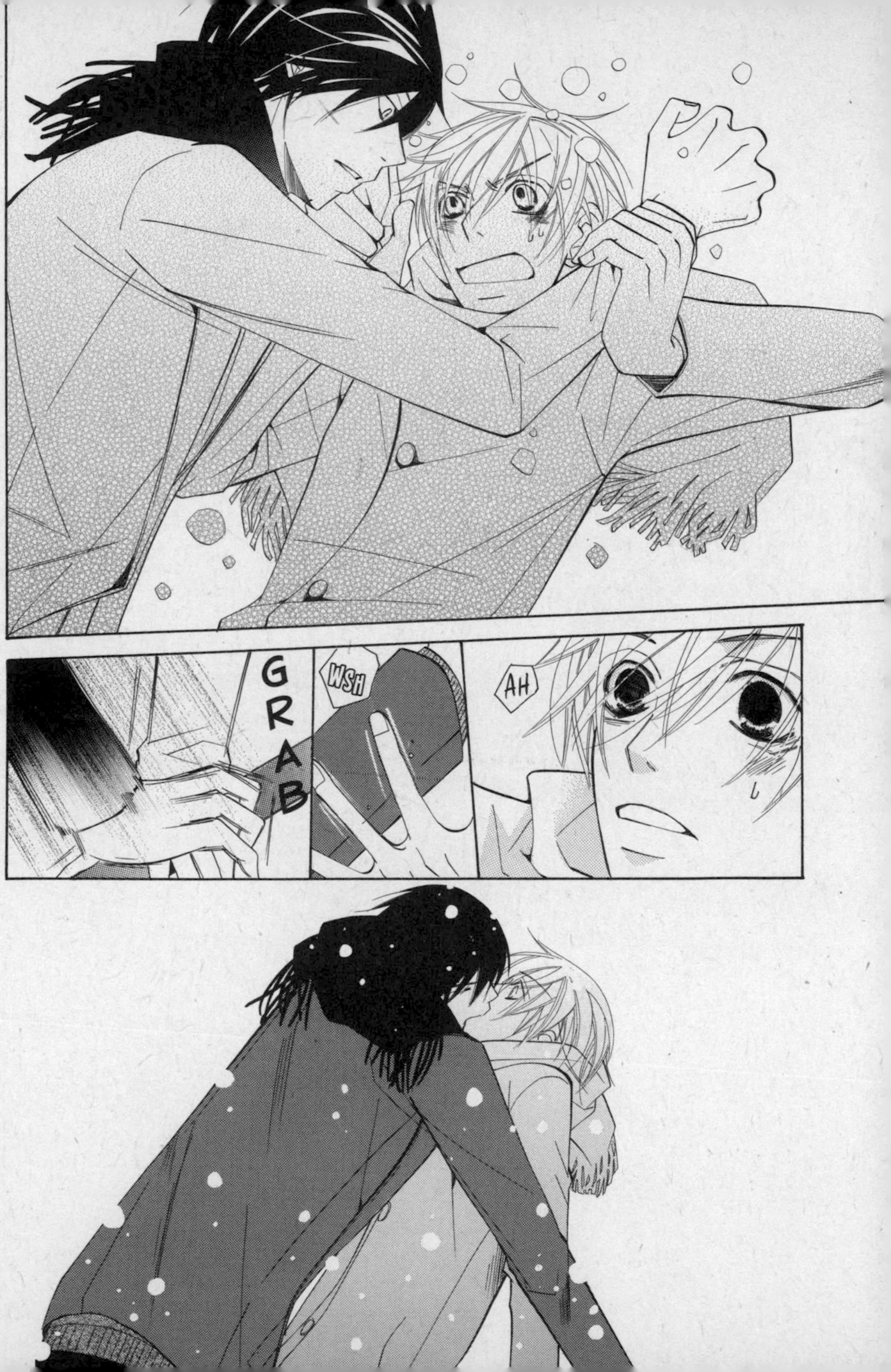
AH
WSH
GRAB

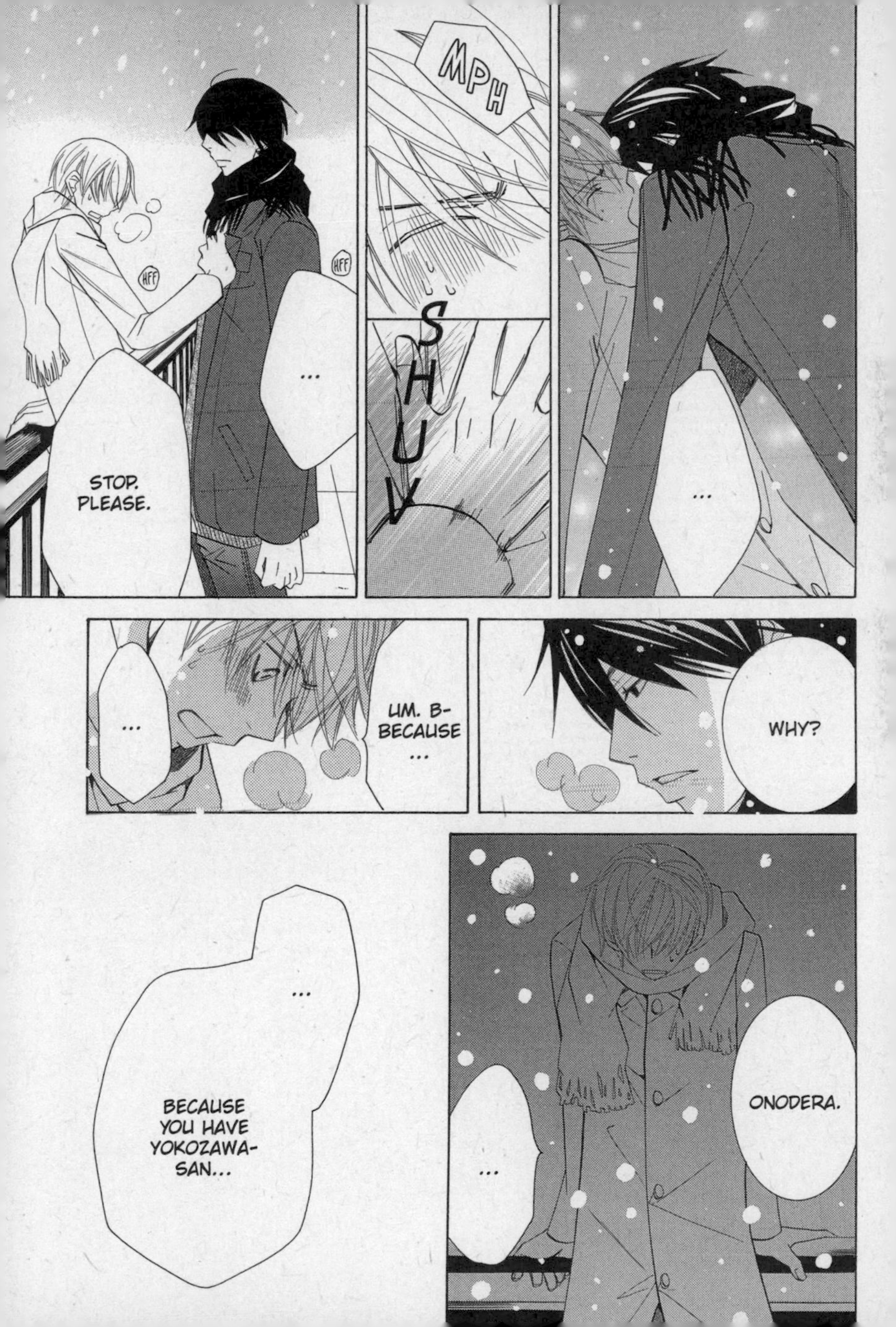
...
MPH
SHUV
HFF
...
HFF
STOP. PLEASE.
WHY?
UM. B-BECAUSE ...
...
ONODERA.
...
...
BECAUSE YOU HAVE YOKOZAWA-SAN...

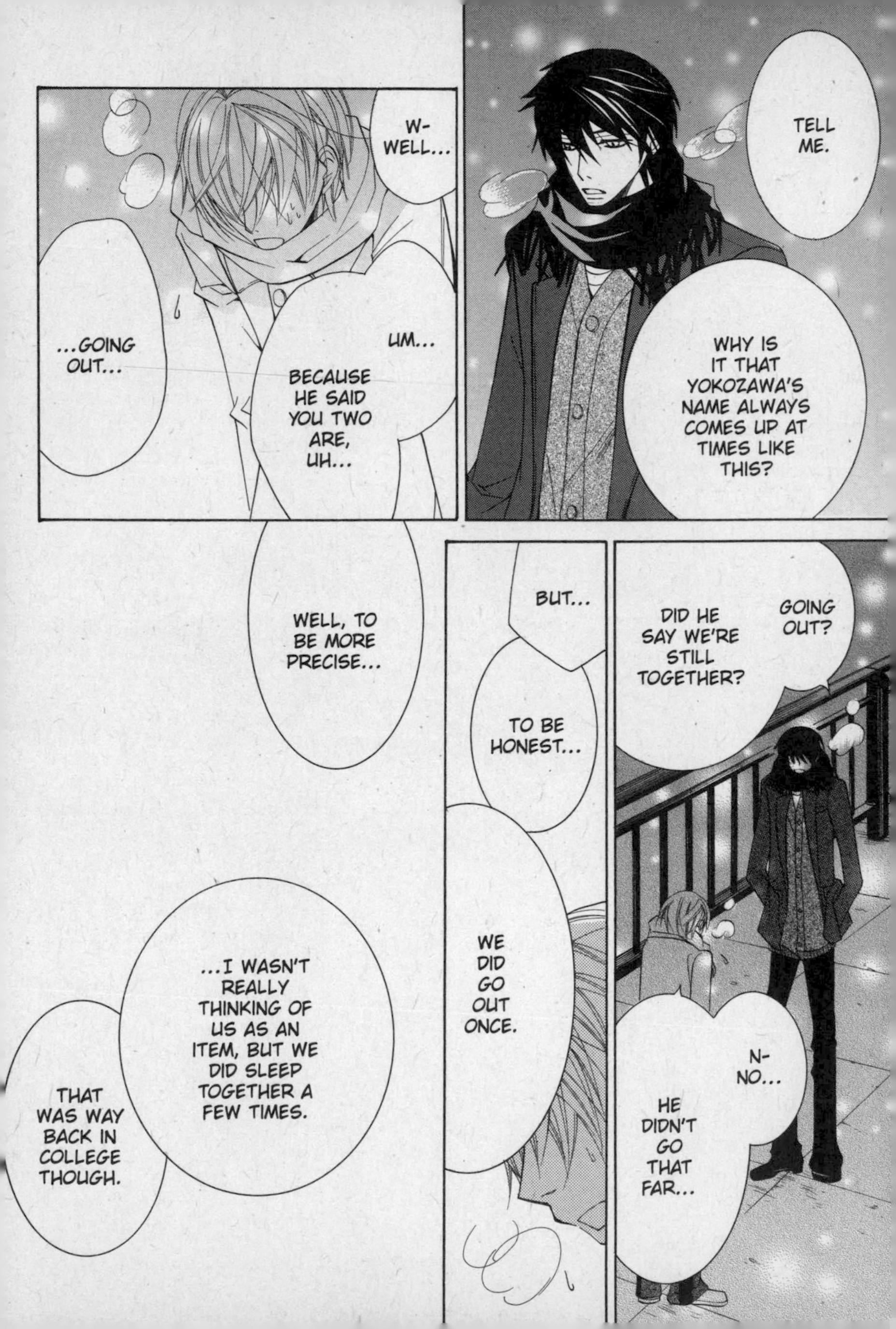
TELL ME.
WHY IS IT THAT YOKOZAWA'S NAME ALWAYS COMES UP AT TIMES LIKE THIS?
W-WELL...
UM...
BECAUSE HE SAID YOU TWO ARE, UH...
...GOING OUT...
GOING OUT?
DID HE SAY WE'RE STILL TOGETHER?
N-NO...
HE DIDN'T GO THAT FAR...
BUT...
TO BE HONEST...
WE DID GO OUT ONCE.
WELL, TO BE MORE PRECISE...
...I WASN'T REALLY THINKING OF US AS AN ITEM, BUT WE DID SLEEP TOGETHER A FEW TIMES.
THAT WAS WAY BACK IN COLLEGE THOUGH.

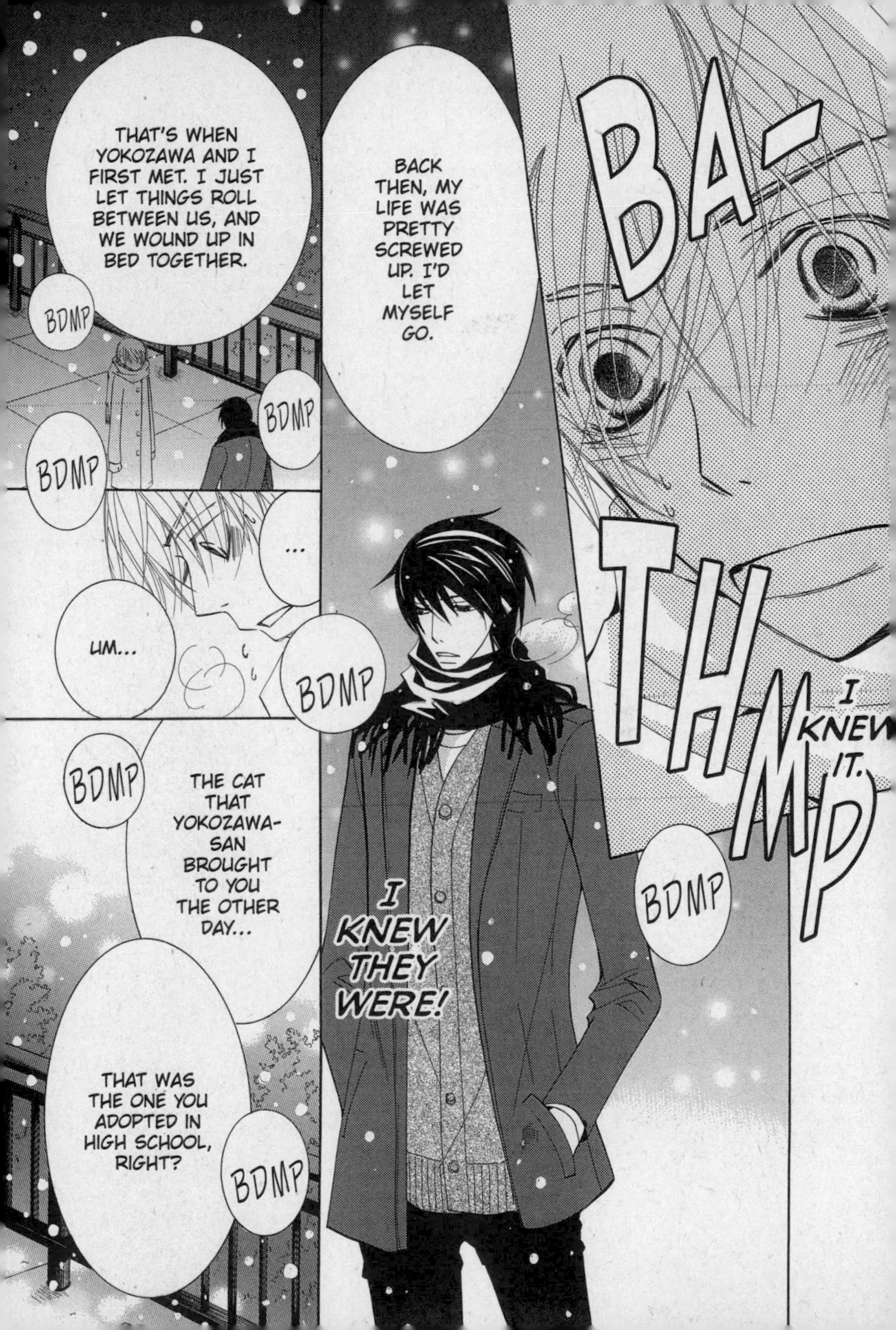
BA-THUMP
I KNEW IT.
BDMP
BACK THEN, MY LIFE WAS PRETTY SCREWED UP. I'D LET MYSELF GO.
I KNEW THEY WERE!
THAT'S WHEN YOKOZAWA AND I FIRST MET. I JUST LET THINGS ROLL BETWEEN US, AND WE WOUND UP IN BED TOGETHER.
BDMP
BDMP
BDMP
...
UM...
BDMP
THE CAT THAT YOKOZAWA-SAN BROUGHT TO YOU THE OTHER DAY...
BDMP
THAT WAS THE ONE YOU ADOPTED IN HIGH SCHOOL, RIGHT?
BDMP

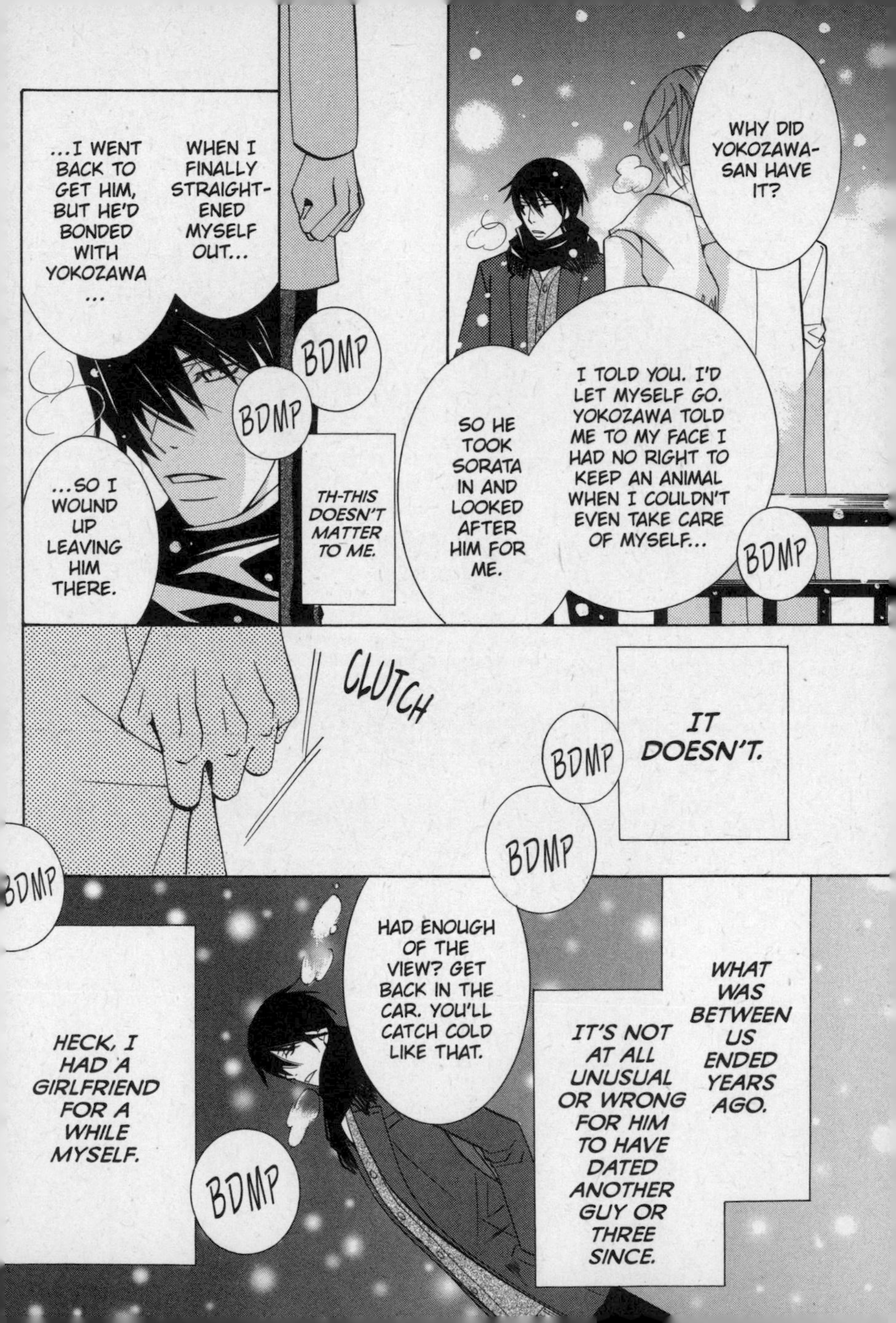
WHY DID YOKOZAWA-SAN HAVE IT?
I TOLD YOU. I'D LET MYSELF GO. YOKOZAWA TOLD ME TO MY FACE I HAD NO RIGHT TO KEEP AN ANIMAL WHEN I COULDN'T EVEN TAKE CARE OF MYSELF...
BDMP
SO HE TOOK SORATA IN AND LOOKED AFTER HIM FOR ME.
TH-THIS DOESN'T MATTER TO ME.
BDMP
BDMP
WHEN I FINALLY STRAIGHT-ENED MYSELF OUT...
...I WENT BACK TO GET HIM, BUT HE'D BONDED WITH YOKOZAWA...
...SO I WOUND UP LEAVING HIM THERE.
IT DOESN'T.
BDMP
BDMP
CLUTCH
BDMP
WHAT WAS BETWEEN US ENDED YEARS AGO.
IT'S NOT AT ALL UNUSUAL OR WRONG FOR HIM TO HAVE DATED ANOTHER GUY OR THREE SINCE.
HAD ENOUGH OF THE VIEW? GET BACK IN THE CAR. YOU'LL CATCH COLD LIKE THAT.
HECK, I HAD A GIRLFRIEND FOR A WHILE MYSELF.
BDMP

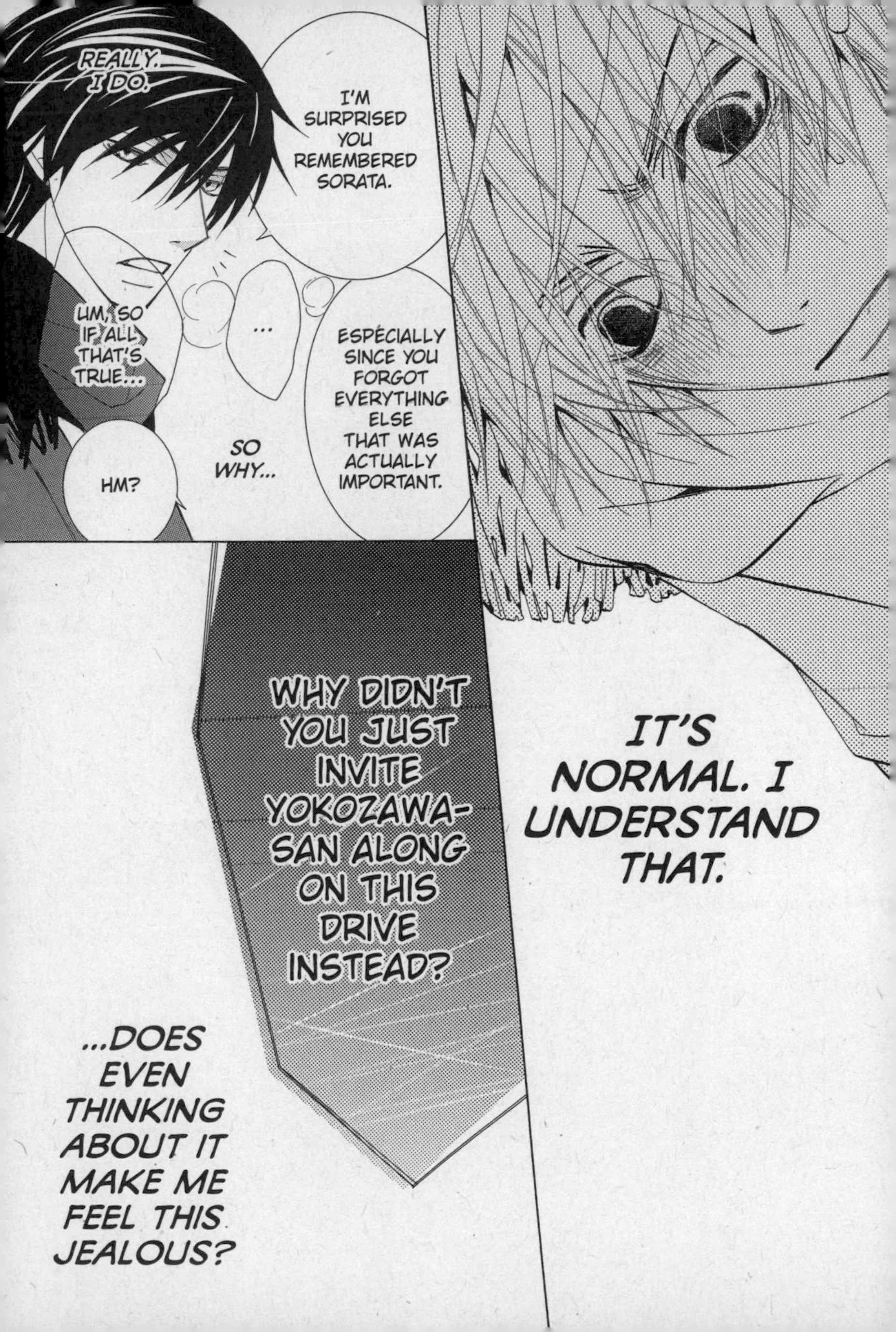
I'M SURPRISED YOU REMEMBERED SORATA.
ESPECIALLY SINCE YOU FORGOT EVERYTHING ELSE THAT WAS ACTUALLY IMPORTANT.
REALLY. I DO.
...
UM, SO IF ALL THAT'S TRUE...
SO WHY...
HM?
IT'S NORMAL. I UNDERSTAND THAT.
WHY DIDN'T YOU JUST INVITE YOKOZAWA-SAN ALONG ON THIS DRIVE INSTEAD?
...DOES EVEN THINKING ABOUT IT MAKE ME FEEL THIS JEALOUS?

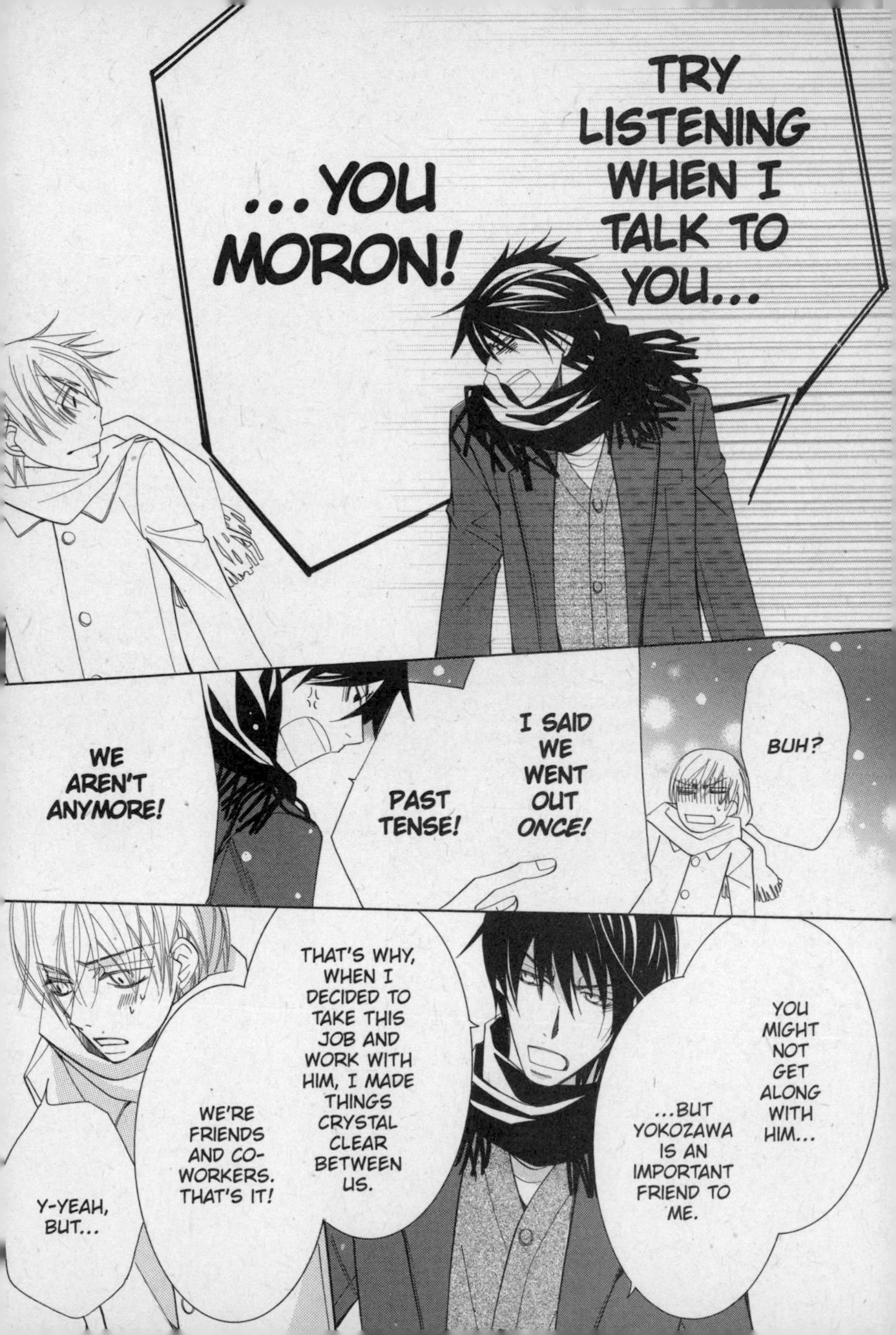
TRY LISTENING WHEN I TALK TO YOU...
...YOU MORON!
BUH?
I SAID WE WENT OUT ONCE!
PAST TENSE!
WE AREN'T ANYMORE!
YOU MIGHT NOT GET ALONG WITH HIM...
...BUT YOKOZAWA IS AN IMPORTANT FRIEND TO ME.
THAT'S WHY, WHEN I DECIDED TO TAKE THIS JOB AND WORK WITH HIM, I MADE THINGS CRYSTAL CLEAR BETWEEN US.
WE'RE FRIENDS AND CO-WORKERS. THAT'S IT!
Y-YEAH, BUT...

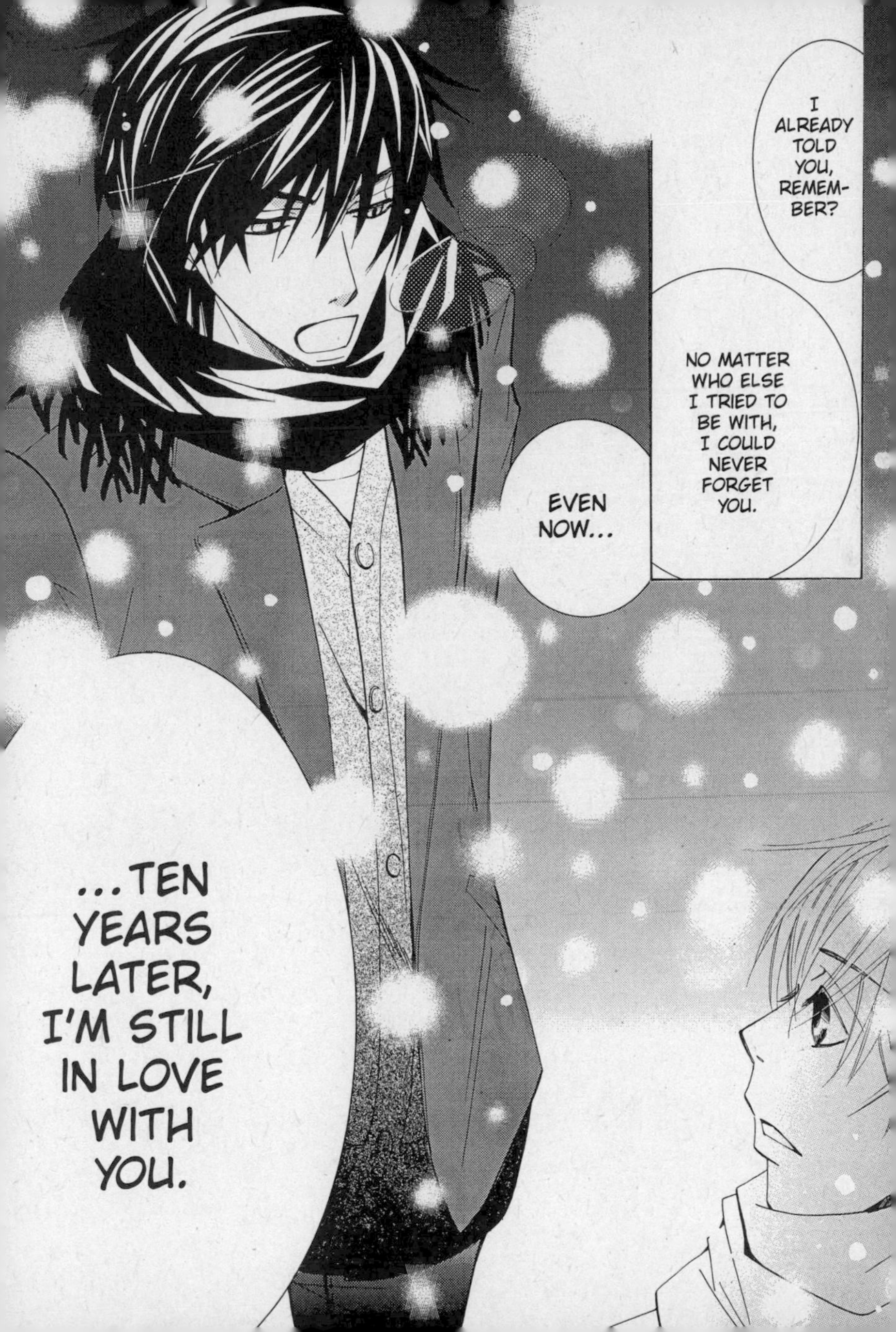
I ALREADY TOLD YOU, REMEMBER?
NO MATTER WHO ELSE I TRIED TO BE WITH, I COULD NEVER FORGET YOU.
EVEN NOW...
...TEN YEARS LATER, I'M STILL IN LOVE WITH YOU.

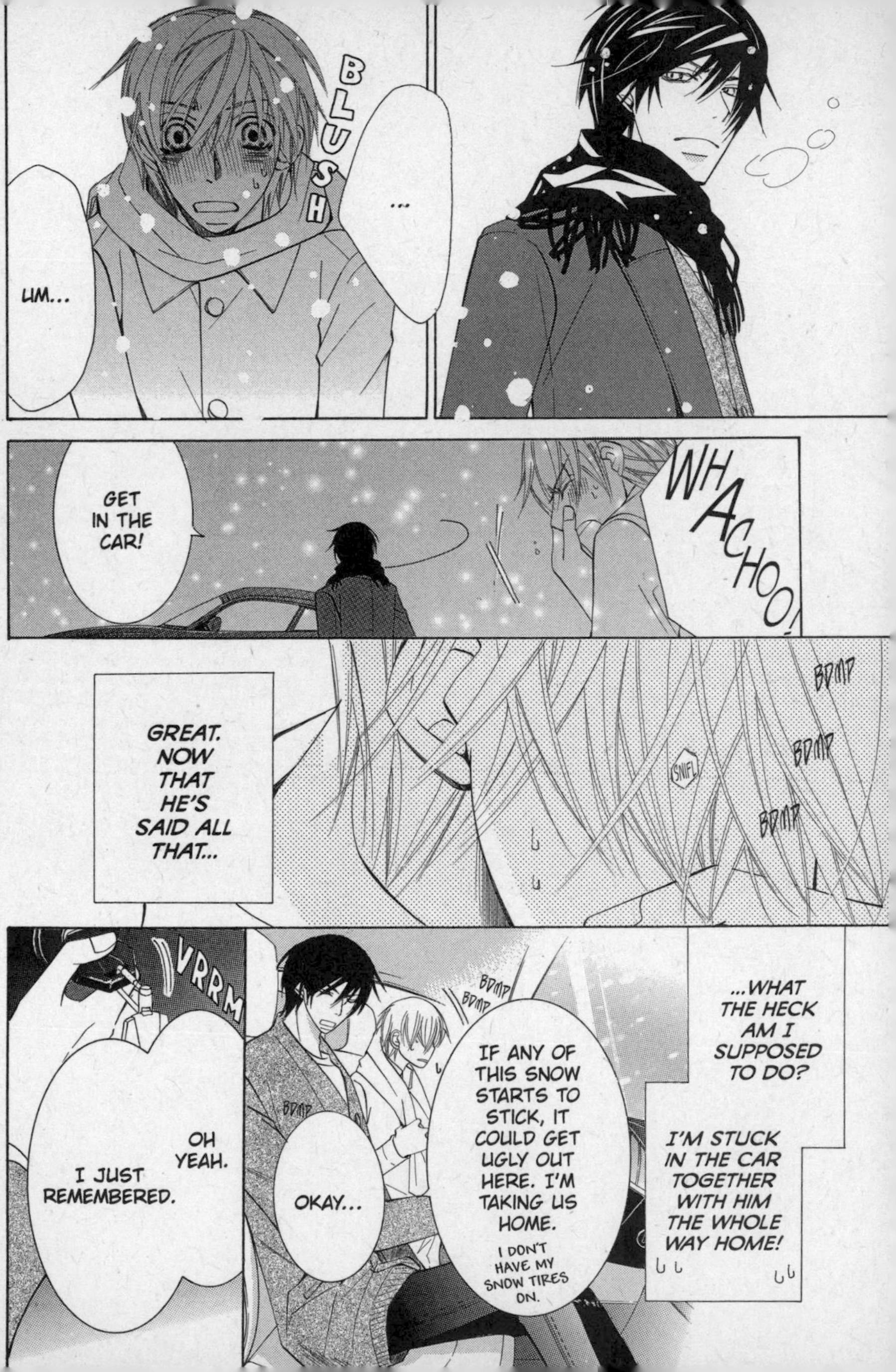
BLUSH
...
UM...
WHACHOO!
GET IN THE CAR!
BDMP
BDMP
SNIFL
BDMP
GREAT. NOW THAT HE'S SAID ALL THAT...
...WHAT THE HECK AM I SUPPOSED TO DO?
I'M STUCK IN THE CAR TOGETHER WITH HIM THE WHOLE WAY HOME!
BDMP
BDMP
IF ANY OF THIS SNOW STARTS TO STICK, IT COULD GET UGLY OUT HERE. I'M TAKING US HOME.
I DON'T HAVE MY SNOW TIRES ON.
BDMP
OKAY...
VRRM
OH YEAH. I JUST REMEMBERED.

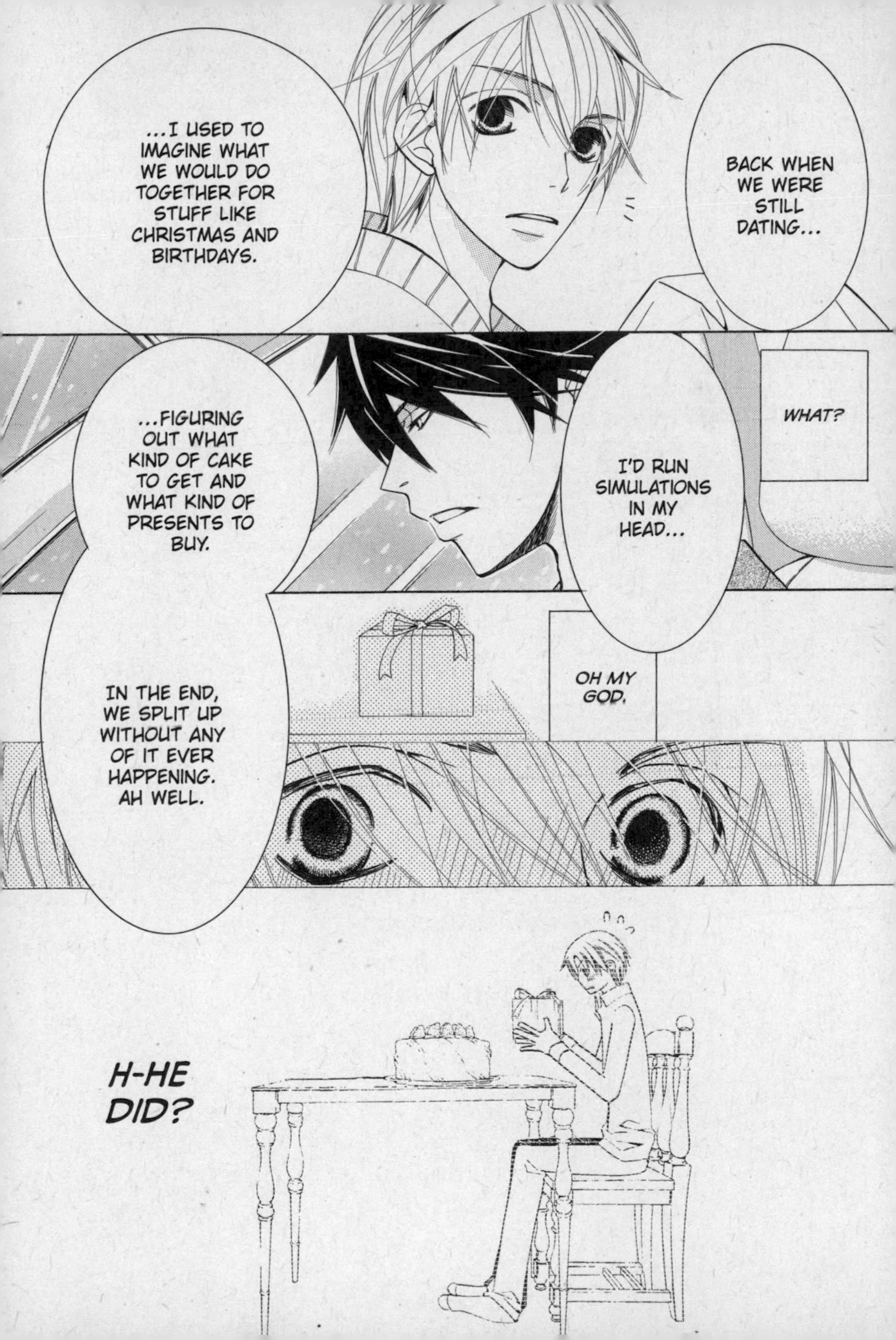
BACK WHEN WE WERE STILL DATING...
...I USED TO IMAGINE WHAT WE WOULD DO TOGETHER FOR STUFF LIKE CHRISTMAS AND BIRTHDAYS.
WHAT?
I'D RUN SIMULATIONS IN MY HEAD...
...FIGURING OUT WHAT KIND OF CAKE TO GET AND WHAT KIND OF PRESENTS TO BUY.
OH MY GOD.
IN THE END, WE SPLIT UP WITHOUT ANY OF IT EVER HAPPENING. AH WELL.
H-HE DID?

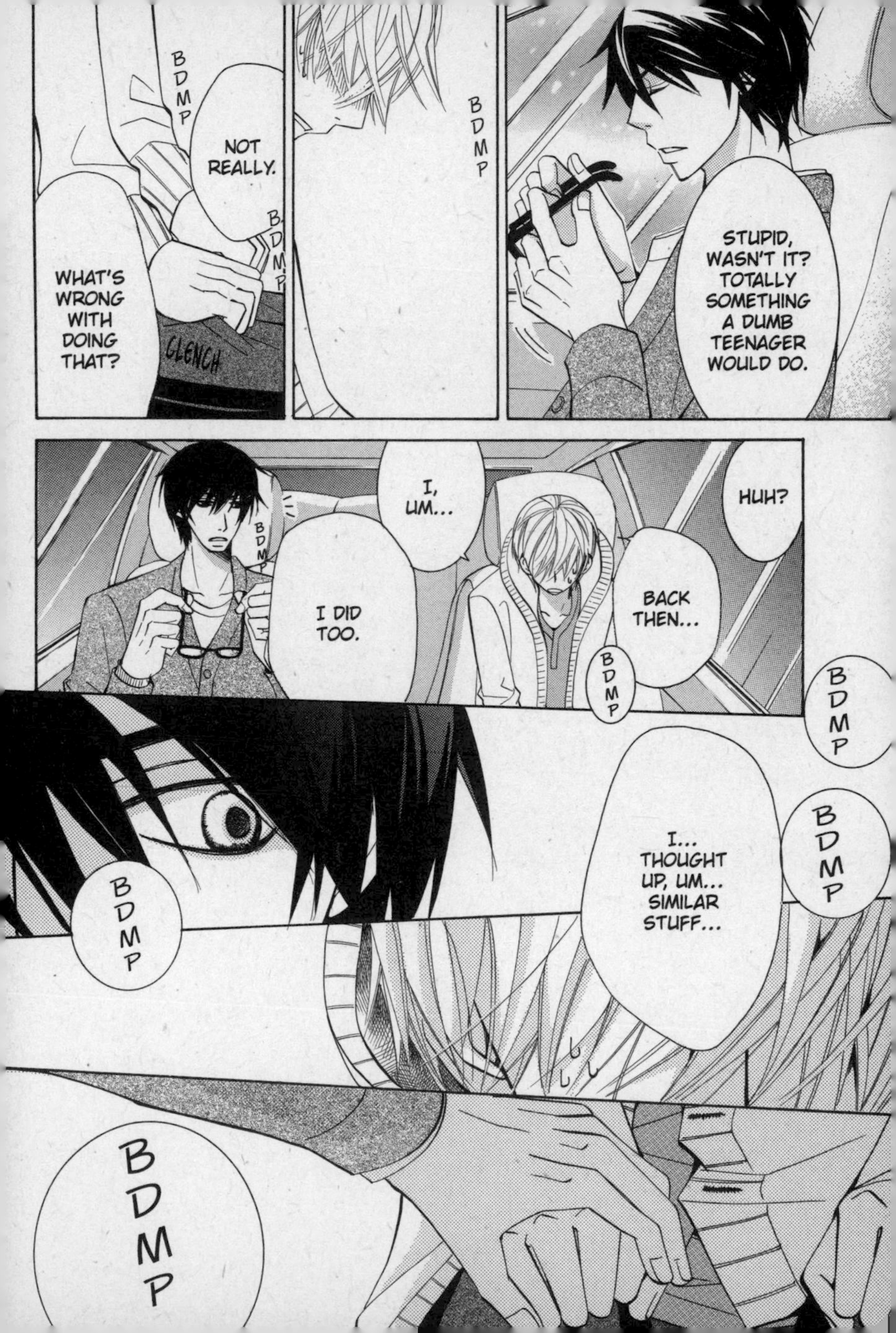
STUPID, WASN'T IT? TOTALLY SOMETHING A DUMB TEENAGER WOULD DO.
BDMP
BDMP
NOT REALLY.
BDMP
WHAT'S WRONG WITH DOING THAT?
CLENCH
HUH?
BACK THEN...
BDMP
I, UM...
I DID TOO.
BDMP
BDMP
I... THOUGHT UP, UM... SIMILAR STUFF...
BDMP
BDMP
BDMP

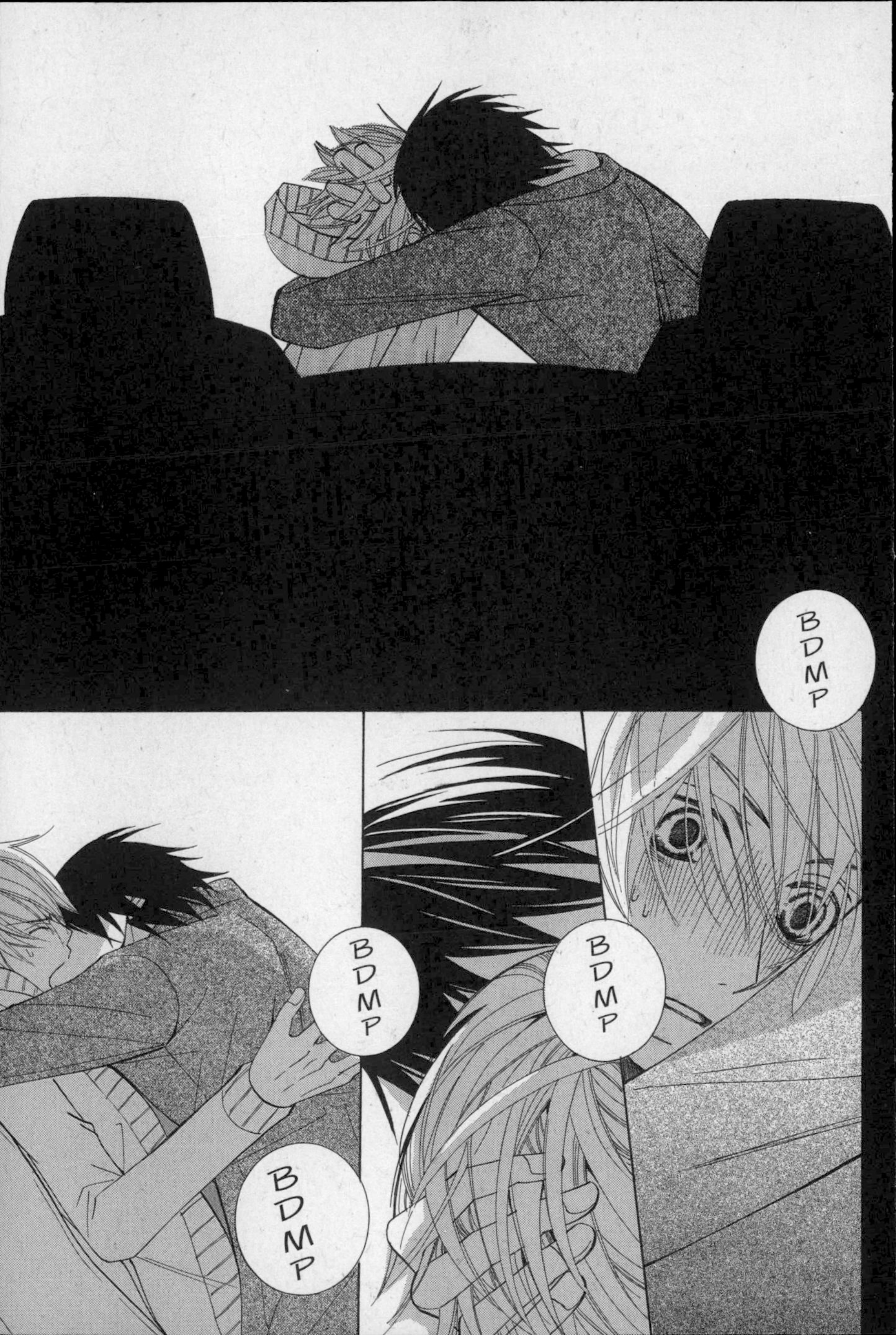
BDMP
BDMP
BDMP
BDMP

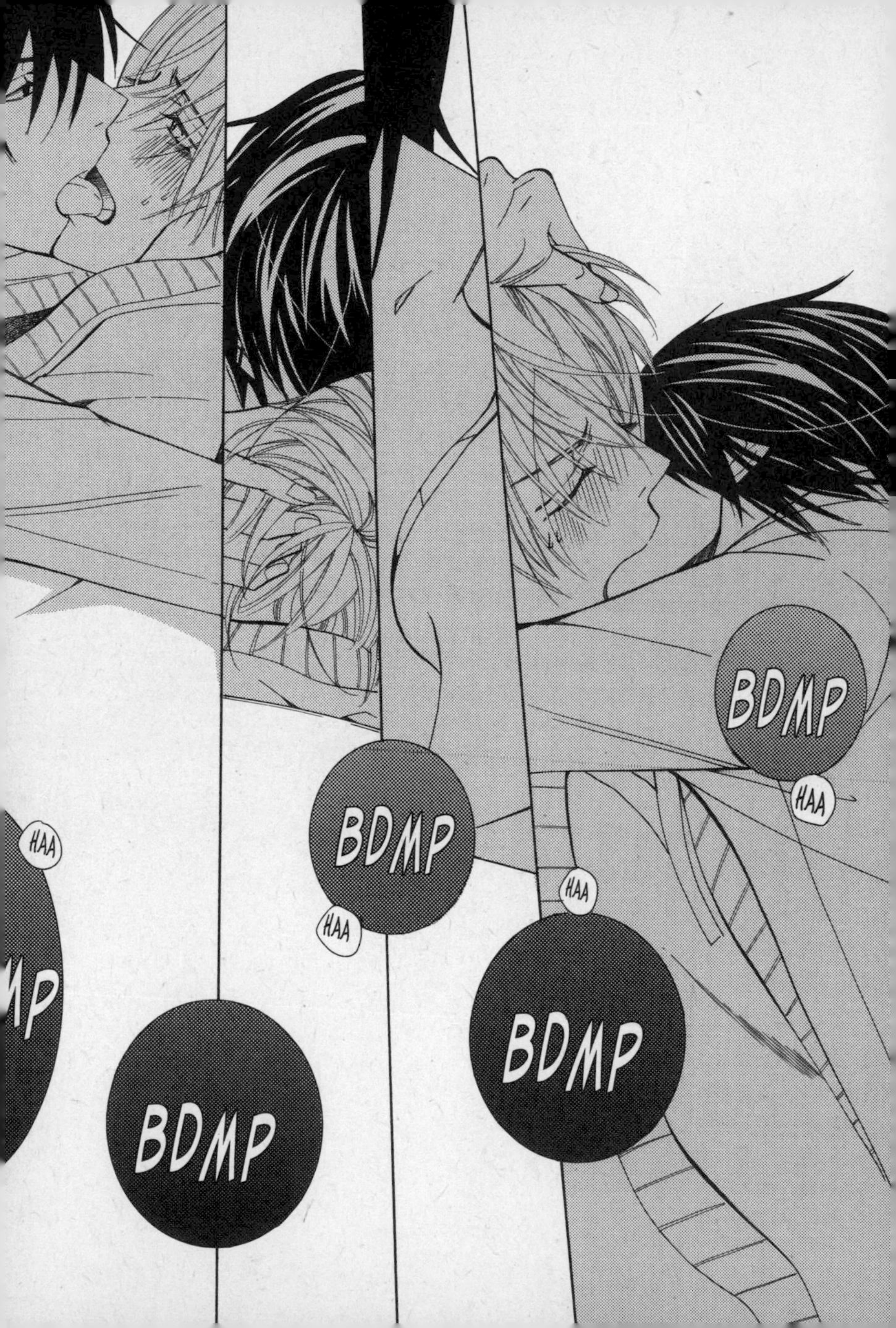
BDMP
HAA
HAA
BDMP
BDMP
HAA
BDMP
HAA

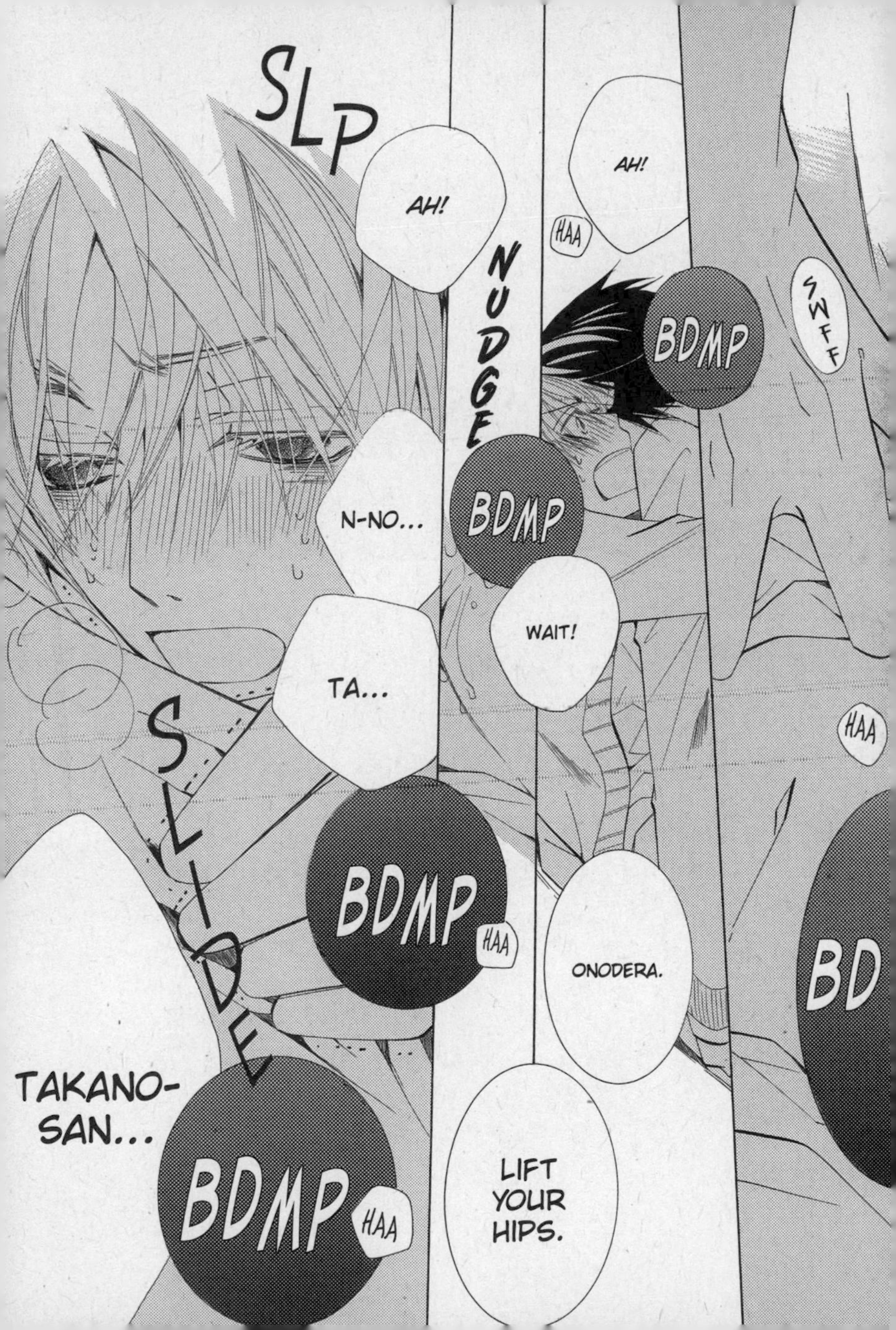
SWFF
HAA
BD
AH!
HAA
BDMP
ONODERA.
LIFT YOUR HIPS.
NUDGE
BDMP
WAIT!
SLP
AH!
N-NO...
TA...
SLIDE
BDMP
HAA
TAKANO-SAN...
BDMP
HAA

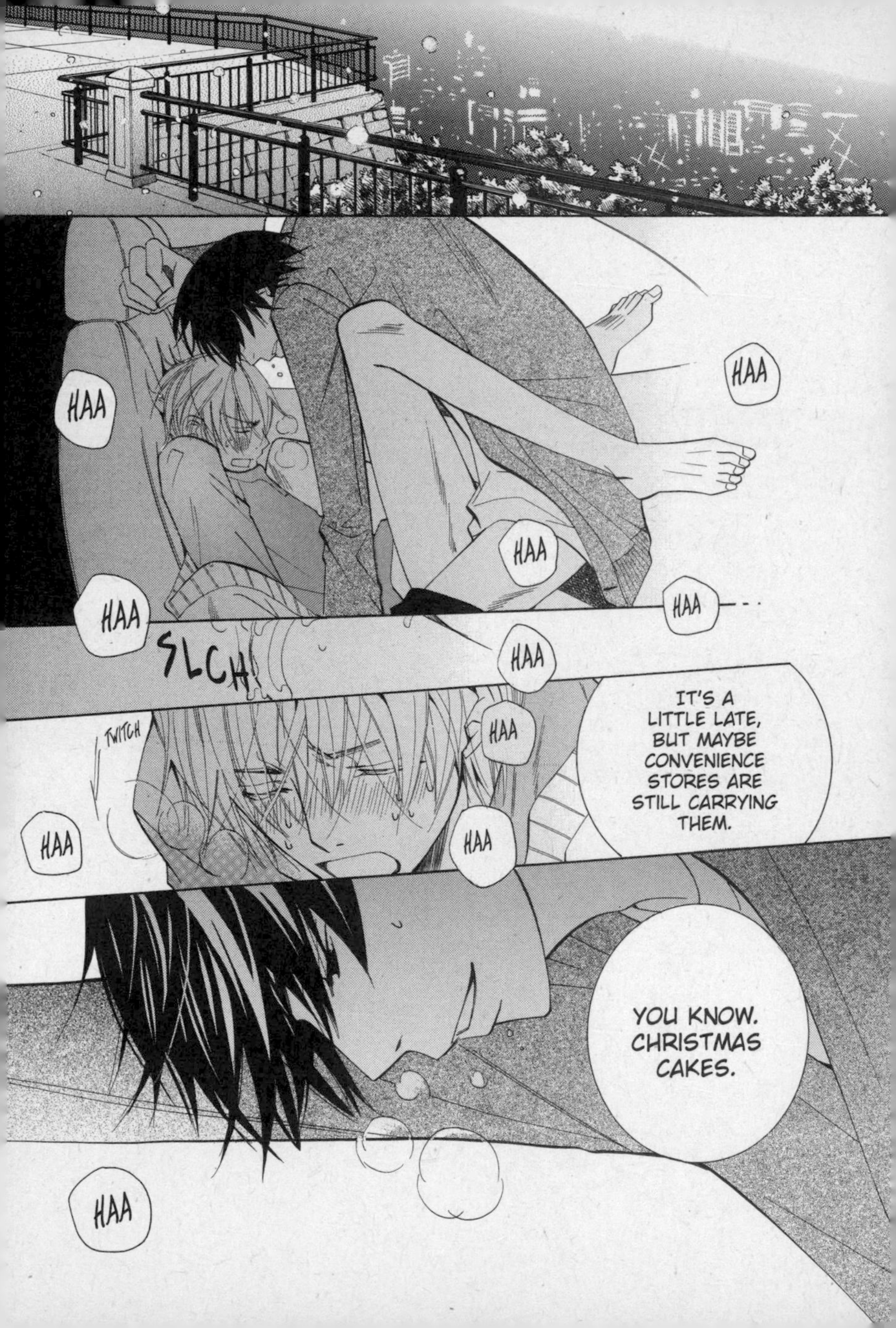
HAA
HAA
HAA
HAA---
HAA
HAA
SLCH!
IT'S A LITTLE LATE, BUT MAYBE CONVENIENCE STORES ARE STILL CARRYING THEM.
HAA
TWITCH
HAA
HAA
YOU KNOW. CHRISTMAS CAKES.
HAA

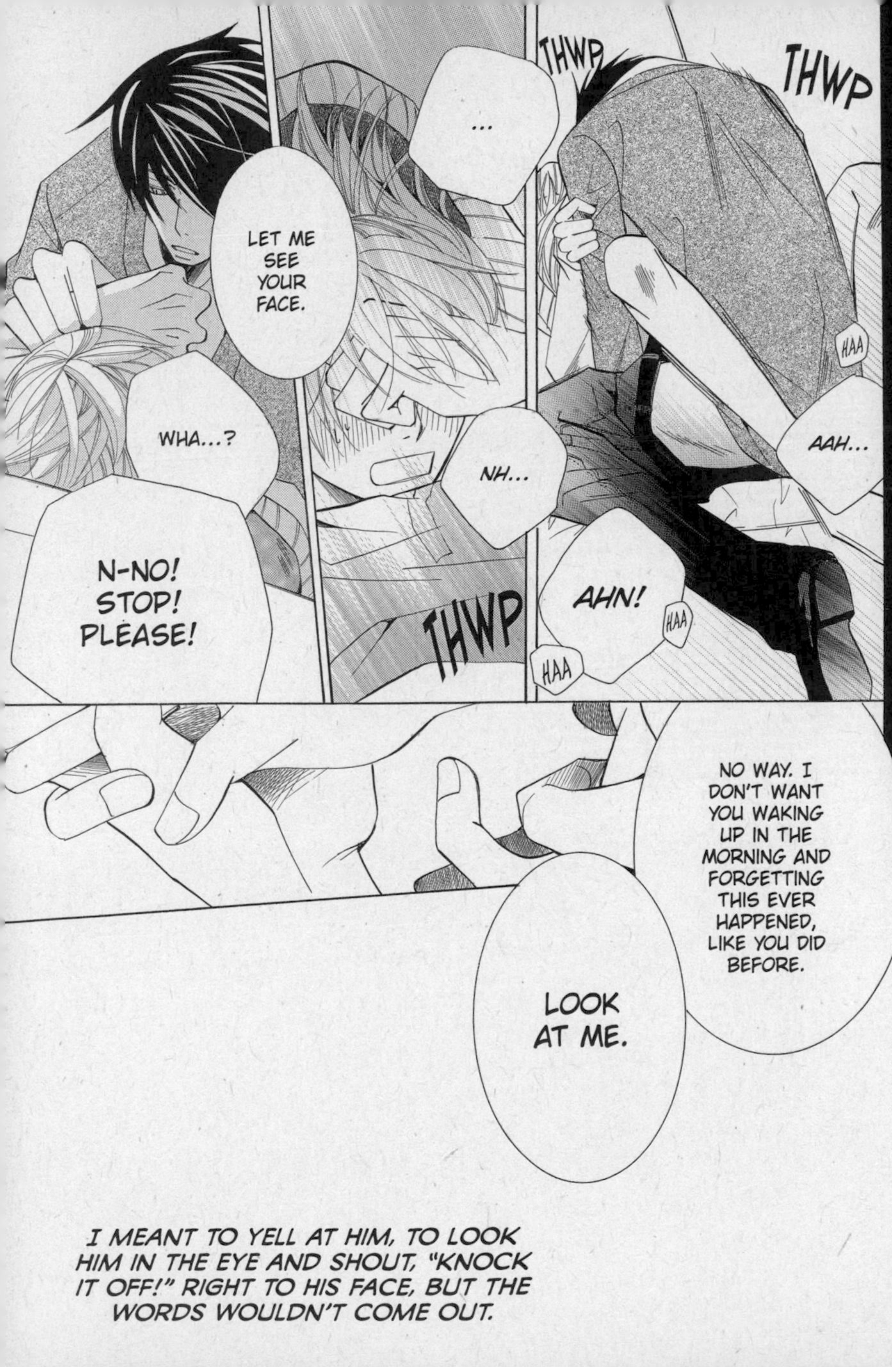
THWP
THWP
HAA
AAH...
AHN!
HAA
HAA
...
NH...
THWP
LET ME SEE YOUR FACE.
WHA...?
N-NO! STOP! PLEASE!
NO WAY. I DON'T WANT YOU WAKING UP IN THE MORNING AND FORGETTING THIS EVER HAPPENED, LIKE YOU DID BEFORE.
LOOK AT ME.
I MEANT TO YELL AT HIM, TO LOOK HIM IN THE EYE AND SHOUT, "KNOCK IT OFF!" RIGHT TO HIS FACE, BUT THE WORDS WOULDN'T COME OUT.

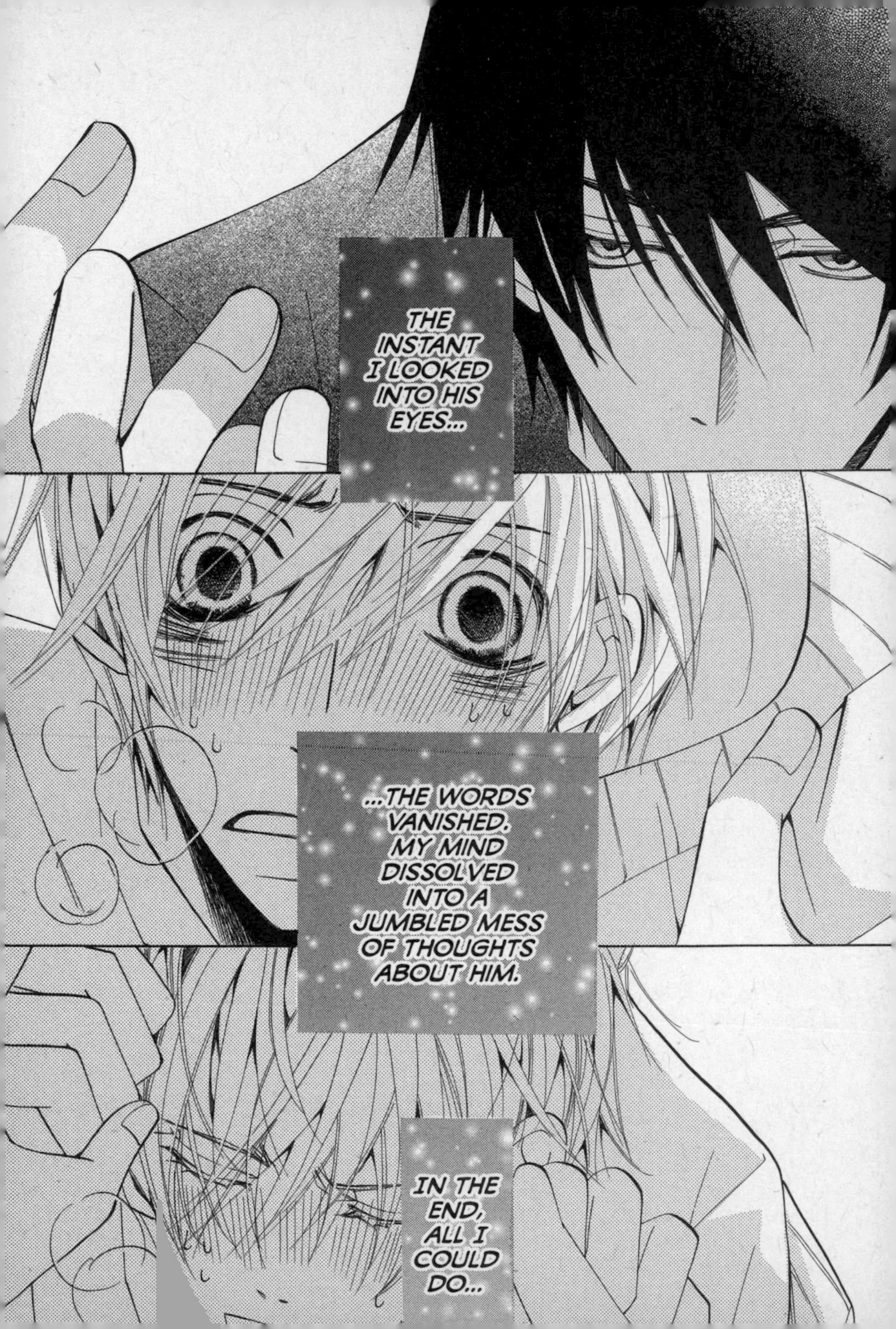
THE INSTANT I LOOKED INTO HIS EYES...
...THE WORDS VANISHED. MY MIND DISSOLVED INTO A JUMBLED MESS OF THOUGHTS ABOUT HIM.
IN THE END, ALL I COULD DO...

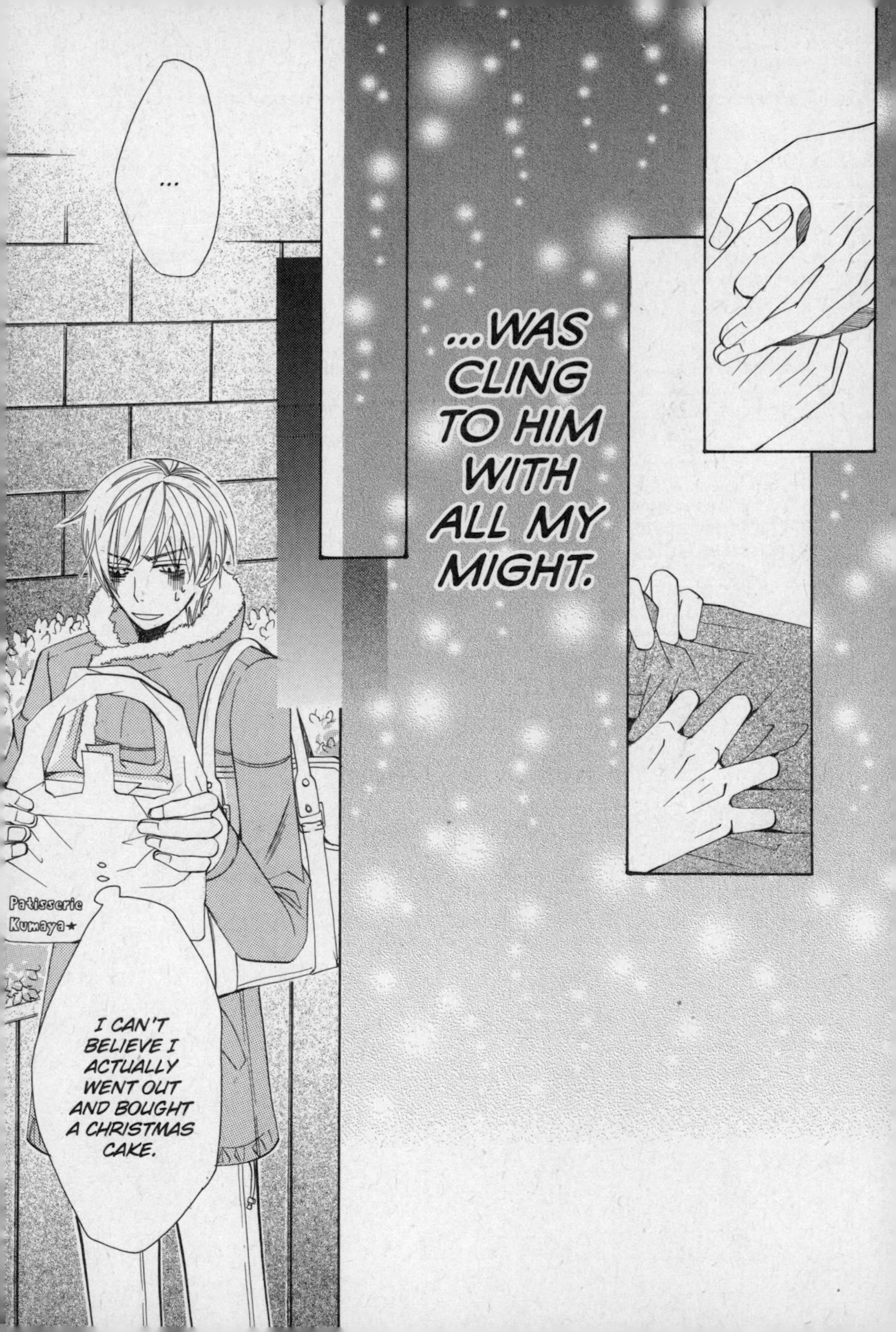
...WAS CLING TO HIM WITH ALL MY MIGHT.
...
Patisserie Kumaya★
I CAN'T BELIEVE I ACTUALLY WENT OUT AND BOUGHT A CHRISTMAS CAKE.

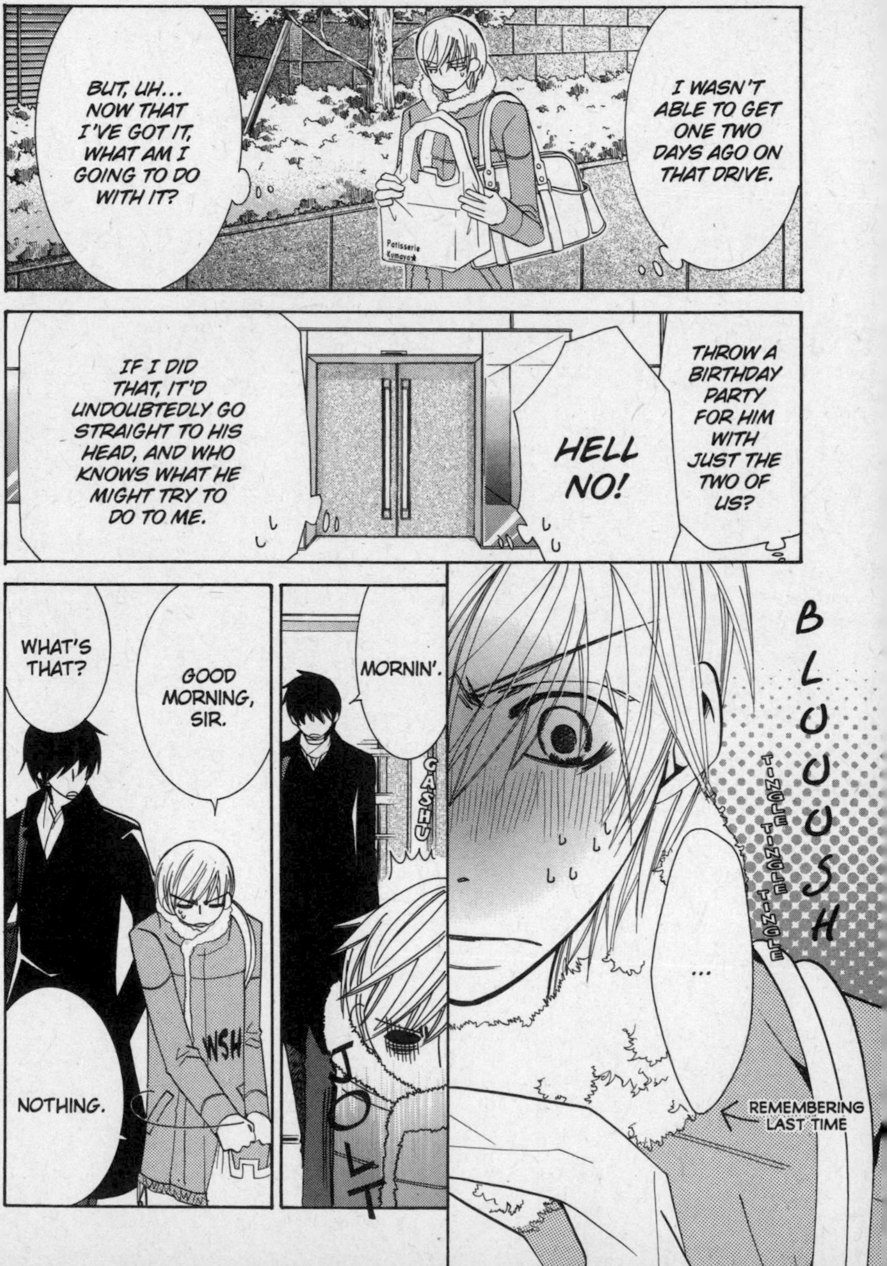
I WASN'T ABLE TO GET ONE TWO DAYS AGO ON THAT DRIVE.
BUT, UH... NOW THAT I'VE GOT IT, WHAT AM I GOING TO DO WITH IT?
Patisserie Kumaya★
THROW A BIRTHDAY PARTY FOR HIM WITH JUST THE TWO OF US?
HELL NO!
IF I DID THAT, IT'D UNDOUBTEDLY GO STRAIGHT TO HIS HEAD, AND WHO KNOWS WHAT HE MIGHT TRY TO DO TO ME.
BLUUSH
TINGLE TINGLE TINGLE
...
REMEMBERING LAST TIME
MORNIN'.
GASHU
JOLT
GOOD MORNING, SIR.
WHAT'S THAT?
WSW
NOTHING.

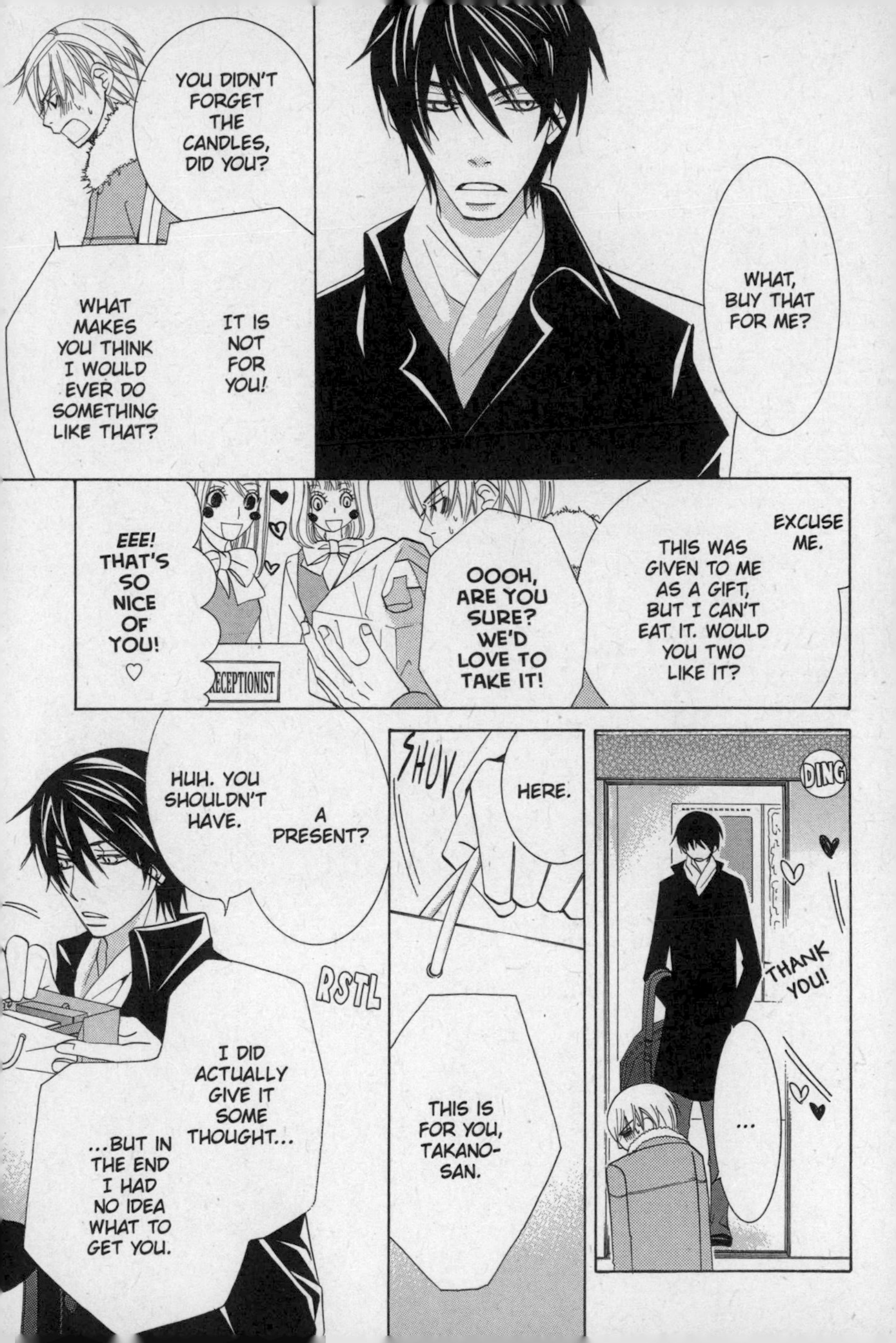
WHAT, BUY THAT FOR ME?
YOU DIDN'T FORGET THE CANDLES, DID YOU?
IT IS NOT FOR YOU!
WHAT MAKES YOU THINK I WOULD EVER DO SOMETHING LIKE THAT?
EXCUSE ME.
THIS WAS GIVEN TO ME AS A GIFT, BUT I CAN'T EAT IT. WOULD YOU TWO LIKE IT?
OOOH, ARE YOU SURE? WE'D LOVE TO TAKE IT!
EEE! THAT'S SO NICE OF YOU! ♡
RECEPTIONIST
DING
THANK YOU!
...
HERE.
SHUV
RSTL
THIS IS FOR YOU, TAKANO-SAN.
A PRESENT?
HUH. YOU SHOULDN'T HAVE.
I DID ACTUALLY GIVE IT SOME THOUGHT...
...BUT IN THE END I HAD NO IDEA WHAT TO GET YOU.

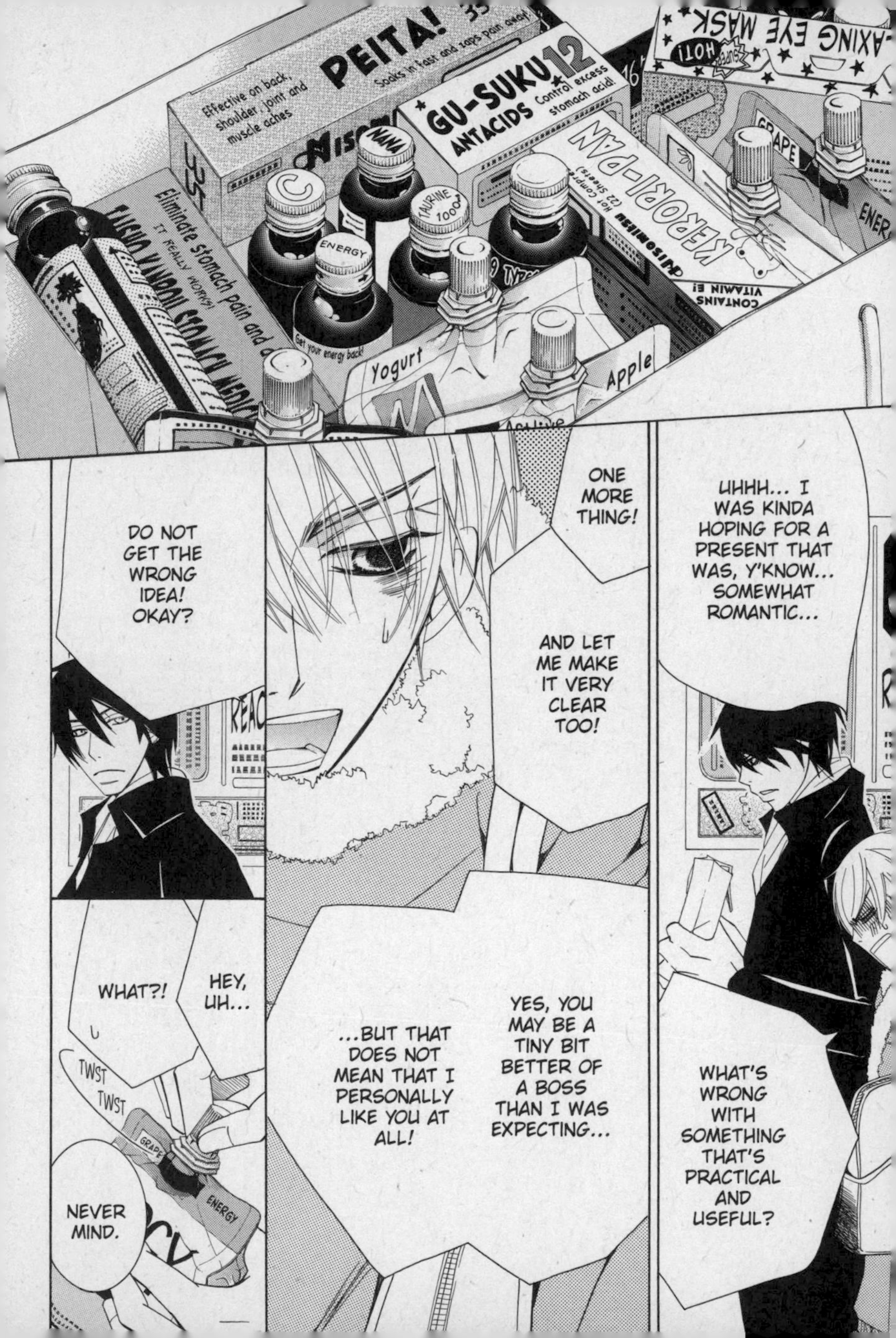
PEITA!
Soaks in fast and zaps pain away!
Effective on back, shoulder, joint and muscle aches
GU-SUKU 12
ANTACIDS
Control excess stomach acid!
SUPER HOT!
GRAPE
KERORI-PAN
Hot Compress (22 Sheets)
Misomitsu
CONTAINS VITAMIN E!
NANA
TAURINE 1000
ENERGY
Get your energy back!
Eliminate stomach pain and
IT REALLY WORKS!
Yogurt
Apple
UHHH... I WAS KINDA HOPING FOR A PRESENT THAT WAS, Y'KNOW... SOMEWHAT ROMANTIC...
WHAT'S WRONG WITH SOMETHING THAT'S PRACTICAL AND USEFUL?
ONE MORE THING!
AND LET ME MAKE IT VERY CLEAR TOO!
YES, YOU MAY BE A TINY BIT BETTER OF A BOSS THAN I WAS EXPECTING...
...BUT THAT DOES NOT MEAN THAT I PERSONALLY LIKE YOU AT ALL!
DO NOT GET THE WRONG IDEA! OKAY?
HEY, UH...
WHAT?!
TWST
TWST
GRAPE
ENERGY
NEVER MIND.

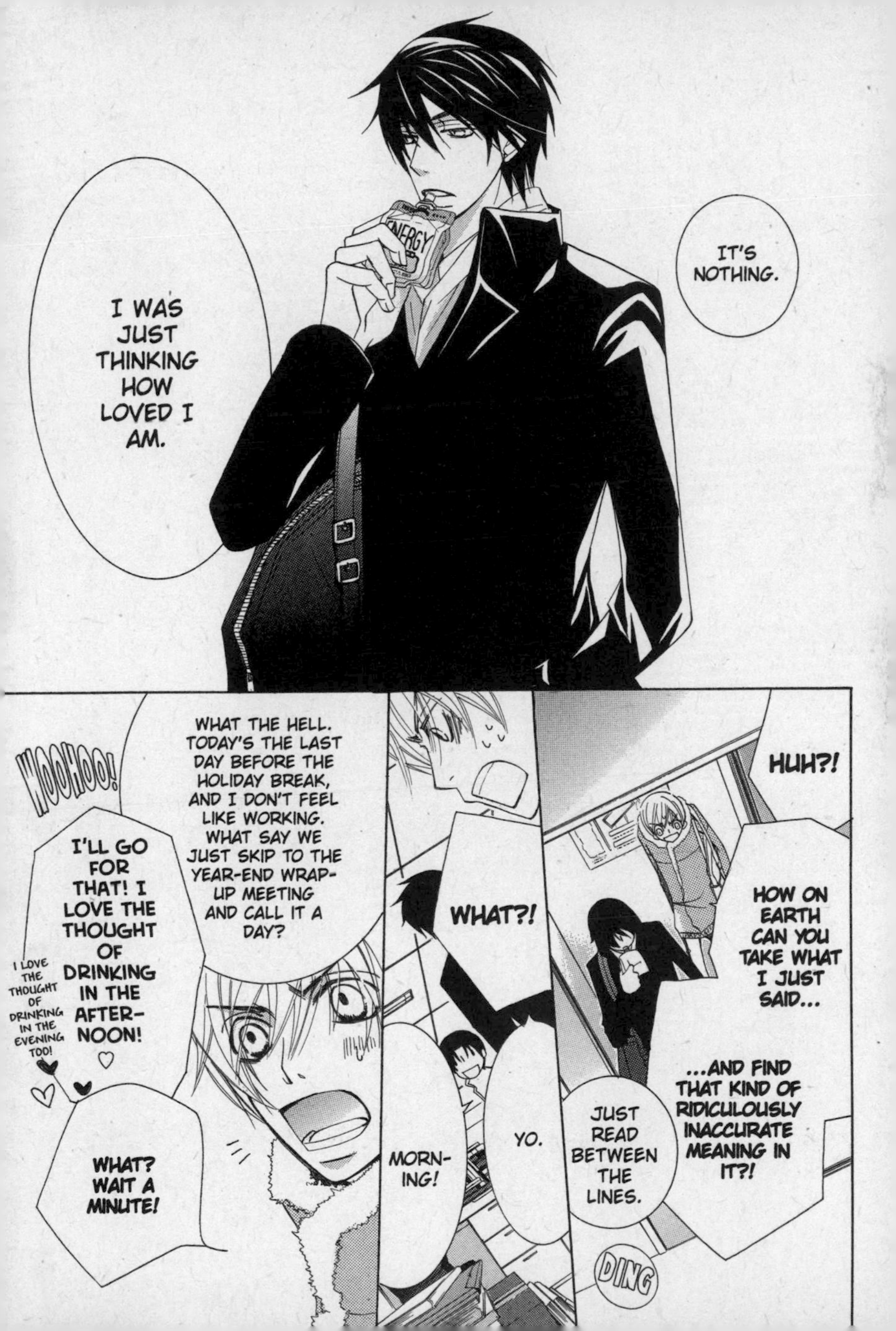
IT'S NOTHING.
I WAS JUST THINKING HOW LOVED I AM.
HUH?!
HOW ON EARTH CAN YOU TAKE WHAT I JUST SAID...
...AND FIND THAT KIND OF RIDICULOUSLY INACCURATE MEANING IN IT?!
JUST READ BETWEEN THE LINES.
DING
WHAT?!
YO.
MORN-ING!
WHAT THE HELL. TODAY'S THE LAST DAY BEFORE THE HOLIDAY BREAK, AND I DON'T FEEL LIKE WORKING. WHAT SAY WE JUST SKIP TO THE YEAR-END WRAP-UP MEETING AND CALL IT A DAY?
WOOHOO!
I'LL GO FOR THAT! I LOVE THE THOUGHT OF DRINKING IN THE AFTER-NOON!
I LOVE THE THOUGHT OF DRINKING IN THE EVENING TOO!
WHAT? WAIT A MINUTE!

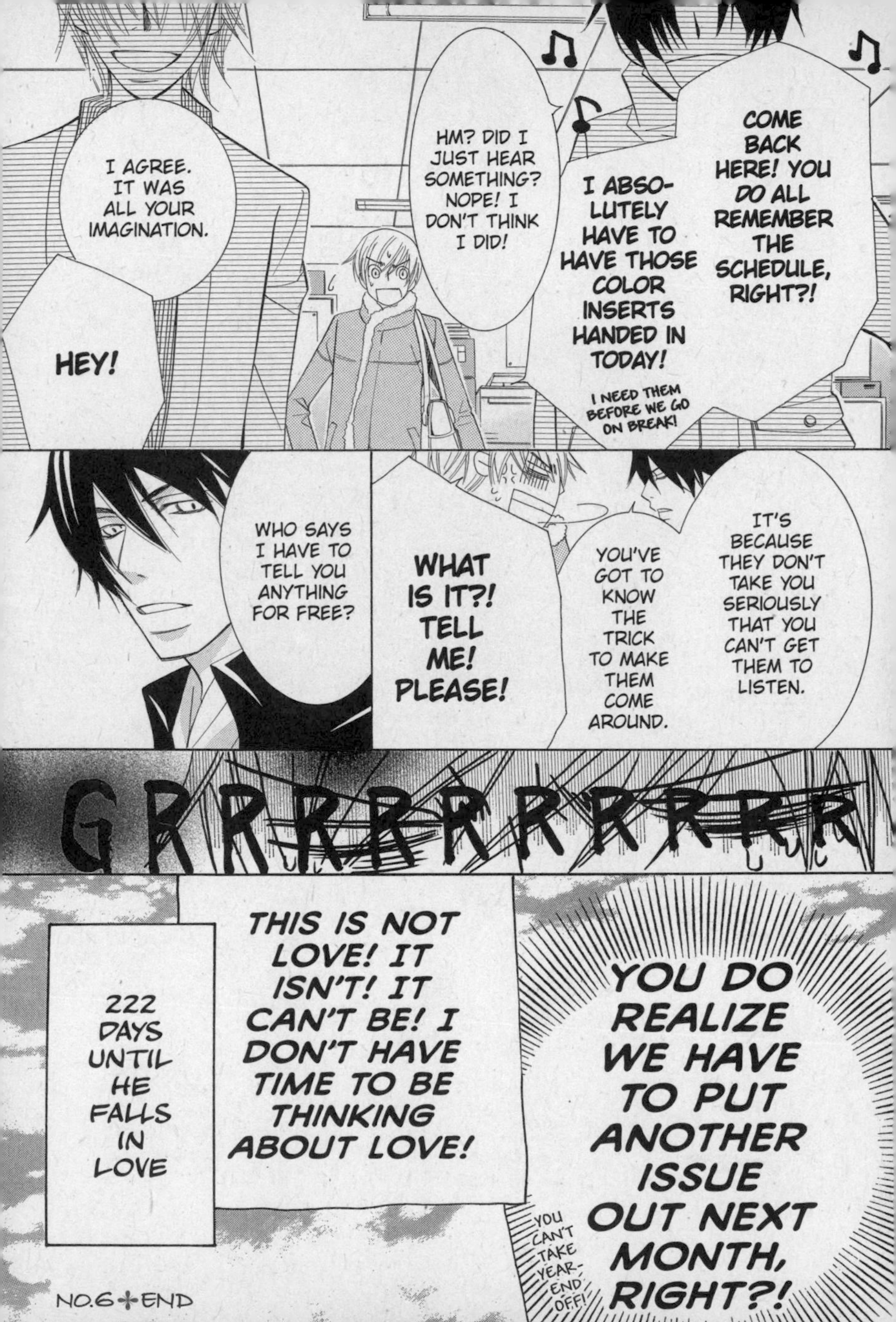
COME BACK HERE! YOU DO ALL REMEMBER THE SCHEDULE, RIGHT?!
I ABSOLUTELY HAVE TO HAVE THOSE COLOR INSERTS HANDED IN TODAY!
I NEED THEM BEFORE WE GO ON BREAK!
HM? DID I JUST HEAR SOMETHING? NOPE! I DON'T THINK I DID!
I AGREE. IT WAS ALL YOUR IMAGINATION.
HEY!
IT'S BECAUSE THEY DON'T TAKE YOU SERIOUSLY THAT YOU CAN'T GET THEM TO LISTEN.
YOU'VE GOT TO KNOW THE TRICK TO MAKE THEM COME AROUND.
WHAT IS IT?! TELL ME! PLEASE!
WHO SAYS I HAVE TO TELL YOU ANYTHING FOR FREE?
GRRRRRRRRRRR
YOU DO REALIZE WE HAVE TO PUT ANOTHER ISSUE OUT NEXT MONTH, RIGHT?!
YOU CAN'T TAKE YEAR-END OFF!
THIS IS NOT LOVE! IT ISN'T! IT CAN'T BE! I DON'T HAVE TIME TO BE THINKING ABOUT LOVE!
222 DAYS UNTIL HE FALLS IN LOVE
NO.6 ✦ END

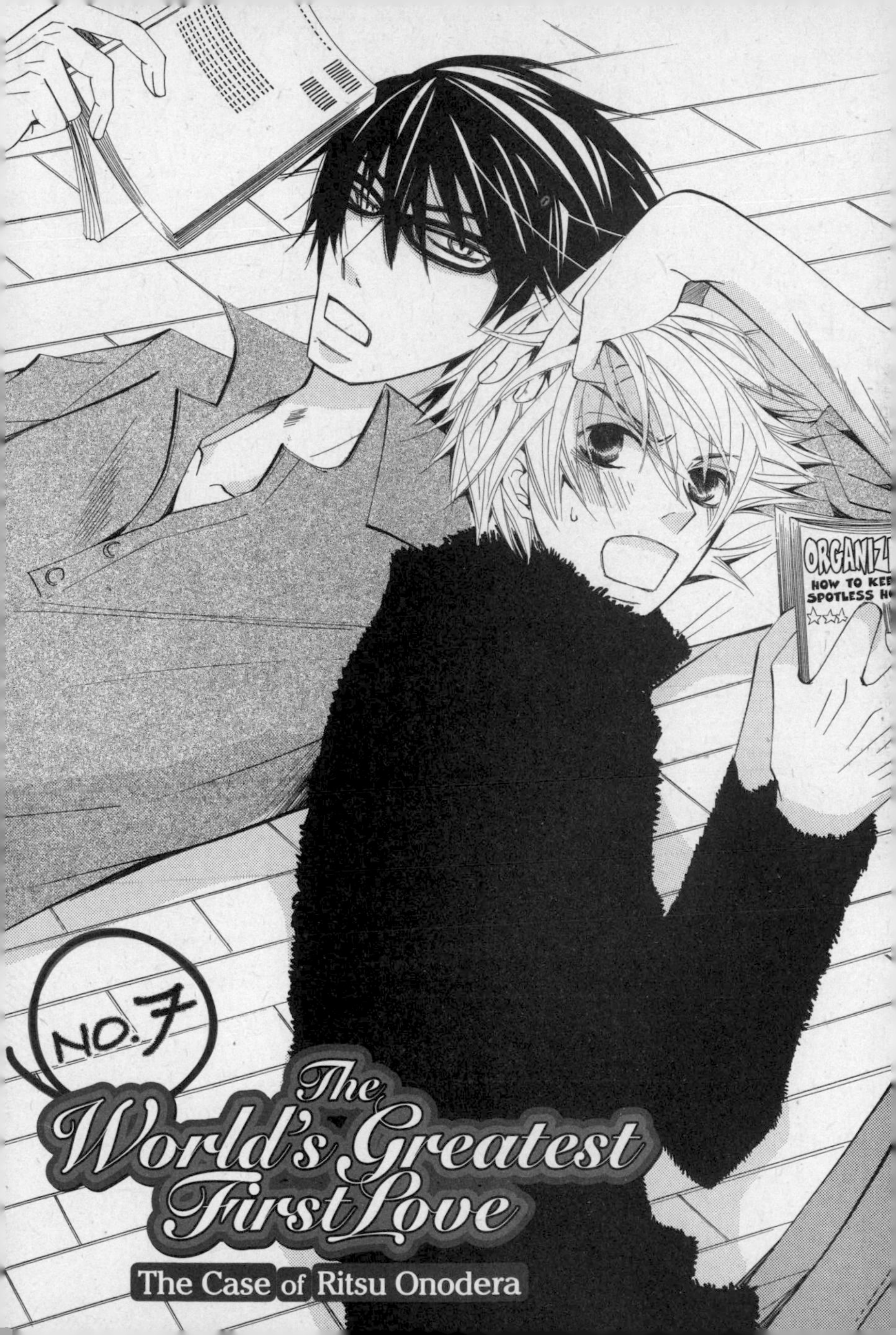
ORGANIZ
HOW TO KEE
SPOTLESS H
NO.7
The World's Greatest First Love
The Case of Ritsu Onodera

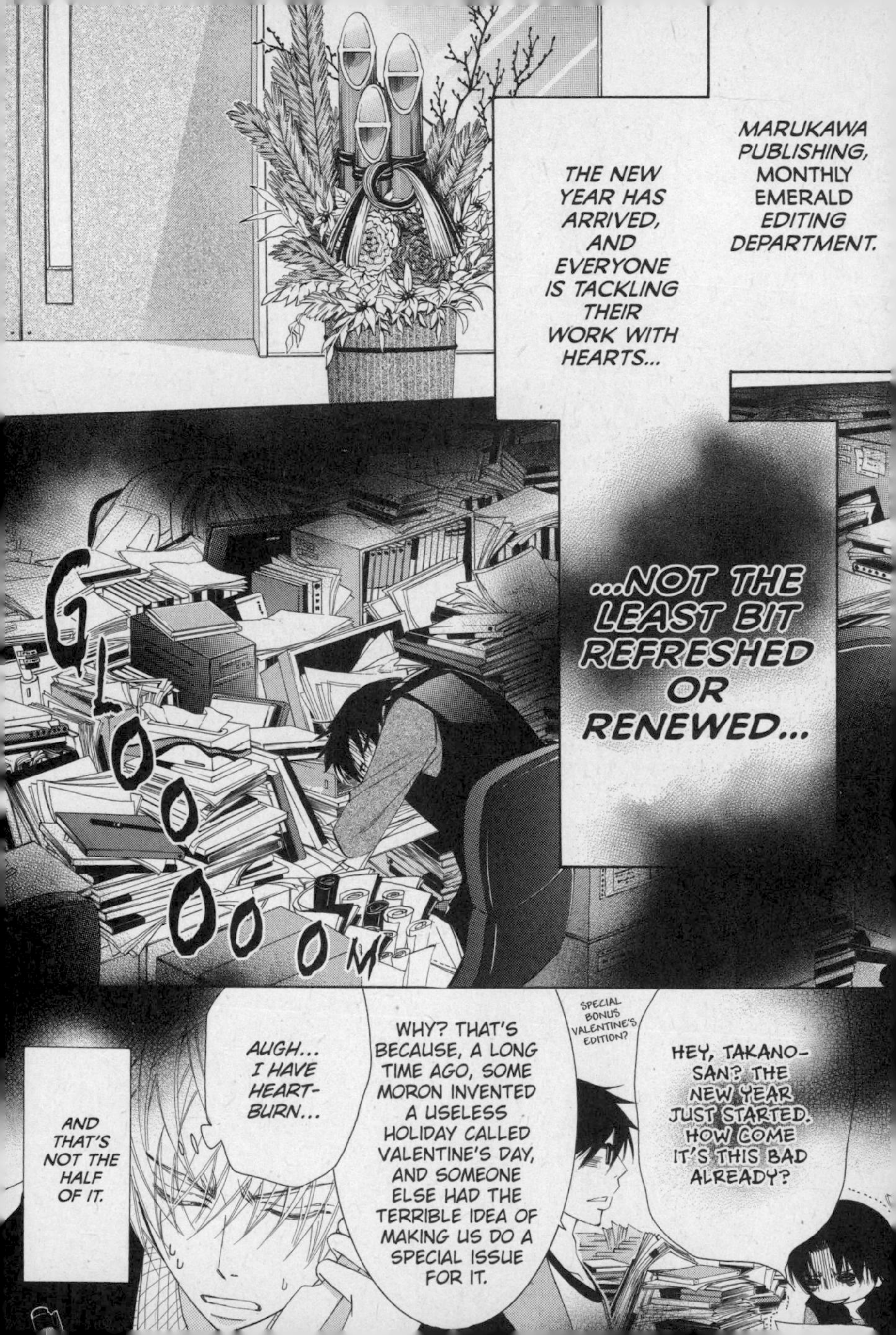
MARUKAWA PUBLISHING, MONTHLY EMERALD EDITING DEPARTMENT.
THE NEW YEAR HAS ARRIVED, AND EVERYONE IS TACKLING THEIR WORK WITH HEARTS...
...NOT THE LEAST BIT REFRESHED OR RENEWED...
GLOOOOOOM
HEY, TAKANO-SAN? THE NEW YEAR JUST STARTED. HOW COME IT'S THIS BAD ALREADY?
SPECIAL BONUS VALENTINE'S EDITION?
WHY? THAT'S BECAUSE, A LONG TIME AGO, SOME MORON INVENTED A USELESS HOLIDAY CALLED VALENTINE'S DAY, AND SOMEONE ELSE HAD THE TERRIBLE IDEA OF MAKING US DO A SPECIAL ISSUE FOR IT.
AUGH... I HAVE HEART-BURN...
AND THAT'S NOT THE HALF OF IT.

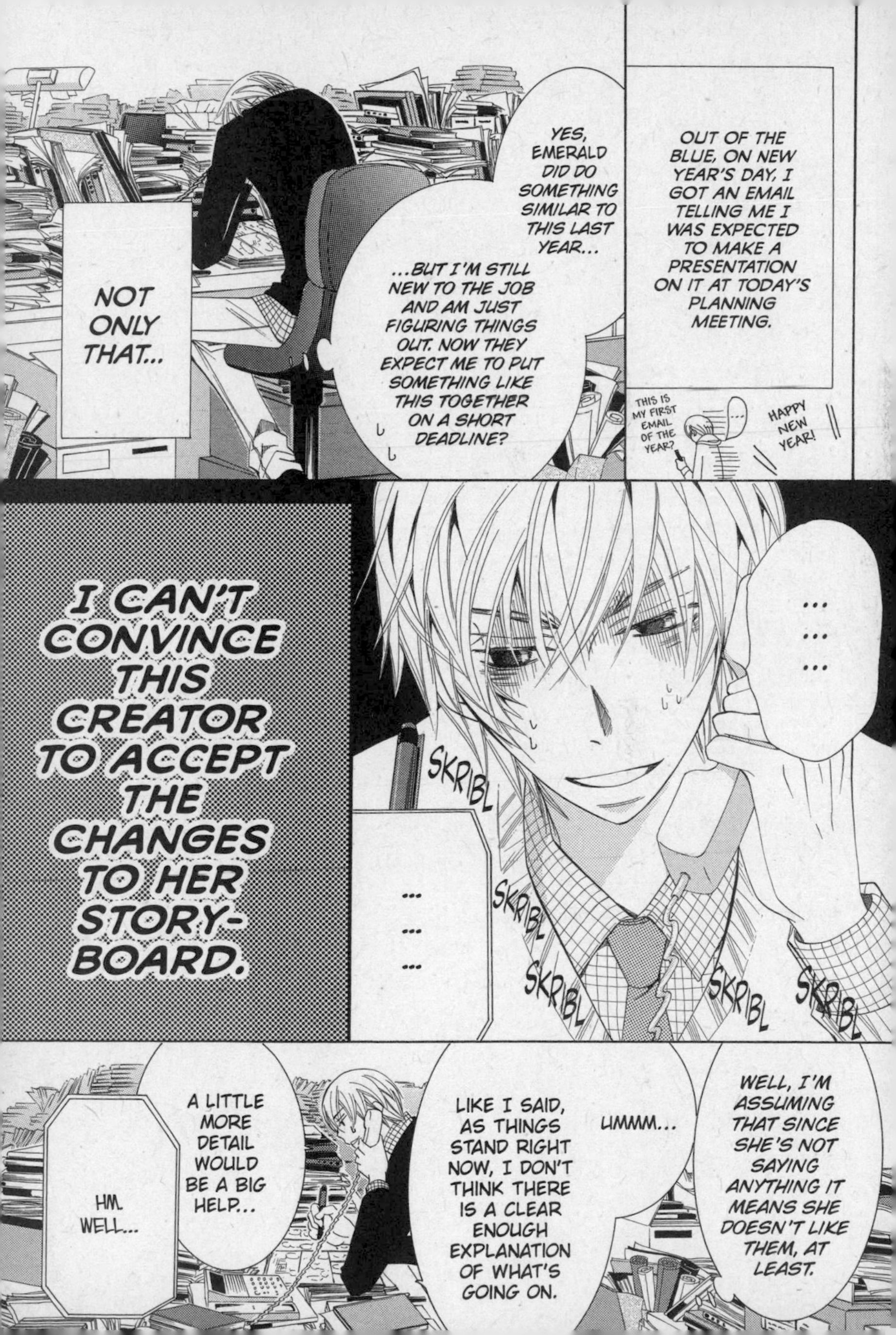
OUT OF THE BLUE, ON NEW YEAR'S DAY, I GOT AN EMAIL TELLING ME I WAS EXPECTED TO MAKE A PRESENTATION ON IT AT TODAY'S PLANNING MEETING.
HAPPY NEW YEAR!
...
THIS IS MY FIRST EMAIL OF THE YEAR?
YES, EMERALD DID DO SOMETHING SIMILAR TO THIS LAST YEAR...
...BUT I'M STILL NEW TO THE JOB AND AM JUST FIGURING THINGS OUT. NOW THEY EXPECT ME TO PUT SOMETHING LIKE THIS TOGETHER ON A SHORT DEADLINE?
NOT ONLY THAT...
... ...
SKRIBL
SKRIBL
SKRIBL
SKRIBL
SKRIBL
... ...
I CAN'T CONVINCE THIS CREATOR TO ACCEPT THE CHANGES TO HER STORY-BOARD.
WELL, I'M ASSUMING THAT SINCE SHE'S NOT SAYING ANYTHING IT MEANS SHE DOESN'T LIKE THEM, AT LEAST.
UMMM...
LIKE I SAID, AS THINGS STAND RIGHT NOW, I DON'T THINK THERE IS A CLEAR ENOUGH EXPLANATION OF WHAT'S GOING ON.
A LITTLE MORE DETAIL WOULD BE A BIG HELP...
HM. WELL...

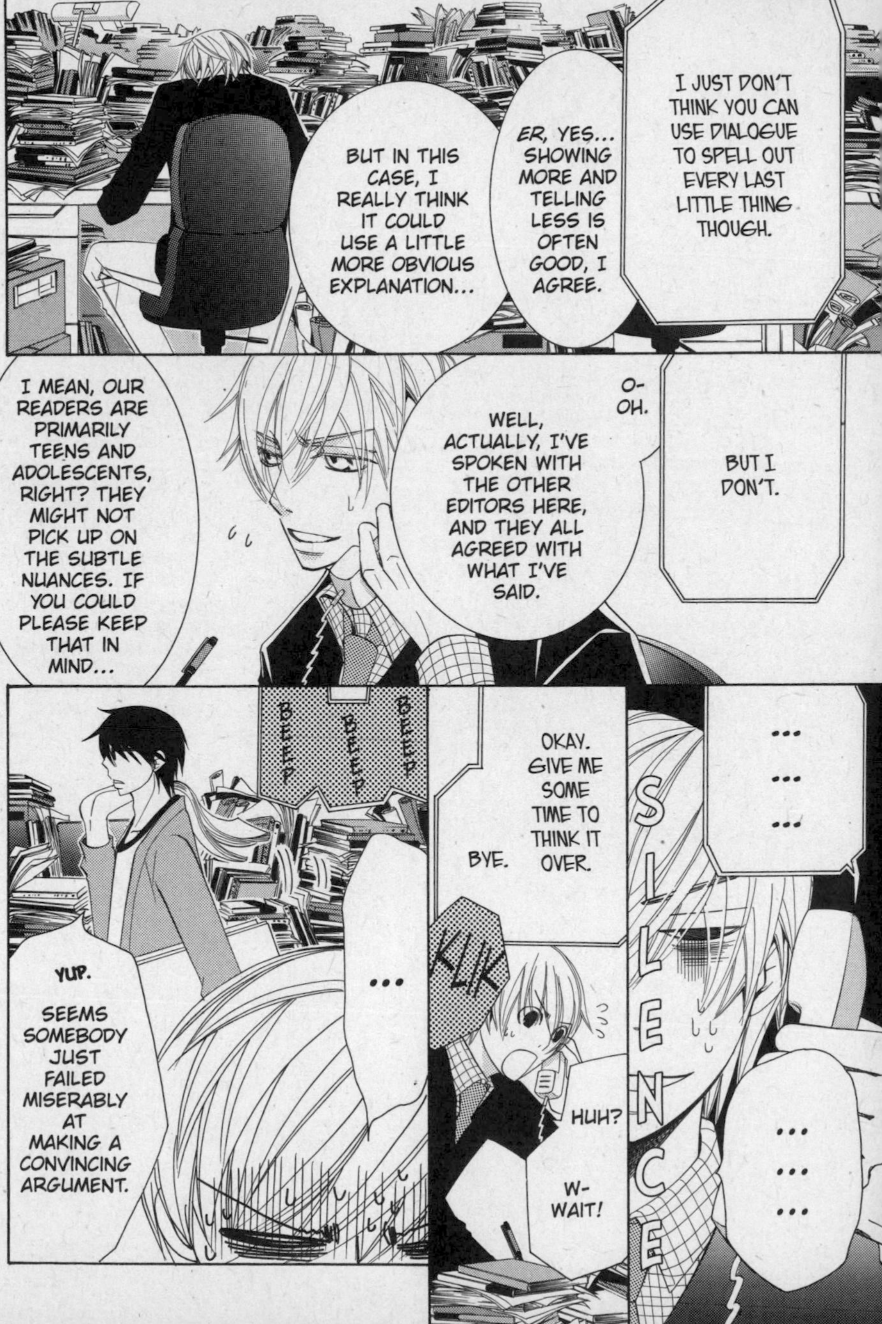
I JUST DON'T THINK YOU CAN USE DIALOGUE TO SPELL OUT EVERY LAST LITTLE THING THOUGH.
ER, YES... SHOWING MORE AND TELLING LESS IS OFTEN GOOD, I AGREE.
BUT IN THIS CASE, I REALLY THINK IT COULD USE A LITTLE MORE OBVIOUS EXPLANATION...
BUT I DON'T.
O-OH.
WELL, ACTUALLY, I'VE SPOKEN WITH THE OTHER EDITORS HERE, AND THEY ALL AGREED WITH WHAT I'VE SAID.
I MEAN, OUR READERS ARE PRIMARILY TEENS AND ADOLESCENTS, RIGHT? THEY MIGHT NOT PICK UP ON THE SUBTLE NUANCES. IF YOU COULD PLEASE KEEP THAT IN MIND...
... ...
SILENCE
... ...
OKAY. GIVE ME SOME TIME TO THINK IT OVER.
BYE.
KLIK
HUH?
W-WAIT!
BEEP
BEEP
BEEP
...
YUP.
SEEMS SOMEBODY JUST FAILED MISERABLY AT MAKING A CONVINCING ARGUMENT.

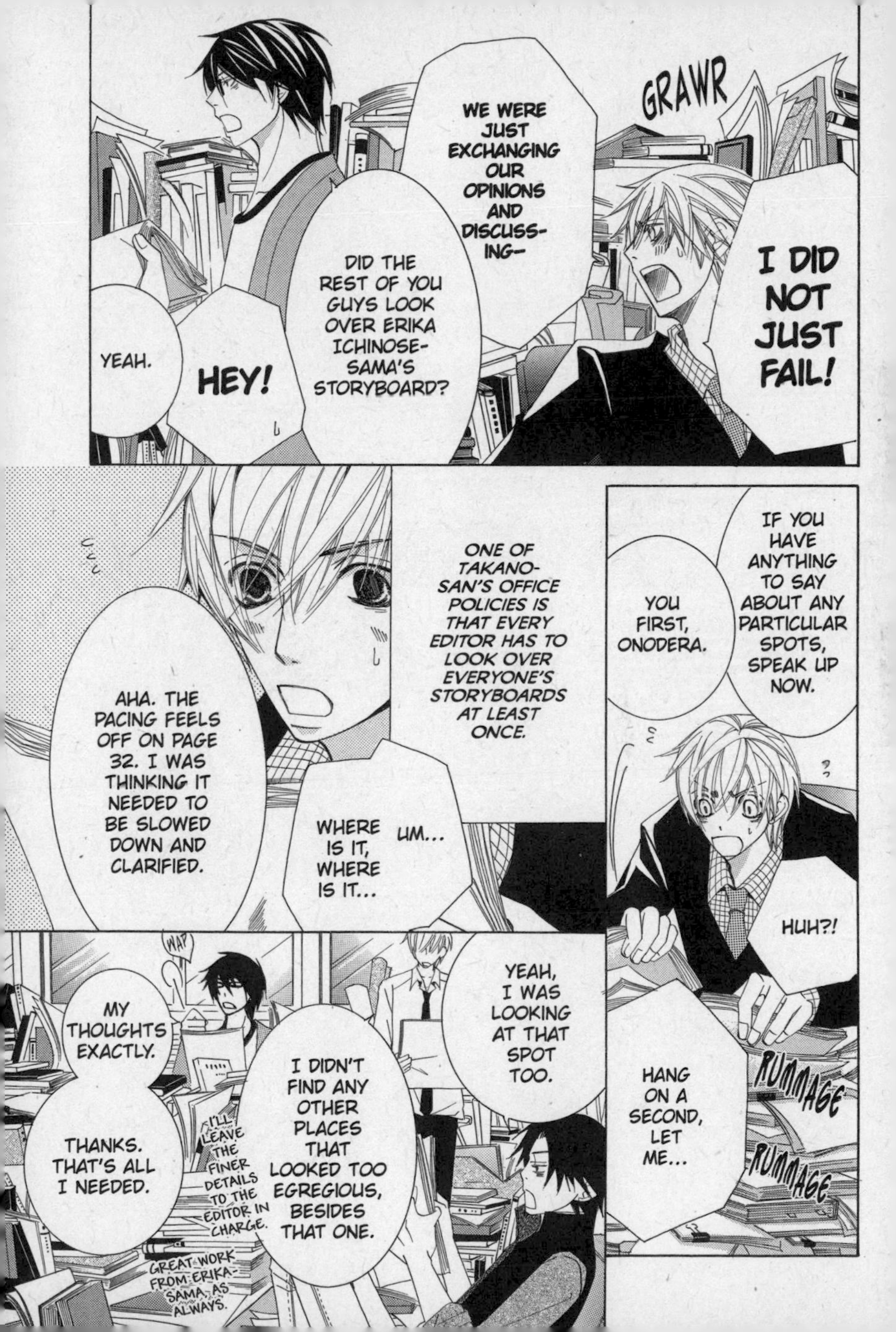
I DID NOT JUST FAIL!
GRAWR
WE WERE JUST EXCHANGING OUR OPINIONS AND DISCUSSING-
DID THE REST OF YOU GUYS LOOK OVER ERIKA ICHINOSE-SAMA'S STORYBOARD?
HEY!
YEAH.
IF YOU HAVE ANYTHING TO SAY ABOUT ANY PARTICULAR SPOTS, SPEAK UP NOW.
YOU FIRST, ONODERA.
HUH?!
RUMMAGE
RUMMAGE
HANG ON A SECOND, LET ME...
ONE OF TAKANO-SAN'S OFFICE POLICIES IS THAT EVERY EDITOR HAS TO LOOK OVER EVERYONE'S STORYBOARDS AT LEAST ONCE.
UM...
WHERE IS IT, WHERE IS IT...
AHA. THE PACING FEELS OFF ON PAGE 32. I WAS THINKING IT NEEDED TO BE SLOWED DOWN AND CLARIFIED.
YEAH, I WAS LOOKING AT THAT SPOT TOO.
I DIDN'T FIND ANY OTHER PLACES THAT LOOKED TOO EGREGIOUS, BESIDES THAT ONE.
I'LL LEAVE THE FINER DETAILS TO THE EDITOR IN CHARGE.
WAP?
MY THOUGHTS EXACTLY.
THANKS. THAT'S ALL I NEEDED.
GREAT WORK FROM ERIKA-SAMA, AS ALWAYS.

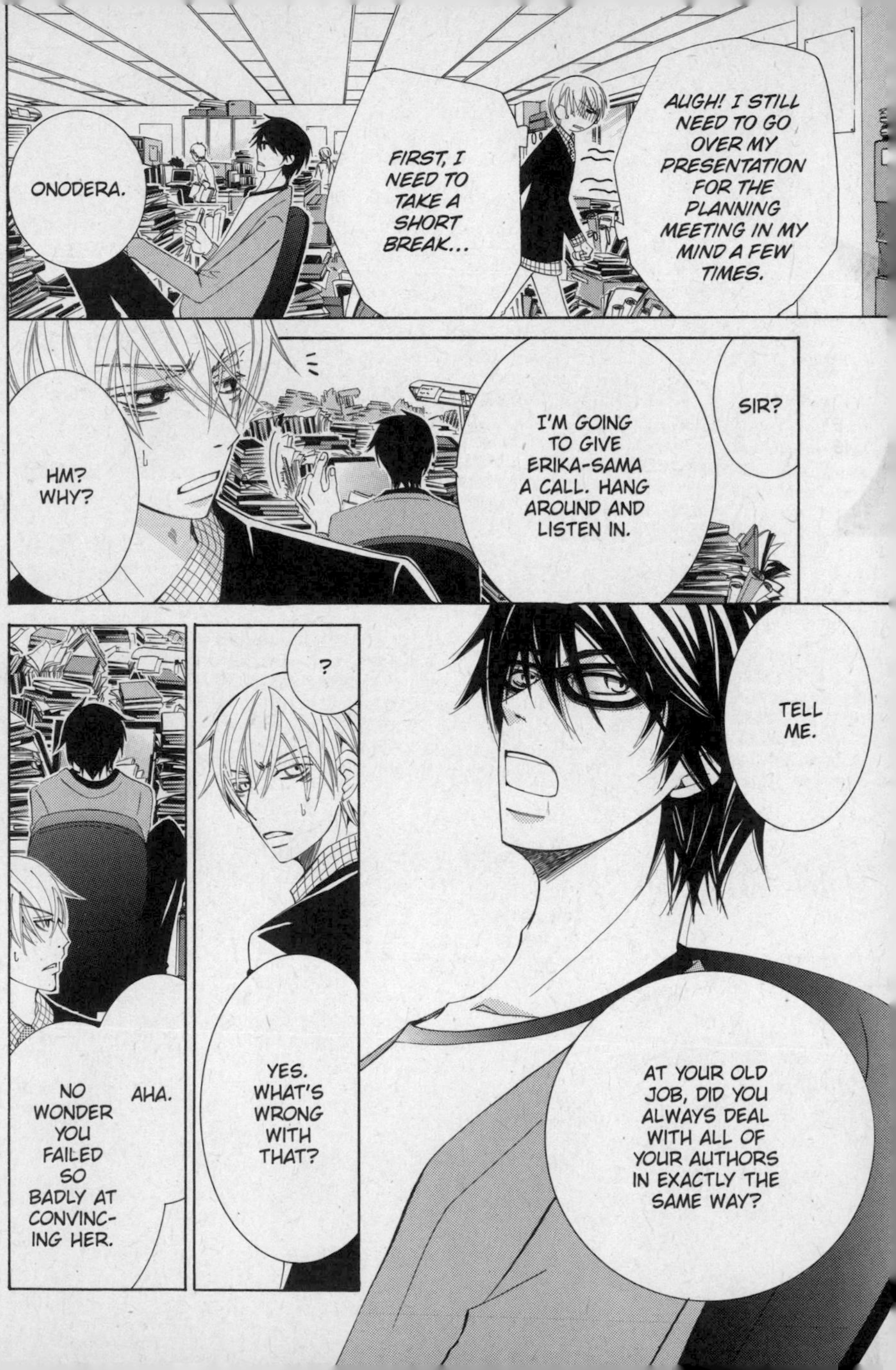
AUGH! I STILL NEED TO GO OVER MY PRESENTATION FOR THE PLANNING MEETING IN MY MIND A FEW TIMES.
FIRST, I NEED TO TAKE A SHORT BREAK...
ONODERA.
SIR?
I'M GOING TO GIVE ERIKA-SAMA A CALL. HANG AROUND AND LISTEN IN.
HM? WHY?
TELL ME.
AT YOUR OLD JOB, DID YOU ALWAYS DEAL WITH ALL OF YOUR AUTHORS IN EXACTLY THE SAME WAY?
?
YES. WHAT'S WRONG WITH THAT?
AHA.
NO WONDER YOU FAILED SO BADLY AT CONVINC-ING HER.

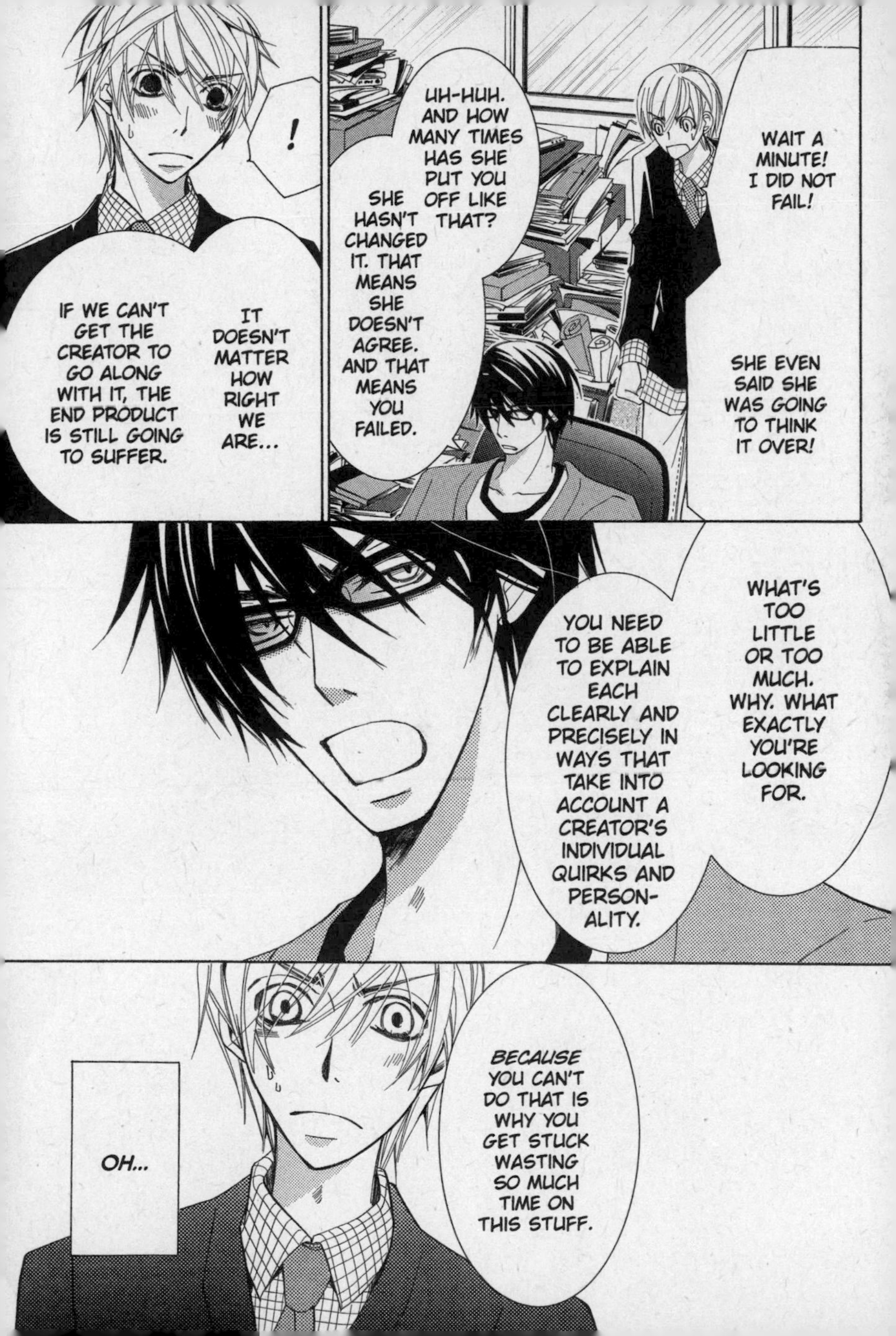
WAIT A MINUTE! I DID NOT FAIL!
SHE EVEN SAID SHE WAS GOING TO THINK IT OVER!
UH-HUH. AND HOW MANY TIMES HAS SHE PUT YOU OFF LIKE THAT?
SHE HASN'T CHANGED IT. THAT MEANS SHE DOESN'T AGREE. AND THAT MEANS YOU FAILED.
!
IT DOESN'T MATTER HOW RIGHT WE ARE...
IF WE CAN'T GET THE CREATOR TO GO ALONG WITH IT, THE END PRODUCT IS STILL GOING TO SUFFER.
WHAT'S TOO LITTLE OR TOO MUCH. WHY. WHAT EXACTLY YOU'RE LOOKING FOR.
YOU NEED TO BE ABLE TO EXPLAIN EACH CLEARLY AND PRECISELY IN WAYS THAT TAKE INTO ACCOUNT A CREATOR'S INDIVIDUAL QUIRKS AND PERSON-ALITY.
BECAUSE YOU CAN'T DO THAT IS WHY YOU GET STUCK WASTING SO MUCH TIME ON THIS STUFF.
OH...

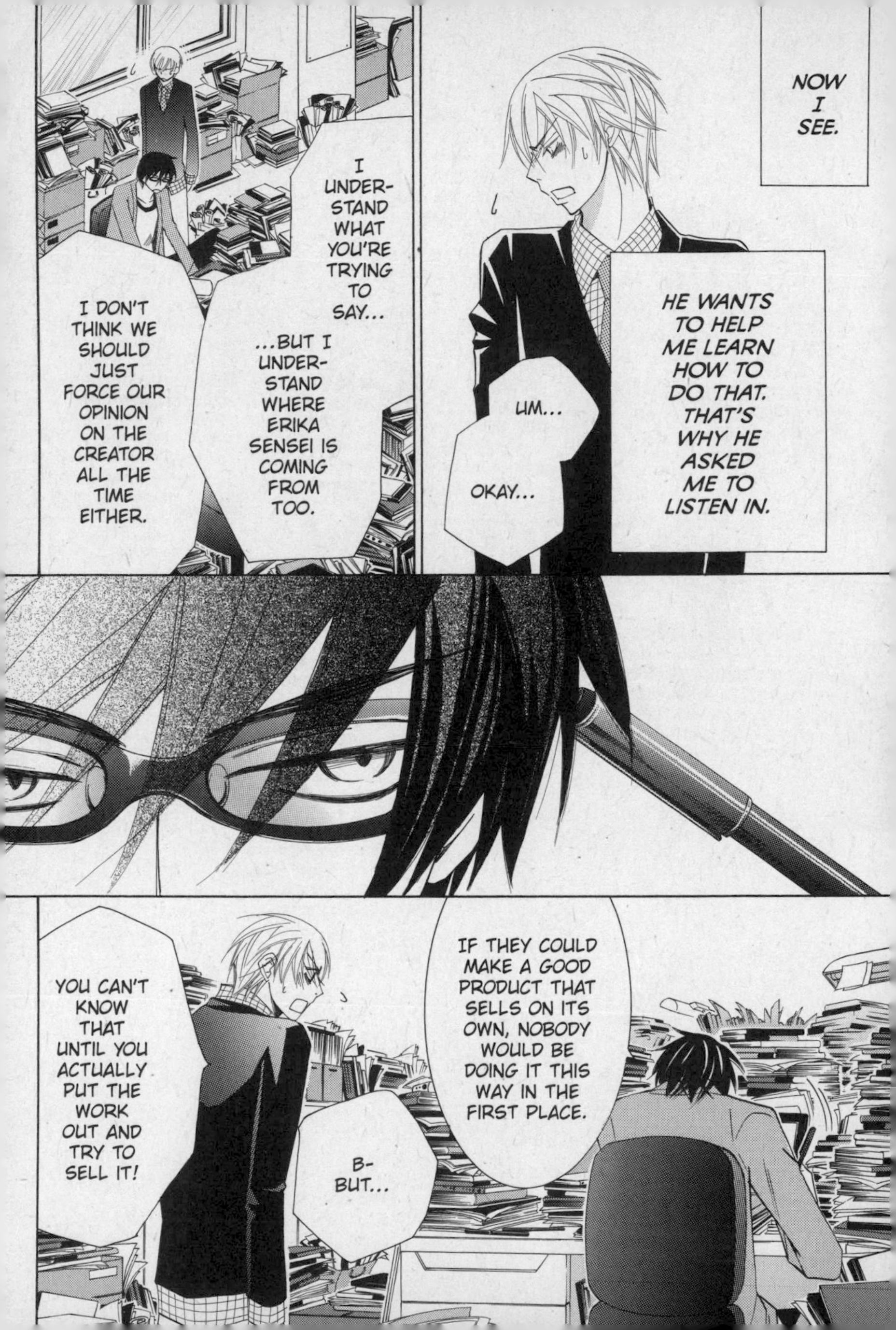
NOW I SEE.
HE WANTS TO HELP ME LEARN HOW TO DO THAT. THAT'S WHY HE ASKED ME TO LISTEN IN.
UM... OKAY...
I UNDER-STAND WHAT YOU'RE TRYING TO SAY...
...BUT I UNDER-STAND WHERE ERIKA SENSEI IS COMING FROM TOO.
I DON'T THINK WE SHOULD JUST FORCE OUR OPINION ON THE CREATOR ALL THE TIME EITHER.
IF THEY COULD MAKE A GOOD PRODUCT THAT SELLS ON ITS OWN, NOBODY WOULD BE DOING IT THIS WAY IN THE FIRST PLACE.
B-BUT...
YOU CAN'T KNOW THAT UNTIL YOU ACTUALLY PUT THE WORK OUT AND TRY TO SELL IT!

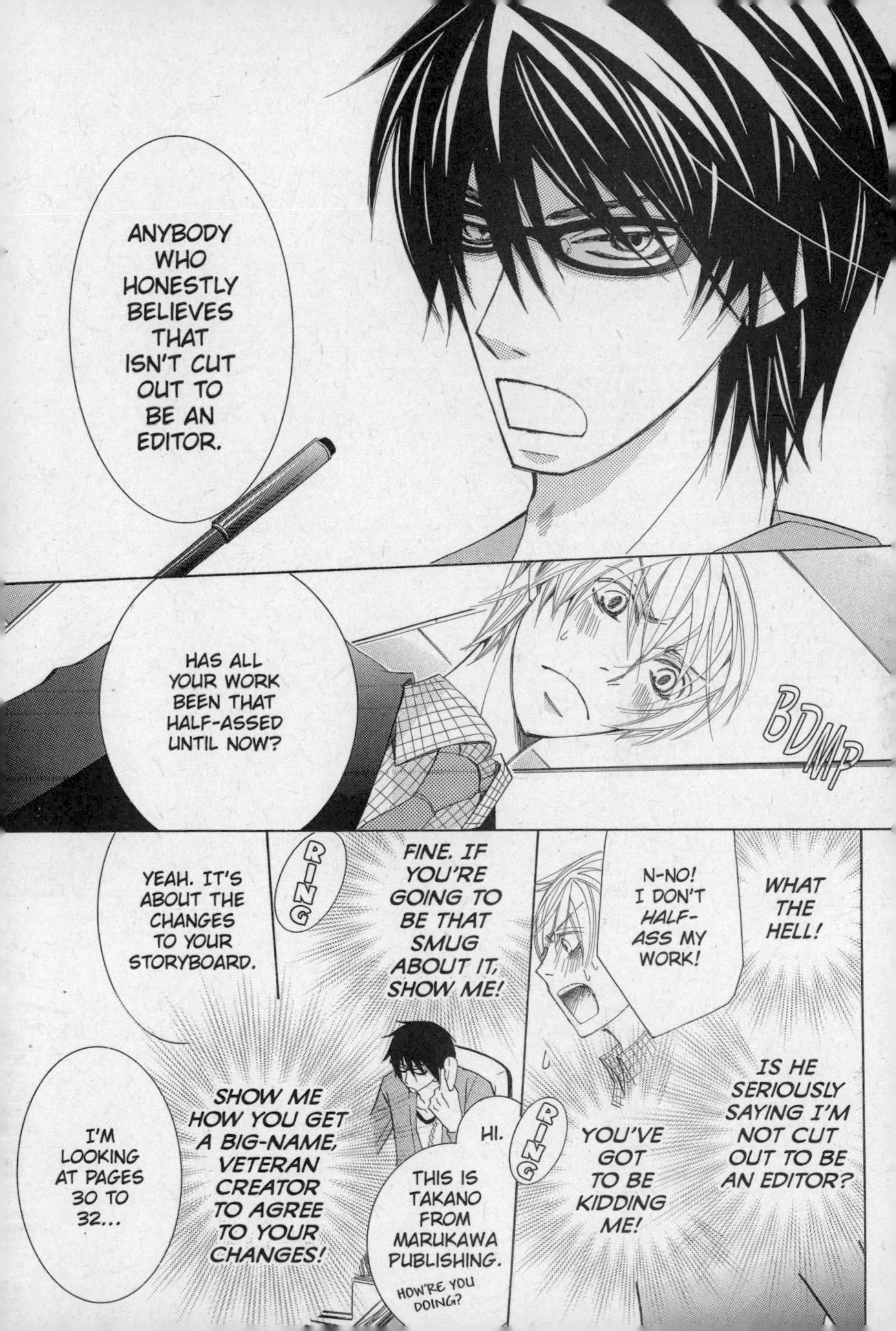
ANYBODY WHO HONESTLY BELIEVES THAT ISN'T CUT OUT TO BE AN EDITOR.
BDMP
HAS ALL YOUR WORK BEEN THAT HALF-ASSED UNTIL NOW?
WHAT THE HELL!
N-NO! I DON'T HALF-ASS MY WORK!
FINE. IF YOU'RE GOING TO BE THAT SMUG ABOUT IT, SHOW ME!
RING
YEAH. IT'S ABOUT THE CHANGES TO YOUR STORYBOARD.
IS HE SERIOUSLY SAYING I'M NOT CUT OUT TO BE AN EDITOR?
YOU'VE GOT TO BE KIDDING ME!
RING
HI.
THIS IS TAKANO FROM MARUKAWA PUBLISHING.
HOW'RE YOU DOING?
SHOW ME HOW YOU GET A BIG-NAME, VETERAN CREATOR TO AGREE TO YOUR CHANGES!
I'M LOOKING AT PAGES 30 TO 32...

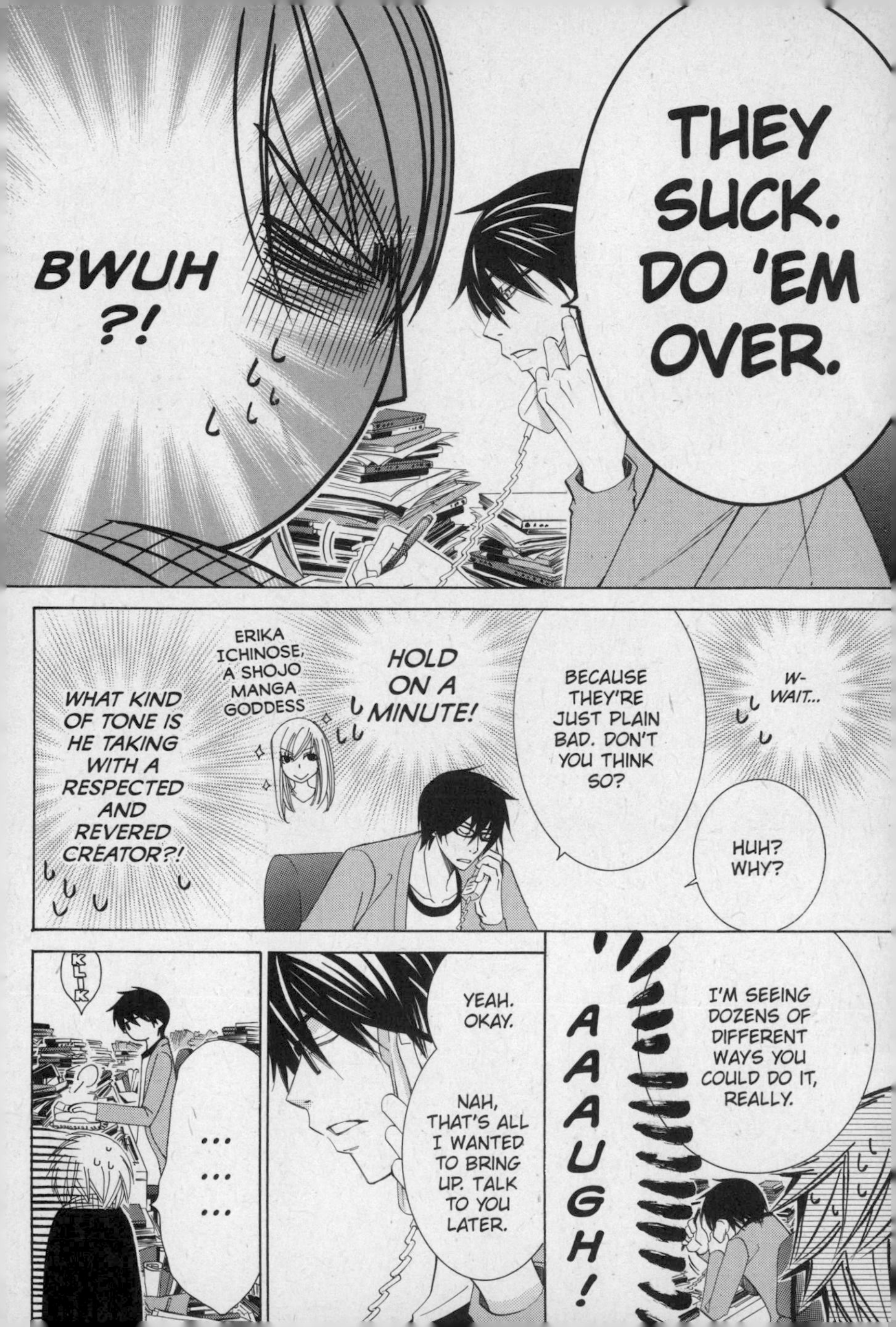
THEY SUCK. DO 'EM OVER.
BWUH ?!
W-WAIT...
HUH? WHY?
BECAUSE THEY'RE JUST PLAIN BAD. DON'T YOU THINK SO?
HOLD ON A MINUTE!
ERIKA ICHINOSE, A SHOJO MANGA GODDESS
WHAT KIND OF TONE IS HE TAKING WITH A RESPECTED AND REVERED CREATOR?!
I'M SEEING DOZENS OF DIFFERENT WAYS YOU COULD DO IT, REALLY.
AAAAUGH!
YEAH. OKAY.
NAH, THAT'S ALL I WANTED TO BRING UP. TALK TO YOU LATER.
KLIK
...
...
...

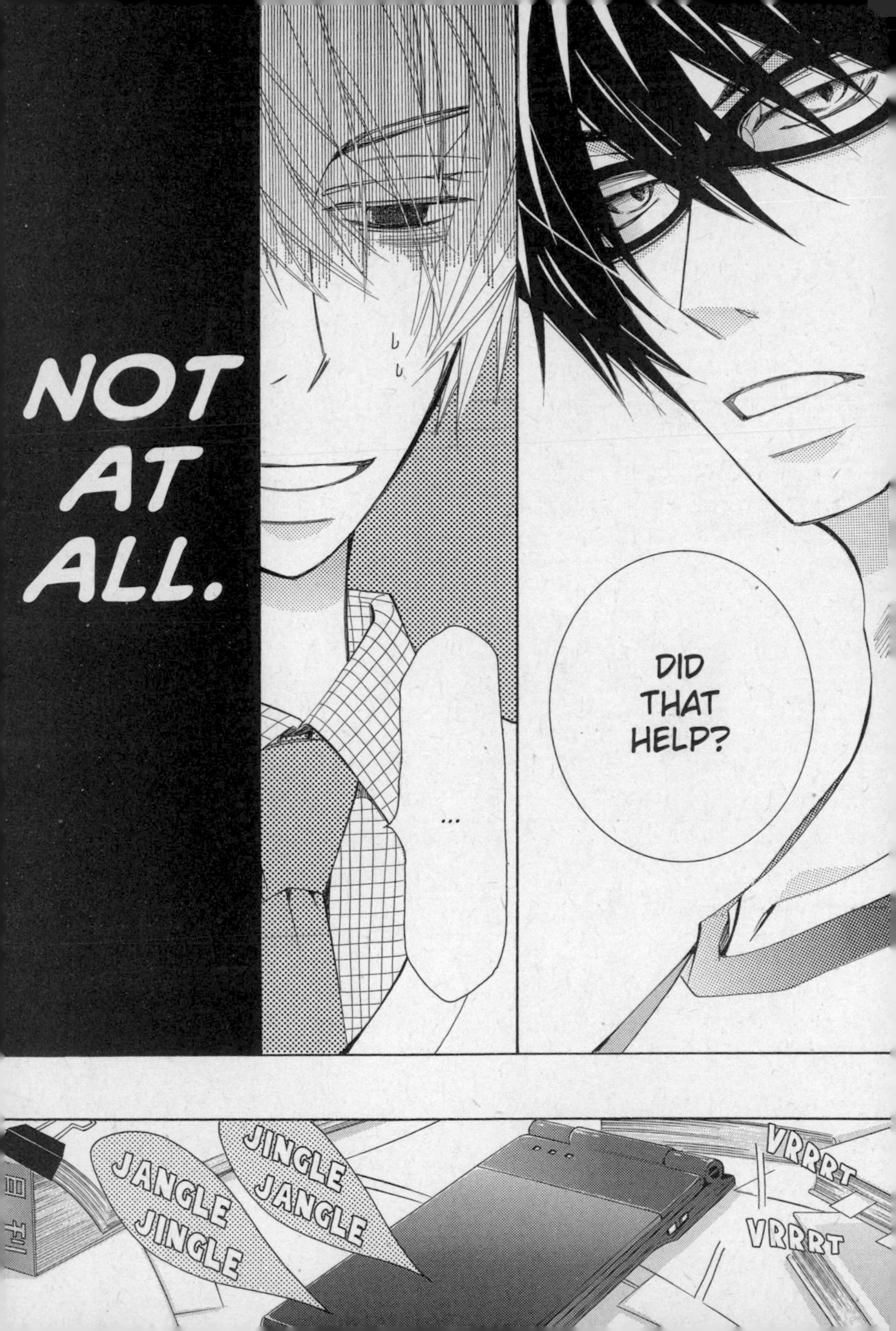
DID THAT HELP?
...
NOT AT ALL.
VRRRT
VRRRT
JINGLE JANGLE
JANGLE JINGLE

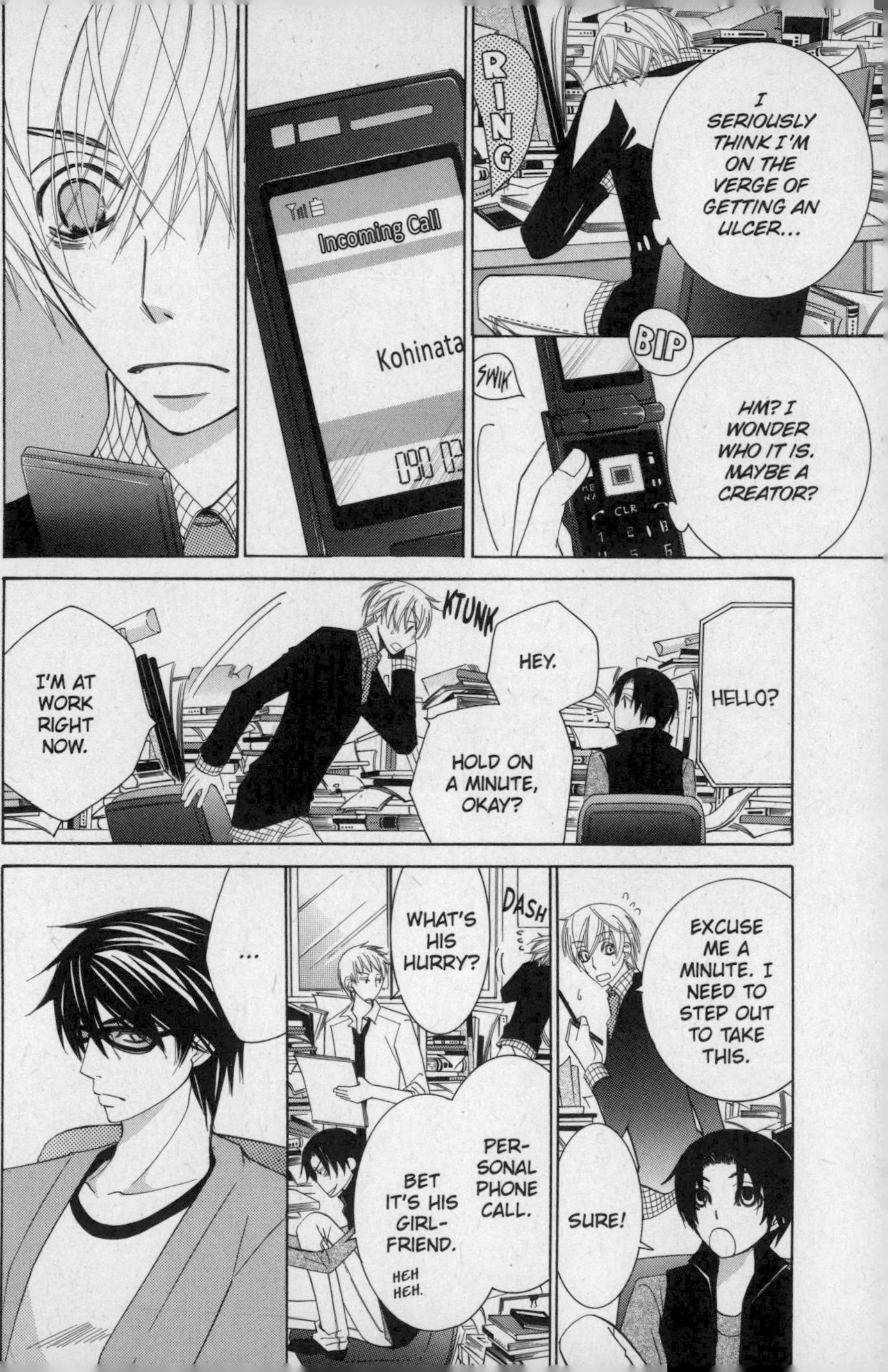
RING
I SERIOUSLY THINK I'M ON THE VERGE OF GETTING AN ULCER...
BIP
SWIK
HM? I WONDER WHO IT IS. MAYBE A CREATOR?
Incoming Call
Kohinata
090 03
HELLO?
HEY.
KTUNK
HOLD ON A MINUTE, OKAY?
I'M AT WORK RIGHT NOW.
EXCUSE ME A MINUTE. I NEED TO STEP OUT TO TAKE THIS.
SURE!
DASH
WHAT'S HIS HURRY?
PERSONAL PHONE CALL.
BET IT'S HIS GIRLFRIEND.
HEH HEH.
...

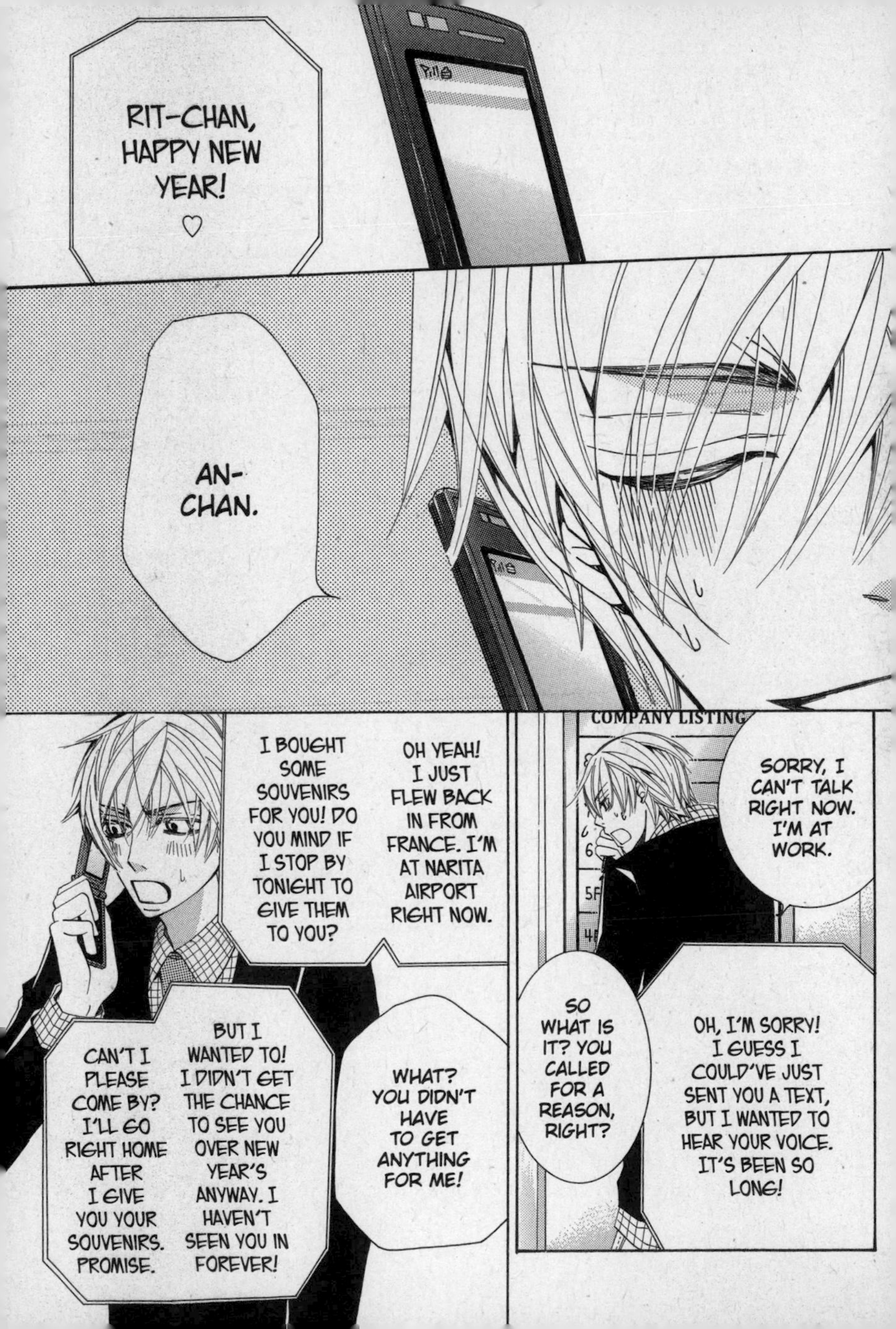
RIT-CHAN, HAPPY NEW YEAR! ♡
AN-CHAN.
COMPANY LISTING
SORRY, I CAN'T TALK RIGHT NOW. I'M AT WORK.
OH, I'M SORRY! I GUESS I COULD'VE JUST SENT YOU A TEXT, BUT I WANTED TO HEAR YOUR VOICE. IT'S BEEN SO LONG!
SO WHAT IS IT? YOU CALLED FOR A REASON, RIGHT?
OH YEAH! I JUST FLEW BACK IN FROM FRANCE. I'M AT NARITA AIRPORT RIGHT NOW.
I BOUGHT SOME SOUVENIRS FOR YOU! DO YOU MIND IF I STOP BY TONIGHT TO GIVE THEM TO YOU?
WHAT? YOU DIDN'T HAVE TO GET ANYTHING FOR ME!
BUT I WANTED TO! I DIDN'T GET THE CHANCE TO SEE YOU OVER NEW YEAR'S ANYWAY. I HAVEN'T SEEN YOU IN FOREVER!
CAN'T I PLEASE COME BY? I'LL GO RIGHT HOME AFTER I GIVE YOU YOUR SOUVENIRS. PROMISE.

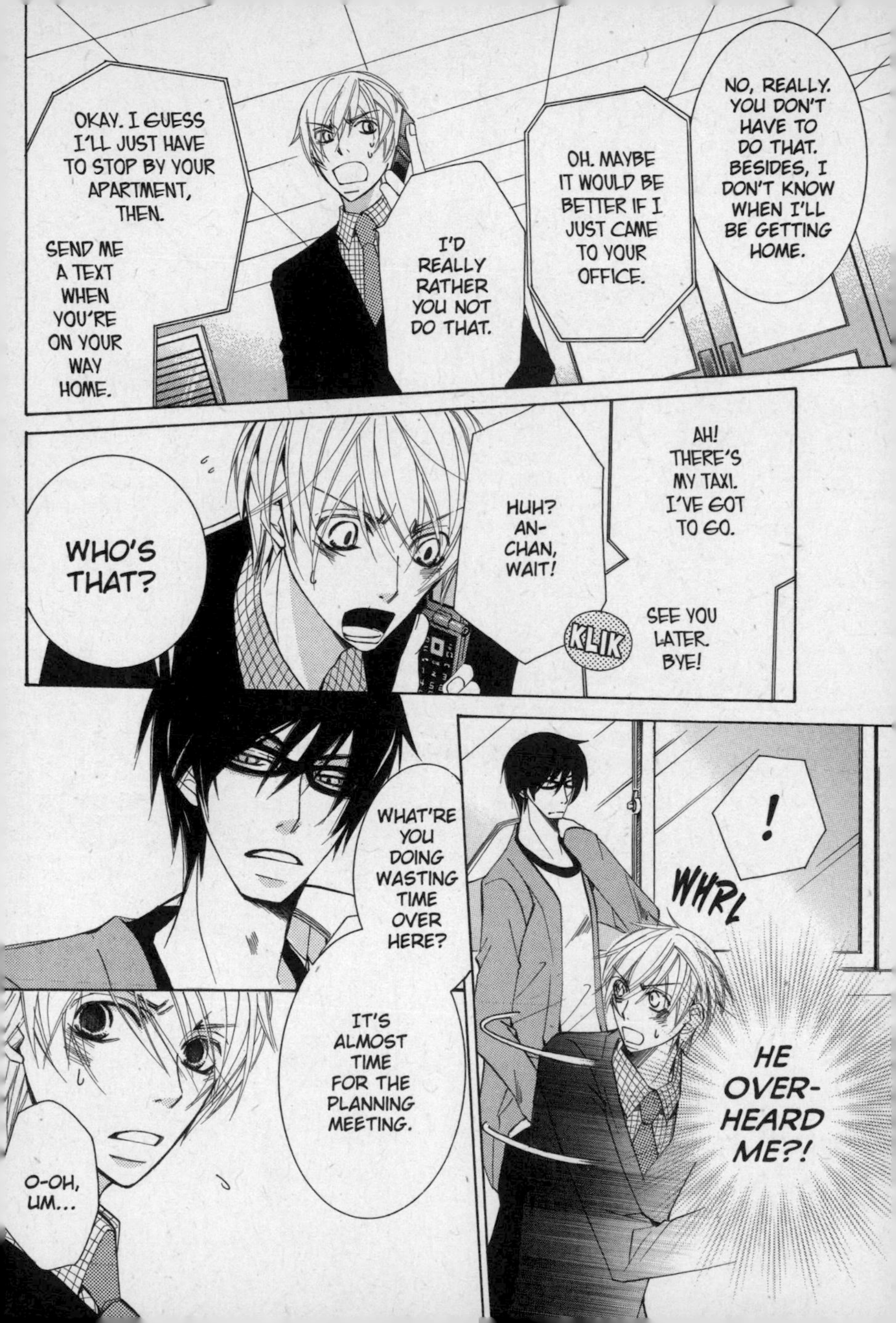
NO, REALLY. YOU DON'T HAVE TO DO THAT. BESIDES, I DON'T KNOW WHEN I'LL BE GETTING HOME.
OH. MAYBE IT WOULD BE BETTER IF I JUST CAME TO YOUR OFFICE.
I'D REALLY RATHER YOU NOT DO THAT.
OKAY. I GUESS I'LL JUST HAVE TO STOP BY YOUR APARTMENT, THEN.
SEND ME A TEXT WHEN YOU'RE ON YOUR WAY HOME.
AH! THERE'S MY TAXI. I'VE GOT TO GO.
HUH? AN-CHAN, WAIT!
KLIK
SEE YOU LATER. BYE!
WHO'S THAT?
!
WHRL
HE OVER-HEARD ME?!
WHAT'RE YOU DOING WASTING TIME OVER HERE?
IT'S ALMOST TIME FOR THE PLANNING MEETING.
O-OH, UM...

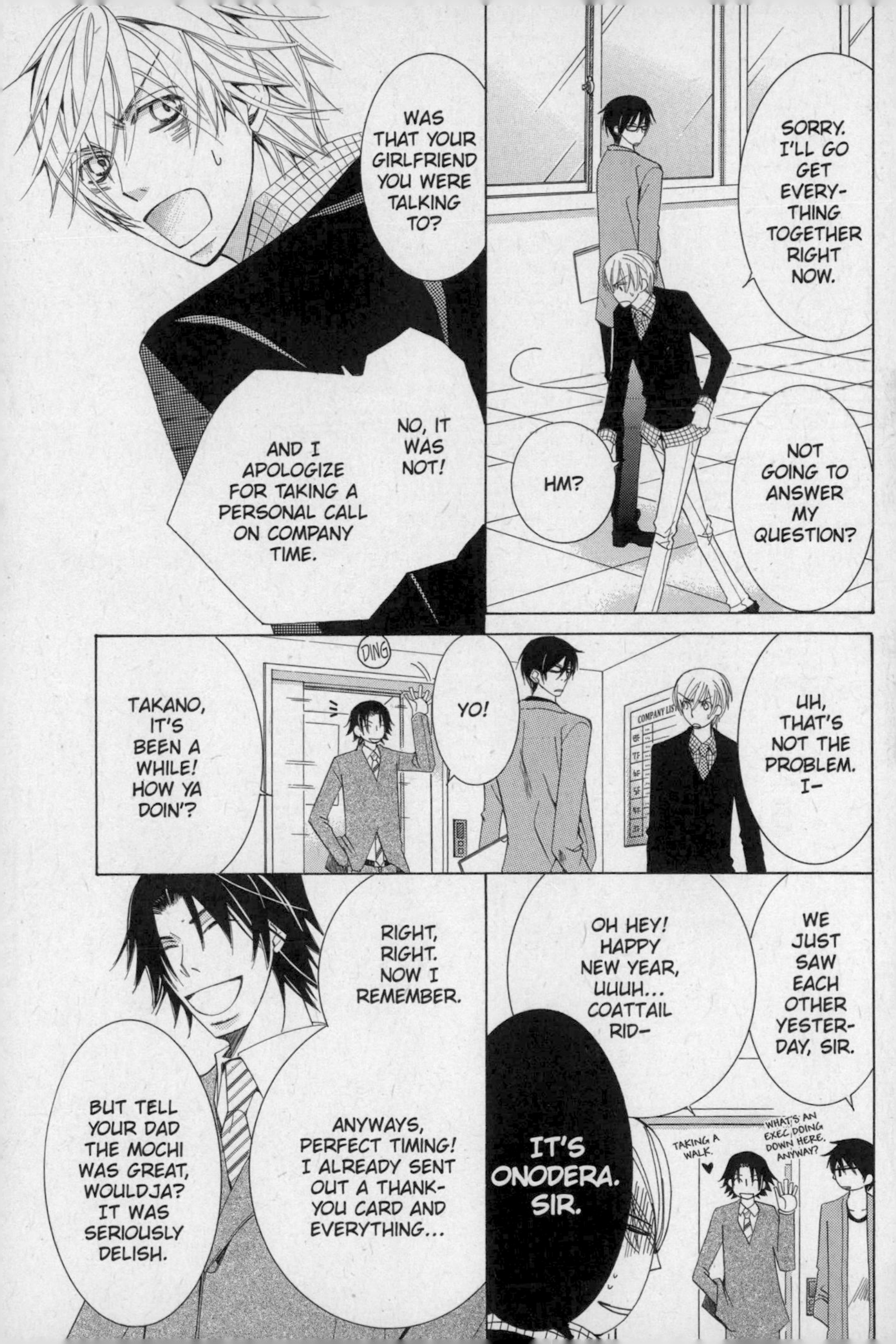
SORRY. I'LL GO GET EVERY-THING TOGETHER RIGHT NOW.
NOT GOING TO ANSWER MY QUESTION?
HM?
WAS THAT YOUR GIRLFRIEND YOU WERE TALKING TO?
NO, IT WAS NOT!
AND I APOLOGIZE FOR TAKING A PERSONAL CALL ON COMPANY TIME.
UH, THAT'S NOT THE PROBLEM. I–
DING
YO!
TAKANO, IT'S BEEN A WHILE! HOW YA DOIN'?
WE JUST SAW EACH OTHER YESTER-DAY, SIR.
OH HEY! HAPPY NEW YEAR, UUUH... COATTAIL RID–
IT'S ONODERA. SIR.
WHAT'S AN EXEC DOING DOWN HERE, ANYWAY?
TAKING A WALK.
RIGHT, RIGHT. NOW I REMEMBER.
ANYWAYS, PERFECT TIMING! I ALREADY SENT OUT A THANK-YOU CARD AND EVERYTHING...
BUT TELL YOUR DAD THE MOCHI WAS GREAT, WOULDJA? IT WAS SERIOUSLY DELISH.

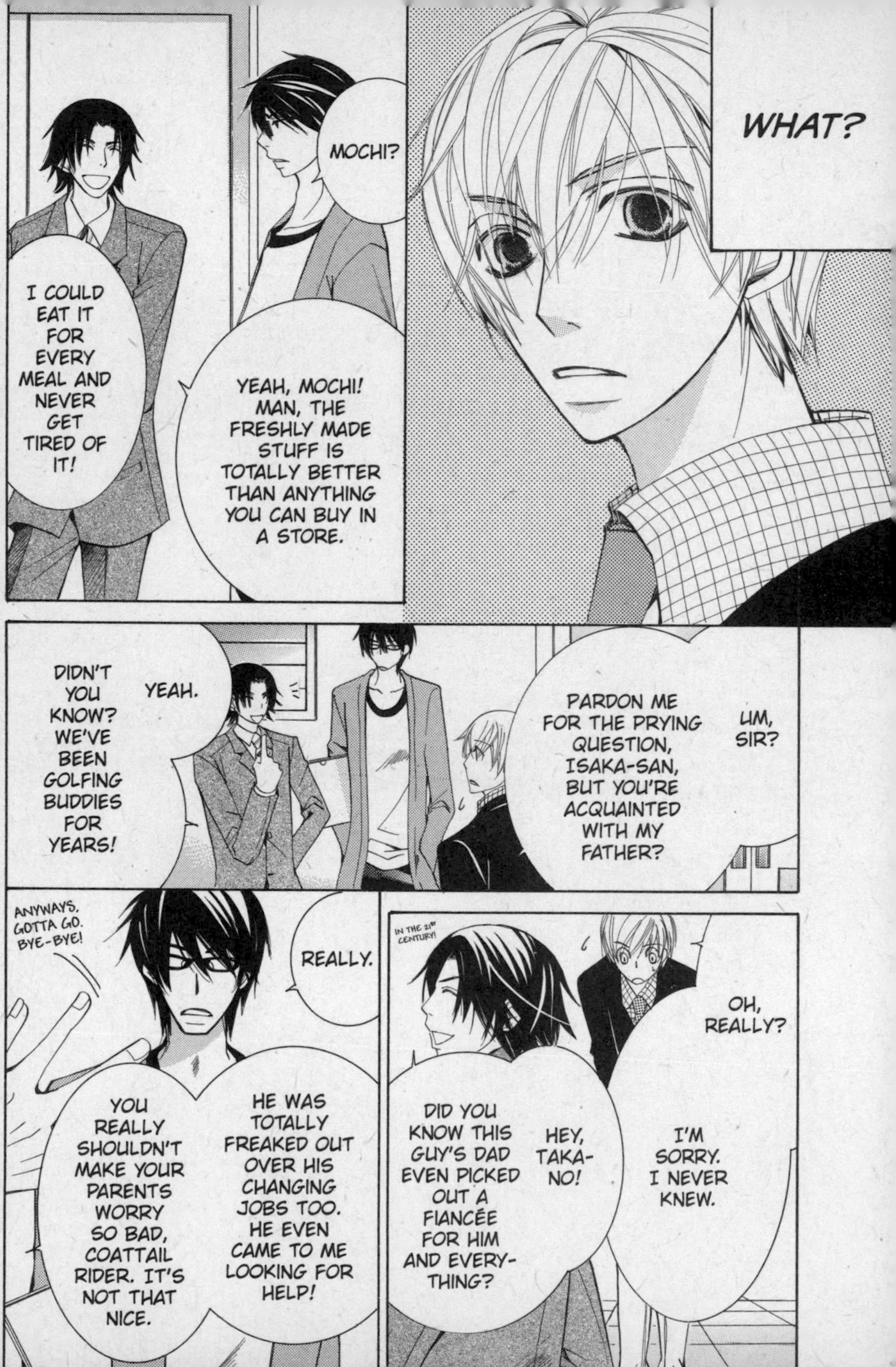
WHAT?
MOCHI?
YEAH, MOCHI! MAN, THE FRESHLY MADE STUFF IS TOTALLY BETTER THAN ANYTHING YOU CAN BUY IN A STORE.
I COULD EAT IT FOR EVERY MEAL AND NEVER GET TIRED OF IT!
UM, SIR?
PARDON ME FOR THE PRYING QUESTION, ISAKA-SAN, BUT YOU'RE ACQUAINTED WITH MY FATHER?
YEAH.
DIDN'T YOU KNOW? WE'VE BEEN GOLFING BUDDIES FOR YEARS!
OH, REALLY?
I'M SORRY. I NEVER KNEW.
HEY, TAKA-NO!
DID YOU KNOW THIS GUY'S DAD EVEN PICKED OUT A FIANCÉE FOR HIM AND EVERY-THING?
IN THE 21ST CENTURY!
REALLY.
HE WAS TOTALLY FREAKED OUT OVER HIS CHANGING JOBS TOO. HE EVEN CAME TO ME LOOKING FOR HELP!
YOU REALLY SHOULDN'T MAKE YOUR PARENTS WORRY SO BAD, COATTAIL RIDER. IT'S NOT THAT NICE.
ANYWAYS, GOTTA GO. BYE-BYE!

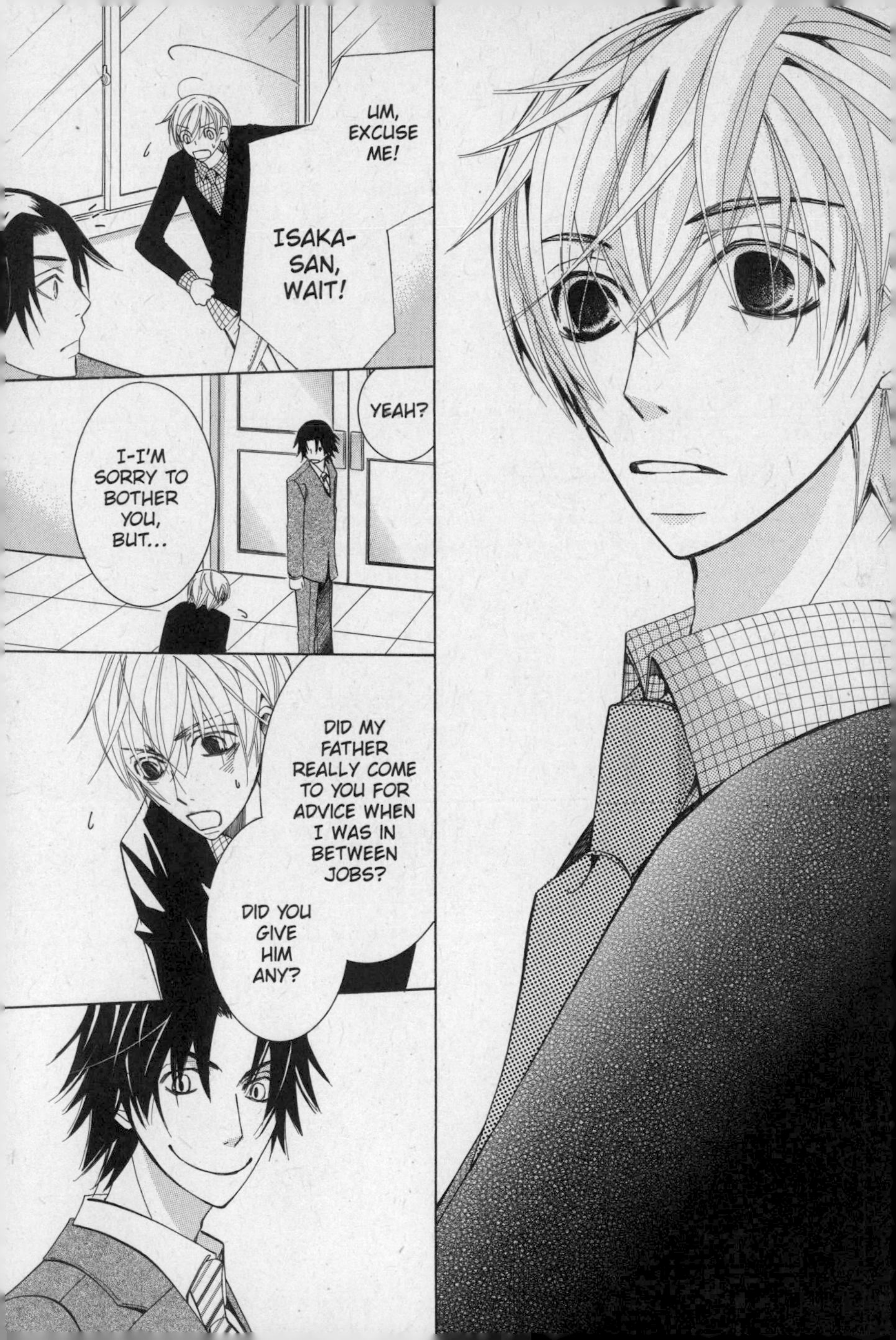
UM, EXCUSE ME!
ISAKA-SAN, WAIT!
YEAH?
I-I'M SORRY TO BOTHER YOU, BUT...
DID MY FATHER REALLY COME TO YOU FOR ADVICE WHEN I WAS IN BETWEEN JOBS?
DID YOU GIVE HIM ANY?

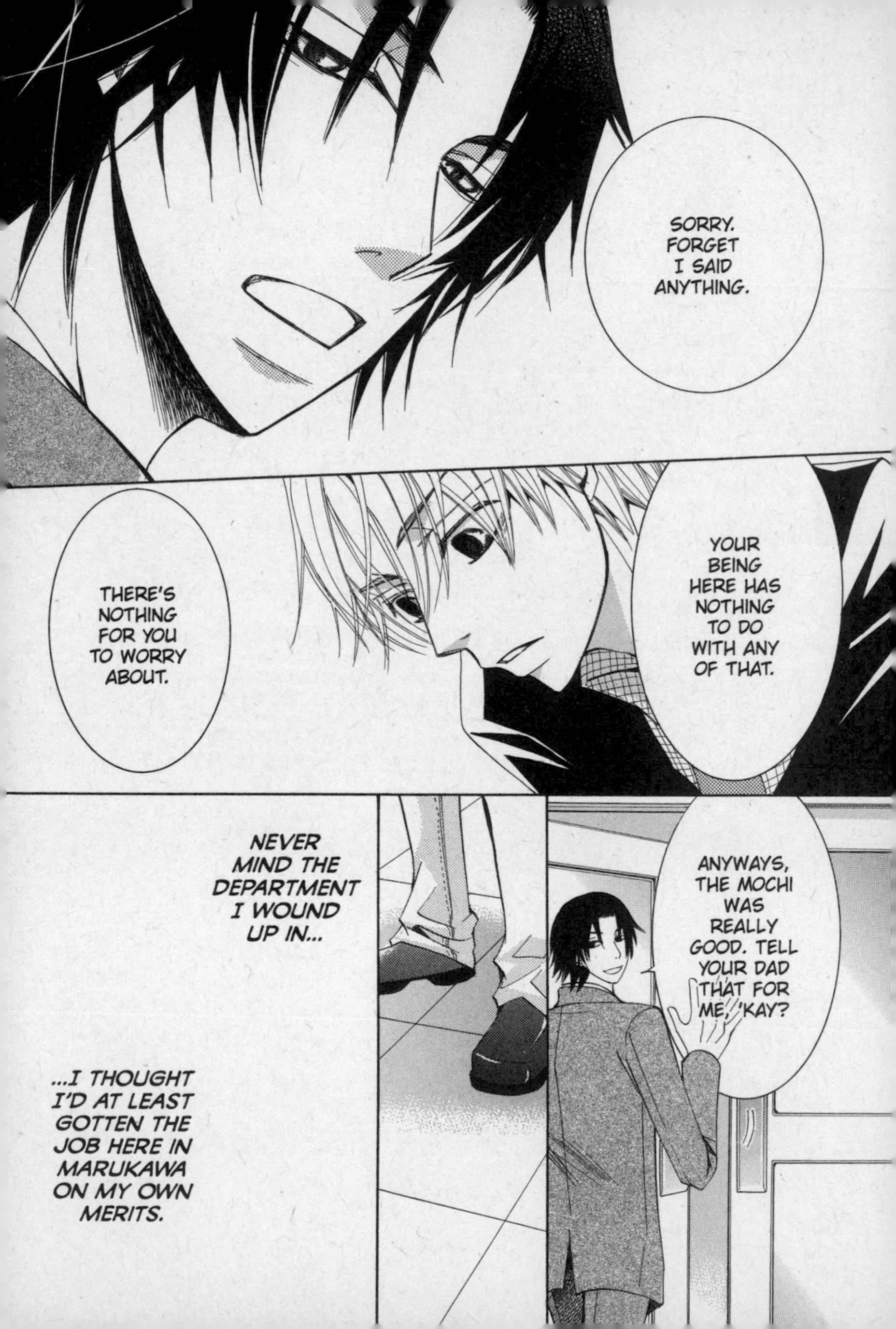
SORRY. FORGET I SAID ANYTHING.
YOUR BEING HERE HAS NOTHING TO DO WITH ANY OF THAT.
THERE'S NOTHING FOR YOU TO WORRY ABOUT.
ANYWAYS, THE MOCHI WAS REALLY GOOD. TELL YOUR DAD THAT FOR ME, 'KAY?
NEVER MIND THE DEPARTMENT I WOUND UP IN...
...I THOUGHT I'D AT LEAST GOTTEN THE JOB HERE IN MARUKAWA ON MY OWN MERITS.

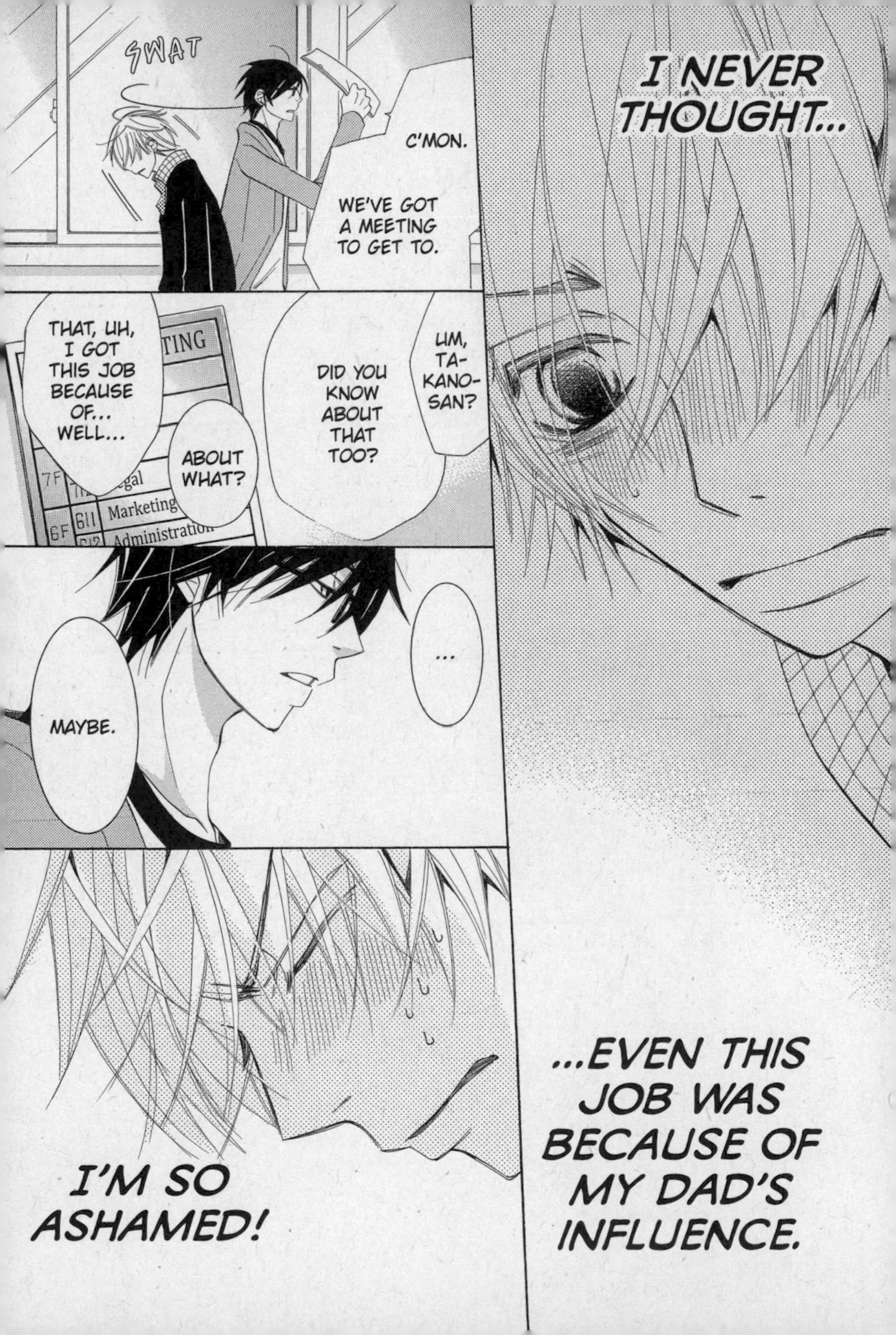
I NEVER THOUGHT...
...EVEN THIS JOB WAS BECAUSE OF MY DAD'S INFLUENCE.
SWAT
C'MON.
WE'VE GOT A MEETING TO GET TO.
UM, TA-KANO-SAN?
DID YOU KNOW ABOUT THAT TOO?
ABOUT WHAT?
THAT, UH, I GOT THIS JOB BECAUSE OF... WELL...
Marketing
Administration
...
MAYBE.
I'M SO ASHAMED!

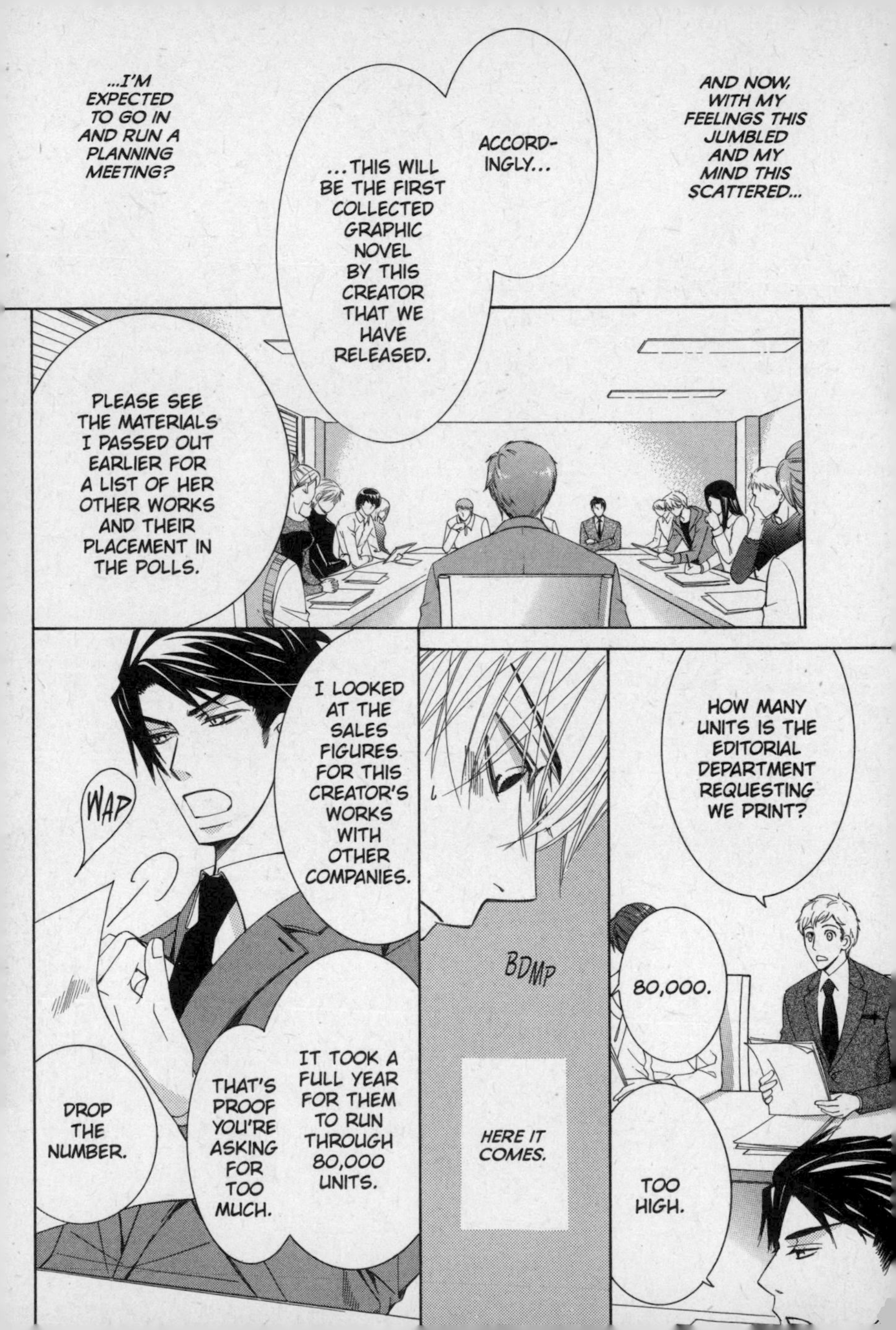

AND NOW, WITH MY FEELINGS THIS JUMBLED AND MY MIND THIS SCATTERED...
...I'M EXPECTED TO GO IN AND RUN A PLANNING MEETING?
ACCORD-INGLY...
...THIS WILL BE THE FIRST COLLECTED GRAPHIC NOVEL BY THIS CREATOR THAT WE HAVE RELEASED.
PLEASE SEE THE MATERIALS I PASSED OUT EARLIER FOR A LIST OF HER OTHER WORKS AND THEIR PLACEMENT IN THE POLLS.
HOW MANY UNITS IS THE EDITORIAL DEPARTMENT REQUESTING WE PRINT?
80,000.
TOO HIGH.
BDMP
HERE IT COMES.
I LOOKED AT THE SALES FIGURES FOR THIS CREATOR'S WORKS WITH OTHER COMPANIES.
WAP
IT TOOK A FULL YEAR FOR THEM TO RUN THROUGH 80,000 UNITS.
THAT'S PROOF YOU'RE ASKING FOR TOO MUCH.
DROP THE NUMBER.

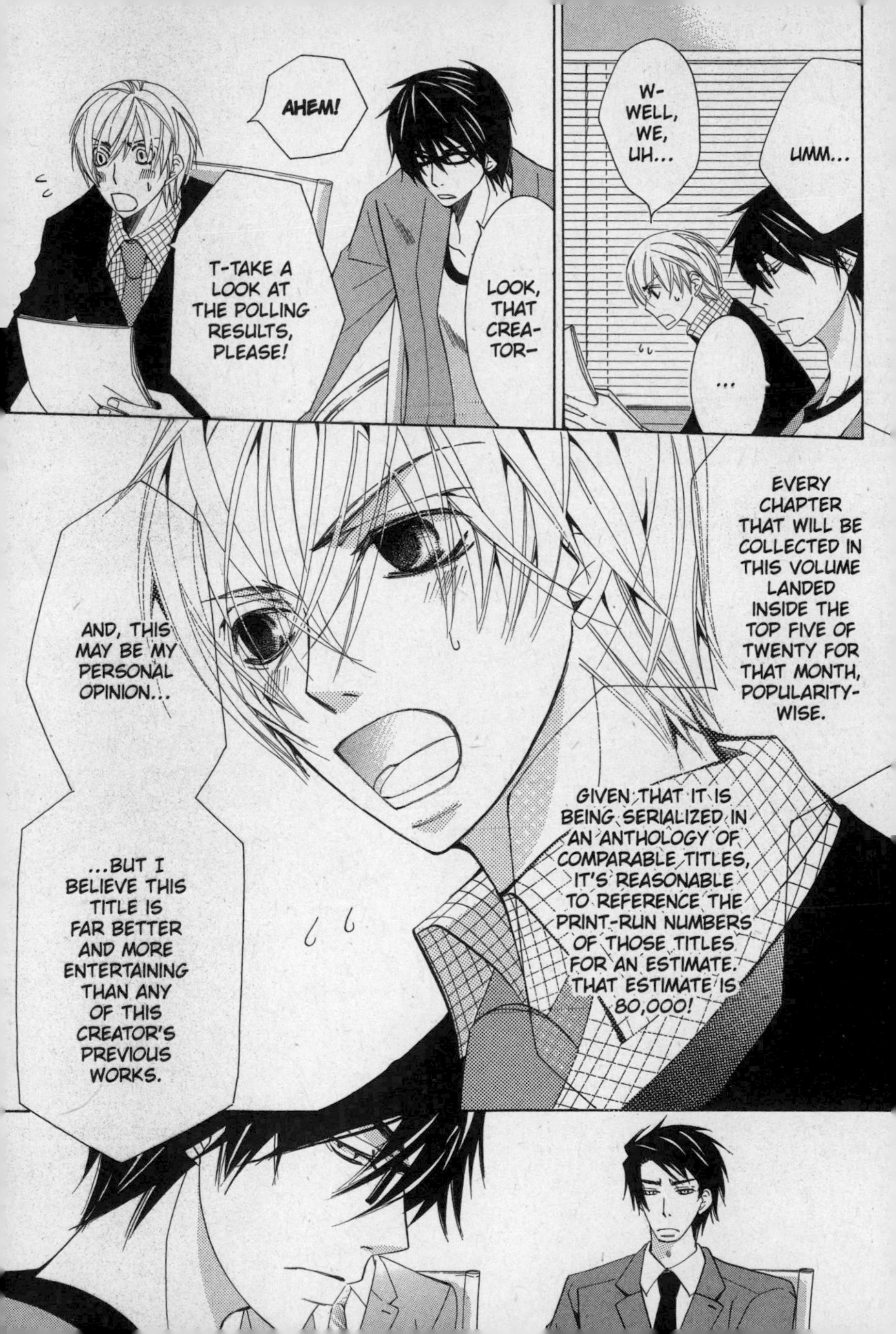
UMM...
W-WELL, WE, UH...
...
AHEM!
LOOK, THAT CREATOR-
T-TAKE A LOOK AT THE POLLING RESULTS, PLEASE!
EVERY CHAPTER THAT WILL BE COLLECTED IN THIS VOLUME LANDED INSIDE THE TOP FIVE OF TWENTY FOR THAT MONTH, POPULARITY-WISE.
GIVEN THAT IT IS BEING SERIALIZED IN AN ANTHOLOGY OF COMPARABLE TITLES, IT'S REASONABLE TO REFERENCE THE PRINT-RUN NUMBERS OF THOSE TITLES FOR AN ESTIMATE. THAT ESTIMATE IS 80,000!
AND, THIS MAY BE MY PERSONAL OPINION...
...BUT I BELIEVE THIS TITLE IS FAR BETTER AND MORE ENTERTAINING THAN ANY OF THIS CREATOR'S PREVIOUS WORKS.

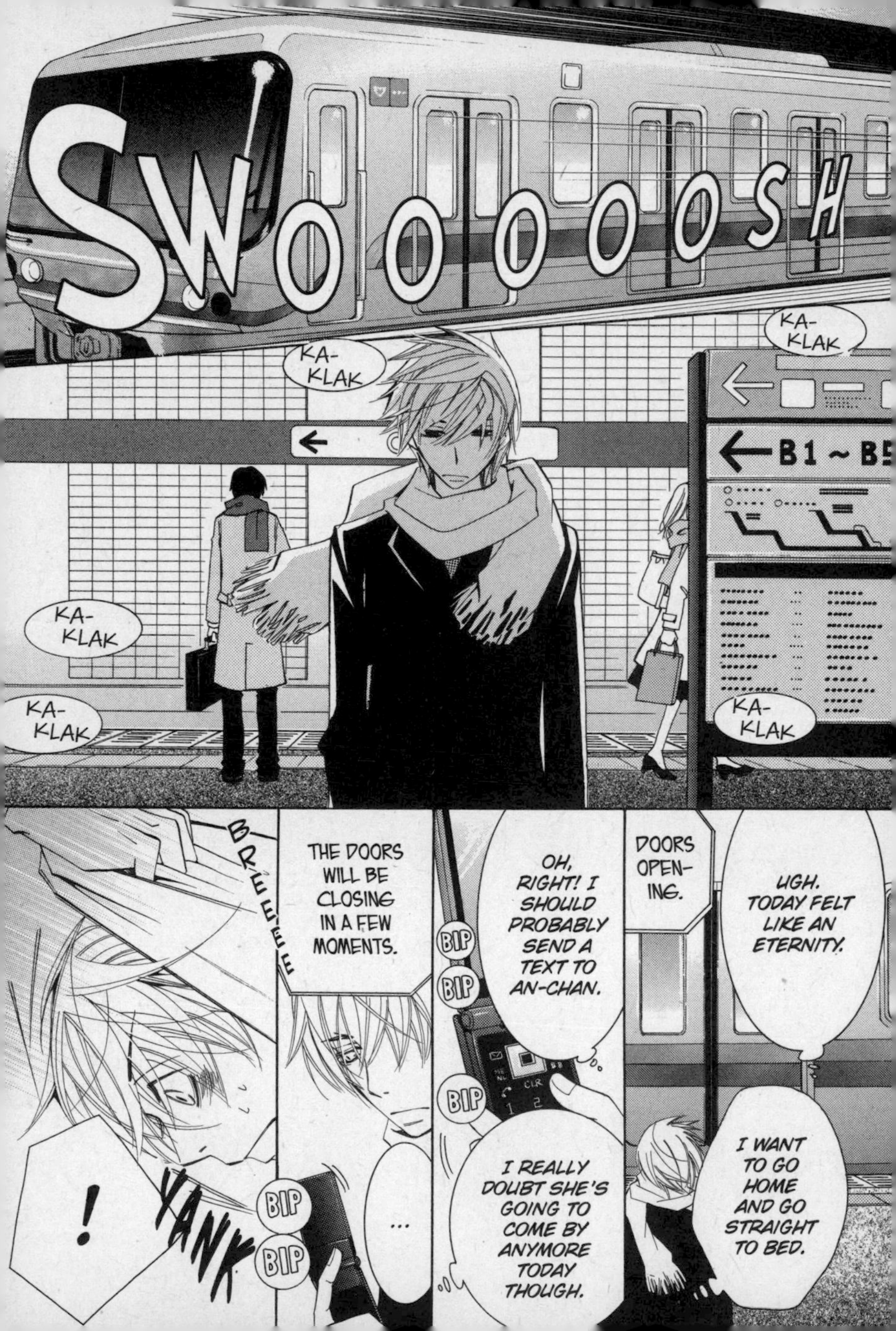
SWOOOOOSH
KA-KLAK
KA-KLAK
KA-KLAK
KA-KLAK
KA-KLAK
← B1 ~ B5
UGH. TODAY FELT LIKE AN ETERNITY.
DOORS OPENING.
I WANT TO GO HOME AND GO STRAIGHT TO BED.
OH, RIGHT! I SHOULD PROBABLY SEND A TEXT TO AN-CHAN.
BIP
BIP
BIP
I REALLY DOUBT SHE'S GOING TO COME BY ANYMORE TODAY THOUGH.
THE DOORS WILL BE CLOSING IN A FEW MOMENTS.
...
BIP
BIP
BREEEEE
!
YANK

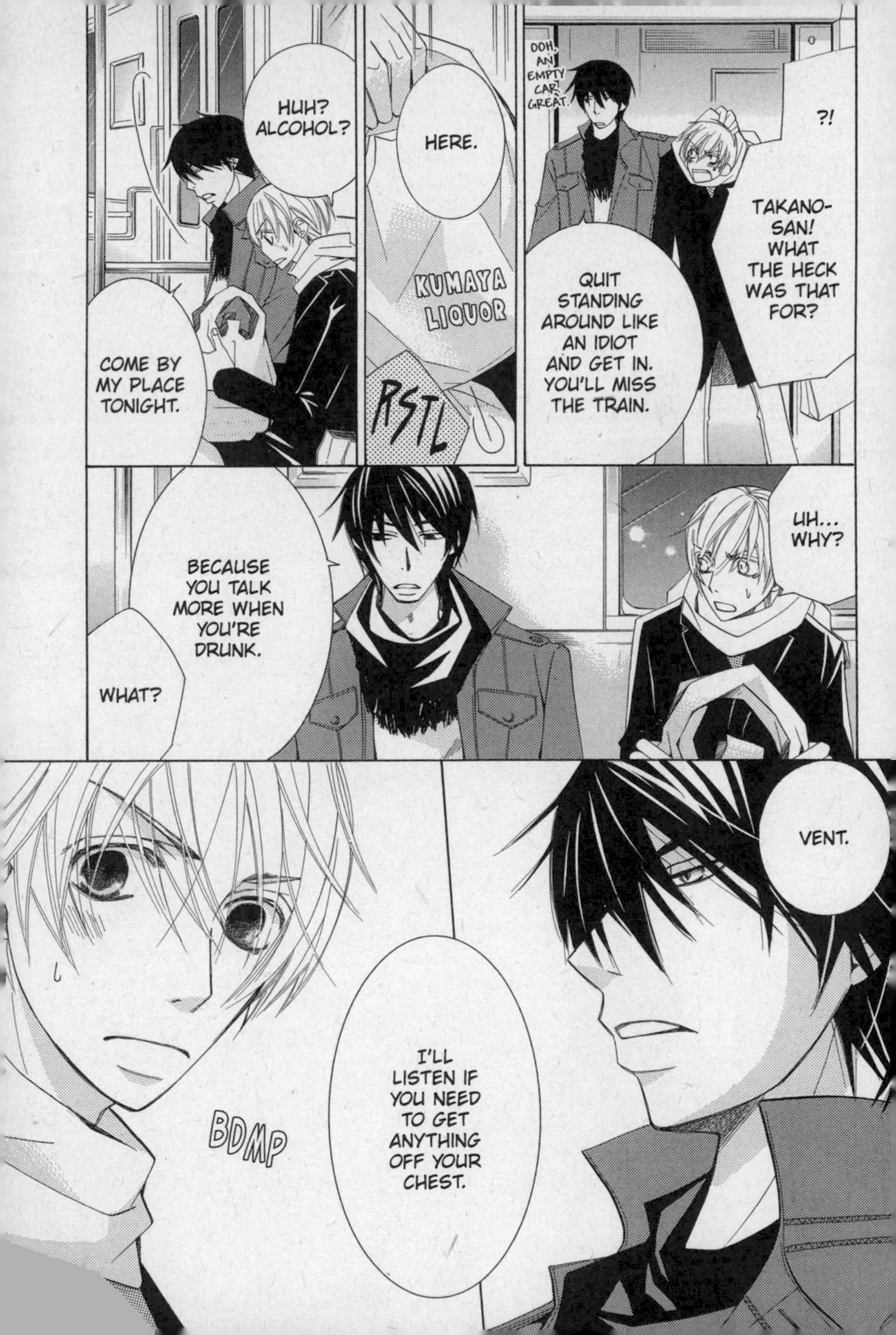
?!
TAKANO-SAN! WHAT THE HECK WAS THAT FOR?
OOH, AN EMPTY CAR! GREAT.
QUIT STANDING AROUND LIKE AN IDIOT AND GET IN. YOU'LL MISS THE TRAIN.
HERE.
KUMAYA LIQUOR
RSTL
HUH? ALCOHOL?
COME BY MY PLACE TONIGHT.
UH... WHY?
BECAUSE YOU TALK MORE WHEN YOU'RE DRUNK.
WHAT?
VENT.
I'LL LISTEN IF YOU NEED TO GET ANYTHING OFF YOUR CHEST.
BDMP

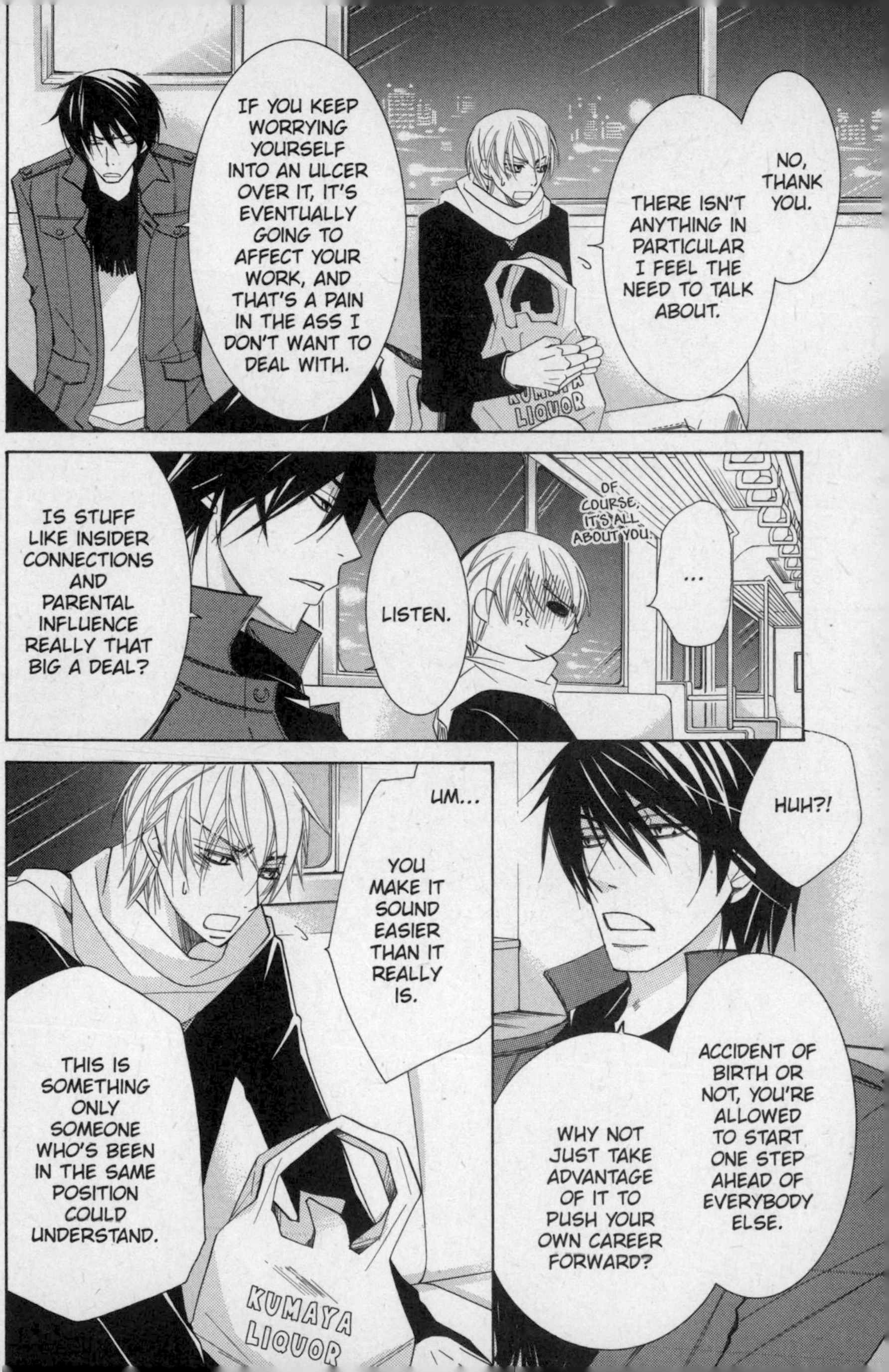
NO, THANK YOU.
THERE ISN'T ANYTHING IN PARTICULAR I FEEL THE NEED TO TALK ABOUT.
IF YOU KEEP WORRYING YOURSELF INTO AN ULCER OVER IT, IT'S EVENTUALLY GOING TO AFFECT YOUR WORK, AND THAT'S A PAIN IN THE ASS I DON'T WANT TO DEAL WITH.
...
OF COURSE, IT'S ALL ABOUT YOU.
LISTEN.
IS STUFF LIKE INSIDER CONNECTIONS AND PARENTAL INFLUENCE REALLY THAT BIG A DEAL?
HUH?!
ACCIDENT OF BIRTH OR NOT, YOU'RE ALLOWED TO START ONE STEP AHEAD OF EVERYBODY ELSE.
WHY NOT JUST TAKE ADVANTAGE OF IT TO PUSH YOUR OWN CAREER FORWARD?
UM...
YOU MAKE IT SOUND EASIER THAN IT REALLY IS.
THIS IS SOMETHING ONLY SOMEONE WHO'S BEEN IN THE SAME POSITION COULD UNDERSTAND.
KUMAYA LIQUOR

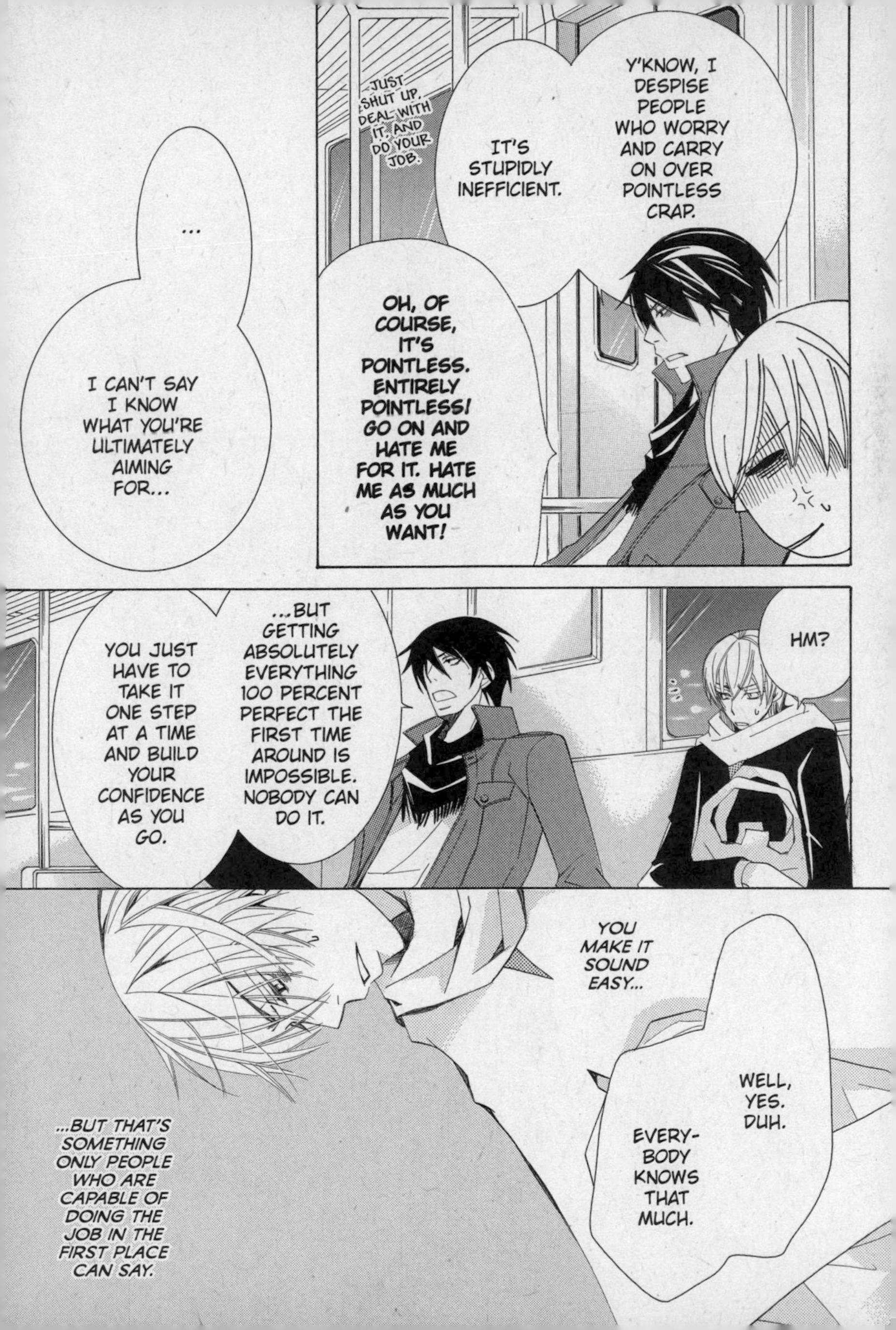
Y'KNOW, I DESPISE PEOPLE WHO WORRY AND CARRY ON OVER POINTLESS CRAP.
IT'S STUPIDLY INEFFICIENT.
JUST SHUT UP, DEAL WITH IT, AND DO YOUR JOB.
OH, OF COURSE, IT'S POINTLESS. ENTIRELY POINTLESS! GO ON AND HATE ME FOR IT. HATE ME AS MUCH AS YOU WANT!
...
I CAN'T SAY I KNOW WHAT YOU'RE ULTIMATELY AIMING FOR...
HM?
...BUT GETTING ABSOLUTELY EVERYTHING 100 PERCENT PERFECT THE FIRST TIME AROUND IS IMPOSSIBLE. NOBODY CAN DO IT.
YOU JUST HAVE TO TAKE IT ONE STEP AT A TIME AND BUILD YOUR CONFIDENCE AS YOU GO.
YOU MAKE IT SOUND EASY...
WELL, YES. DUH.
EVERY-BODY KNOWS THAT MUCH.
...BUT THAT'S SOMETHING ONLY PEOPLE WHO ARE CAPABLE OF DOING THE JOB IN THE FIRST PLACE CAN SAY.

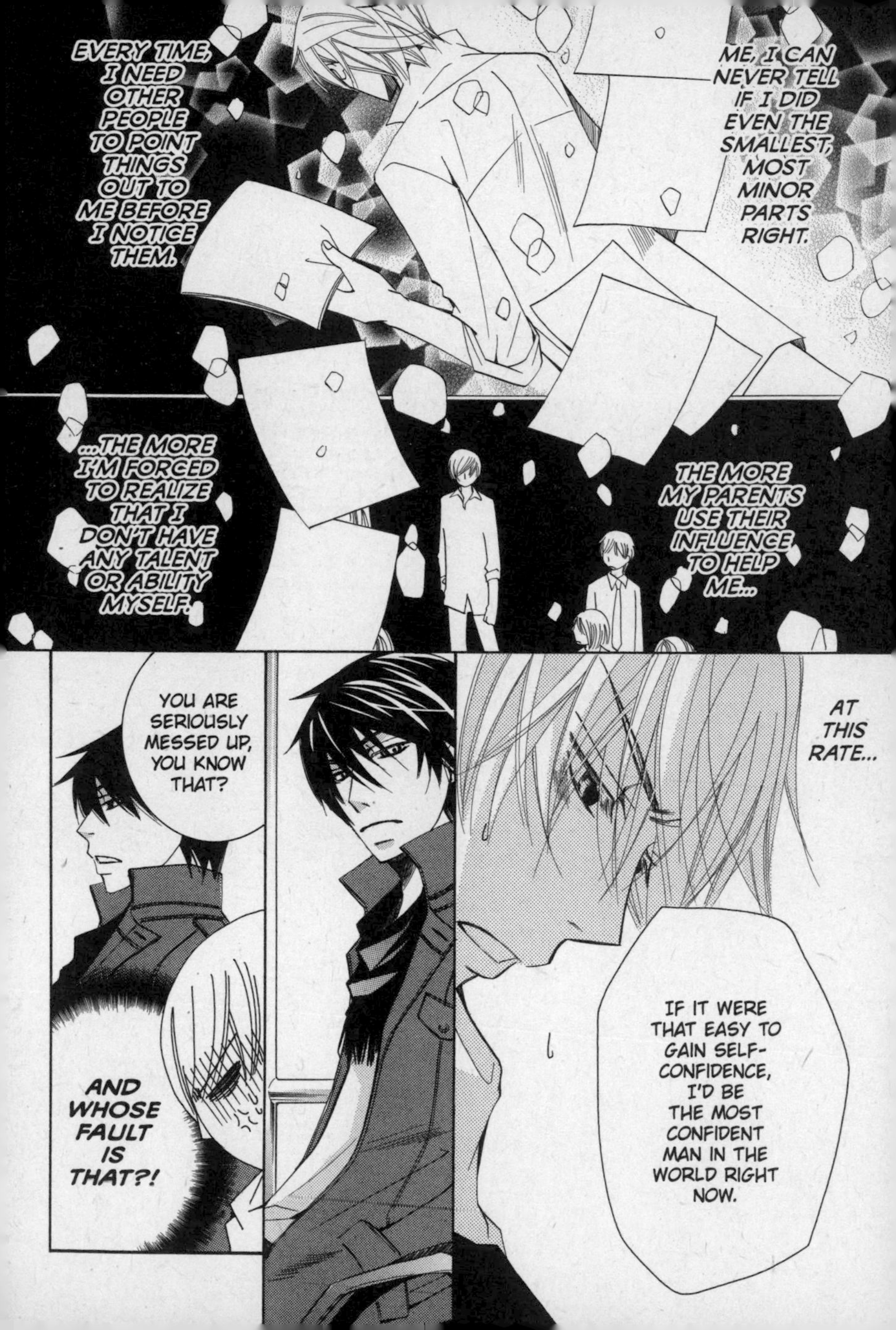

ME, I CAN NEVER TELL IF I DID EVEN THE SMALLEST, MOST MINOR PARTS RIGHT.
EVERY TIME, I NEED OTHER PEOPLE TO POINT THINGS OUT TO ME BEFORE I NOTICE THEM.
THE MORE MY PARENTS USE THEIR INFLUENCE TO HELP ME...
...THE MORE I'M FORCED TO REALIZE THAT I DON'T HAVE ANY TALENT OR ABILITY MYSELF.
AT THIS RATE...
IF IT WERE THAT EASY TO GAIN SELF-CONFIDENCE, I'D BE THE MOST CONFIDENT MAN IN THE WORLD RIGHT NOW.
YOU ARE SERIOUSLY MESSED UP, YOU KNOW THAT?
AND WHOSE FAULT IS THAT?!

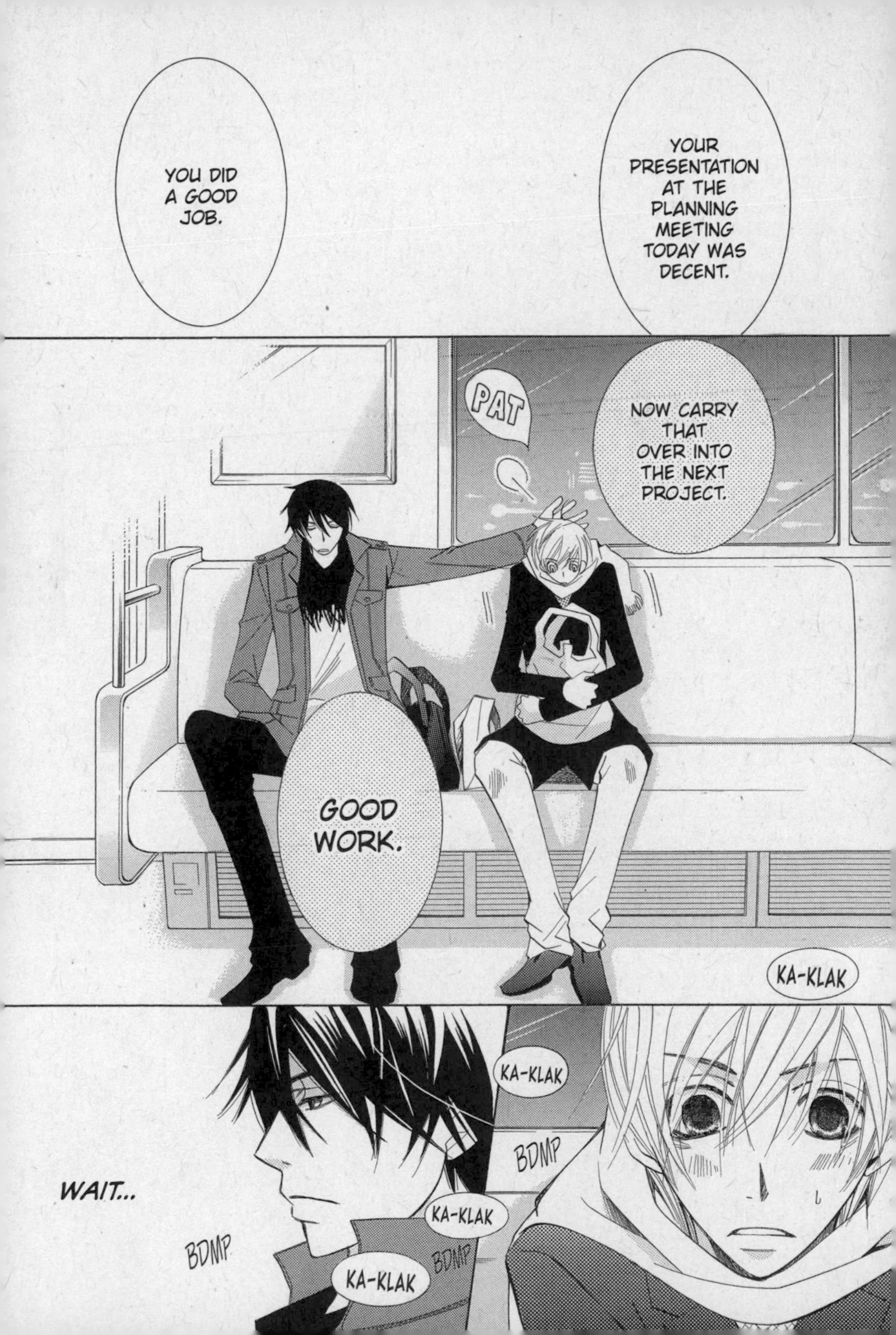
YOUR PRESENTATION AT THE PLANNING MEETING TODAY WAS DECENT.
YOU DID A GOOD JOB.
NOW CARRY THAT OVER INTO THE NEXT PROJECT.
PAT
GOOD WORK.
KA-KLAK
KA-KLAK
BDMP
KA-KLAK
BDMP
KA-KLAK
BDMP
WAIT...

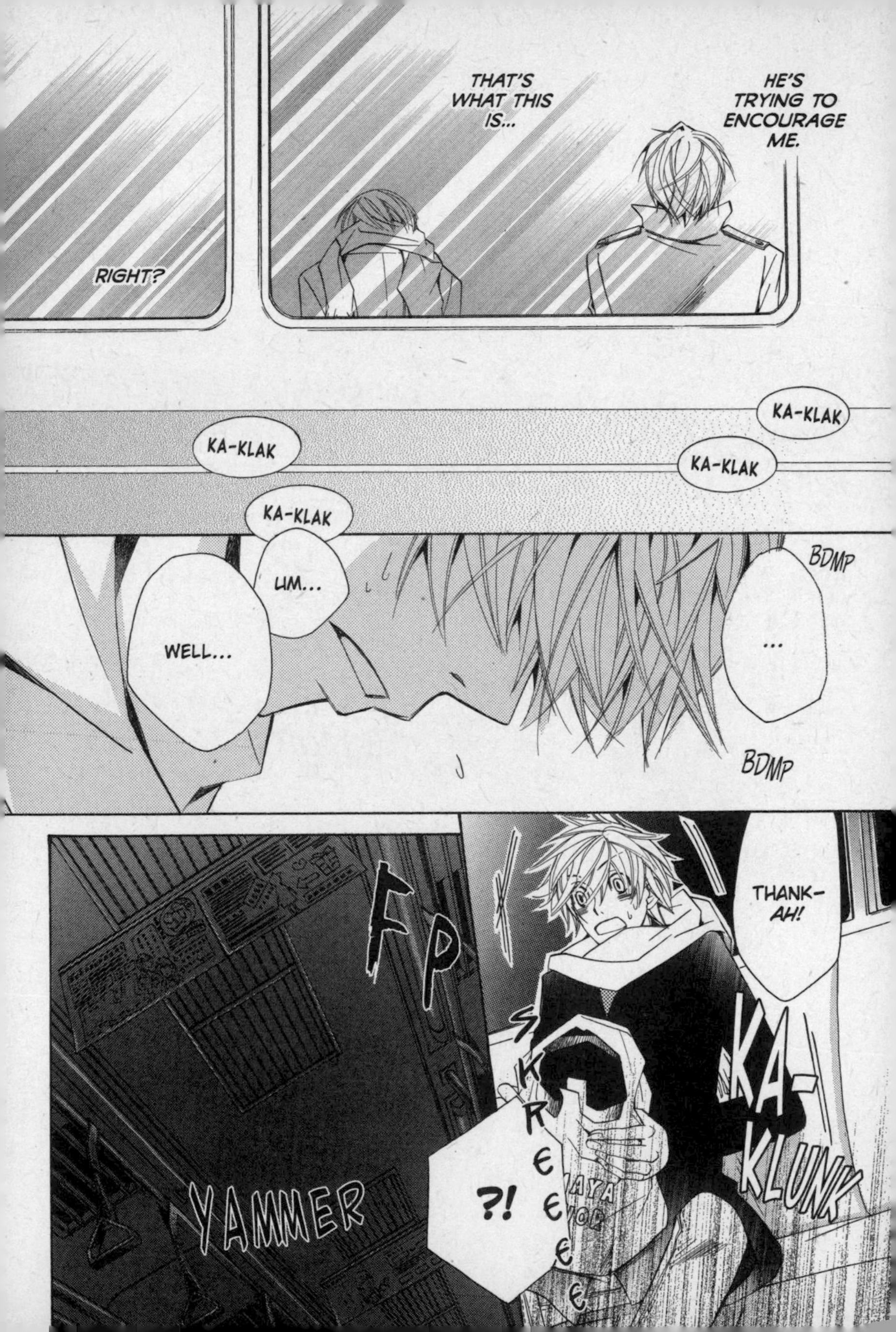
HE'S TRYING TO ENCOURAGE ME.
THAT'S WHAT THIS IS...
RIGHT?
KA-KLAK
KA-KLAK
KA-KLAK
KA-KLAK
BDMP
...
BDMP
UM...
WELL...
THANK- AH!
KA-KLUNK
SKREEEEE
?!
FP
YAMMER

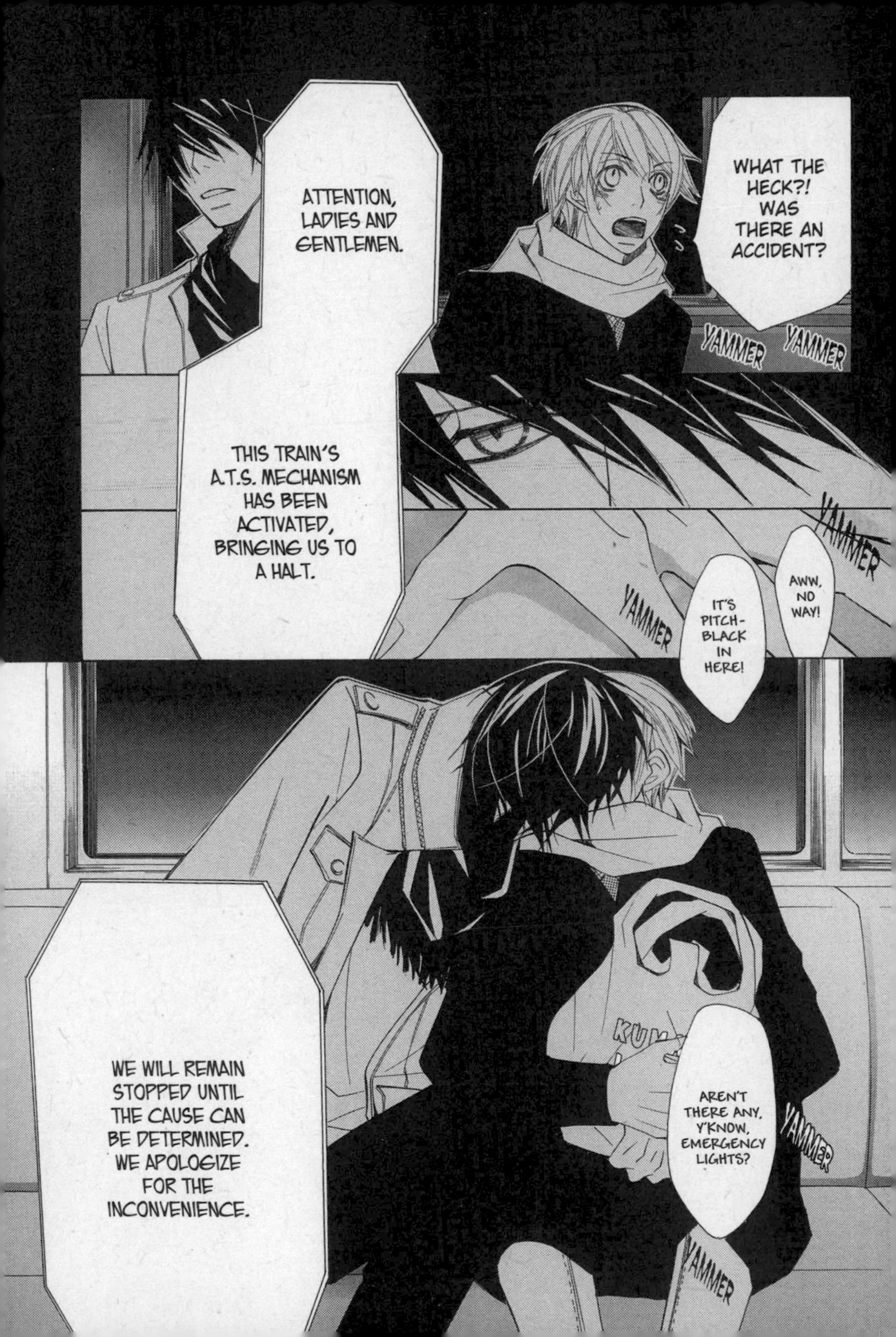
WHAT THE HECK?! WAS THERE AN ACCIDENT?
YAMMER YAMMER
ATTENTION, LADIES AND GENTLEMEN.
YAMMER
AWW, NO WAY!
IT'S PITCH-BLACK IN HERE!
YAMMER
THIS TRAIN'S A.T.S. MECHANISM HAS BEEN ACTIVATED, BRINGING US TO A HALT.
AREN'T THERE ANY, Y'KNOW, EMERGENCY LIGHTS?
YAMMER
YAMMER
WE WILL REMAIN STOPPED UNTIL THE CAUSE CAN BE DETERMINED. WE APOLOGIZE FOR THE INCONVENIENCE.

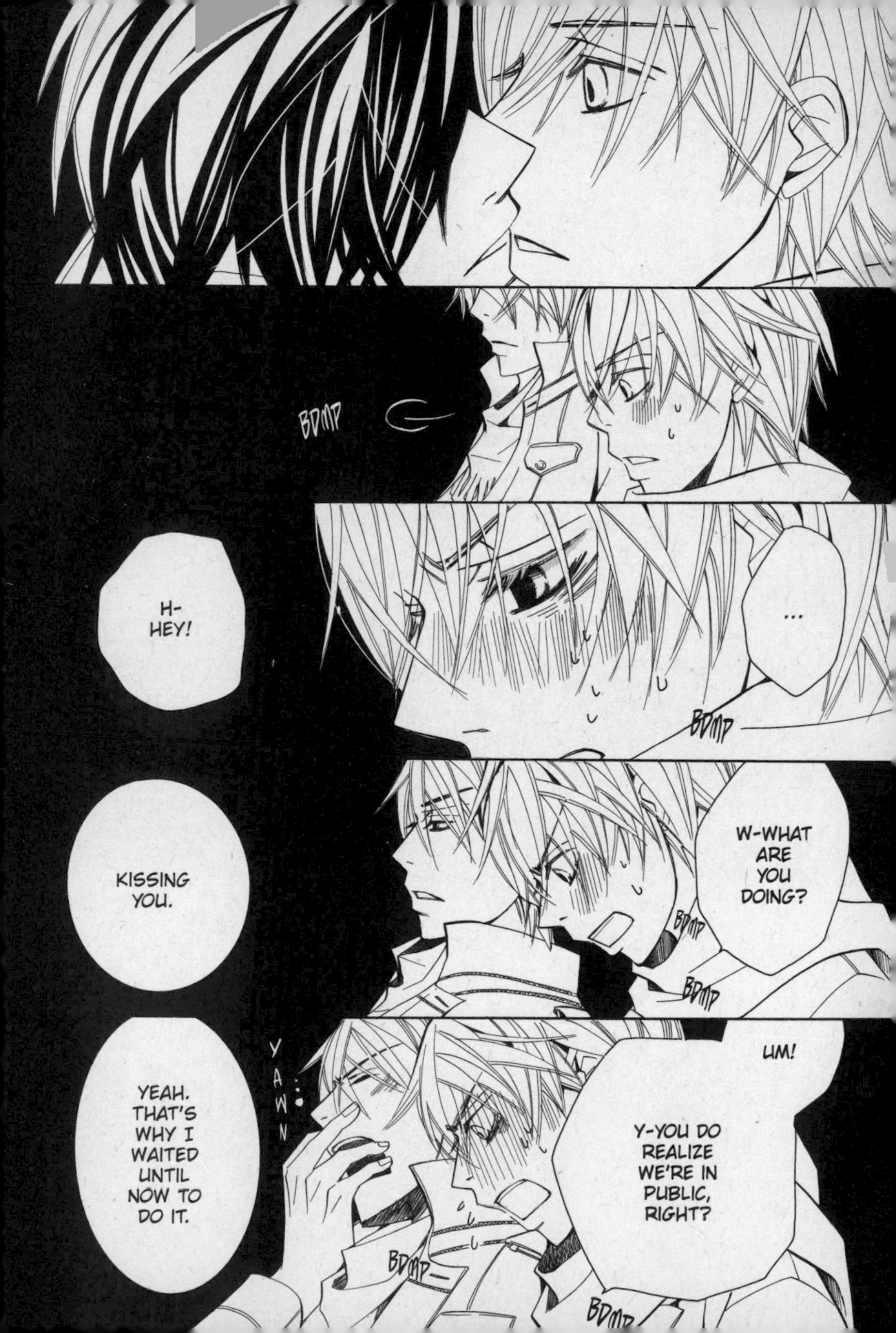
BDMP
...
H- HEY!
BDMP
W-WHAT ARE YOU DOING?
BDMP
BDMP
KISSING YOU.
UM!
Y-YOU DO REALIZE WE'RE IN PUBLIC, RIGHT?
BDMP
BDMP
YAWN
YEAH. THAT'S WHY I WAITED UNTIL NOW TO DO IT.

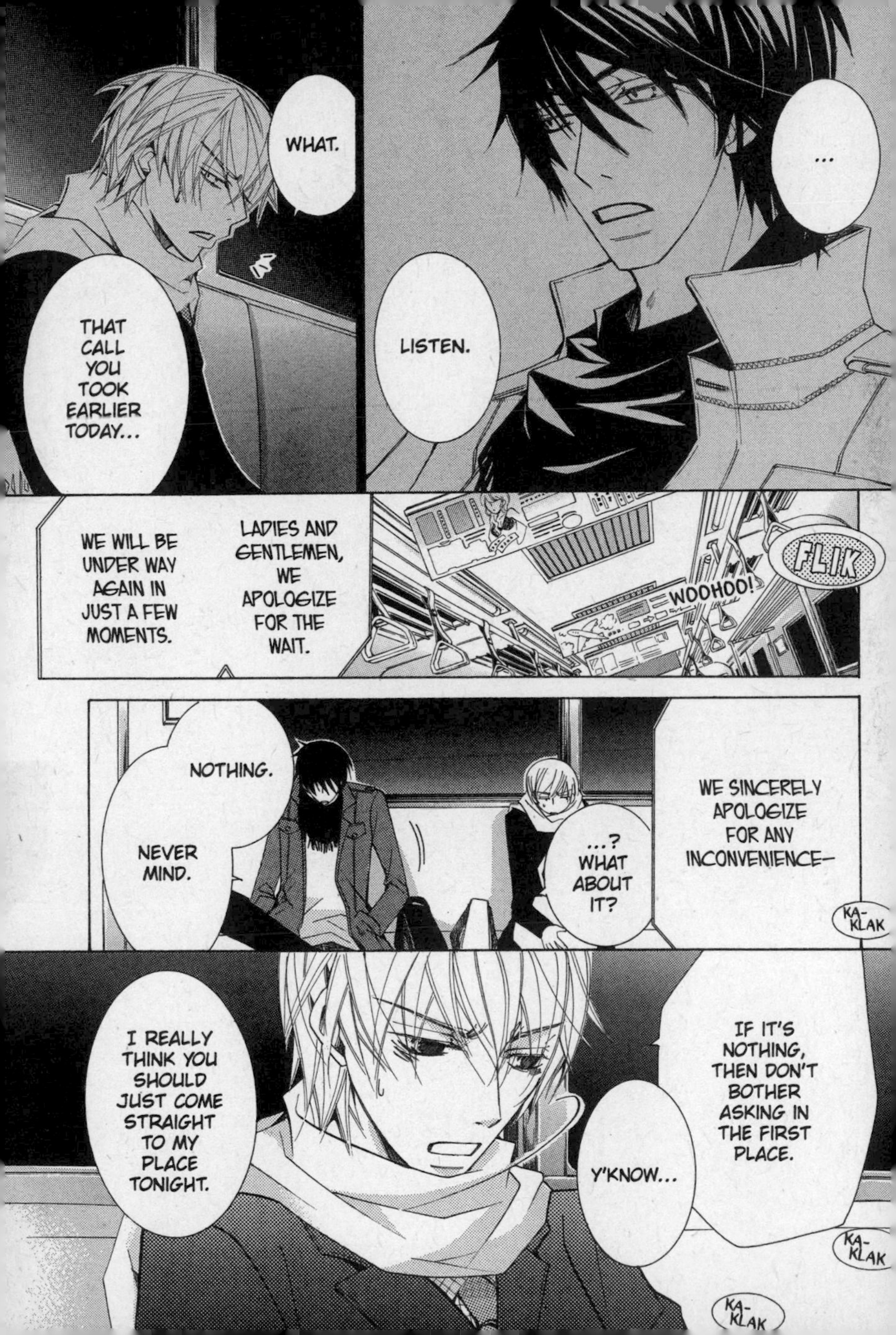
...
LISTEN.
WHAT.
THAT CALL YOU TOOK EARLIER TODAY...
FLIK
WOOHOO!
LADIES AND GENTLEMEN, WE APOLOGIZE FOR THE WAIT.
WE WILL BE UNDER WAY AGAIN IN JUST A FEW MOMENTS.
WE SINCERELY APOLOGIZE FOR ANY INCONVENIENCE—
KA-KLAK
...? WHAT ABOUT IT?
NOTHING.
NEVER MIND.
IF IT'S NOTHING, THEN DON'T BOTHER ASKING IN THE FIRST PLACE.
KA-KLAK
Y'KNOW...
I REALLY THINK YOU SHOULD JUST COME STRAIGHT TO MY PLACE TONIGHT.
KA-KLAK

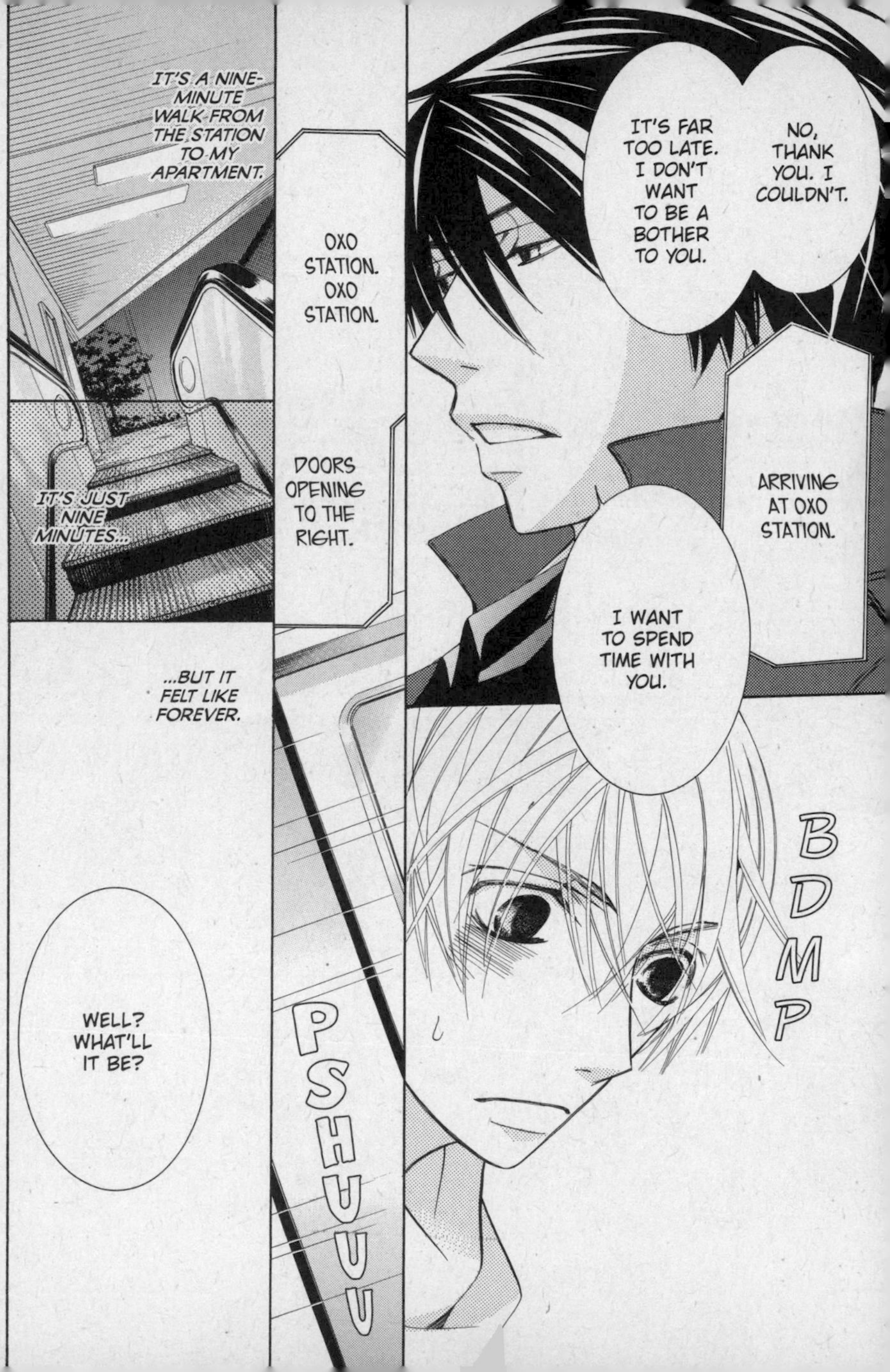
NO, THANK YOU. I COULDN'T.
IT'S FAR TOO LATE. I DON'T WANT TO BE A BOTHER TO YOU.
ARRIVING AT OXO STATION.
I WANT TO SPEND TIME WITH YOU.
BDMP
OXO STATION. OXO STATION.
DOORS OPENING TO THE RIGHT.
PSHUUU
IT'S A NINE-MINUTE WALK FROM THE STATION TO MY APARTMENT.
IT'S JUST NINE MINUTES...
...BUT IT FELT LIKE FOREVER.
WELL? WHAT'LL IT BE?

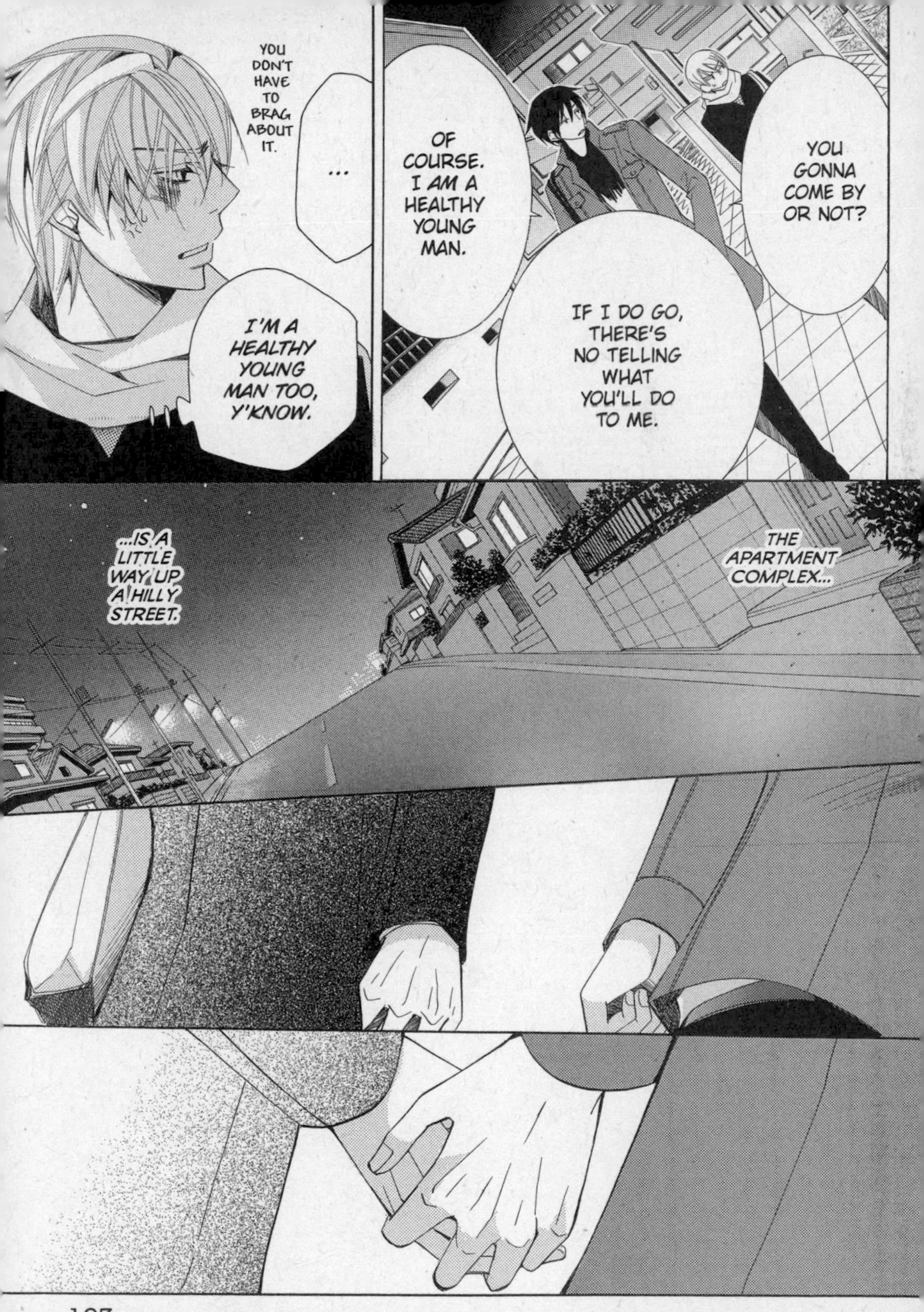
YOU GONNA COME BY OR NOT?
IF I DO GO, THERE'S NO TELLING WHAT YOU'LL DO TO ME.
OF COURSE. I AM A HEALTHY YOUNG MAN.
...
YOU DON'T HAVE TO BRAG ABOUT IT.
I'M A HEALTHY YOUNG MAN TOO, Y'KNOW.
THE APARTMENT COMPLEX...
...IS A LITTLE WAY UP A HILLY STREET.

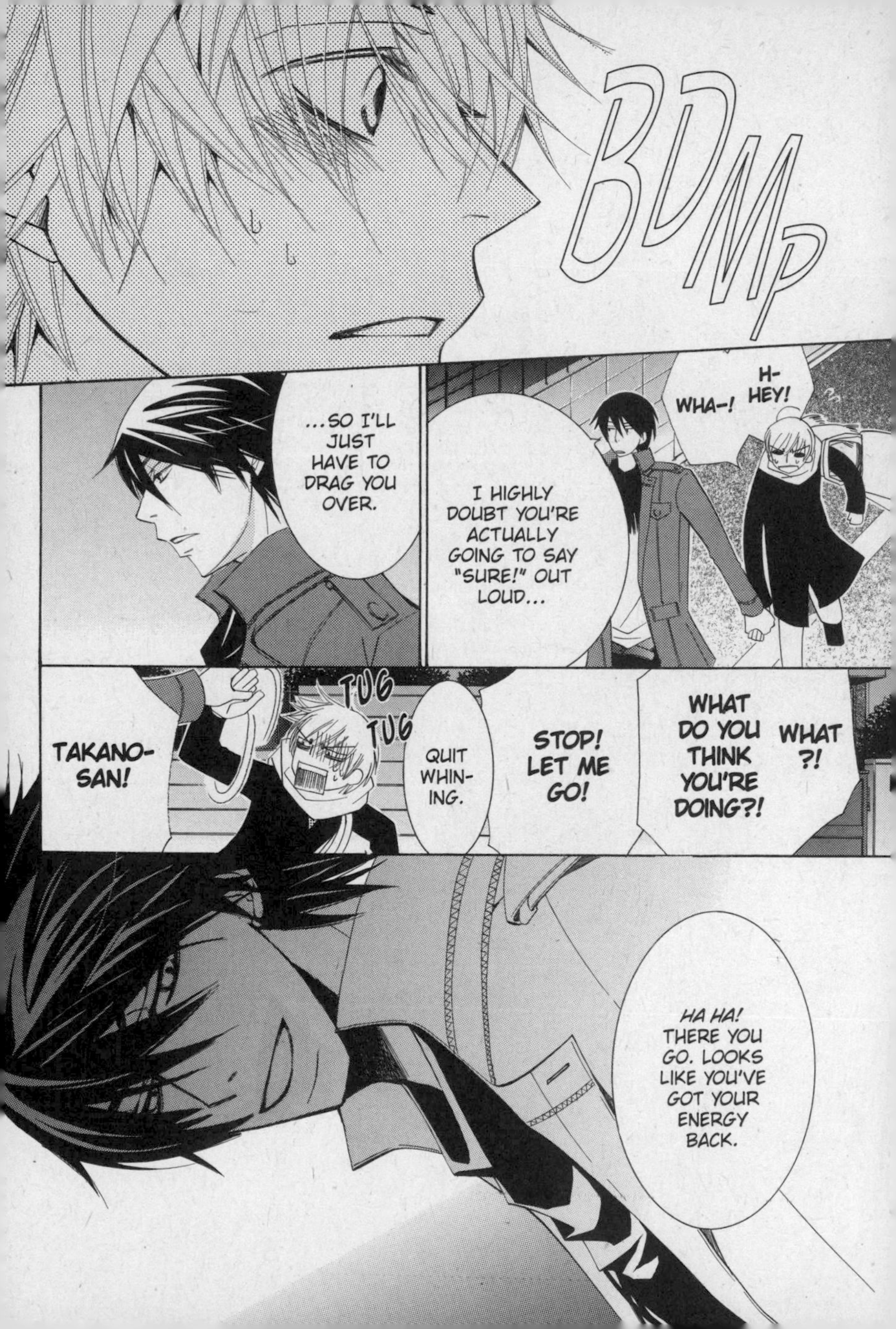
BDMP
H-HEY!
WHA-!
I HIGHLY DOUBT YOU'RE ACTUALLY GOING TO SAY "SURE!" OUT LOUD...
...SO I'LL JUST HAVE TO DRAG YOU OVER.
WHAT ?!
WHAT DO YOU THINK YOU'RE DOING?!
STOP! LET ME GO!
QUIT WHINING.
TUG TUG
TAKANO-SAN!
HA HA! THERE YOU GO. LOOKS LIKE YOU'VE GOT YOUR ENERGY BACK.

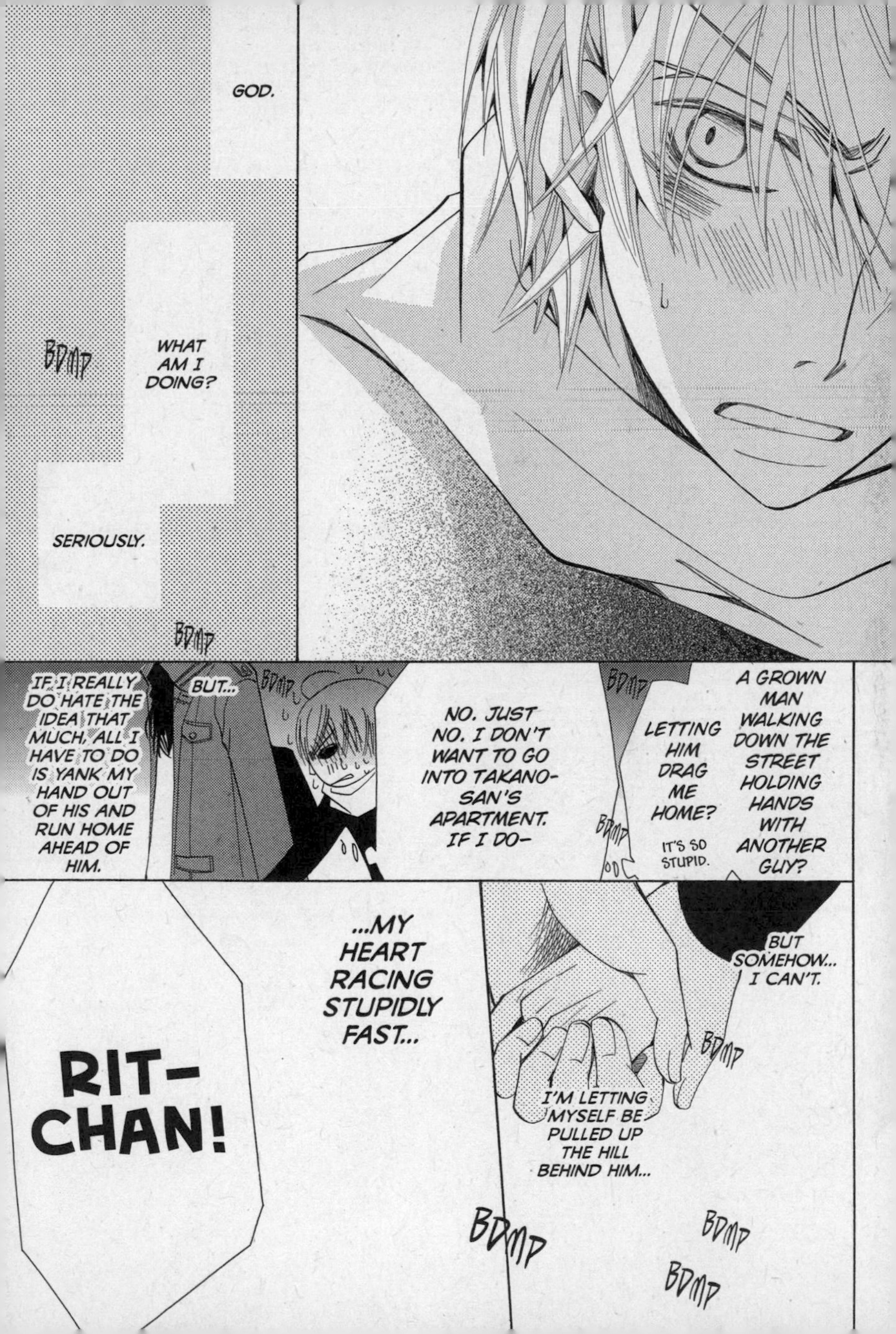
GOD.
WHAT AM I DOING?
BDMP
SERIOUSLY.
BDMP
A GROWN MAN WALKING DOWN THE STREET HOLDING HANDS WITH ANOTHER GUY?
BDMP
LETTING HIM DRAG ME HOME?
IT'S SO STUPID.
BDMP
NO. JUST NO. I DON'T WANT TO GO INTO TAKANO-SAN'S APARTMENT. IF I DO-
BDMP
BUT...
IF I REALLY DO HATE THE IDEA THAT MUCH, ALL I HAVE TO DO IS YANK MY HAND OUT OF HIS AND RUN HOME AHEAD OF HIM.
BUT SOMEHOW... I CAN'T.
BDMP
I'M LETTING MYSELF BE PULLED UP THE HILL BEHIND HIM...
BDMP
BDMP
BDMP
...MY HEART RACING STUPIDLY FAST...
RIT-CHAN!

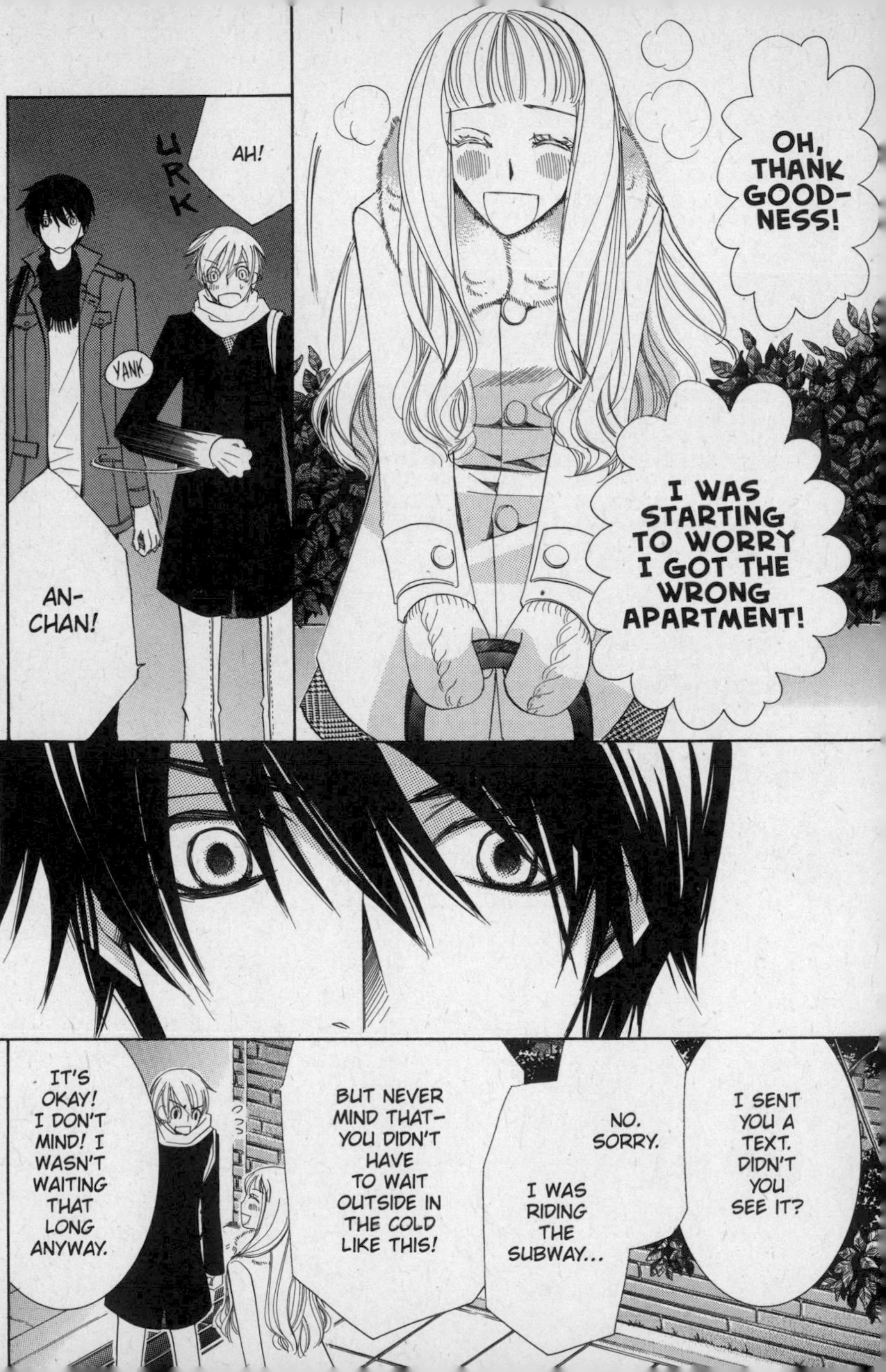
OH, THANK GOOD-NESS!
I WAS STARTING TO WORRY I GOT THE WRONG APARTMENT!
AH!
URK
YANK
AN-CHAN!
I SENT YOU A TEXT. DIDN'T YOU SEE IT?
NO. SORRY.
I WAS RIDING THE SUBWAY...
BUT NEVER MIND THAT—YOU DIDN'T HAVE TO WAIT OUTSIDE IN THE COLD LIKE THIS!
IT'S OKAY! I DON'T MIND! I WASN'T WAITING THAT LONG ANYWAY.

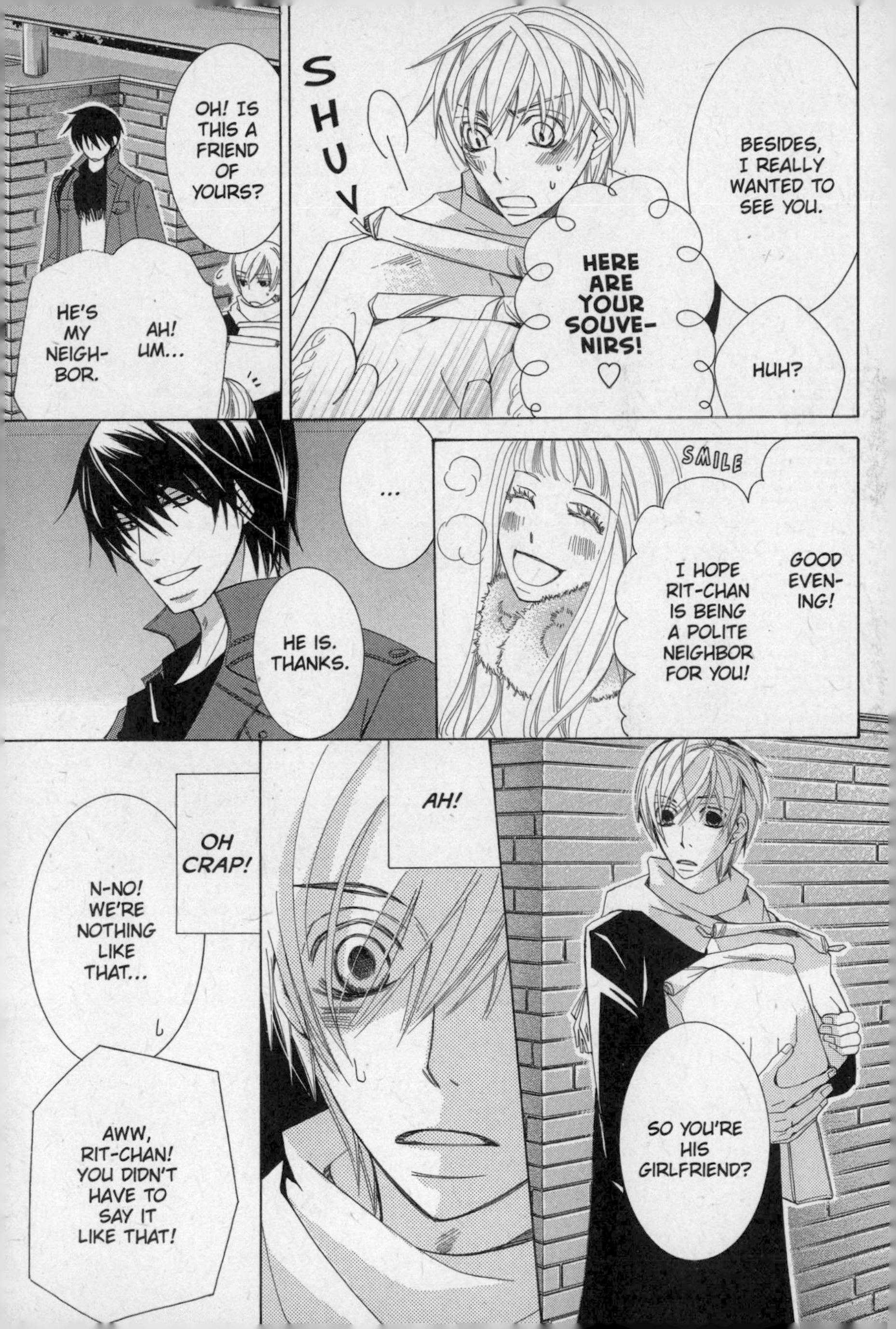
BESIDES, I REALLY WANTED TO SEE YOU.
HUH?
HERE ARE YOUR SOUVENIRS! ♡
SHUV
OH! IS THIS A FRIEND OF YOURS?
AH! UM...
HE'S MY NEIGHBOR.
SMILE
GOOD EVENING!
I HOPE RIT-CHAN IS BEING A POLITE NEIGHBOR FOR YOU!
...
HE IS. THANKS.
SO YOU'RE HIS GIRLFRIEND?
AH!
OH CRAP!
N-NO! WE'RE NOTHING LIKE THAT...
AWW, RIT-CHAN! YOU DIDN'T HAVE TO SAY IT LIKE THAT!

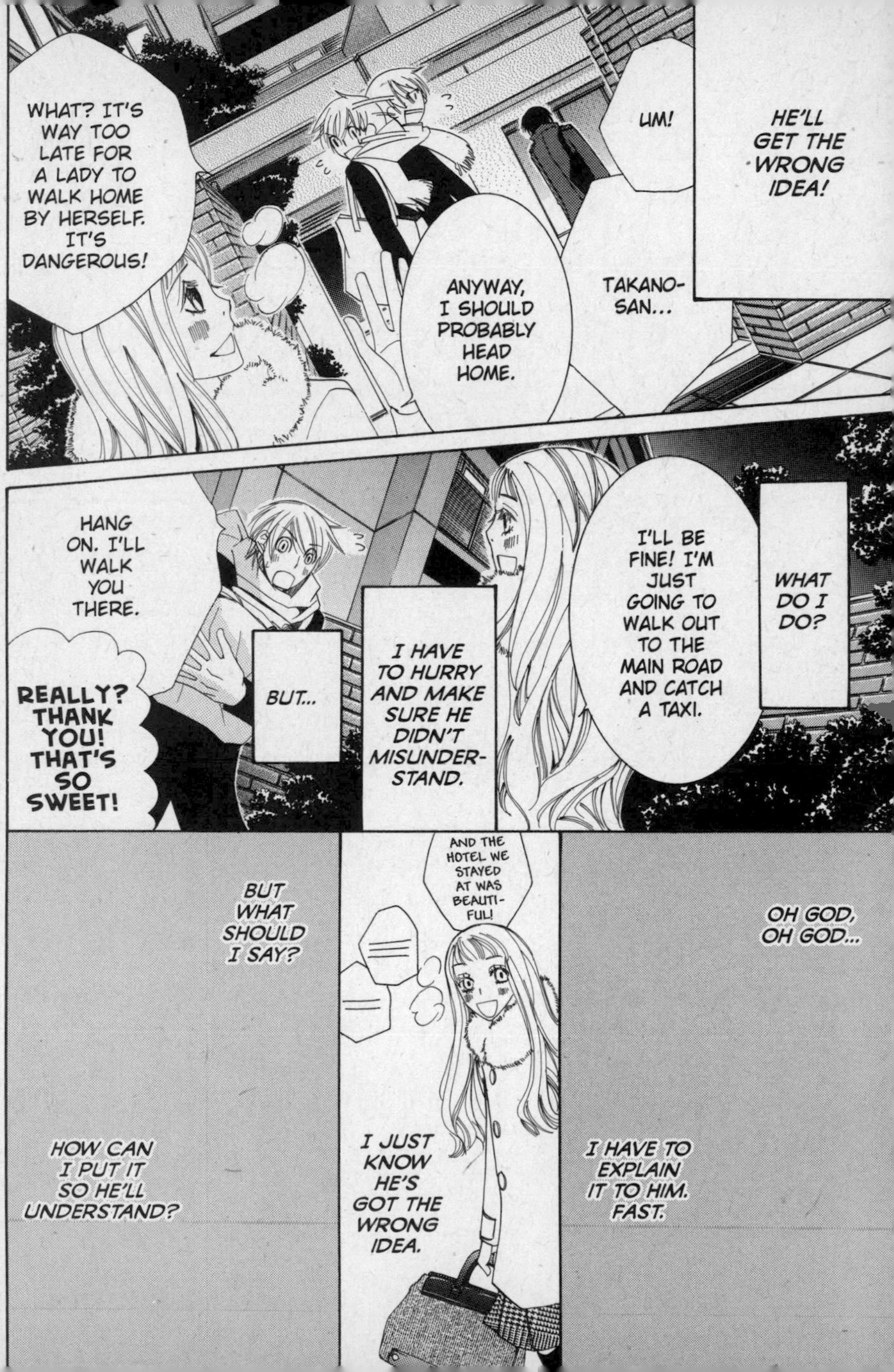
HE'LL GET THE WRONG IDEA!
UM!
TAKANO-SAN...
ANYWAY, I SHOULD PROBABLY HEAD HOME.
WHAT? IT'S WAY TOO LATE FOR A LADY TO WALK HOME BY HERSELF. IT'S DANGEROUS!
WHAT DO I DO?
I'LL BE FINE! I'M JUST GOING TO WALK OUT TO THE MAIN ROAD AND CATCH A TAXI.
I HAVE TO HURRY AND MAKE SURE HE DIDN'T MISUNDERSTAND.
BUT...
HANG ON. I'LL WALK YOU THERE.
REALLY? THANK YOU! THAT'S SO SWEET!
OH GOD, OH GOD...
I HAVE TO EXPLAIN IT TO HIM. FAST.
AND THE HOTEL WE STAYED AT WAS BEAUTIFUL!
I JUST KNOW HE'S GOT THE WRONG IDEA.
BUT WHAT SHOULD I SAY?
HOW CAN I PUT IT SO HE'LL UNDERSTAND?

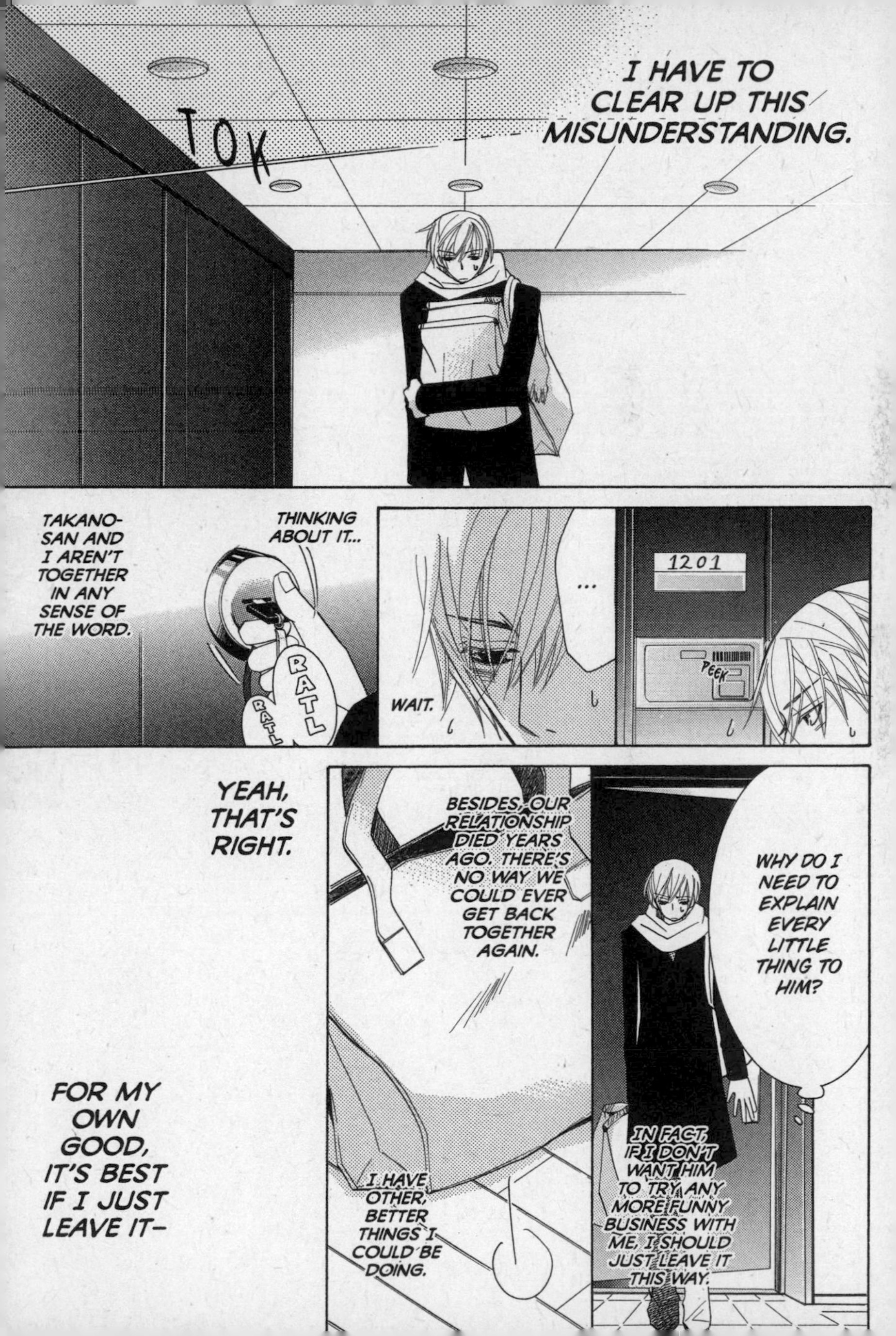
TOK
I HAVE TO CLEAR UP THIS MISUNDERSTANDING.
1201
PEEK
...
WAIT.
THINKING ABOUT IT...
TAKANO-SAN AND I AREN'T TOGETHER IN ANY SENSE OF THE WORD.
RATL
RATL
WHY DO I NEED TO EXPLAIN EVERY LITTLE THING TO HIM?
IN FACT, IF I DON'T WANT HIM TO TRY ANY MORE FUNNY BUSINESS WITH ME, I SHOULD JUST LEAVE IT THIS WAY.
BESIDES, OUR RELATIONSHIP DIED YEARS AGO. THERE'S NO WAY WE COULD EVER GET BACK TOGETHER AGAIN.
I HAVE OTHER, BETTER THINGS I COULD BE DOING.
YEAH, THAT'S RIGHT.
FOR MY OWN GOOD, IT'S BEST IF I JUST LEAVE IT–

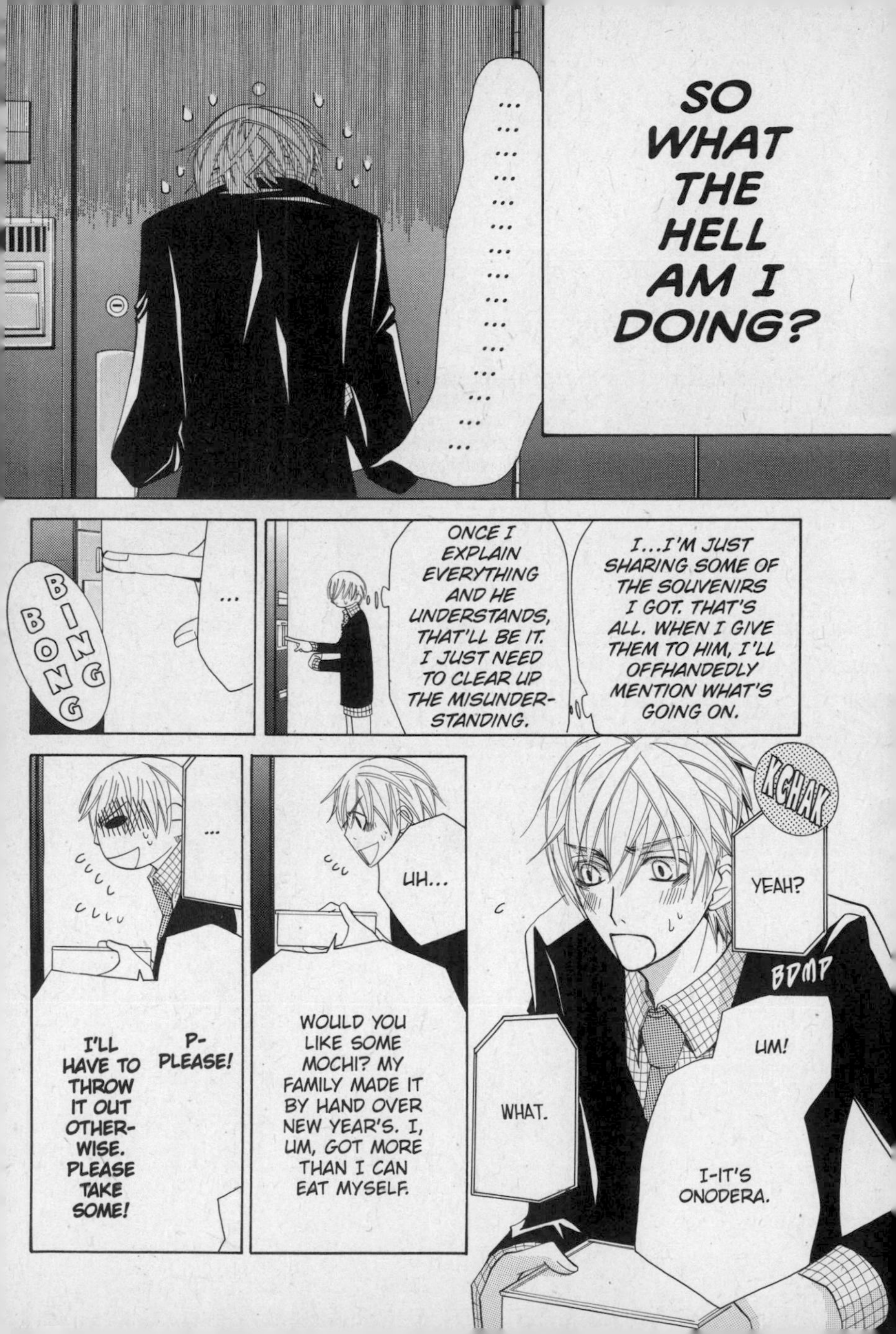

SO WHAT THE HELL AM I DOING?
... ...
I...I'M JUST SHARING SOME OF THE SOUVENIRS I GOT. THAT'S ALL. WHEN I GIVE THEM TO HIM, I'LL OFFHANDEDLY MENTION WHAT'S GOING ON.
ONCE I EXPLAIN EVERYTHING AND HE UNDERSTANDS, THAT'LL BE IT. I JUST NEED TO CLEAR UP THE MISUNDER-STANDING.
...
BING BONG
KCHAK
YEAH?
BDMP
UM!
I-IT'S ONODERA.
WHAT.
UH...
WOULD YOU LIKE SOME MOCHI? MY FAMILY MADE IT BY HAND OVER NEW YEAR'S. I, UM, GOT MORE THAN I CAN EAT MYSELF.
...
P-PLEASE!
I'LL HAVE TO THROW IT OUT OTHER-WISE. PLEASE TAKE SOME!

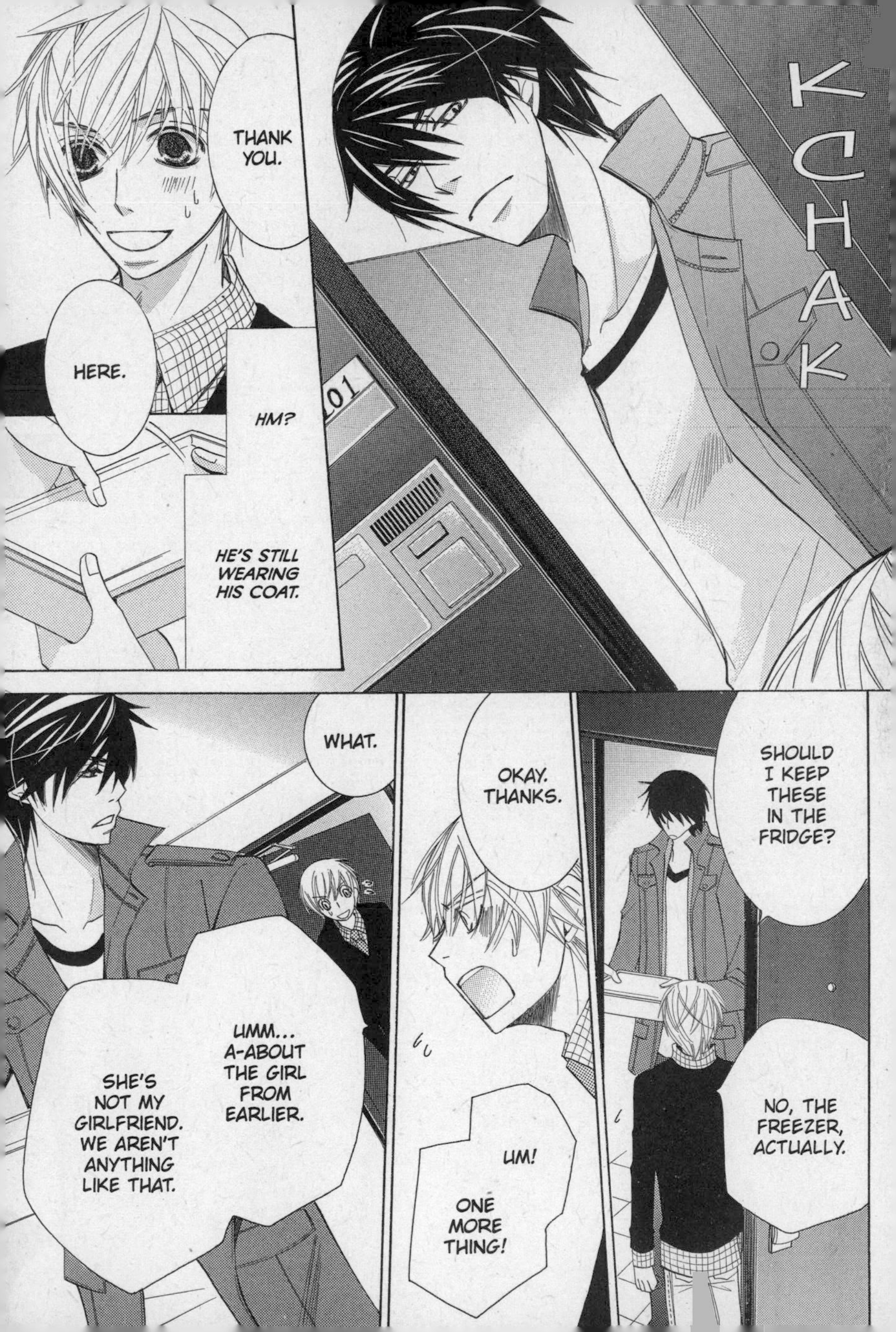
KCHAK
THANK YOU.
HERE.
HM?
HE'S STILL WEARING HIS COAT.
SHOULD I KEEP THESE IN THE FRIDGE?
NO, THE FREEZER, ACTUALLY.
OKAY. THANKS.
UM!
ONE MORE THING!
WHAT.
UMM... A-ABOUT THE GIRL FROM EARLIER.
SHE'S NOT MY GIRLFRIEND. WE AREN'T ANYTHING LIKE THAT.

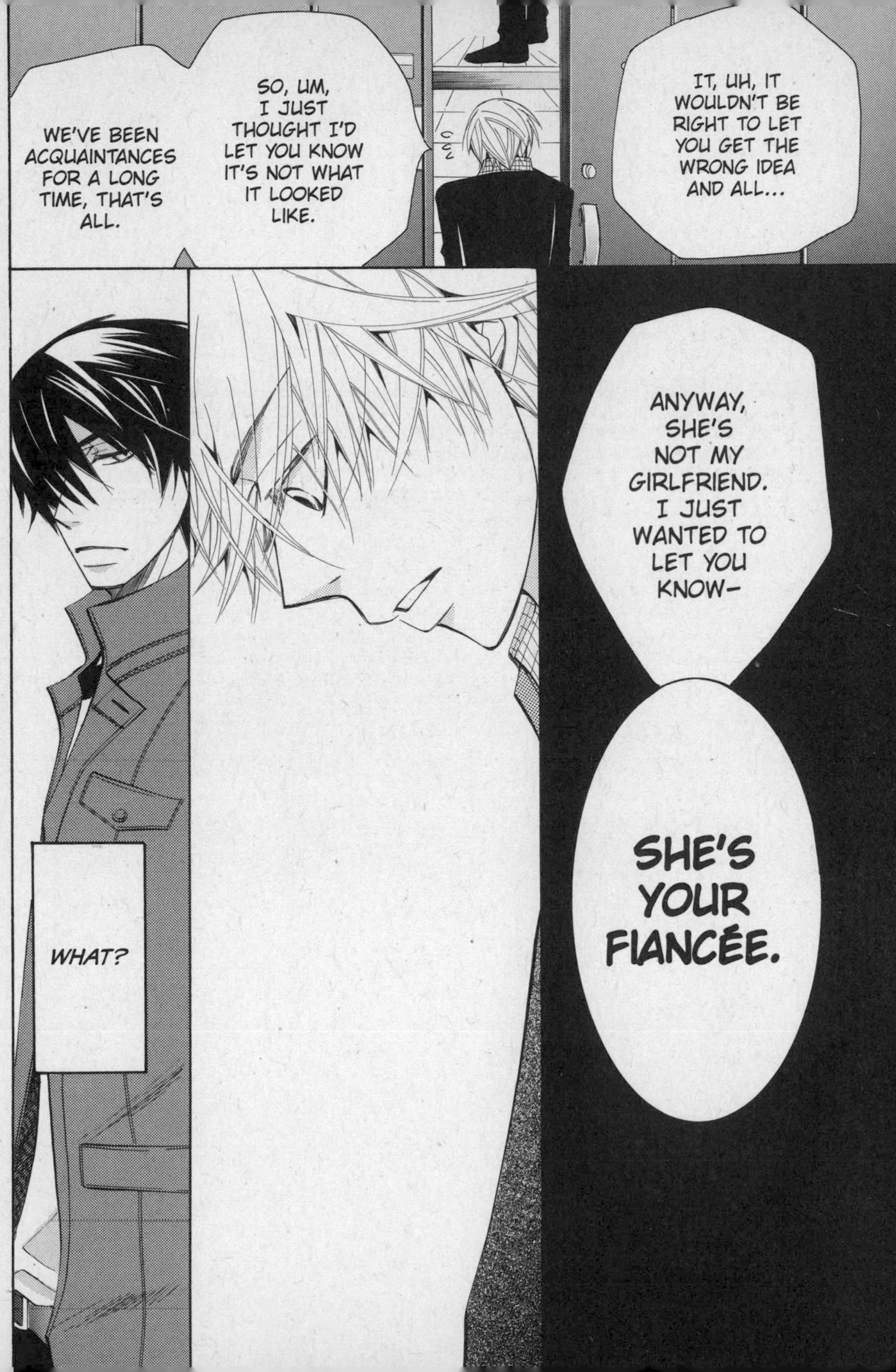
IT, UH, IT WOULDN'T BE RIGHT TO LET YOU GET THE WRONG IDEA AND ALL...
SO, UM, I JUST THOUGHT I'D LET YOU KNOW IT'S NOT WHAT IT LOOKED LIKE.
WE'VE BEEN ACQUAINTANCES FOR A LONG TIME, THAT'S ALL.
ANYWAY, SHE'S NOT MY GIRLFRIEND. I JUST WANTED TO LET YOU KNOW–
SHE'S YOUR FIANCÉE.
WHAT?

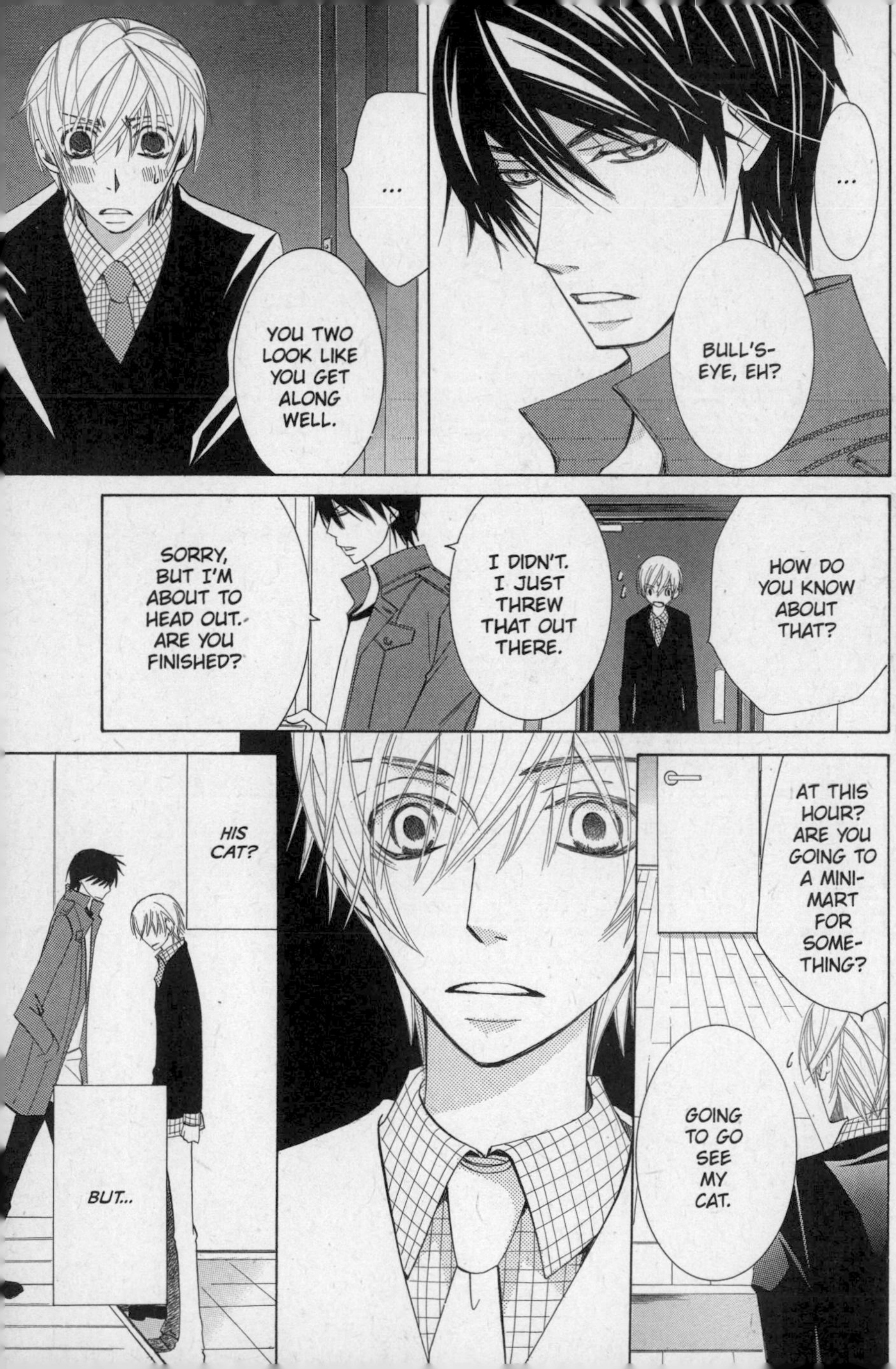
...
BULL'S-EYE, EH?
...
YOU TWO LOOK LIKE YOU GET ALONG WELL.
HOW DO YOU KNOW ABOUT THAT?
I DIDN'T. I JUST THREW THAT OUT THERE.
SORRY, BUT I'M ABOUT TO HEAD OUT. ARE YOU FINISHED?
AT THIS HOUR? ARE YOU GOING TO A MINI-MART FOR SOME-THING?
GOING TO GO SEE MY CAT.
HIS CAT?
BUT...

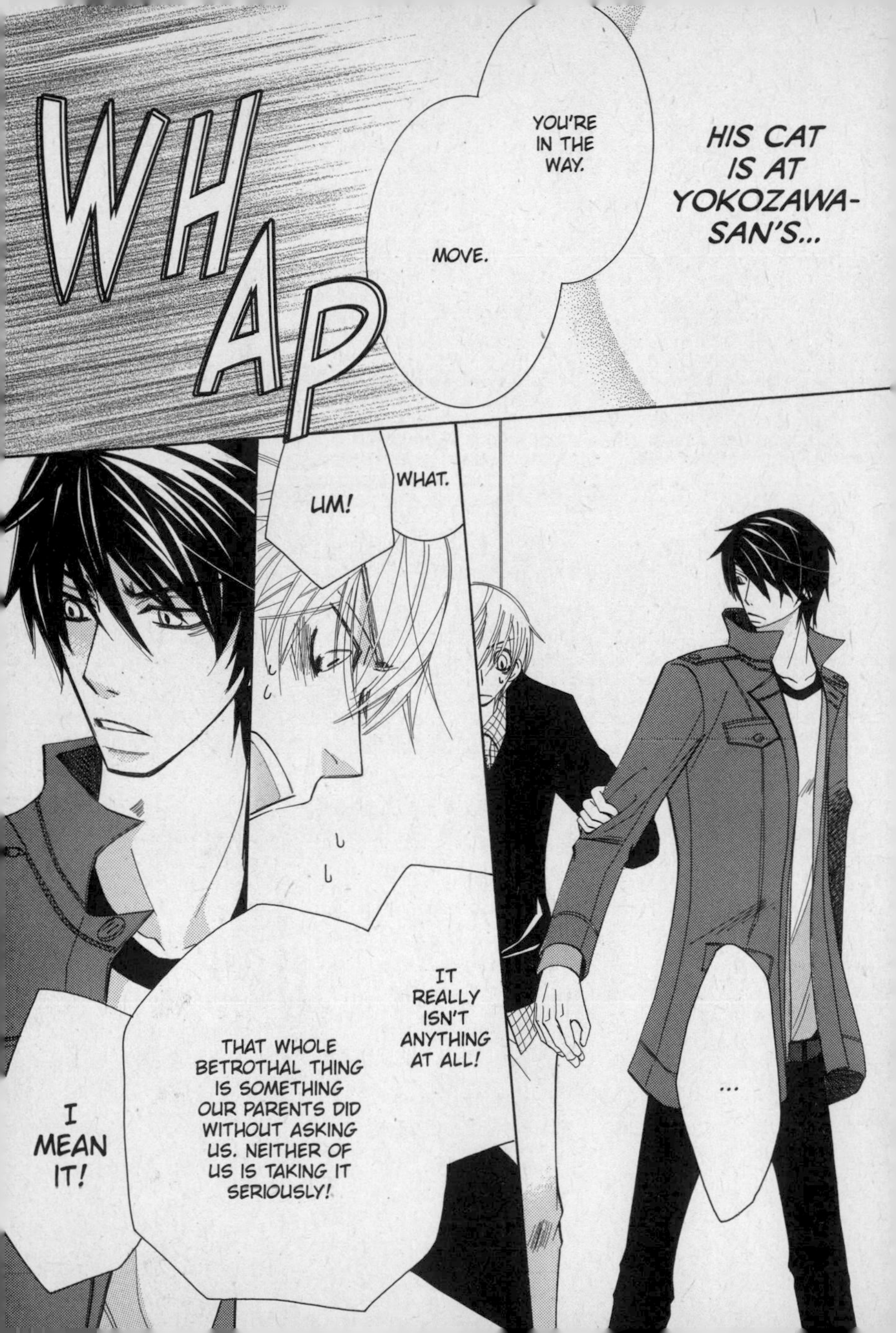
HIS CAT IS AT YOKOZAWA-SAN'S...
YOU'RE IN THE WAY.
MOVE.
WHAP
...
WHAT.
UM!
IT REALLY ISN'T ANYTHING AT ALL!
THAT WHOLE BETROTHAL THING IS SOMETHING OUR PARENTS DID WITHOUT ASKING US. NEITHER OF US IS TAKING IT SERIOUSLY!
I MEAN IT!

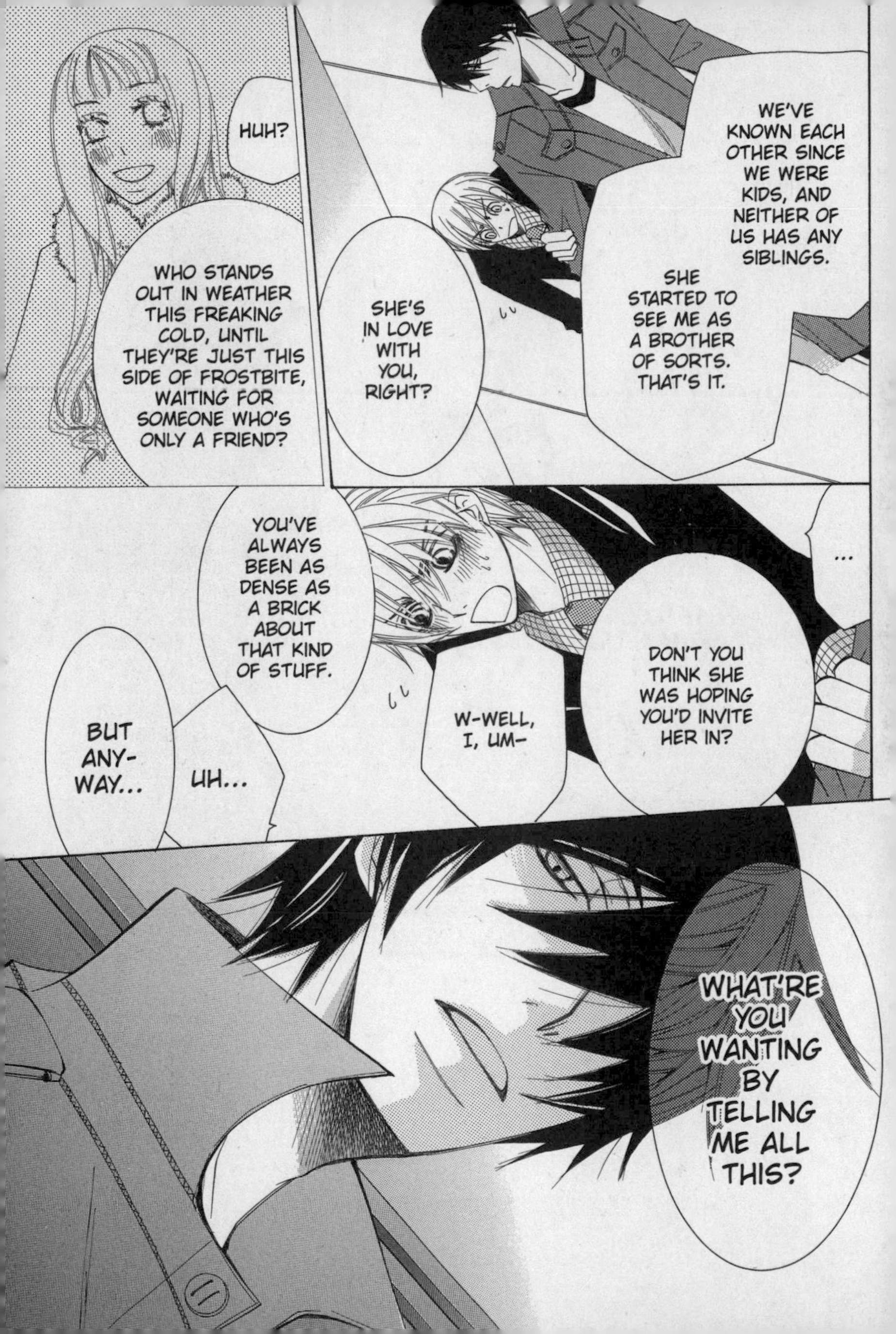
WE'VE KNOWN EACH OTHER SINCE WE WERE KIDS, AND NEITHER OF US HAS ANY SIBLINGS.
SHE STARTED TO SEE ME AS A BROTHER OF SORTS. THAT'S IT.
SHE'S IN LOVE WITH YOU, RIGHT?
HUH?
WHO STANDS OUT IN WEATHER THIS FREAKING COLD, UNTIL THEY'RE JUST THIS SIDE OF FROSTBITE, WAITING FOR SOMEONE WHO'S ONLY A FRIEND?
...
DON'T YOU THINK SHE WAS HOPING YOU'D INVITE HER IN?
W-WELL, I, UM-
YOU'VE ALWAYS BEEN AS DENSE AS A BRICK ABOUT THAT KIND OF STUFF.
UH...
BUT ANY-WAY...
WHAT'RE YOU WANTING BY TELLING ME ALL THIS?

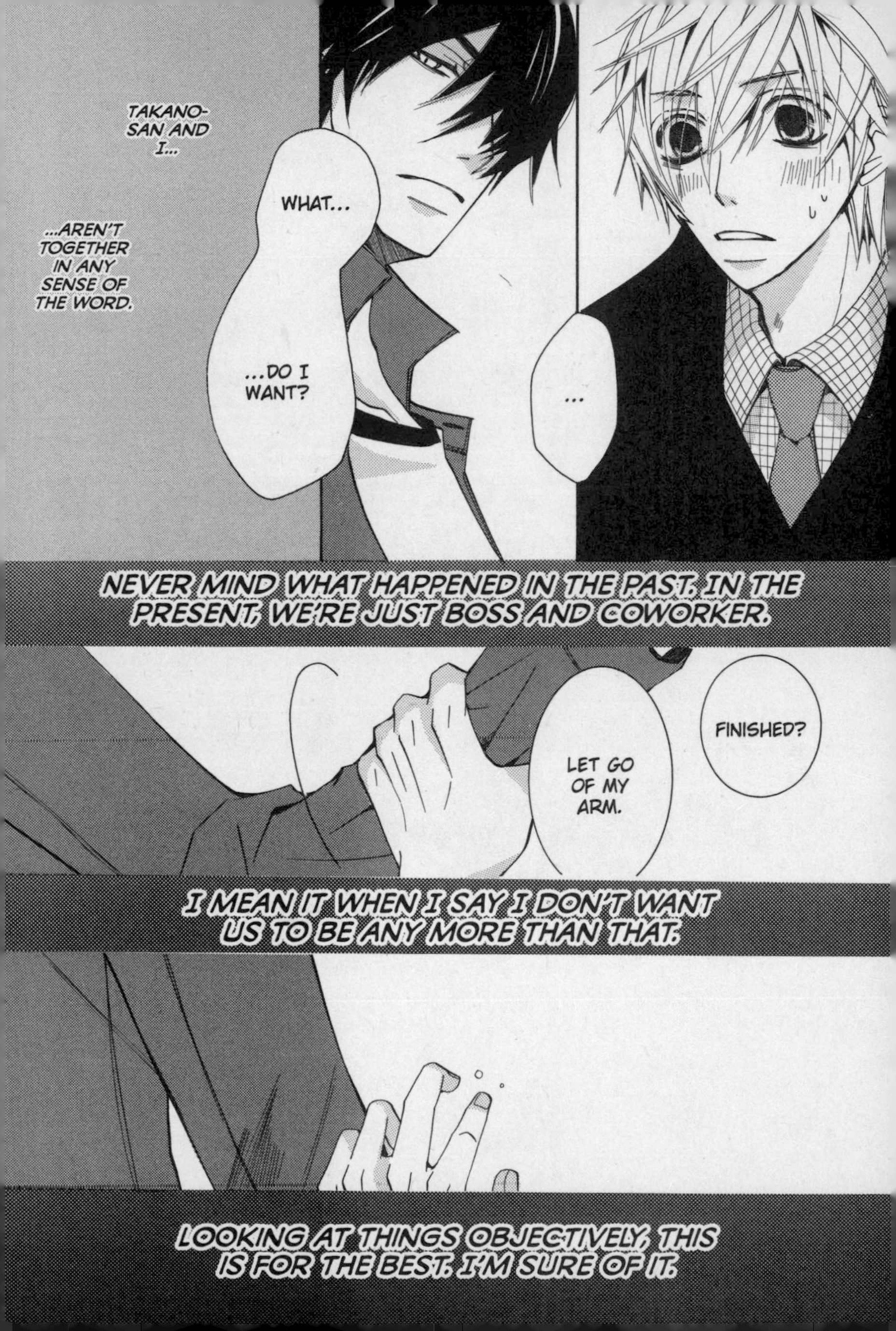
...
WHAT...
...DO I WANT?
TAKANO-SAN AND I...
...AREN'T TOGETHER IN ANY SENSE OF THE WORD.
NEVER MIND WHAT HAPPENED IN THE PAST. IN THE PRESENT, WE'RE JUST BOSS AND COWORKER.
FINISHED?
LET GO OF MY ARM.
I MEAN IT WHEN I SAY I DON'T WANT US TO BE ANY MORE THAN THAT.
LOOKING AT THINGS OBJECTIVELY, THIS IS FOR THE BEST. I'M SURE OF IT.

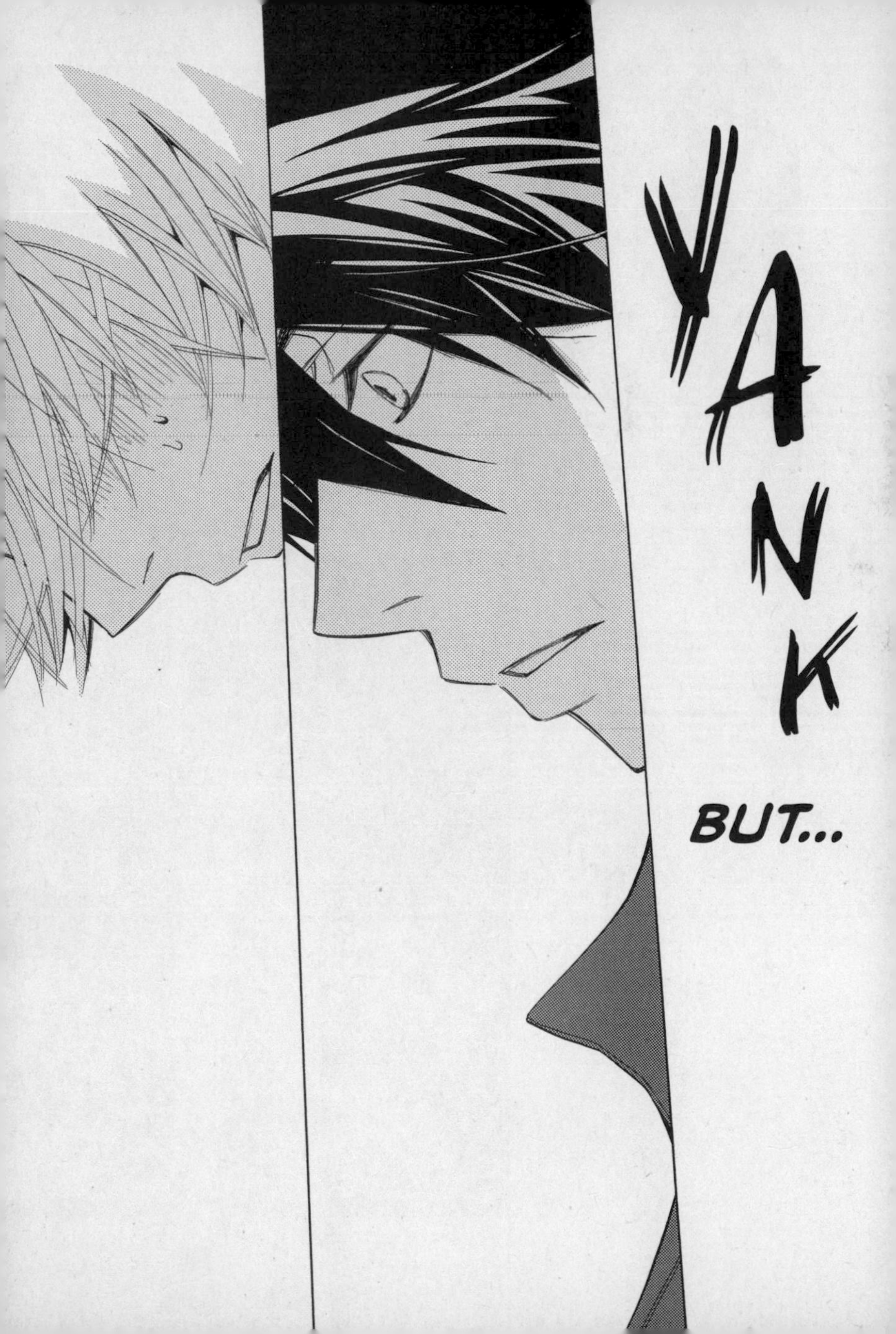
YANK
BUT...

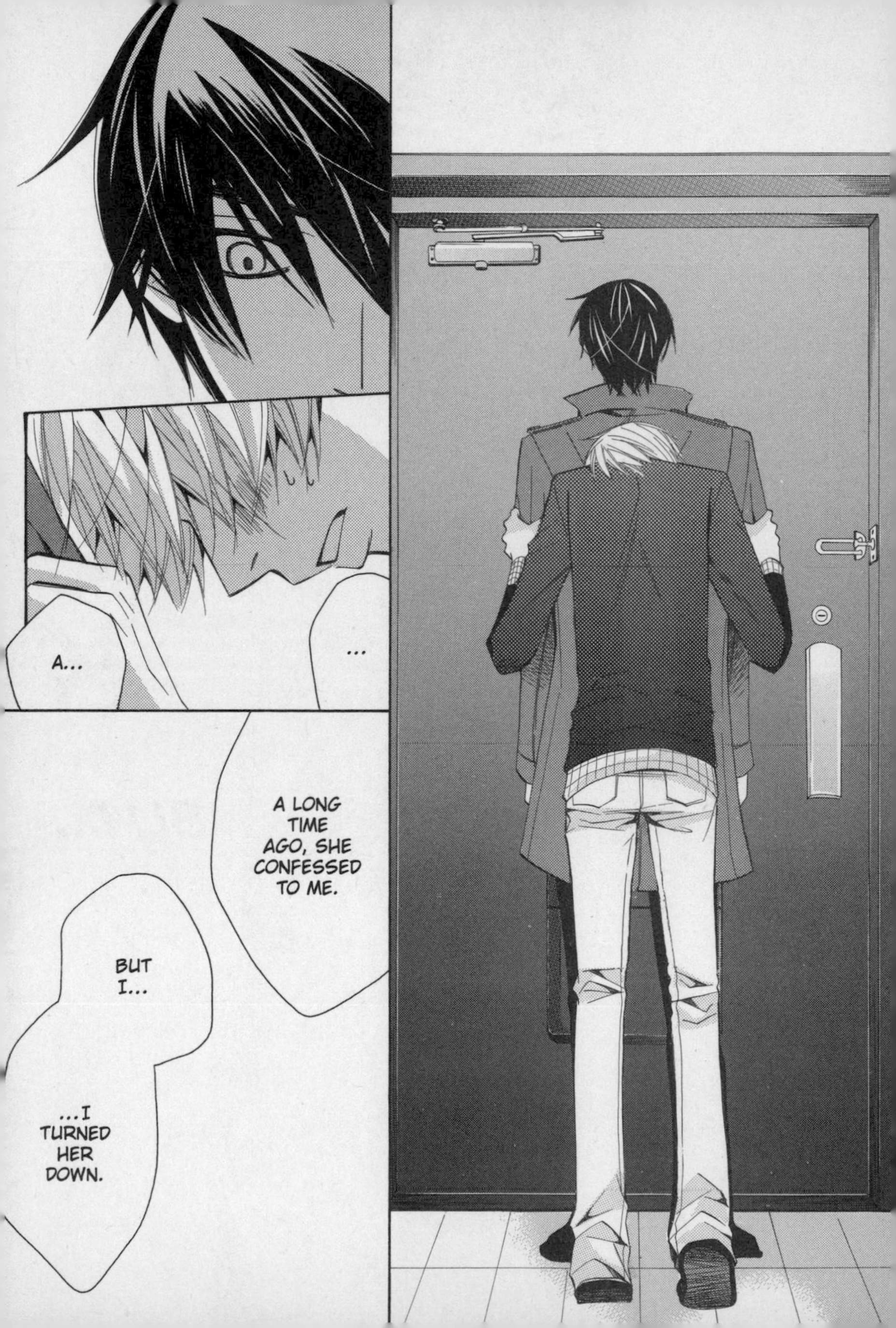
...
A...
A LONG TIME AGO, SHE CONFESSED TO ME.
BUT I...
...I TURNED HER DOWN.

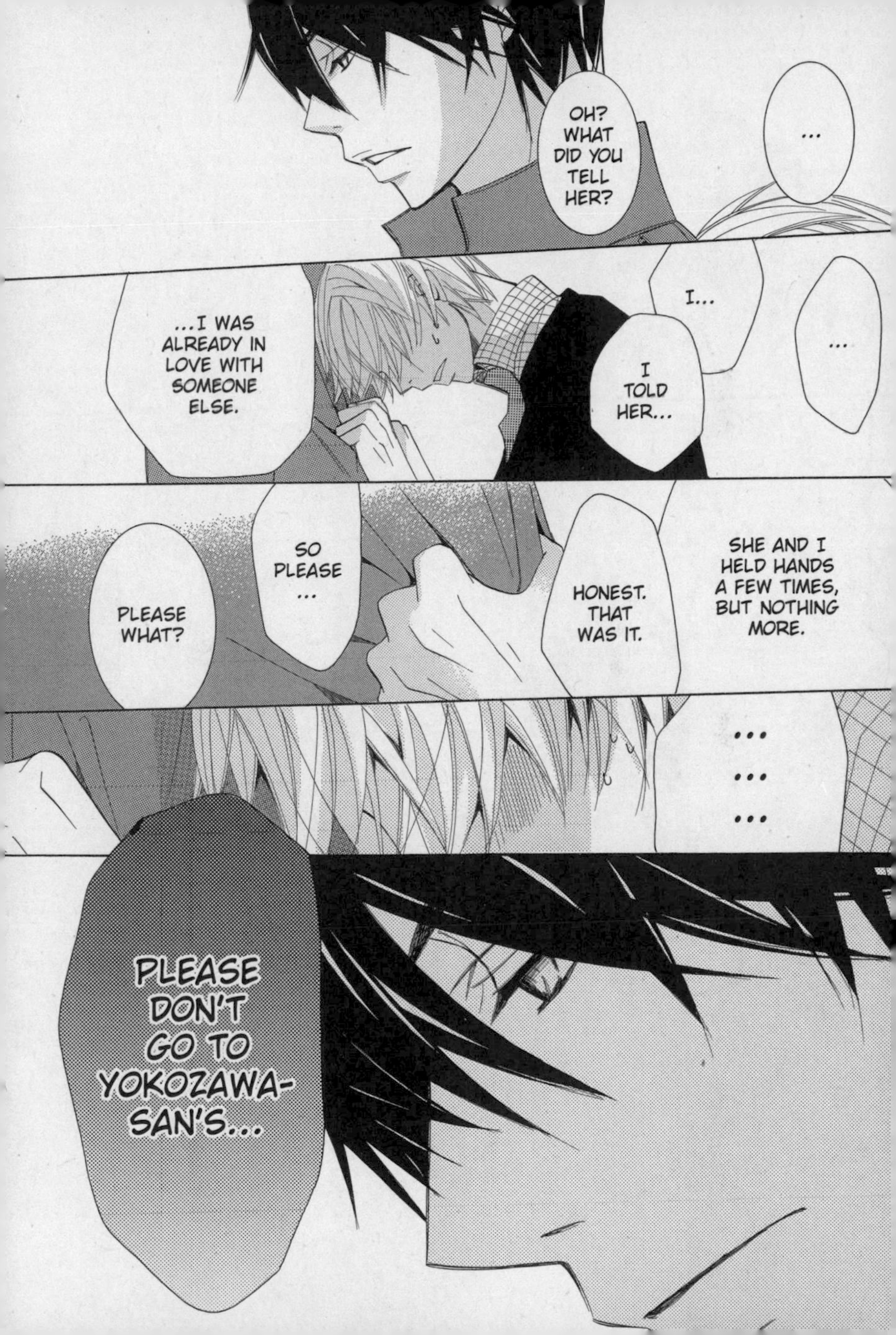
...
OH? WHAT DID YOU TELL HER?
...
I...
I TOLD HER...
...I WAS ALREADY IN LOVE WITH SOMEONE ELSE.
SHE AND I HELD HANDS A FEW TIMES, BUT NOTHING MORE.
HONEST. THAT WAS IT.
SO PLEASE...
PLEASE WHAT?
... ...
PLEASE DON'T GO TO YOKOZAWA-SAN'S...

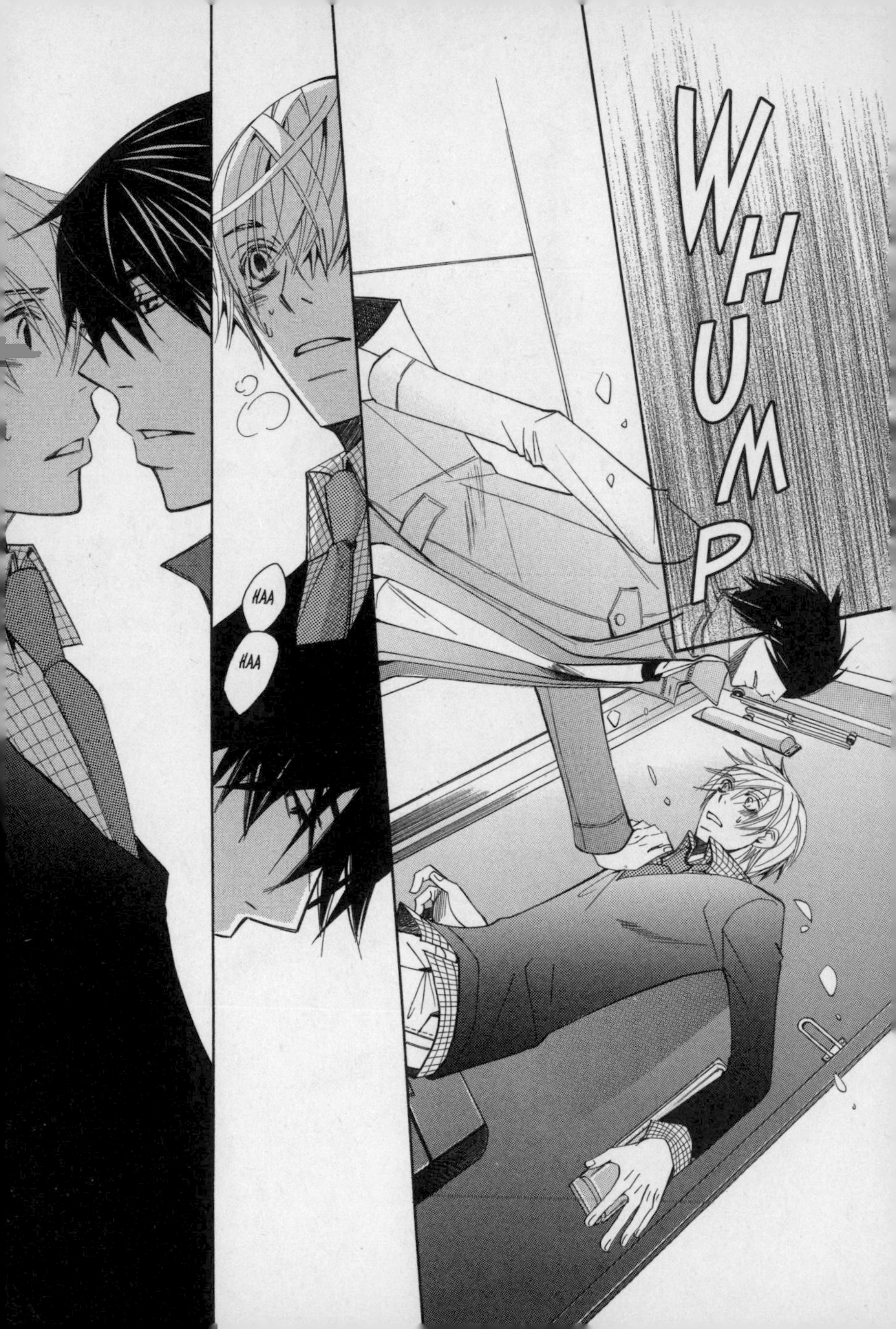
WHUMP
HAA
HAA

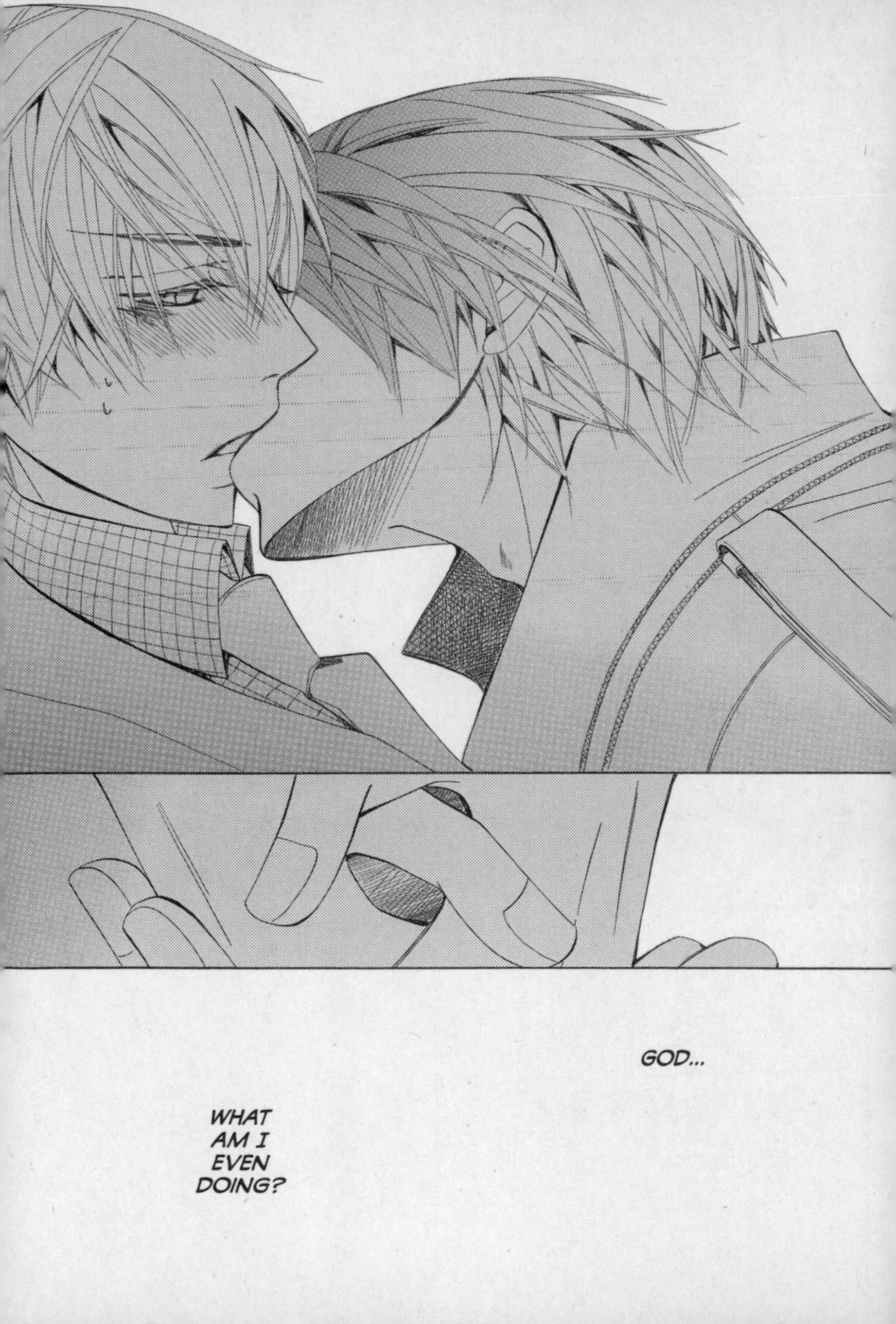
GOD...
WHAT AM I EVEN DOING?

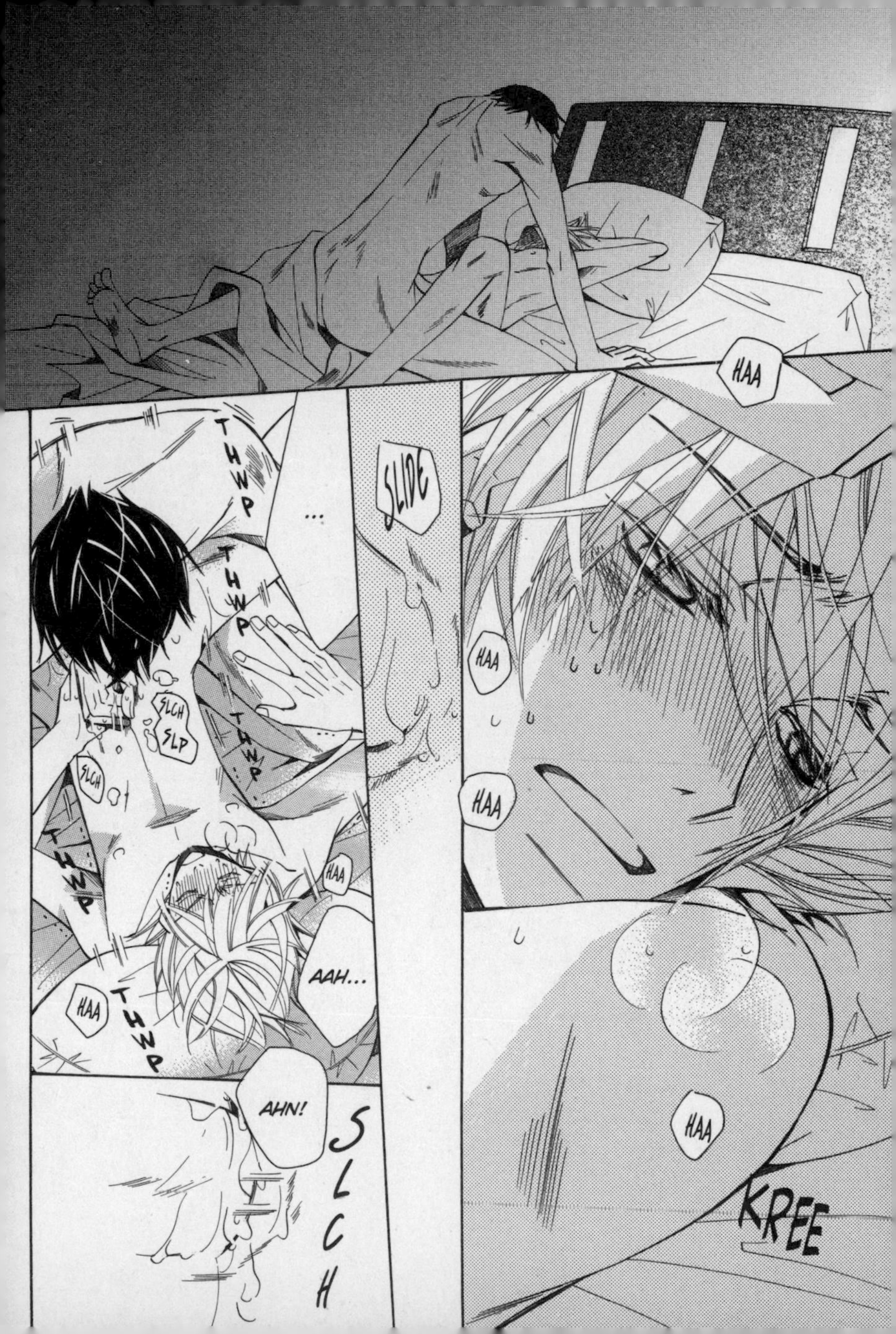
HAA
HAA
HAA
HAA
KREE
SLIDE
THWP
...
THWP
SLCH
SLP
SLCH
THWP
...
HAA
THWP
AAH...
HAA
THWP
AHN!
SLCH

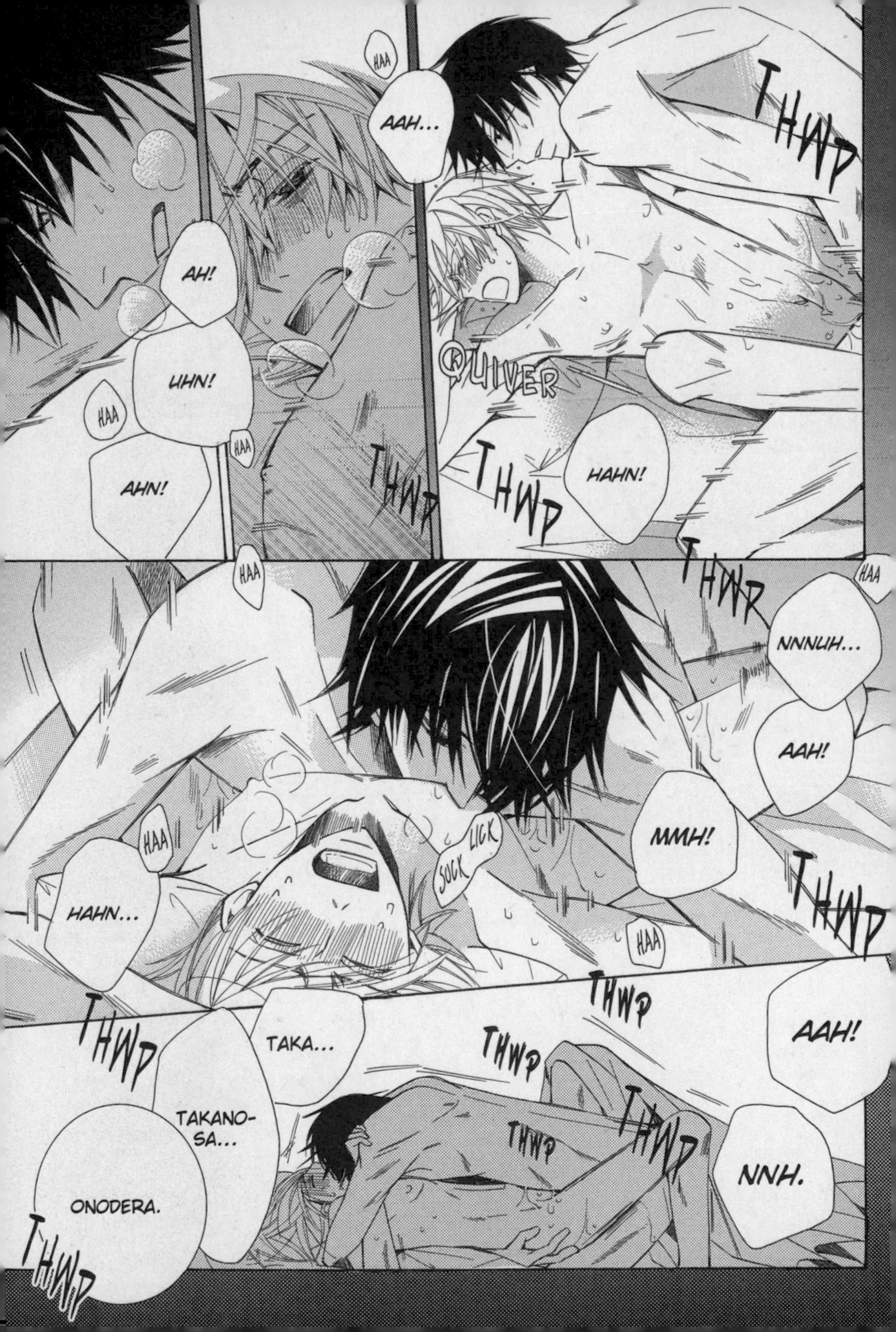
HAA
AAH...
THWP
QUIVER
HAHN!
THWP
AH!
HAA
THWP
UHN!
HAA
AHN!
THWP
HAA
HAA
NNNUH...
AAH!
MMH!
THWP
LICK
SUCK
HAA
HAA
HAHN...
AAH!
THWP
THWP
NNH.
THWP
THWP
TAKA...
TAKANO-SA...
THWP
ONODERA.
THWP

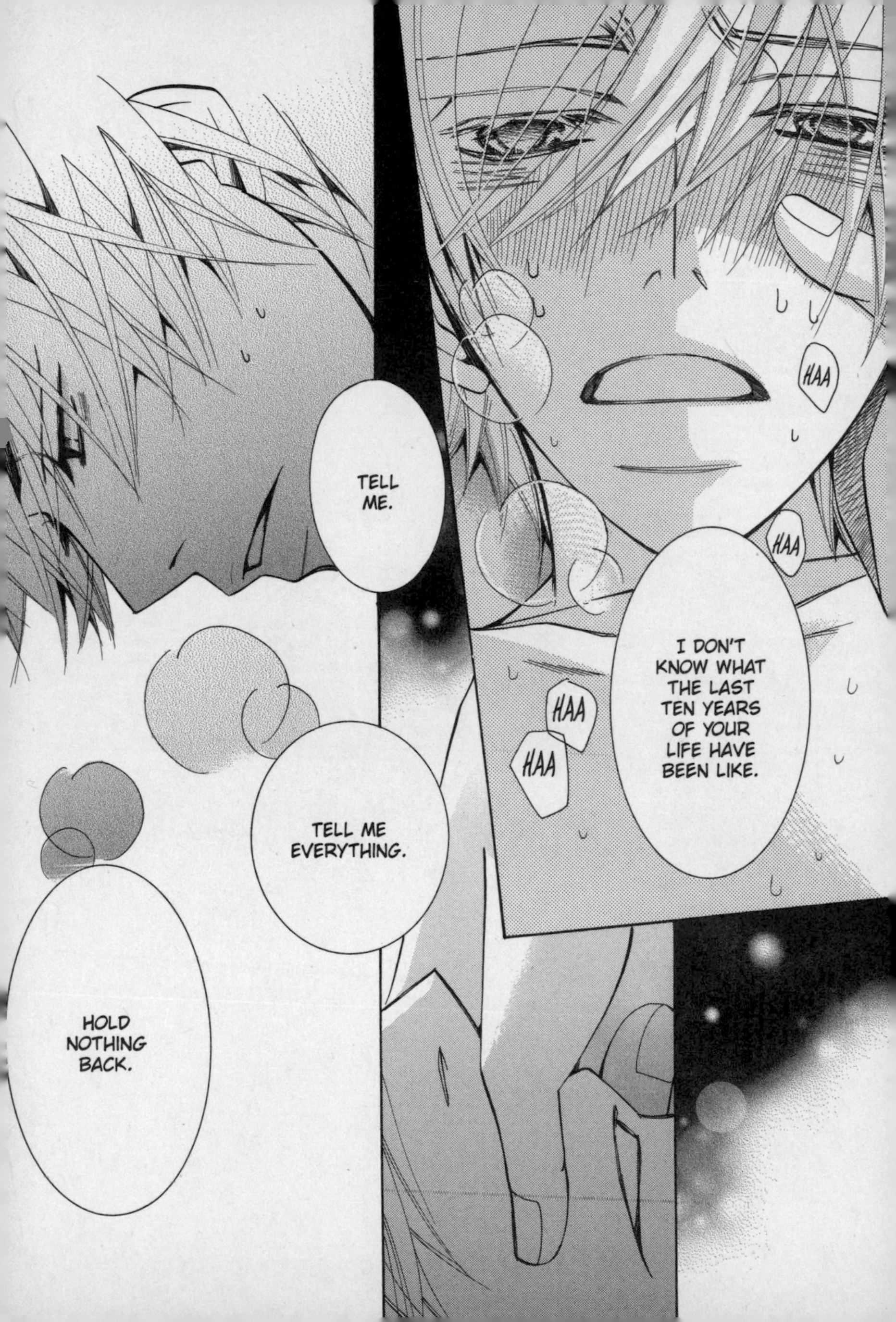
HAA
HAA
I DON'T KNOW WHAT THE LAST TEN YEARS OF YOUR LIFE HAVE BEEN LIKE.
HAA
HAA
TELL ME.
TELL ME EVERYTHING.
HOLD NOTHING BACK.

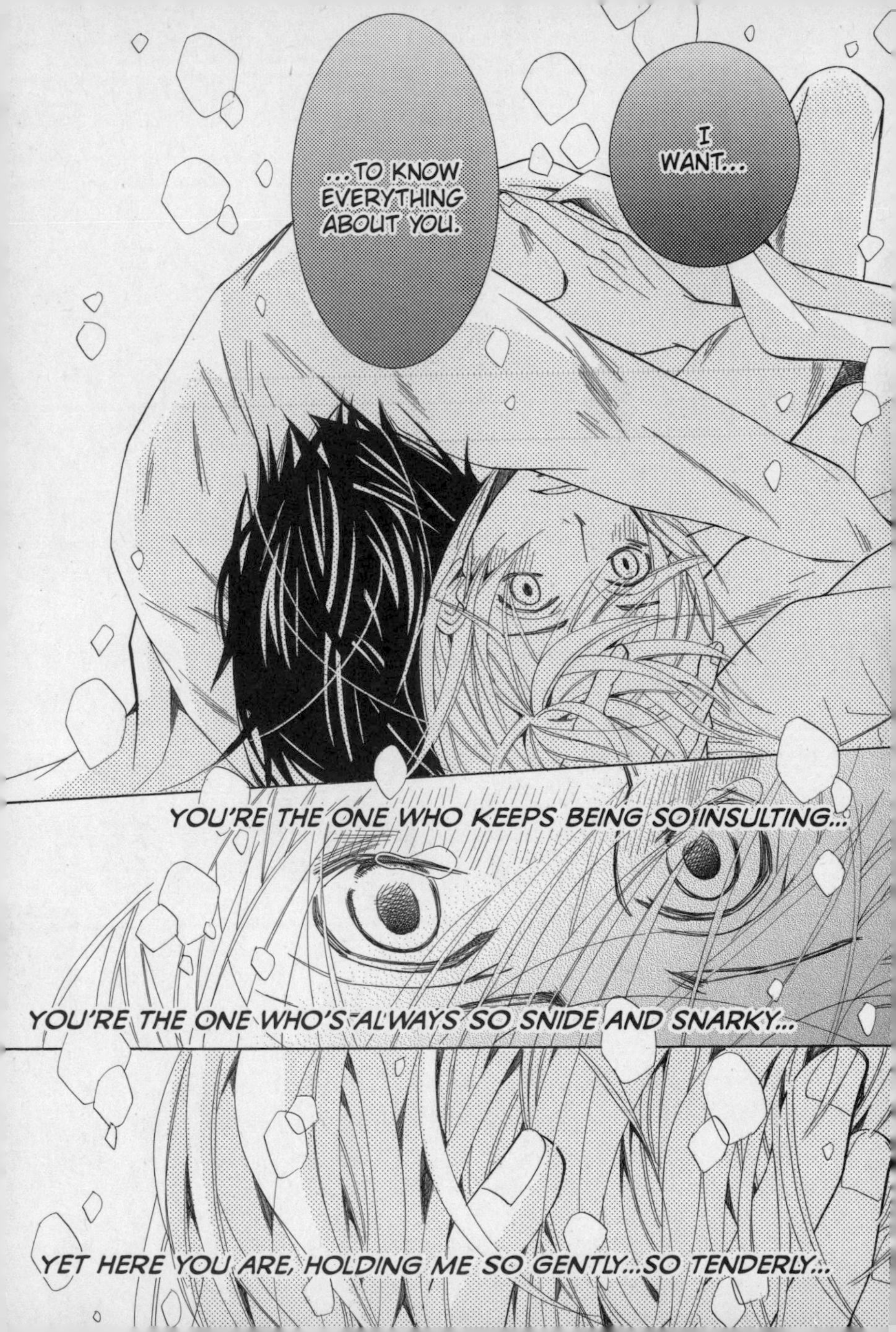
I WANT...
...TO KNOW EVERYTHING ABOUT YOU.
YOU'RE THE ONE WHO KEEPS BEING SO INSULTING...
YOU'RE THE ONE WHO'S ALWAYS SO SNIDE AND SNARKY...
YET HERE YOU ARE, HOLDING ME SO GENTLY...SO TENDERLY...

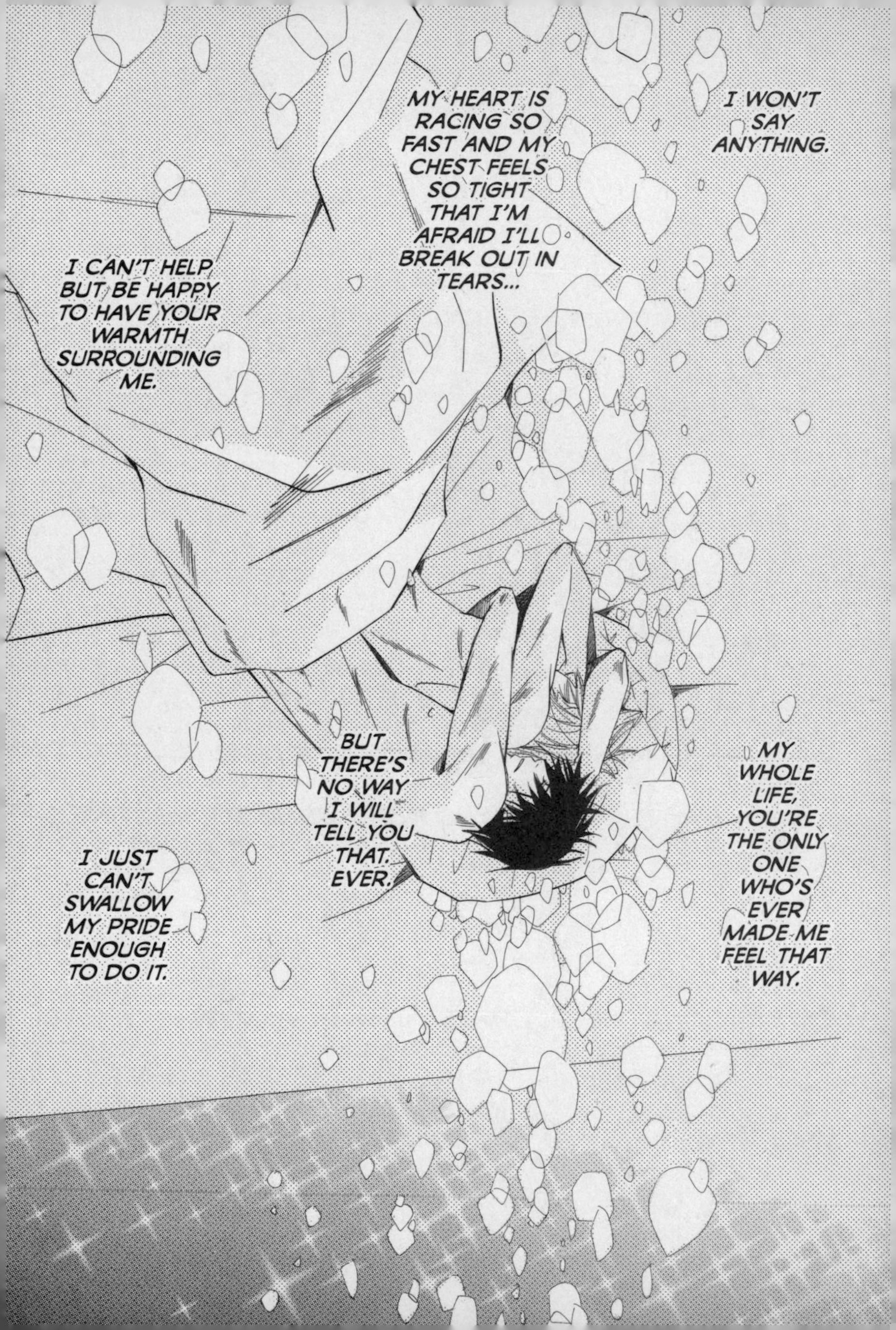
I WON'T SAY ANYTHING.
MY HEART IS RACING SO FAST AND MY CHEST FEELS SO TIGHT THAT I'M AFRAID I'LL BREAK OUT IN TEARS...
I CAN'T HELP BUT BE HAPPY TO HAVE YOUR WARMTH SURROUNDING ME.
MY WHOLE LIFE, YOU'RE THE ONLY ONE WHO'S EVER MADE ME FEEL THAT WAY.
BUT THERE'S NO WAY I WILL TELL YOU THAT. EVER.
I JUST CAN'T SWALLOW MY PRIDE ENOUGH TO DO IT.

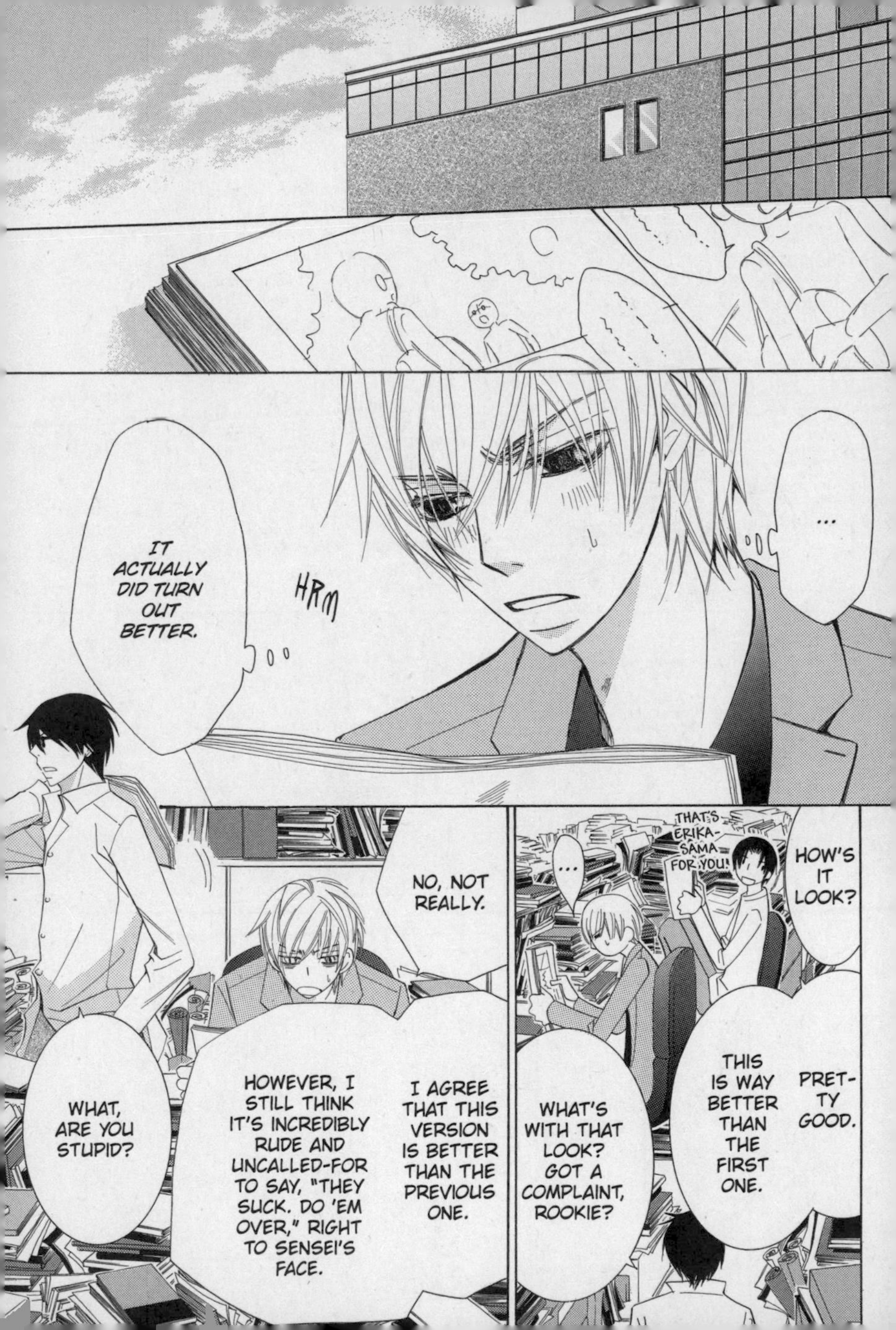
...
HRM
IT ACTUALLY DID TURN OUT BETTER.
HOW'S IT LOOK?
THAT'S ERIKA-SAMA FOR YOU!
...
PRET-TY GOOD.
THIS IS WAY BETTER THAN THE FIRST ONE.
WHAT'S WITH THAT LOOK? GOT A COMPLAINT, ROOKIE?
NO, NOT REALLY.
I AGREE THAT THIS VERSION IS BETTER THAN THE PREVIOUS ONE.
HOWEVER, I STILL THINK IT'S INCREDIBLY RUDE AND UNCALLED-FOR TO SAY, "THEY SUCK. DO 'EM OVER," RIGHT TO SENSEI'S FACE.
WHAT, ARE YOU STUPID?

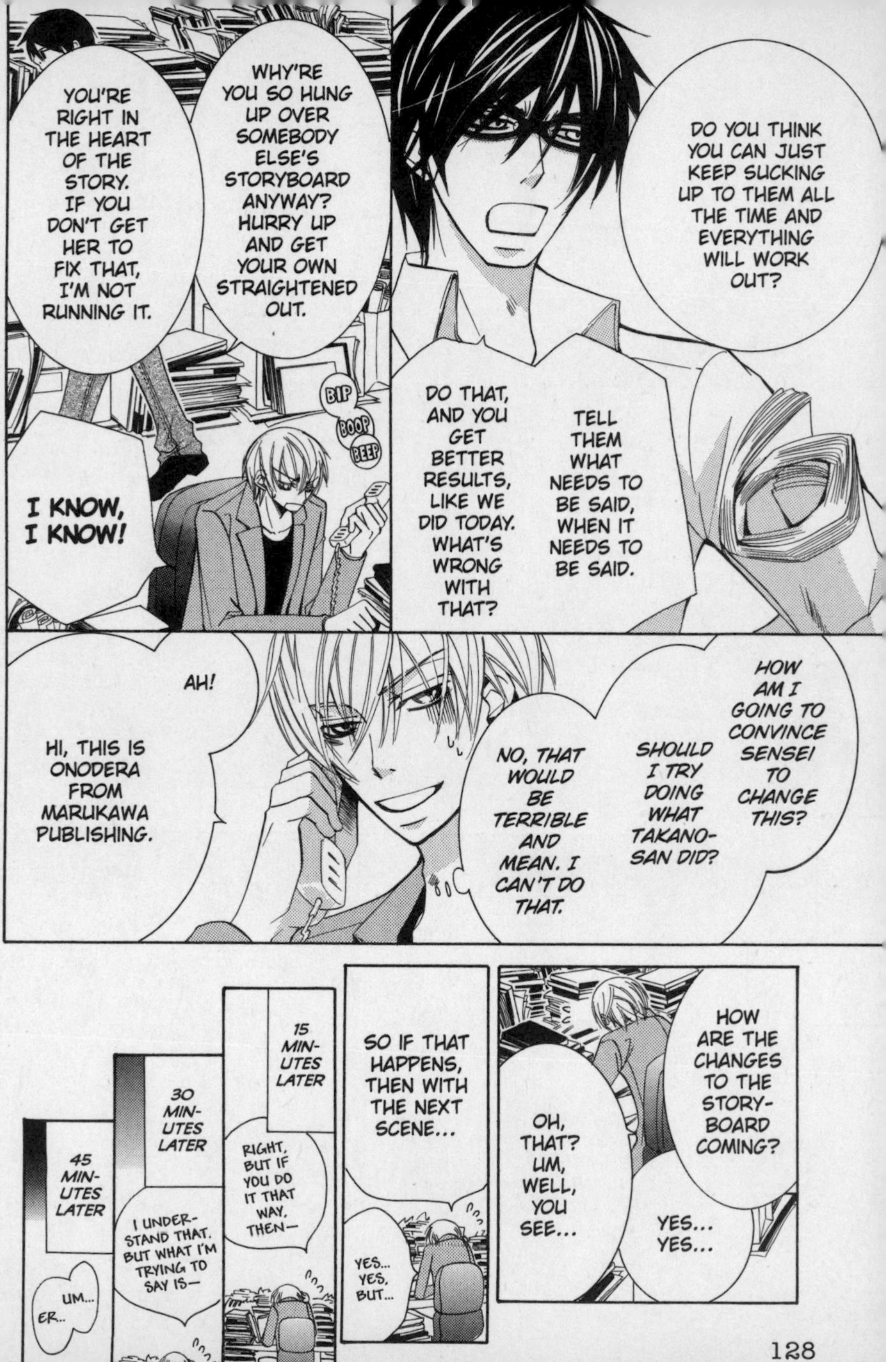
DO YOU THINK YOU CAN JUST KEEP SUCKING UP TO THEM ALL THE TIME AND EVERYTHING WILL WORK OUT?
TELL THEM WHAT NEEDS TO BE SAID, WHEN IT NEEDS TO BE SAID.
DO THAT, AND YOU GET BETTER RESULTS, LIKE WE DID TODAY. WHAT'S WRONG WITH THAT?
WHY'RE YOU SO HUNG UP OVER SOMEBODY ELSE'S STORYBOARD ANYWAY? HURRY UP AND GET YOUR OWN STRAIGHTENED OUT.
YOU'RE RIGHT IN THE HEART OF THE STORY. IF YOU DON'T GET HER TO FIX THAT, I'M NOT RUNNING IT.
BIP
BOOP
BEEP
I KNOW, I KNOW!
HOW AM I GOING TO CONVINCE SENSEI TO CHANGE THIS?
SHOULD I TRY DOING WHAT TAKANO-SAN DID?
NO, THAT WOULD BE TERRIBLE AND MEAN. I CAN'T DO THAT.
AH!
HI, THIS IS ONODERA FROM MARUKAWA PUBLISHING.
HOW ARE THE CHANGES TO THE STORY-BOARD COMING?
YES... YES...
OH, THAT? UM, WELL, YOU SEE...
SO IF THAT HAPPENS, THEN WITH THE NEXT SCENE...
YES... YES, BUT...
15 MIN-UTES LATER
RIGHT, BUT IF YOU DO IT THAT WAY, THEN—
30 MIN-UTES LATER
I UNDER-STAND THAT. BUT WHAT I'M TRYING TO SAY IS—
45 MIN-UTES LATER
UM... ER...

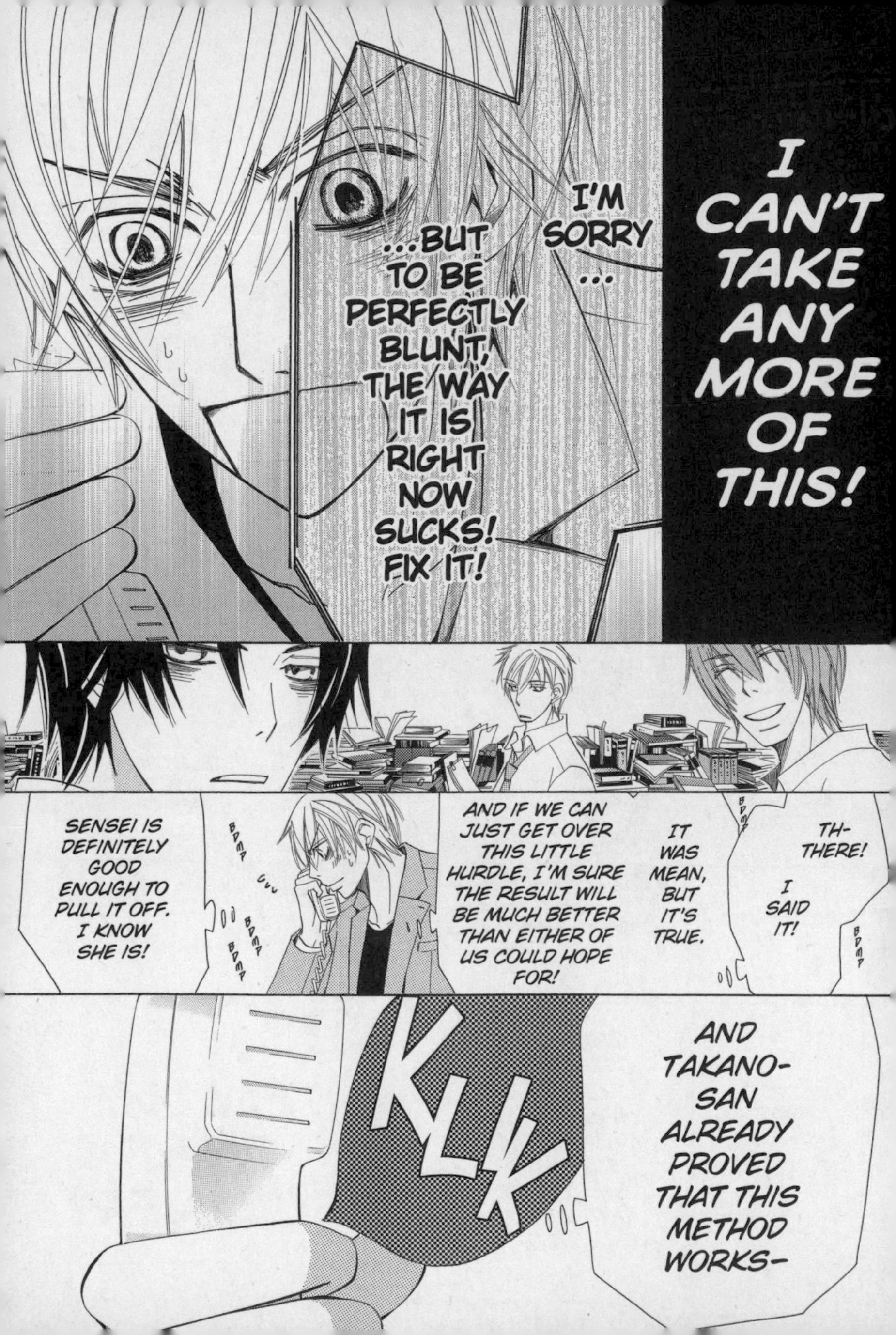
I CAN'T TAKE ANY MORE OF THIS!
I'M SORRY...
...BUT TO BE PERFECTLY BLUNT, THE WAY IT IS RIGHT NOW SUCKS! FIX IT!
TH-THERE!
I SAID IT!
BDMP
BDMP
IT WAS MEAN, BUT IT'S TRUE.
AND IF WE CAN JUST GET OVER THIS LITTLE HURDLE, I'M SURE THE RESULT WILL BE MUCH BETTER THAN EITHER OF US COULD HOPE FOR!
BDMP
BDMP
BDMP
SENSEI IS DEFINITELY GOOD ENOUGH TO PULL IT OFF. I KNOW SHE IS!
AND TAKANO-SAN ALREADY PROVED THAT THIS METHOD WORKS-
KLIK

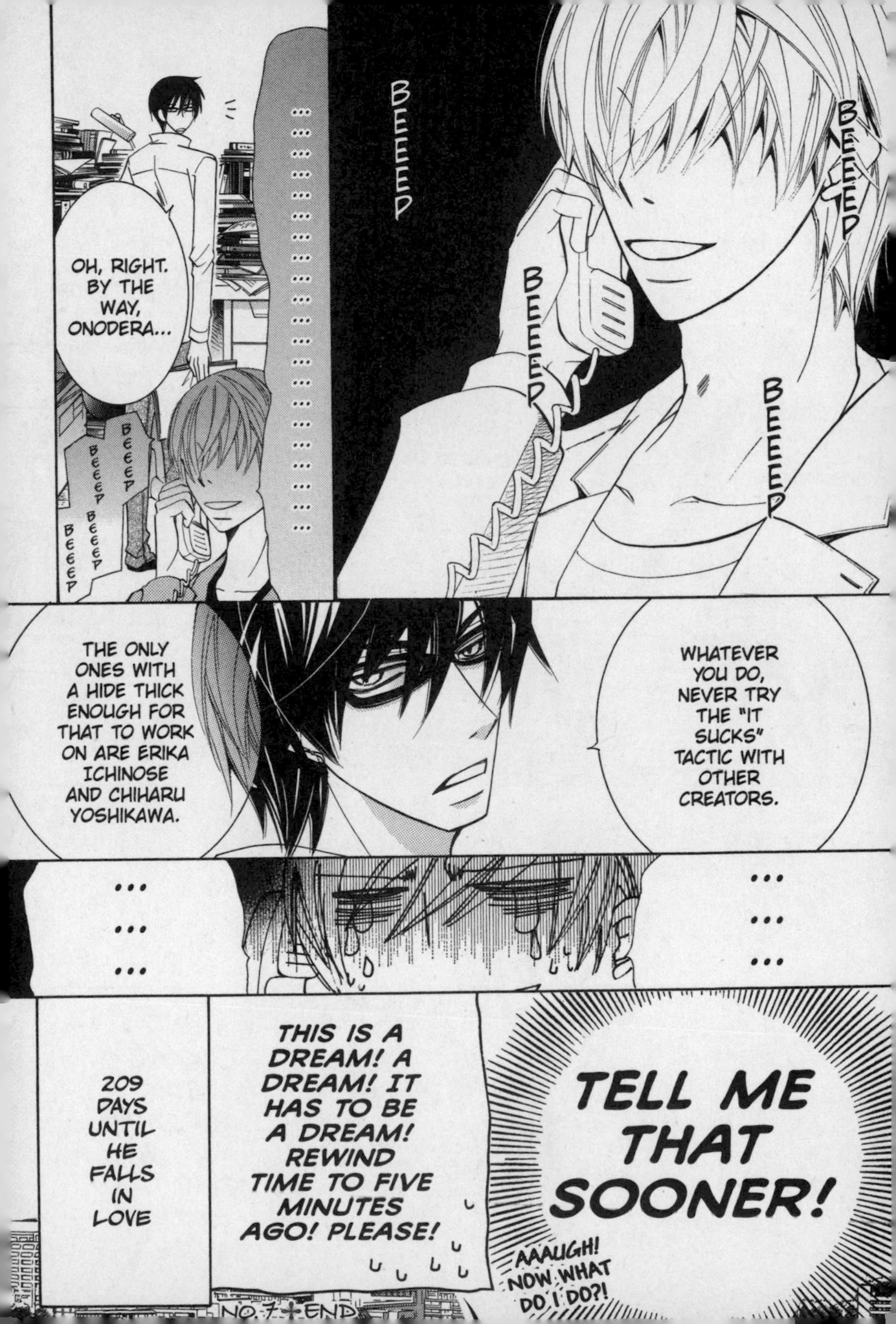

BEEEP
BEEEP
BEEEP
BEEEP
...
OH, RIGHT. BY THE WAY, ONODERA...
BEEEP
BEEEP
BEEEP
BEEEP
WHATEVER YOU DO, NEVER TRY THE "IT SUCKS" TACTIC WITH OTHER CREATORS.
THE ONLY ONES WITH A HIDE THICK ENOUGH FOR THAT TO WORK ON ARE ERIKA ICHINOSE AND CHIHARU YOSHIKAWA.
... ...
... ...
TELL ME THAT SOONER!
AAAUGH! NOW WHAT DO I DO?!
THIS IS A DREAM! A DREAM! IT HAS TO BE A DREAM! REWIND TIME TO FIVE MINUTES AGO! PLEASE!
209 DAYS UNTIL HE FALLS IN LOVE
NO. 7 END

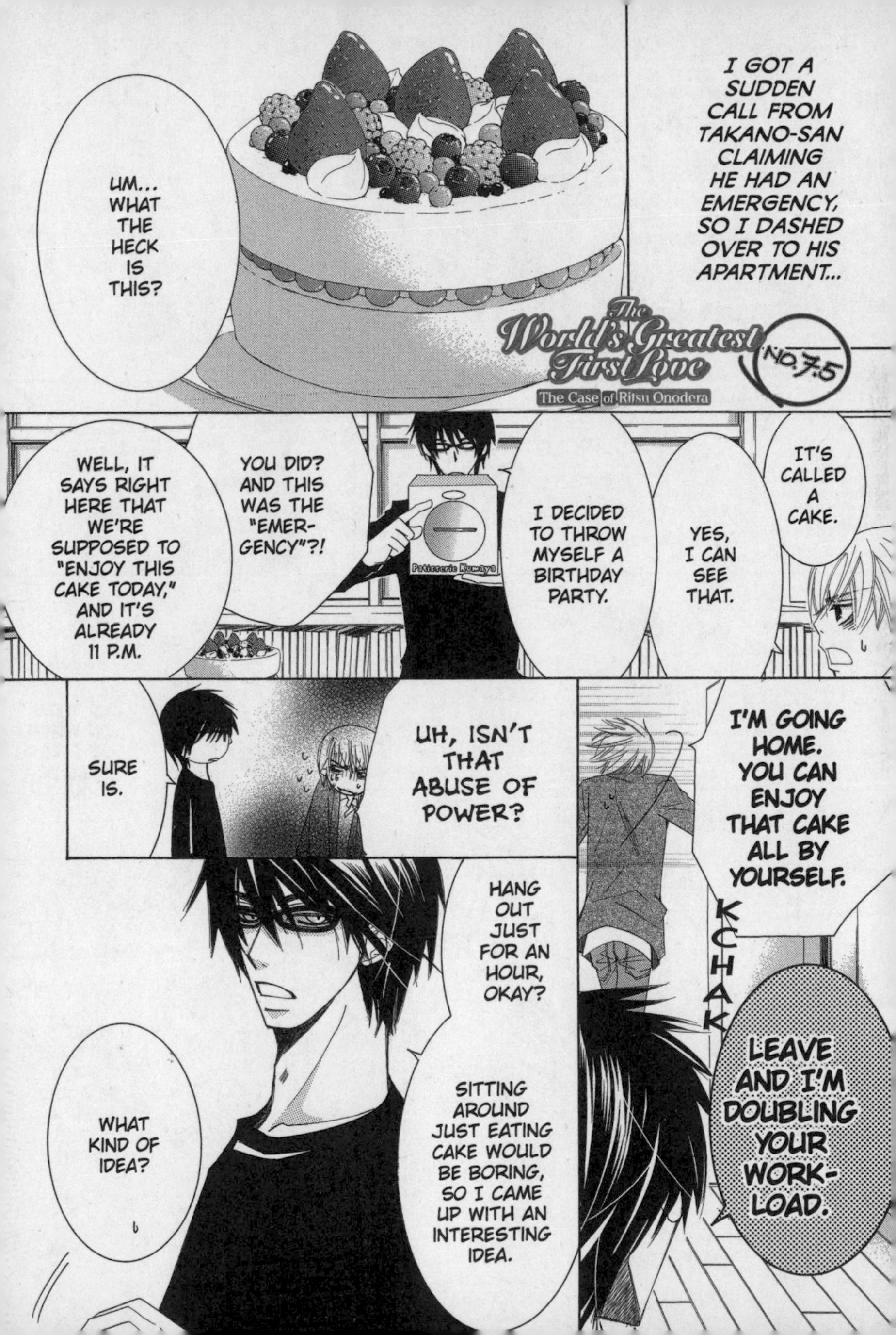
I GOT A SUDDEN CALL FROM TAKANO-SAN CLAIMING HE HAD AN EMERGENCY, SO I DASHED OVER TO HIS APARTMENT...
The World's Greatest First Love
NO.7.5
The Case of Ritsu Onodera
UM... WHAT THE HECK IS THIS?
IT'S CALLED A CAKE.
YES, I CAN SEE THAT.
I DECIDED TO THROW MYSELF A BIRTHDAY PARTY.
YOU DID? AND THIS WAS THE "EMERGENCY"?!
Patisserie Kumaya
WELL, IT SAYS RIGHT HERE THAT WE'RE SUPPOSED TO "ENJOY THIS CAKE TODAY," AND IT'S ALREADY 11 P.M.
I'M GOING HOME. YOU CAN ENJOY THAT CAKE ALL BY YOURSELF.
KCHAK
LEAVE AND I'M DOUBLING YOUR WORKLOAD.
UH, ISN'T THAT ABUSE OF POWER?
SURE IS.
HANG OUT JUST FOR AN HOUR, OKAY?
SITTING AROUND JUST EATING CAKE WOULD BE BORING, SO I CAME UP WITH AN INTERESTING IDEA.
WHAT KIND OF IDEA?

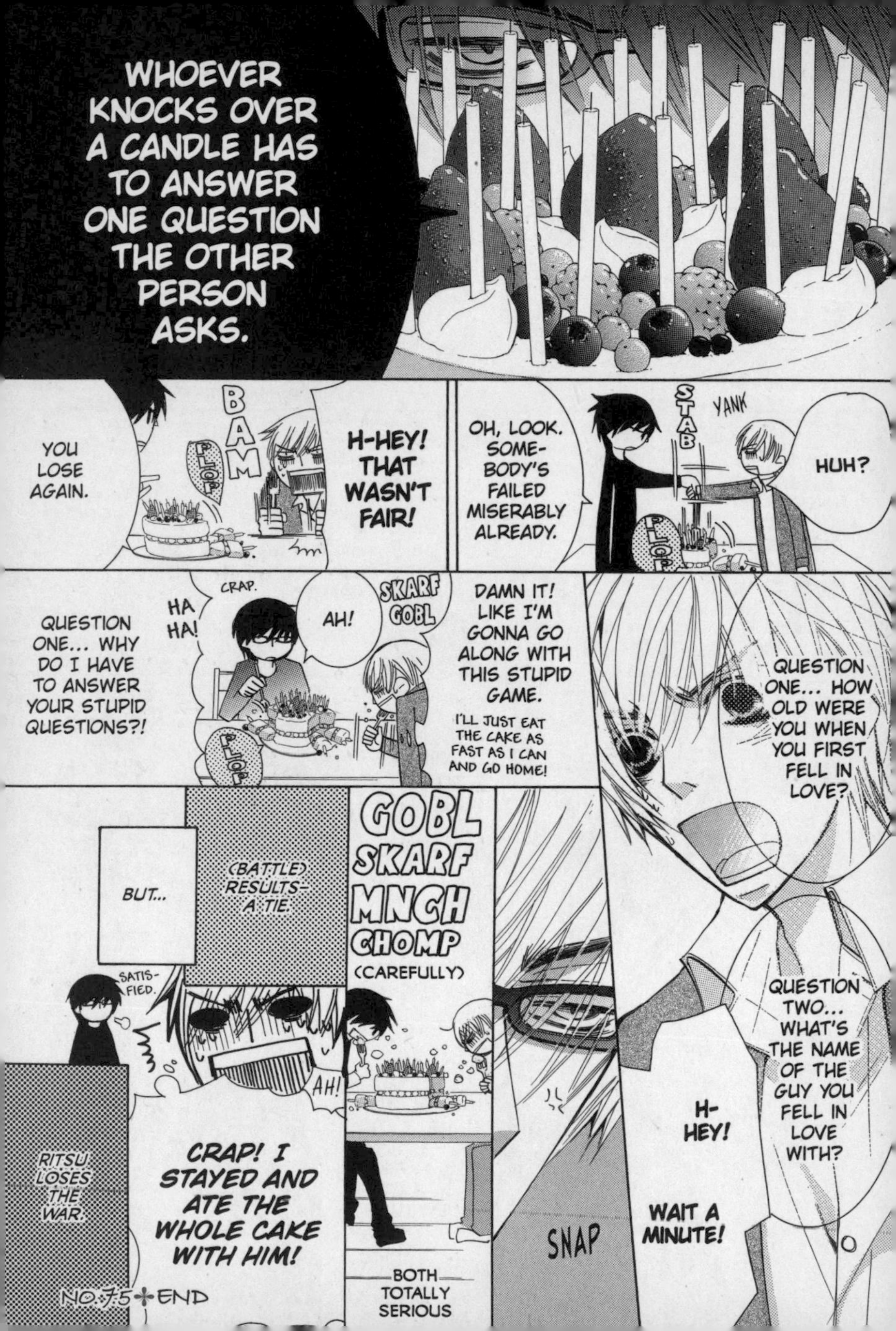
WHOEVER KNOCKS OVER A CANDLE HAS TO ANSWER ONE QUESTION THE OTHER PERSON ASKS.
HUH?
YANK
STAB
OH, LOOK. SOMEBODY'S FAILED MISERABLY ALREADY.
PLOP
H-HEY! THAT WASN'T FAIR!
BAM
PLOP
YOU LOSE AGAIN.
QUESTION ONE... HOW OLD WERE YOU WHEN YOU FIRST FELL IN LOVE?
DAMN IT! LIKE I'M GONNA GO ALONG WITH THIS STUPID GAME.
I'LL JUST EAT THE CAKE AS FAST AS I CAN AND GO HOME!
SKARF GOBL
AH!
CRAP.
HA HA!
QUESTION ONE... WHY DO I HAVE TO ANSWER YOUR STUPID QUESTIONS?!
PLOP
QUESTION TWO... WHAT'S THE NAME OF THE GUY YOU FELL IN LOVE WITH?
H-HEY!
WAIT A MINUTE!
SNAP
GOBL SKARF MNCH CHOMP
(CAREFULLY)
AH!
BOTH TOTALLY SERIOUS
(BATTLE) RESULTS—A TIE.
BUT...
SATIS-FIED.
CRAP! I STAYED AND ATE THE WHOLE CAKE WITH HIM!
RITSU LOSES THE WAR.
NO.7.5 END

MARUKAWA PUBLISHING TERMINOLOGY & JARGON (PART 11)

***NOTE:** ALL OF THE TERMINOLOGY LISTED HEREIN IS SPECIFIC TO MARUKAWA PUBLISHING AND MAY NOT BE APPLICABLE TO THE GENERAL PUBLISHING INDUSTRY.

[YEAR-END]

AT THE END OF THE YEAR, MANY PEOPLE IN THE PUBLISHING BUSINESS, FROM EDITORS TO PRINTERS, WANT TO TAKE TIME OFF. ACCORDINGLY, THE CYCLE SHIFTS FROM THE STANDARD TO A UNIQUE ONE-TIME-ONLY SCHEDULE FOR THE END OF THE YEAR. MOSTLY, THE CHANGE IS FORCED BY RELEASE DATES BEING MOVED AROUND TO ACCOMMODATE THE HOLIDAYS, BUT THERE ARE OCCASIONALLY OTHER REASONS FOR THE SHIFT.

FOR EXAMPLE, MANY COMPANIES ARE CLOSED BETWEEN DECEMBER 25 AND JANUARY 5 FOR THE HOLIDAYS. COPY THAT WOULD NORMALLY BE ON TIME IF SUBMITTED BY THE FIRST OF THE MONTH WOULD IN THIS CASE BE LATE. IN ORDER FOR EVERYTHING TO BE COMPLETE IN TIME FOR PRINTING, THE COPY NEEDS TO BE SUBMITTED A WEEK EARLIER, BY THE 24TH. IN THIS FASHION, THE ENTIRE SCHEDULE IS BUMPED UP, OFTEN SHORTENING DEADLINES ACROSS THE WHOLE CYCLE. IT IS, UNSURPRISINGLY, A SCHEDULE THAT CAN CAUSE A NUMBER OF EDITORS HEARTBURN.

[ANNUAL YEAR-END REPENTANCE MEETING]

AT THE END OF EVERY YEAR, *EMERALD* EDITING DEPARTMENT MANAGING EDITOR YOSHIYUKI HATORI HOLDS A MEETING WITH MEGAHIT SHOJO MANGA CREATOR CHIHARU YOSHIKAWA. TOPICS OF THE MEETING GENERALLY INCLUDE HOW TERRIBLE CHIHARU WAS AT FOLLOWING THE SET SCHEDULE, HOW MANY TIMES HE WAS LATE FOR DEADLINES, POSSIBLE EXCUSES FOR WHY HE CAN'T MANAGE TO BE ON TIME, AND OTHER OBSERVATIONS MADE ABOUT CHIHARU'S ACTIONS ACROSS THE PAST YEAR. ACCORDING TO REPORTS, THIS YEAR'S MOST RECENT MEETING LASTED A FULL FOUR HOURS.

The World's Greatest First Love
The Case of Ritsu Onodera

LOOK! THERE'S A BIG SALE ON DISHWASHERS! I SHOULD PROBABLY GET ONE, DON'T YOU THINK?
WHY NOT SIMPLY HAND WASH THEM DAILY? YOU LIVE ALONE. YOU CAN'T POSSIBLY HAVE THAT MANY TO DO.
THAT'S... TRUE. I GUESS...
Catalogue
YOUR DISHES WILL BE SPARKLING CLEAN!
BIG SALE
DISH-WASHERS

MARUKAWA PUBLISHING TERMINOLOGY & JARGON (PART 12)

***NOTE:** ALL OF THE TERMINOLOGY LISTED HEREIN IS SPECIFIC TO MARUKAWA PUBLISHING AND MAY NOT BE APPLICABLE TO THE GENERAL PUBLISHING INDUSTRY.

[FOUNDRY PROOF]

UNLIKE STANDARD PROOFS FOR FIRST PRINTINGS OR REPRINTINGS, FOUNDRY PROOFS ARE PROOFS THAT ARE PRINTED FOR ONE LAST CHECK OF PAGES THAT UNDERWENT EXTENSIVE REVISION, LAYOUTS THAT REQUIRED SIGNIFICANT CHANGES, OR ANY OTHER COPY THAT HAD TO BE REDONE TO A CONSIDERABLE DEGREE. THIS STEP IS OFTEN SKIPPED DUE TO LACK OF TIME.

[TEST COPY]

AT THE VERY START OF PRINTING, A TEST COPY IS PRINTED AS A SAMPLE. A TEST COPY CAN BE A SINGLE SHEET OR A WHOLE VOLUME OF A BOOK OR MAGAZINE PRINTED AND BOUND TOGETHER SO THAT THE OVERALL BOOK DESIGN CAN BE VIEWED. EDITORS REVIEW THESE COPIES TO BE SURE THERE ARE NO MISTAKES AND ALL LAST-MINUTE CORRECTIONS WERE ACCOUNTED FOR.

[AUTHOR'S PROOF]

WHEN AUTHORS REVISE A GALLEY PROOF, IT'S CALLED AN AUTHOR'S PROOF OR AUTHOR'S REVISION. AUTHORS CAN BE GIVEN GALLEY PROOFS THAT HAVE ALREADY BEEN GONE OVER BY EDITORS, OR A COPY OF THE GALLEY CAN BE PRINTED OFF FOR THE AUTHOR TO WORK ON CONCURRENTLY WITH THE EDITORS. AT MARUKAWA, AUTHOR PROOFS ARE SKIPPED FOR THE MONTHLY ANTHOLOGIES. HOWEVER, SOMETIMES AUTHOR PROOFS ARE REQUESTED WHEN A SERIES IS COLLECTED INTO A TANKOUBON.

The World's Greatest First Love
The Case of Ritsu Onodera

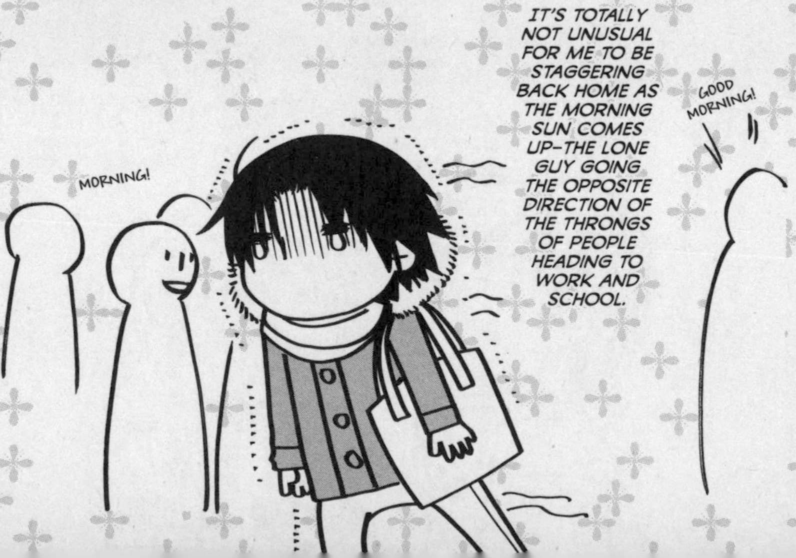
IT'S TOTALLY NOT UNUSUAL FOR ME TO BE STAGGERING BACK HOME AS THE MORNING SUN COMES UP–THE LONE GUY GOING THE OPPOSITE DIRECTION OF THE THRONGS OF PEOPLE HEADING TO WORK AND SCHOOL.
GOOD MORNING!
MORNING!

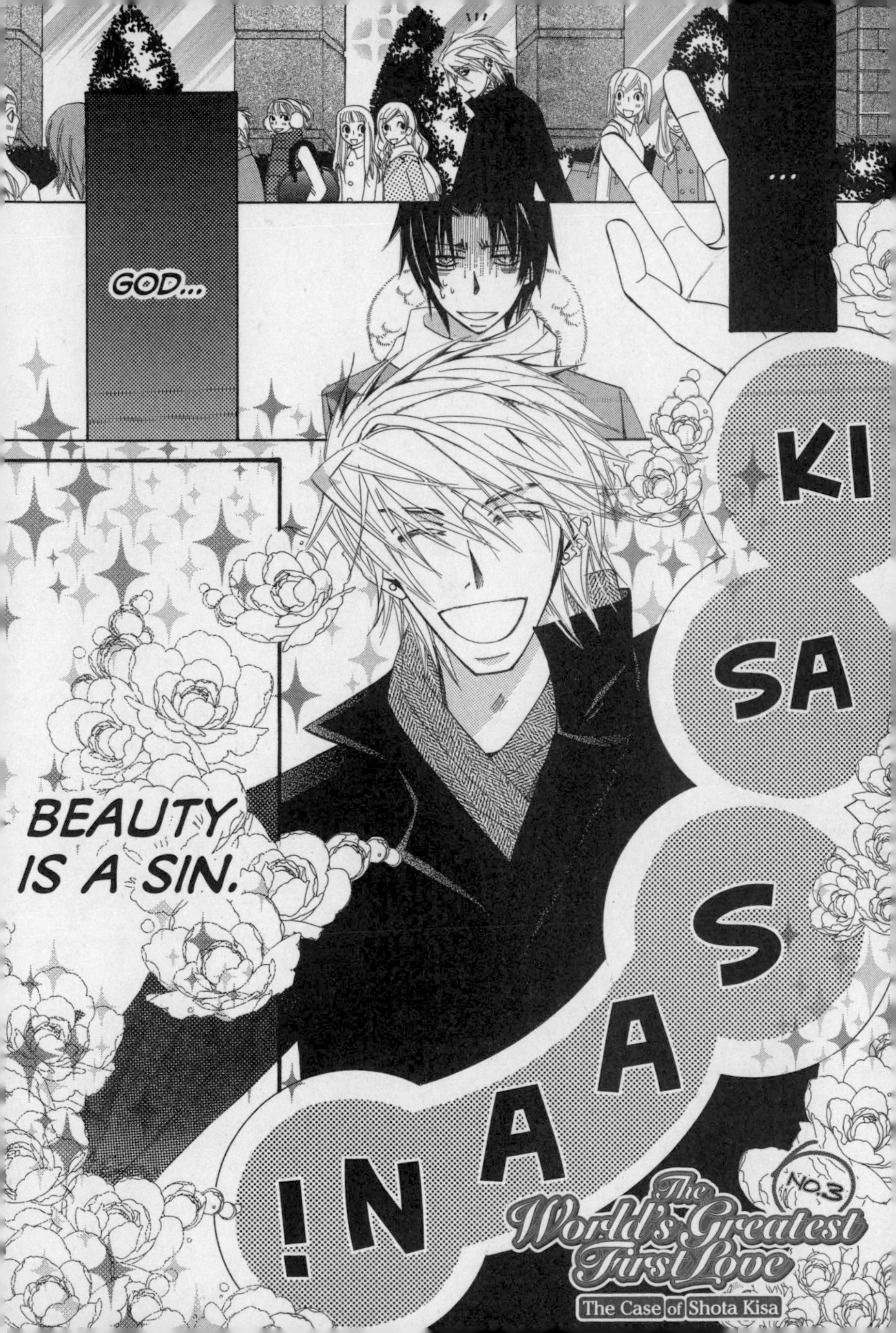
...
GOD...
KISASAAN!
BEAUTY IS A SIN.
NO.3
The World's Greatest First Love
The Case of Shota Kisa

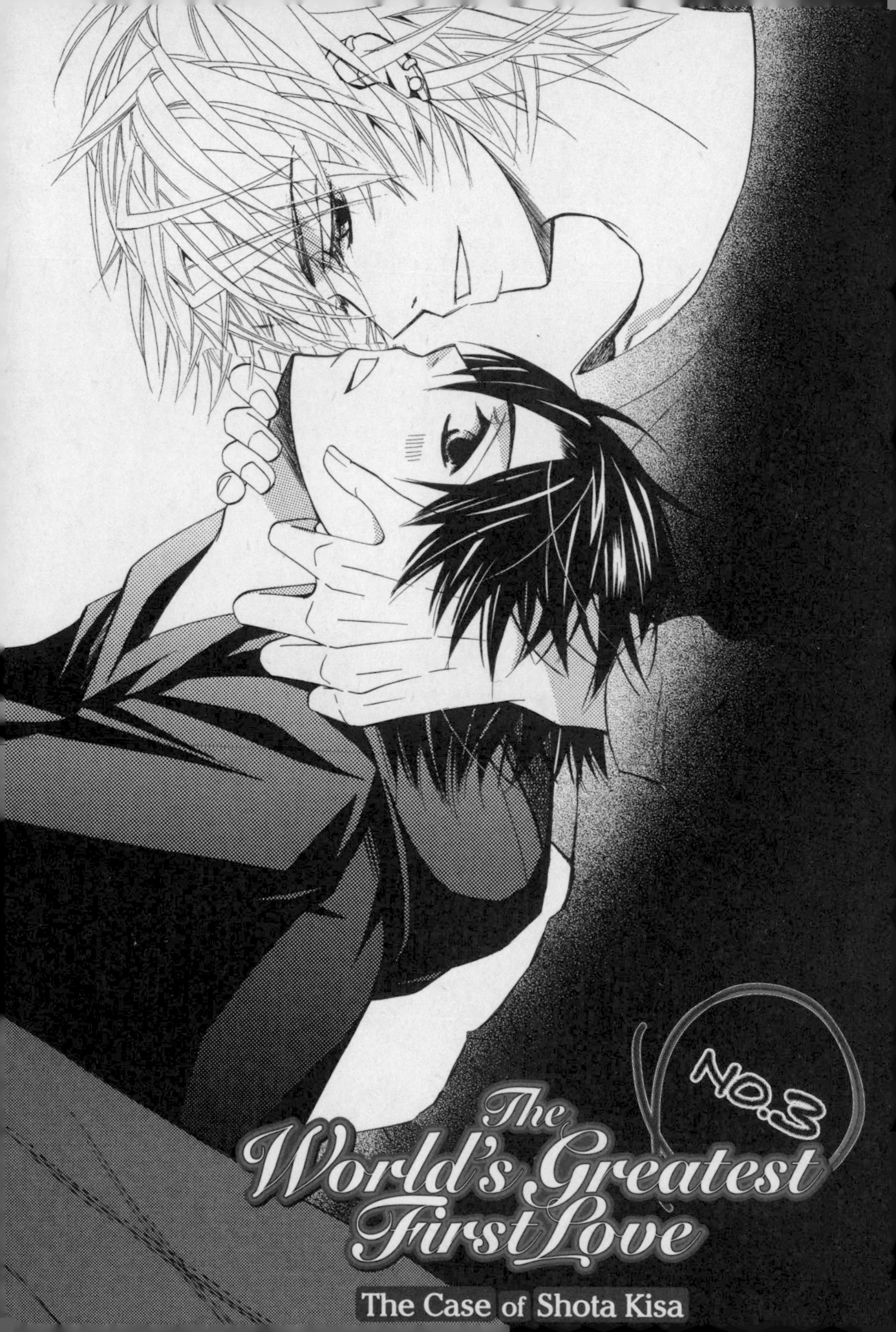

NO.3
The World's Greatest First Love
The Case of Shota Kisa

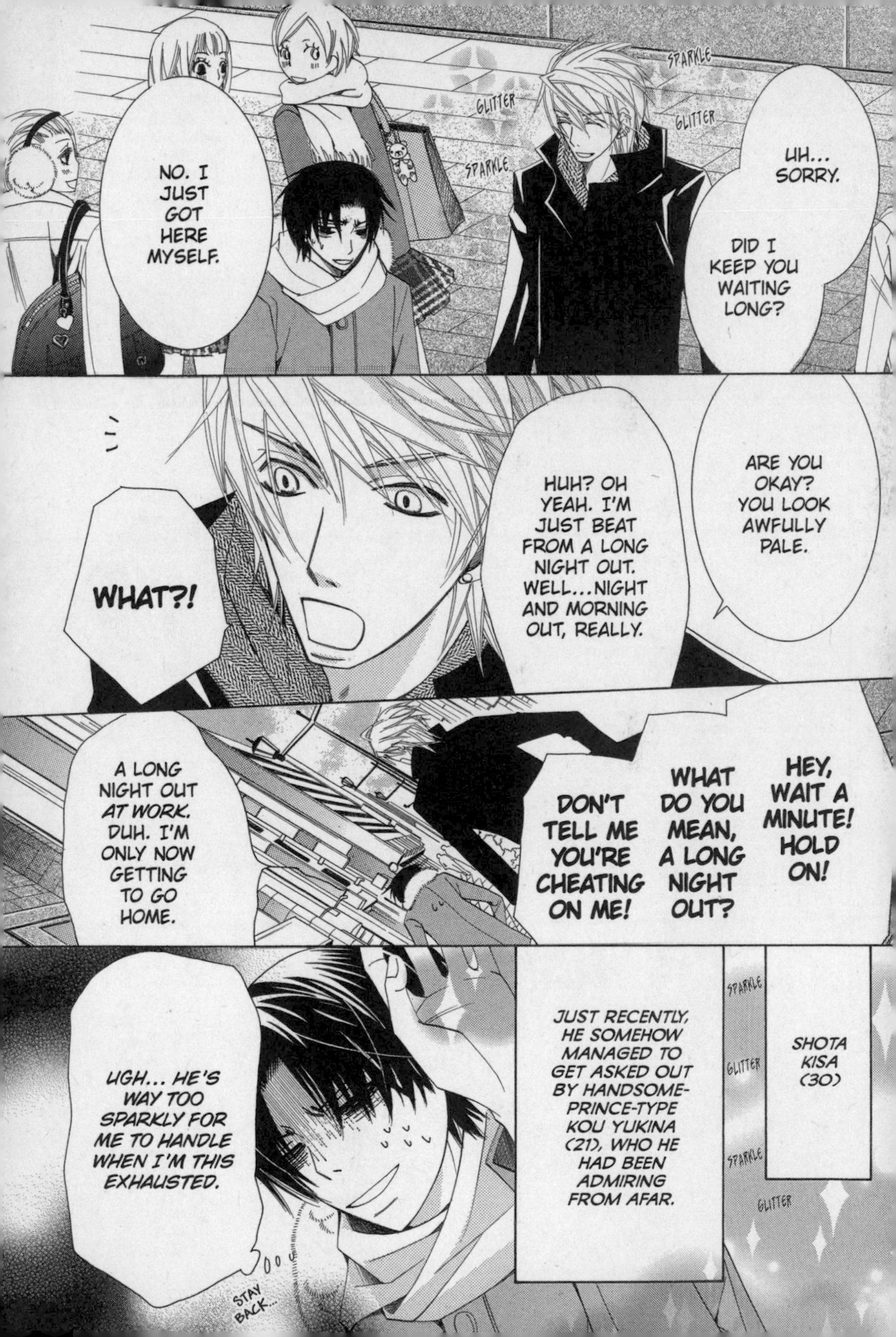
SPARKLE
GLITTER
UH... SORRY.
DID I KEEP YOU WAITING LONG?
GLITTER
SPARKLE
NO. I JUST GOT HERE MYSELF.
ARE YOU OKAY? YOU LOOK AWFULLY PALE.
HUH? OH YEAH. I'M JUST BEAT FROM A LONG NIGHT OUT. WELL...NIGHT AND MORNING OUT, REALLY.
WHAT?!
HEY, WAIT A MINUTE! HOLD ON!
WHAT DO YOU MEAN, A LONG NIGHT OUT?
DON'T TELL ME YOU'RE CHEATING ON ME!
A LONG NIGHT OUT AT WORK. DUH. I'M ONLY NOW GETTING TO GO HOME.
SHOTA KISA (30)
SPARKLE
GLITTER
SPARKLE
GLITTER
JUST RECENTLY, HE SOMEHOW MANAGED TO GET ASKED OUT BY HANDSOME-PRINCE-TYPE KOU YUKINA (21), WHO HE HAD BEEN ADMIRING FROM AFAR.
UGH... HE'S WAY TOO SPARKLY FOR ME TO HANDLE WHEN I'M THIS EXHAUSTED.
STAY BACK...

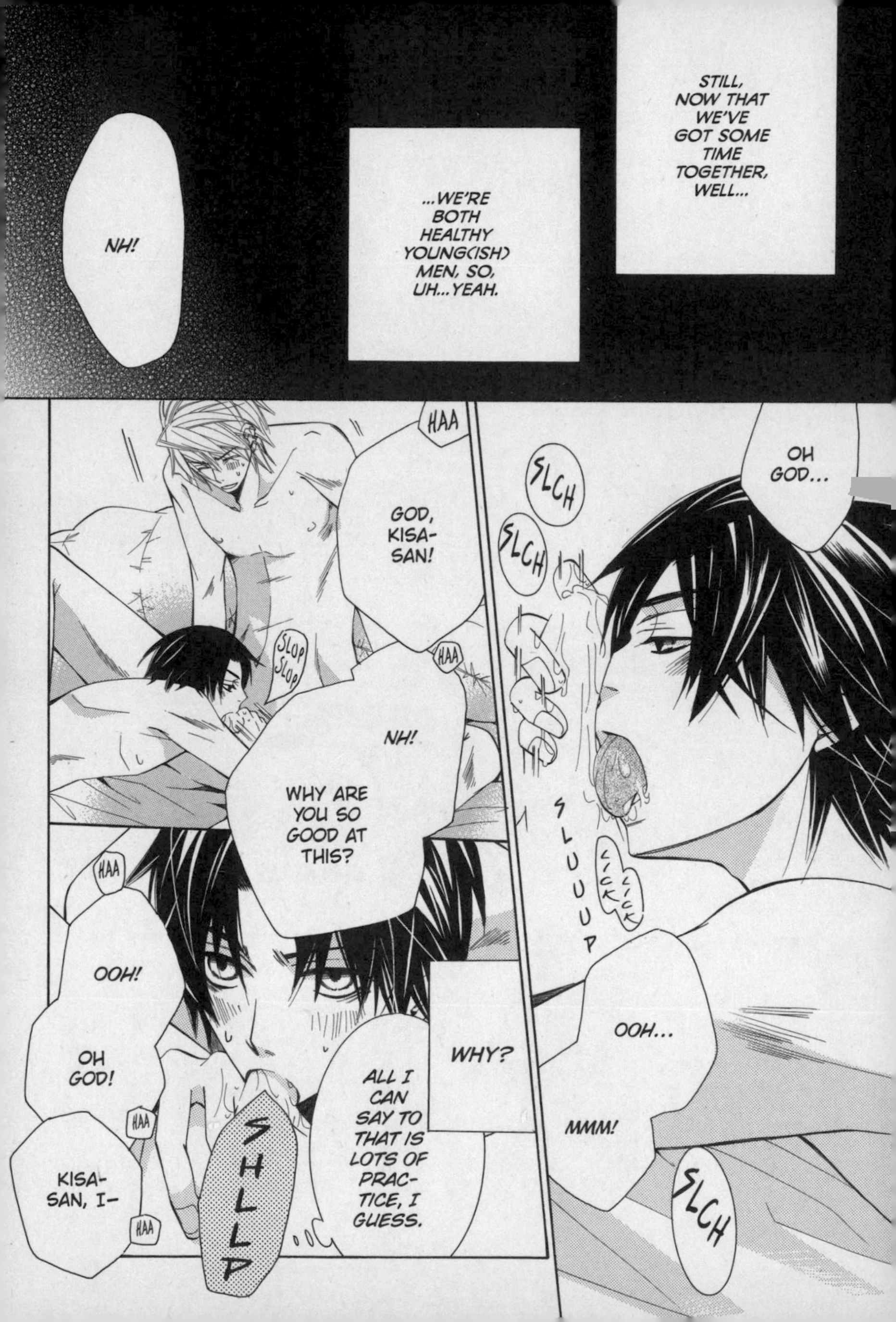
STILL, NOW THAT WE'VE GOT SOME TIME TOGETHER, WELL...
...WE'RE BOTH HEALTHY YOUNG(ISH) MEN, SO, UH...YEAH.
NH!
OH GOD...
SLCH
SLCH
SLUUUP
LICK LICK
OOH...
MMM!
SLCH
HAA
GOD, KISA-SAN!
SLOP SLOP
HAA
NH!
WHY ARE YOU SO GOOD AT THIS?
HAA
WHY?
ALL I CAN SAY TO THAT IS LOTS OF PRAC-TICE, I GUESS.
OOH!
OH GOD!
HAA
SHLLP
KISA-SAN, I-
HAA

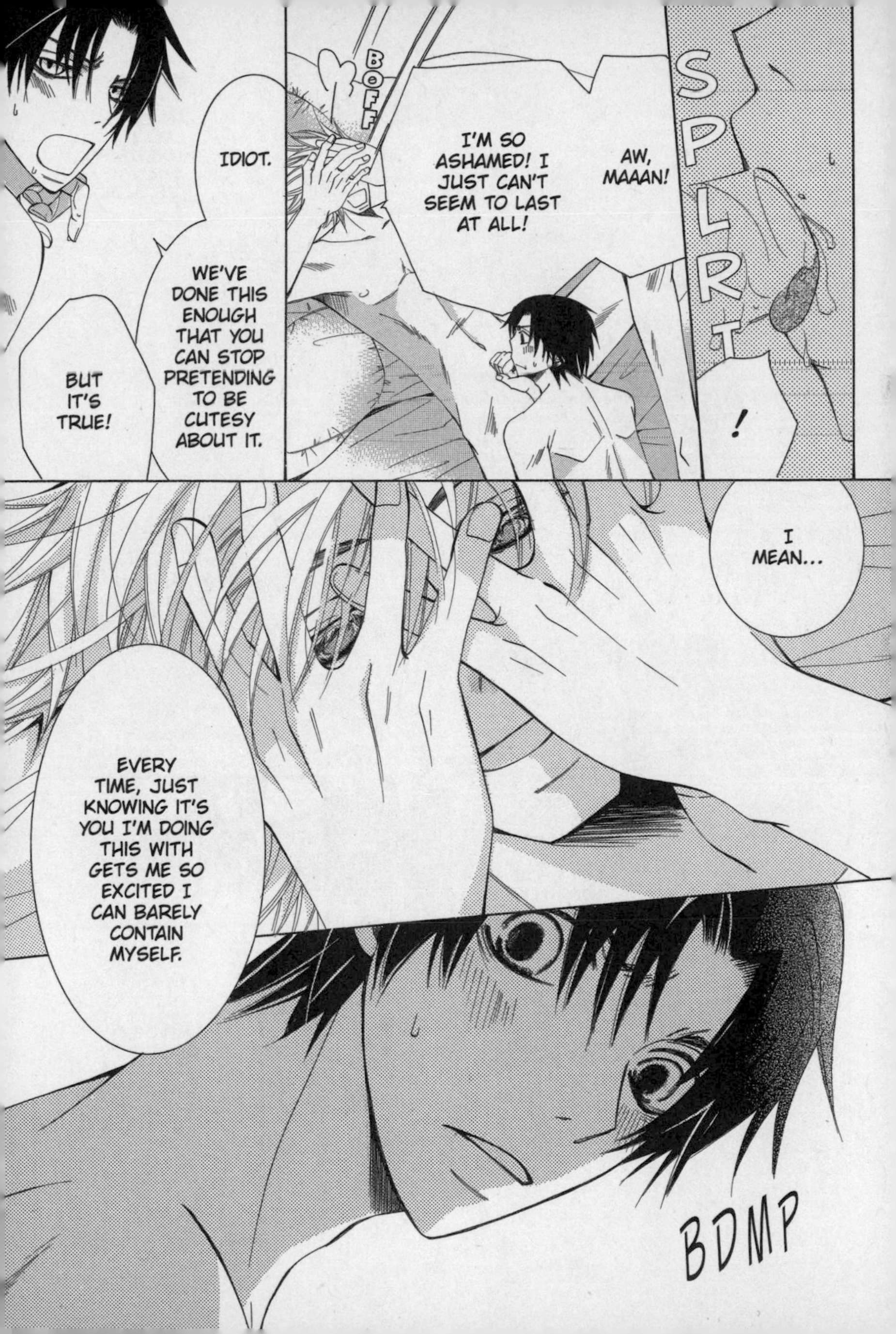
SPLRT
!
AW, MAAAN!
I'M SO ASHAMED! I JUST CAN'T SEEM TO LAST AT ALL!
BOFF
IDIOT.
WE'VE DONE THIS ENOUGH THAT YOU CAN STOP PRETENDING TO BE CUTESY ABOUT IT.
BUT IT'S TRUE!
I MEAN...
EVERY TIME, JUST KNOWING IT'S YOU I'M DOING THIS WITH GETS ME SO EXCITED I CAN BARELY CONTAIN MYSELF.
BDMP

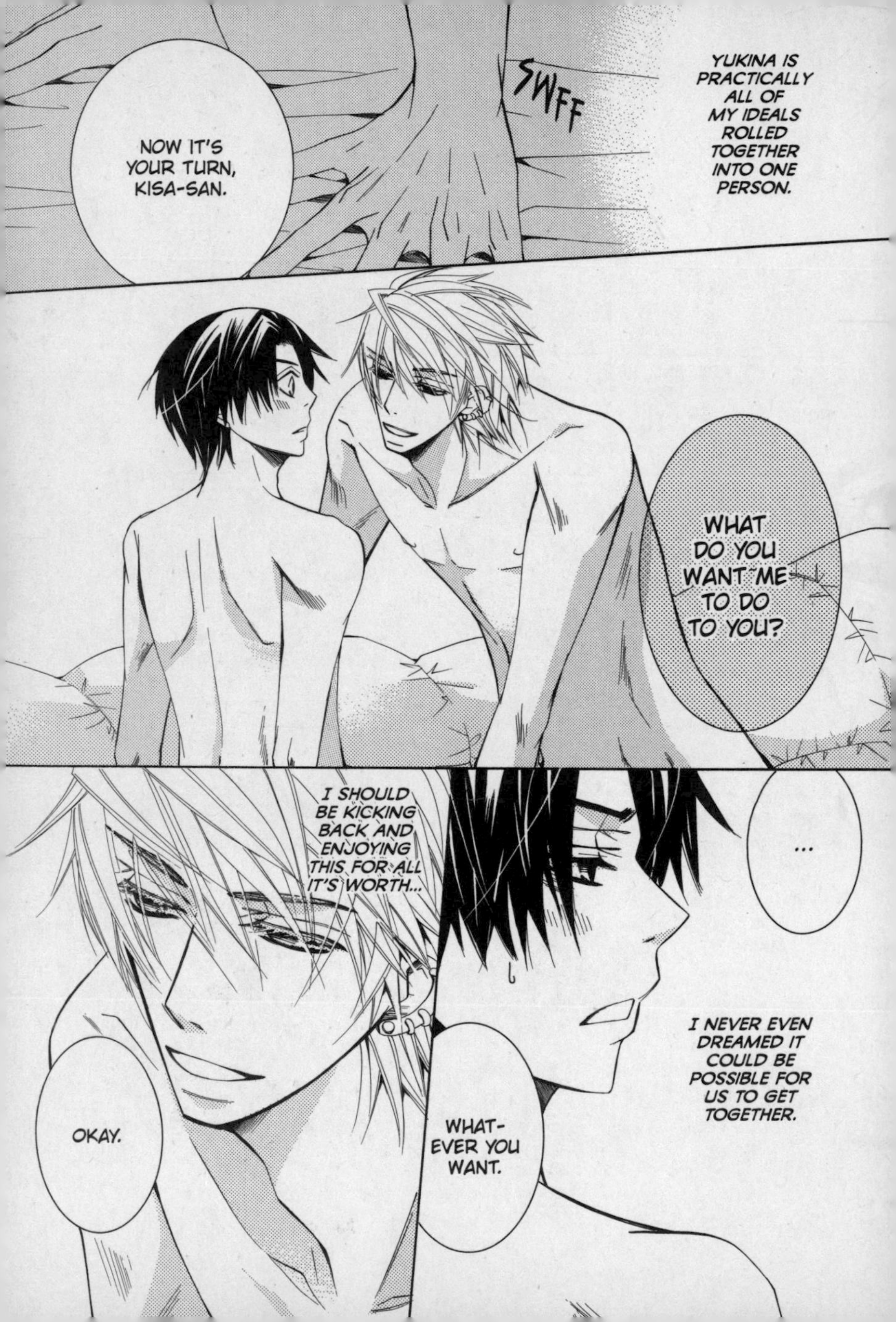
YUKINA IS PRACTICALLY ALL OF MY IDEALS ROLLED TOGETHER INTO ONE PERSON.
SWFF
NOW IT'S YOUR TURN, KISA-SAN.
WHAT DO YOU WANT ME TO DO TO YOU?
...
I SHOULD BE KICKING BACK AND ENJOYING THIS FOR ALL IT'S WORTH...
I NEVER EVEN DREAMED IT COULD BE POSSIBLE FOR US TO GET TOGETHER.
WHAT-EVER YOU WANT.
OKAY.

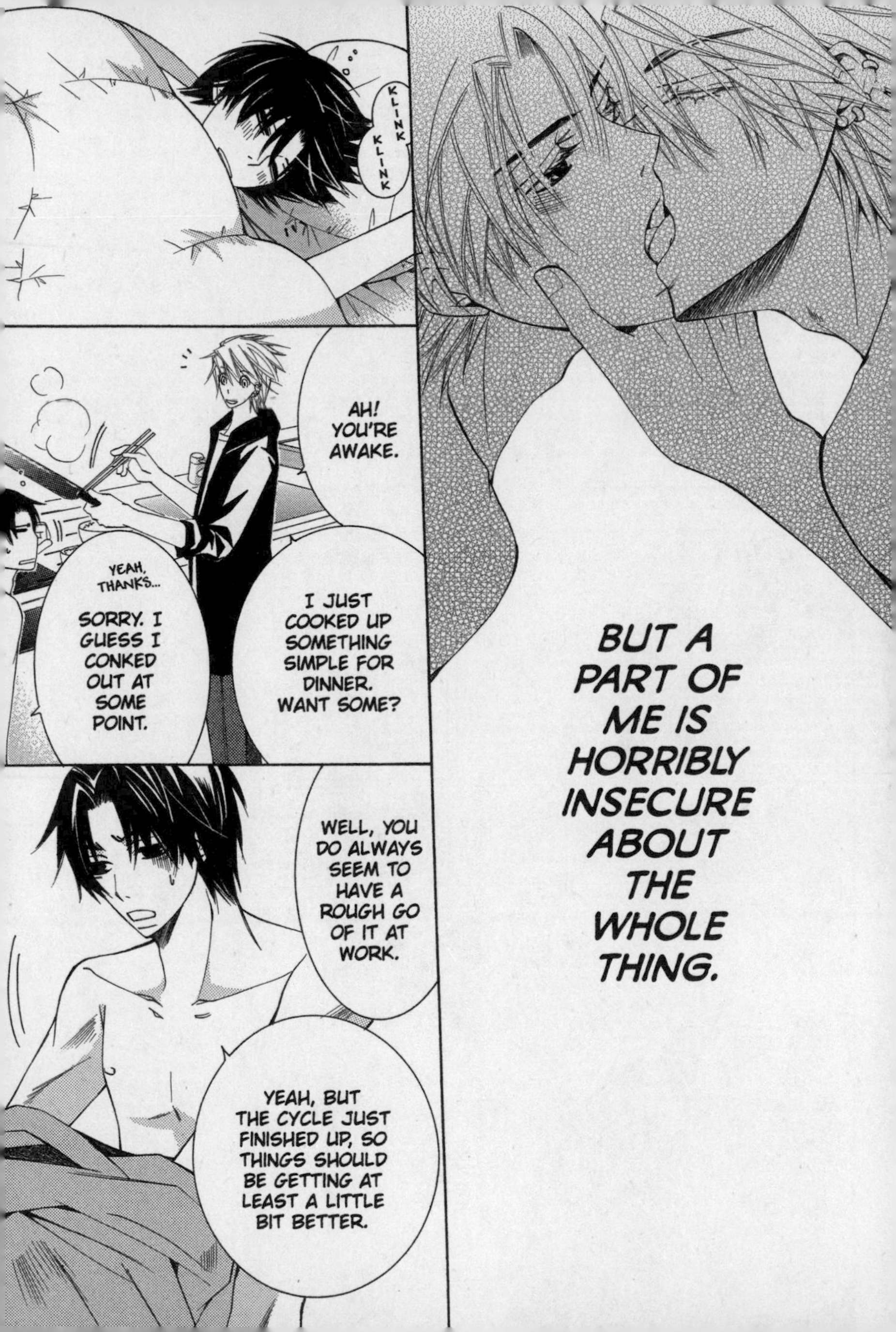
BUT A PART OF ME IS HORRIBLY INSECURE ABOUT THE WHOLE THING.
KLINK KLINK
AH! YOU'RE AWAKE.
I JUST COOKED UP SOMETHING SIMPLE FOR DINNER. WANT SOME?
YEAH, THANKS...
SORRY. I GUESS I CONKED OUT AT SOME POINT.
WELL, YOU DO ALWAYS SEEM TO HAVE A ROUGH GO OF IT AT WORK.
YEAH, BUT THE CYCLE JUST FINISHED UP, SO THINGS SHOULD BE GETTING AT LEAST A LITTLE BIT BETTER.

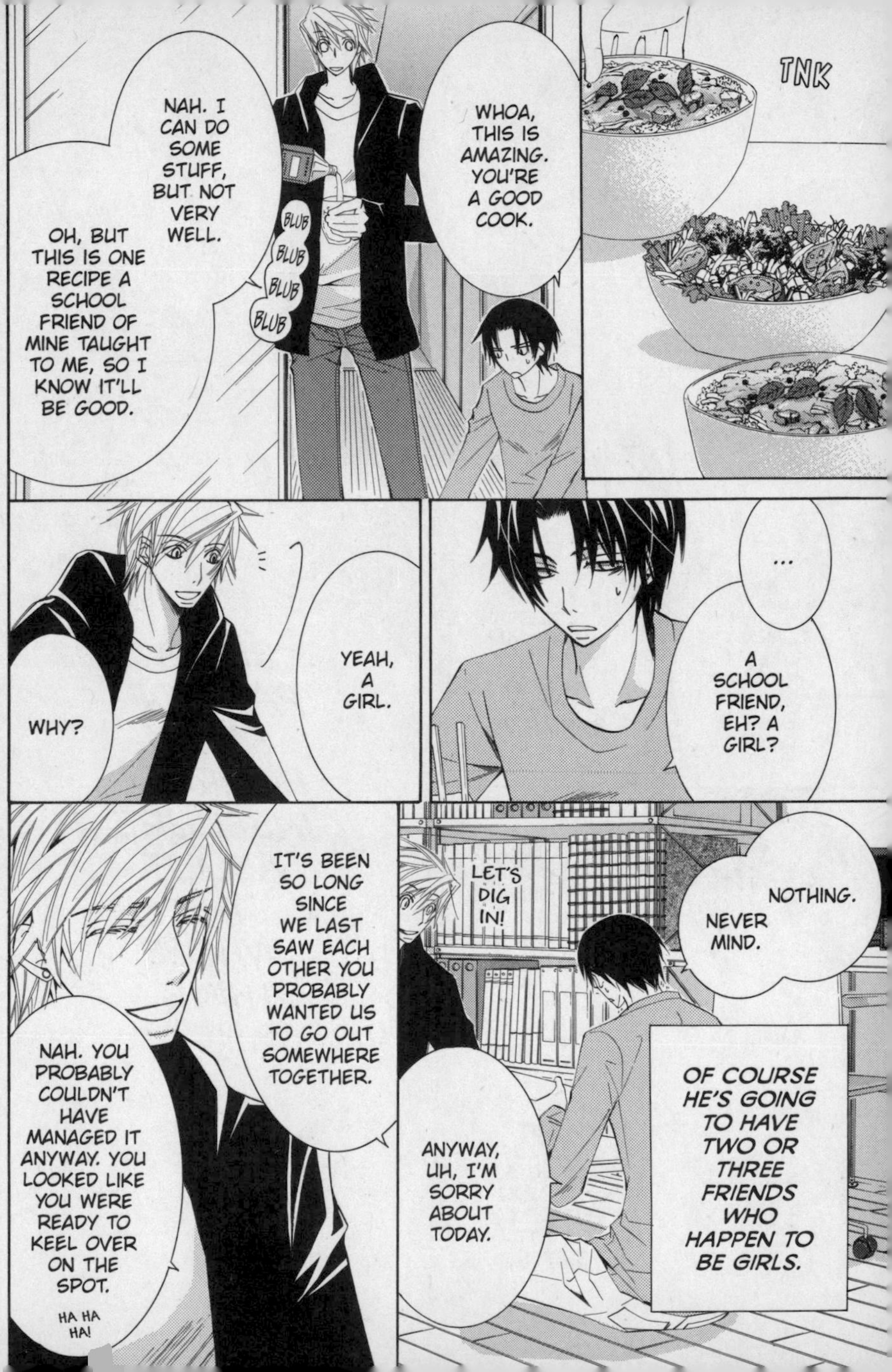
TNK
WHOA, THIS IS AMAZING. YOU'RE A GOOD COOK.
NAH. I CAN DO SOME STUFF, BUT NOT VERY WELL.
BLUB BLUB BLUB BLUB
OH, BUT THIS IS ONE RECIPE A SCHOOL FRIEND OF MINE TAUGHT TO ME, SO I KNOW IT'LL BE GOOD.
...
A SCHOOL FRIEND, EH? A GIRL?
YEAH, A GIRL.
WHY?
NOTHING. NEVER MIND.
LET'S DIG IN!
OF COURSE HE'S GOING TO HAVE TWO OR THREE FRIENDS WHO HAPPEN TO BE GIRLS.
ANYWAY, UH, I'M SORRY ABOUT TODAY.
IT'S BEEN SO LONG SINCE WE LAST SAW EACH OTHER YOU PROBABLY WANTED US TO GO OUT SOMEWHERE TOGETHER.
NAH. YOU PROBABLY COULDN'T HAVE MANAGED IT ANYWAY. YOU LOOKED LIKE YOU WERE READY TO KEEL OVER ON THE SPOT.
HA HA HA!

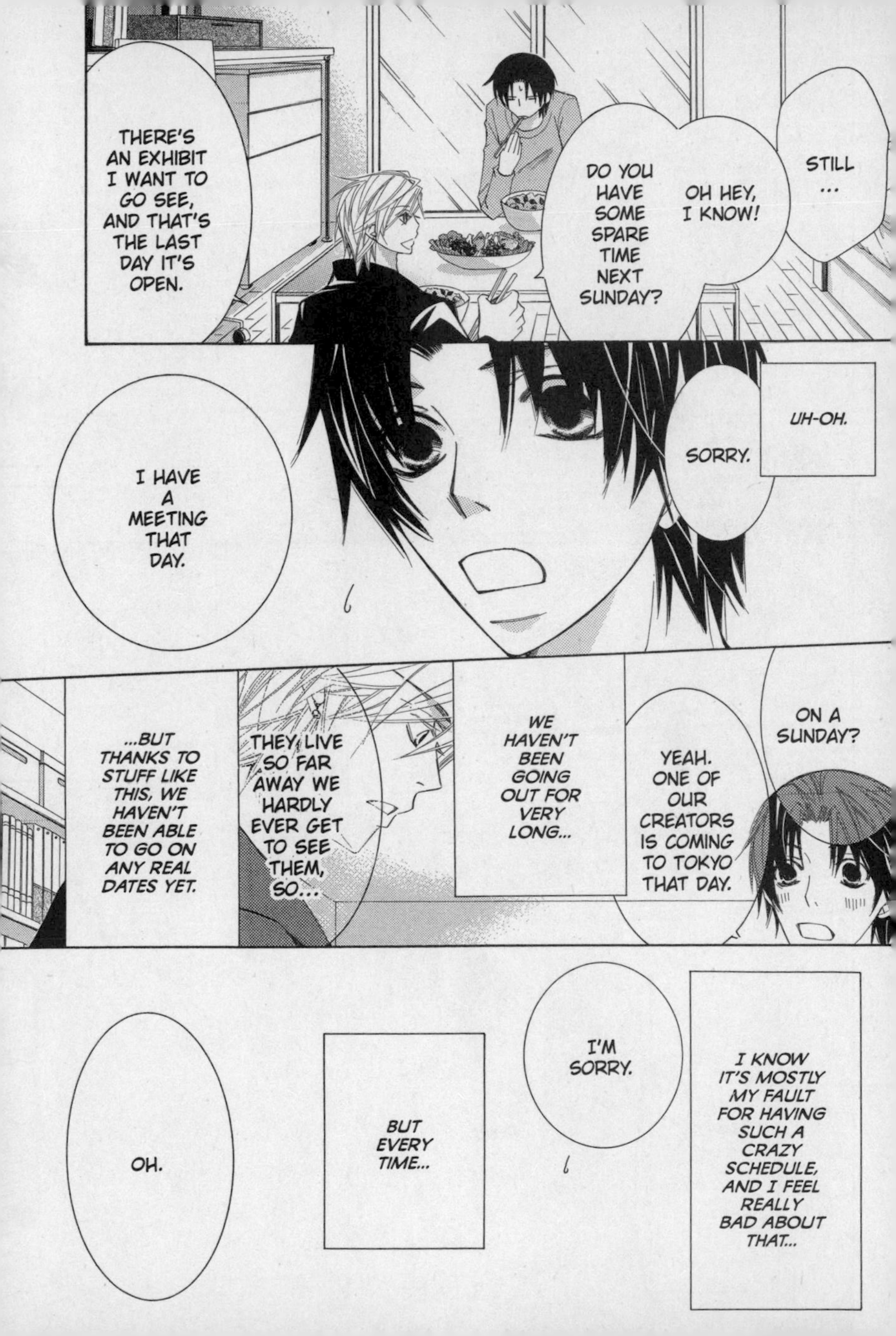
STILL ...
OH HEY, I KNOW!
DO YOU HAVE SOME SPARE TIME NEXT SUNDAY?
THERE'S AN EXHIBIT I WANT TO GO SEE, AND THAT'S THE LAST DAY IT'S OPEN.
UH-OH.
SORRY.
I HAVE A MEETING THAT DAY.
ON A SUNDAY?
YEAH. ONE OF OUR CREATORS IS COMING TO TOKYO THAT DAY.
WE HAVEN'T BEEN GOING OUT FOR VERY LONG...
THEY LIVE SO FAR AWAY WE HARDLY EVER GET TO SEE THEM, SO...
...BUT THANKS TO STUFF LIKE THIS, WE HAVEN'T BEEN ABLE TO GO ON ANY REAL DATES YET.
I KNOW IT'S MOSTLY MY FAULT FOR HAVING SUCH A CRAZY SCHEDULE, AND I FEEL REALLY BAD ABOUT THAT...
I'M SORRY.
BUT EVERY TIME...
OH.

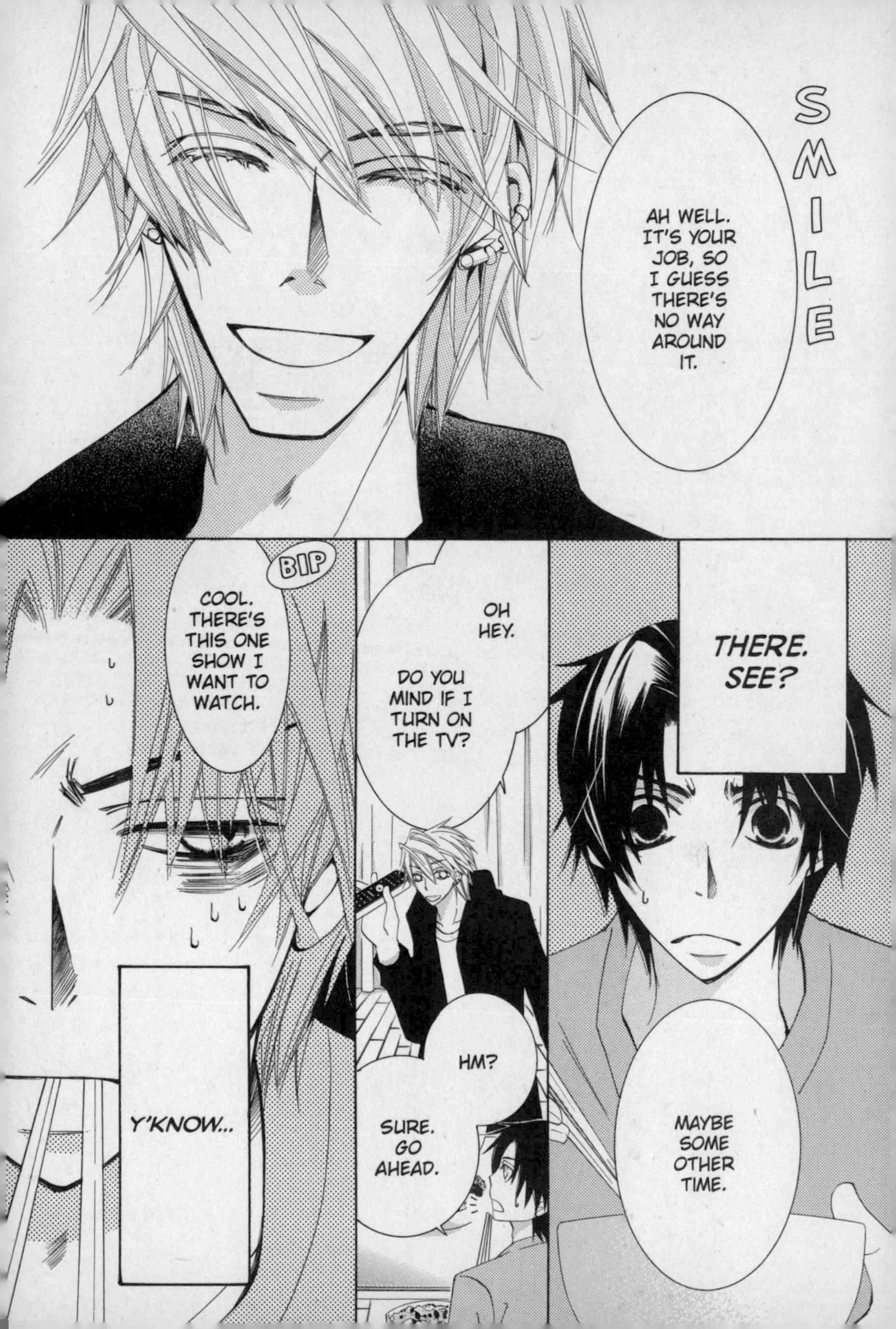
SMILE
AH WELL. IT'S YOUR JOB, SO I GUESS THERE'S NO WAY AROUND IT.
THERE. SEE?
MAYBE SOME OTHER TIME.
OH HEY.
DO YOU MIND IF I TURN ON THE TV?
HM?
SURE. GO AHEAD.
BIP
COOL. THERE'S THIS ONE SHOW I WANT TO WATCH.
Y'KNOW...

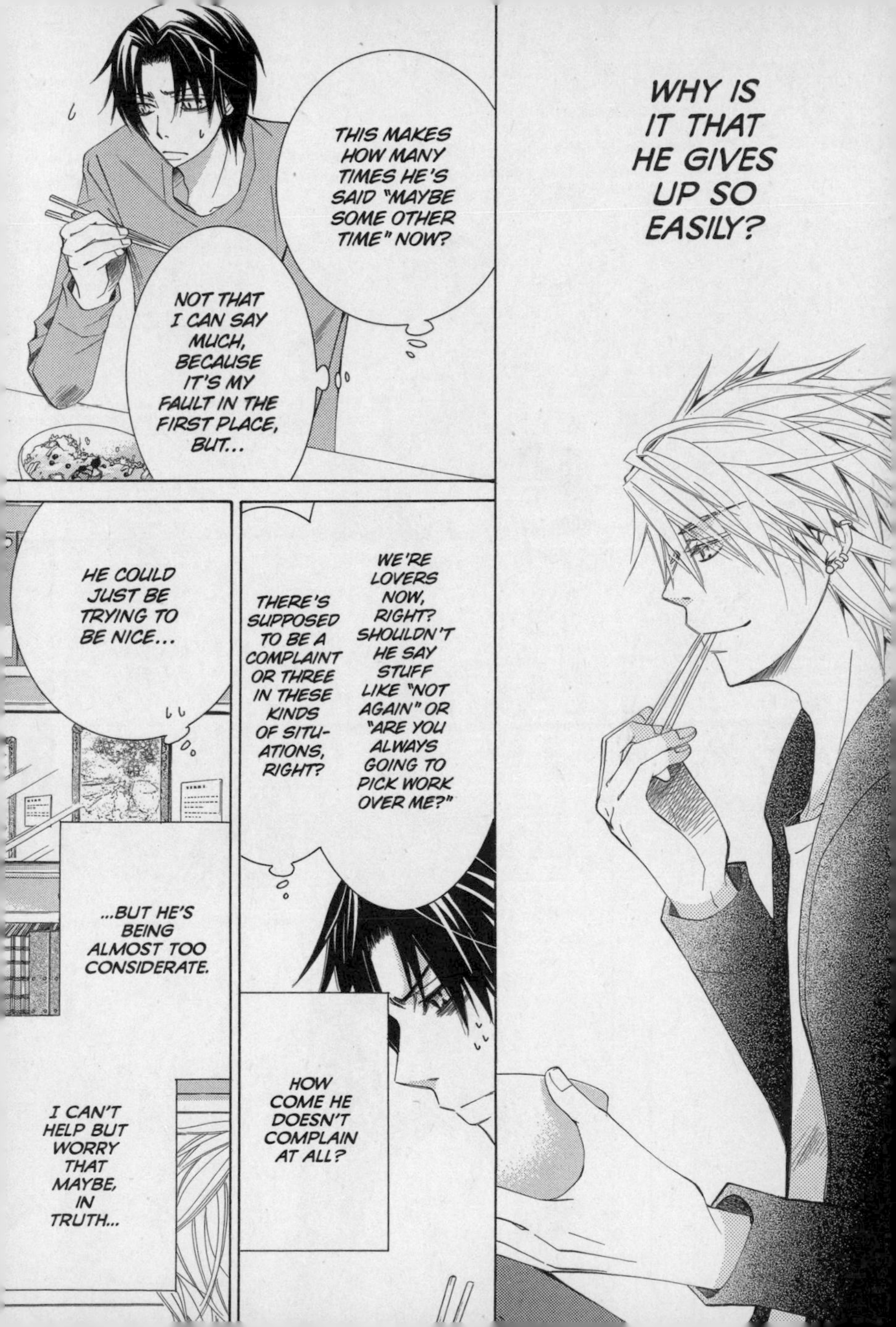
WHY IS IT THAT HE GIVES UP SO EASILY?
THIS MAKES HOW MANY TIMES HE'S SAID "MAYBE SOME OTHER TIME" NOW?
NOT THAT I CAN SAY MUCH, BECAUSE IT'S MY FAULT IN THE FIRST PLACE, BUT...
WE'RE LOVERS NOW, RIGHT? SHOULDN'T HE SAY STUFF LIKE "NOT AGAIN" OR "ARE YOU ALWAYS GOING TO PICK WORK OVER ME?"
THERE'S SUPPOSED TO BE A COMPLAINT OR THREE IN THESE KINDS OF SITUATIONS, RIGHT?
HE COULD JUST BE TRYING TO BE NICE...
...BUT HE'S BEING ALMOST TOO CONSIDERATE.
HOW COME HE DOESN'T COMPLAIN AT ALL?
I CAN'T HELP BUT WORRY THAT MAYBE, IN TRUTH...

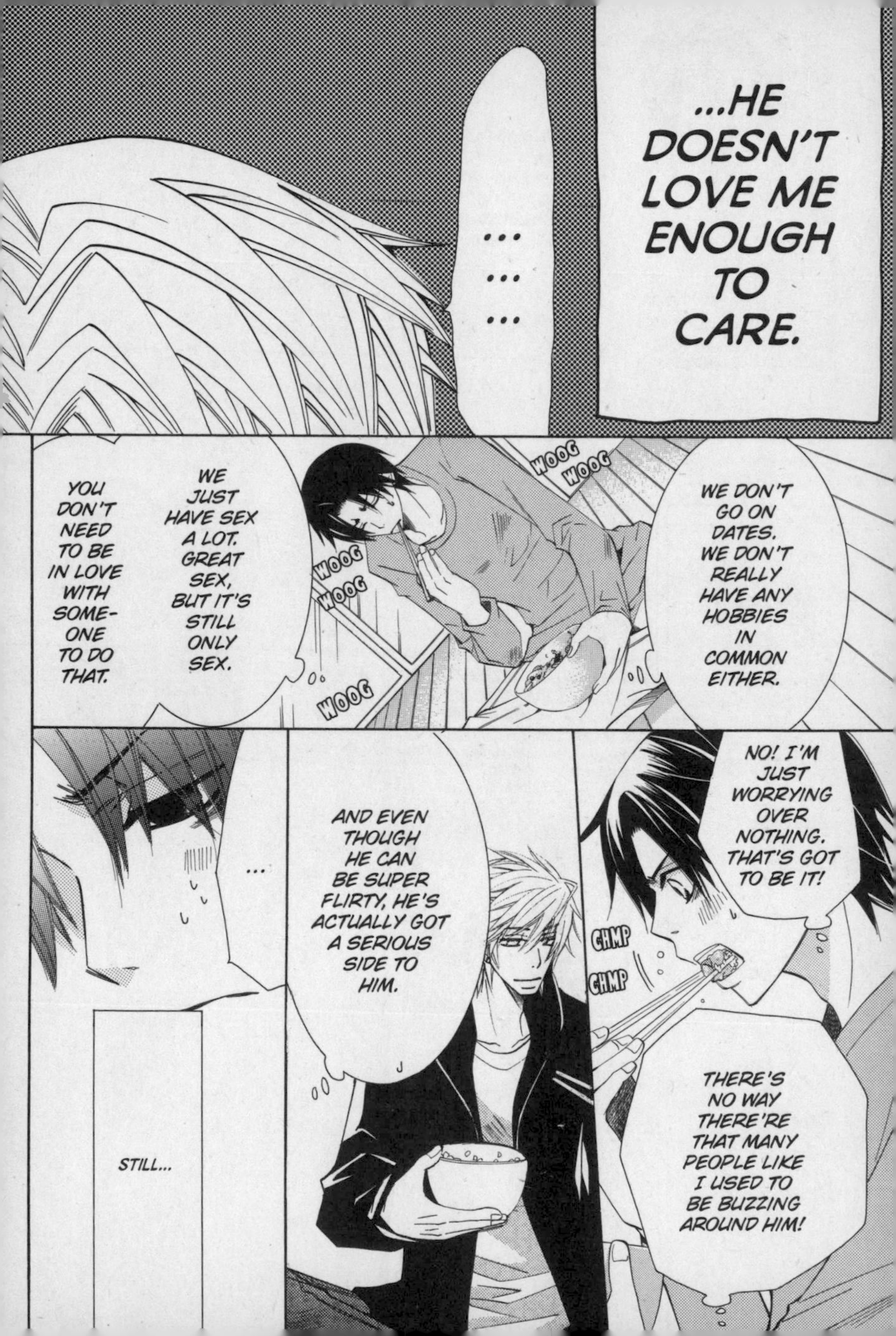
...HE DOESN'T LOVE ME ENOUGH TO CARE.
... ...
WE DON'T GO ON DATES. WE DON'T REALLY HAVE ANY HOBBIES IN COMMON EITHER.
WOOG WOOG
WOOG WOOG
WOOG
WE JUST HAVE SEX A LOT. GREAT SEX, BUT IT'S STILL ONLY SEX.
YOU DON'T NEED TO BE IN LOVE WITH SOME-ONE TO DO THAT.
NO! I'M JUST WORRYING OVER NOTHING. THAT'S GOT TO BE IT!
CHMP
CHMP
THERE'S NO WAY THERE'RE THAT MANY PEOPLE LIKE I USED TO BE BUZZING AROUND HIM!
AND EVEN THOUGH HE CAN BE SUPER FLIRTY, HE'S ACTUALLY GOT A SERIOUS SIDE TO HIM.
...
STILL...

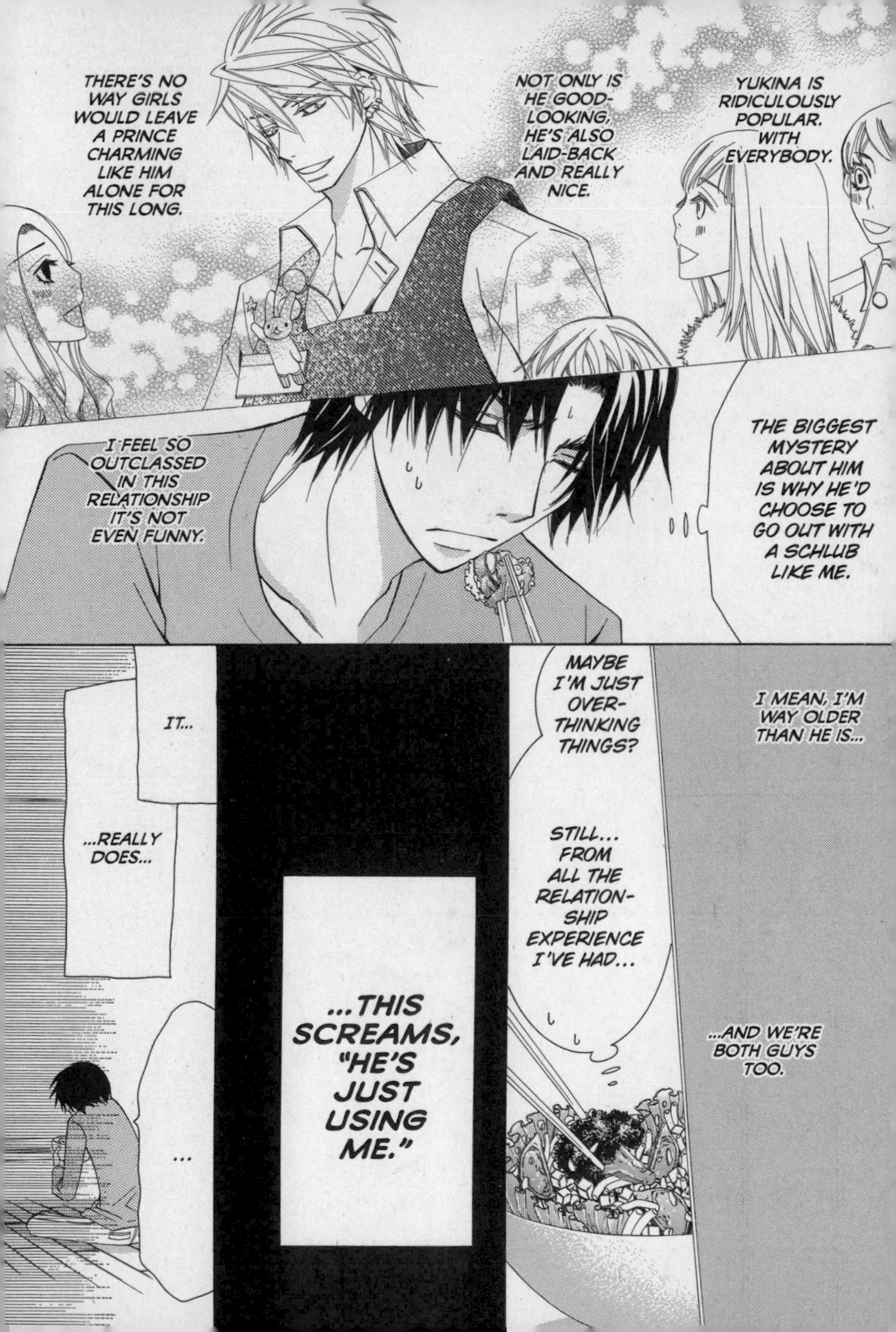
YUKINA IS RIDICULOUSLY POPULAR. WITH EVERYBODY.
NOT ONLY IS HE GOOD-LOOKING, HE'S ALSO LAID-BACK AND REALLY NICE.
THERE'S NO WAY GIRLS WOULD LEAVE A PRINCE CHARMING LIKE HIM ALONE FOR THIS LONG.
THE BIGGEST MYSTERY ABOUT HIM IS WHY HE'D CHOOSE TO GO OUT WITH A SCHLUB LIKE ME.
I FEEL SO OUTCLASSED IN THIS RELATIONSHIP IT'S NOT EVEN FUNNY.
I MEAN, I'M WAY OLDER THAN HE IS...
MAYBE I'M JUST OVER-THINKING THINGS?
...AND WE'RE BOTH GUYS TOO.
STILL... FROM ALL THE RELATION-SHIP EXPERIENCE I'VE HAD...
...THIS SCREAMS, "HE'S JUST USING ME."
IT...
...REALLY DOES...
...

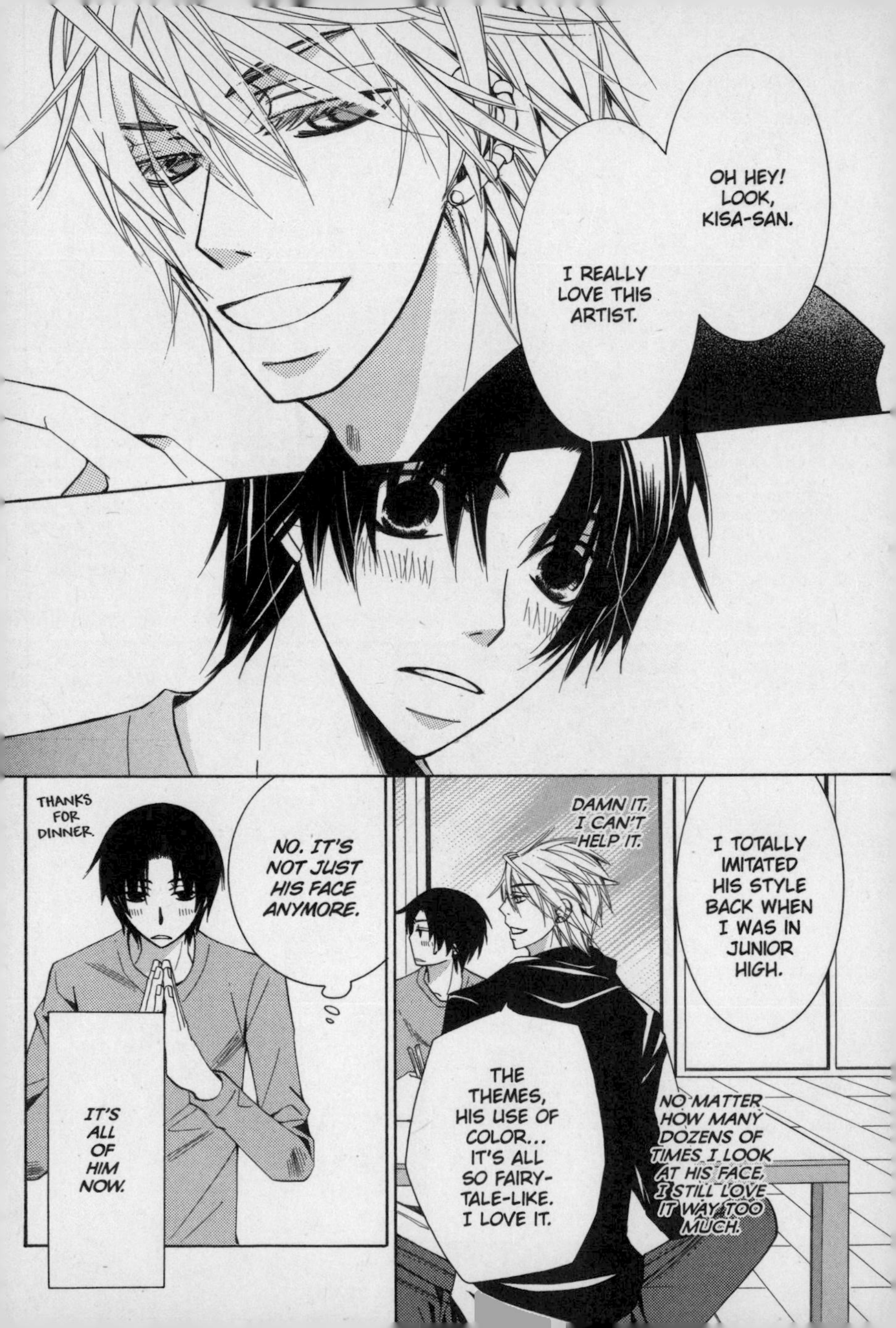
OH HEY! LOOK, KISA-SAN.
I REALLY LOVE THIS ARTIST.
I TOTALLY IMITATED HIS STYLE BACK WHEN I WAS IN JUNIOR HIGH.
DAMN IT, I CAN'T HELP IT.
NO MATTER HOW MANY DOZENS OF TIMES I LOOK AT HIS FACE, I STILL LOVE IT WAY TOO MUCH.
THE THEMES, HIS USE OF COLOR... IT'S ALL SO FAIRY-TALE-LIKE. I LOVE IT.
NO. IT'S NOT JUST HIS FACE ANYMORE.
THANKS FOR DINNER.
IT'S ALL OF HIM NOW.

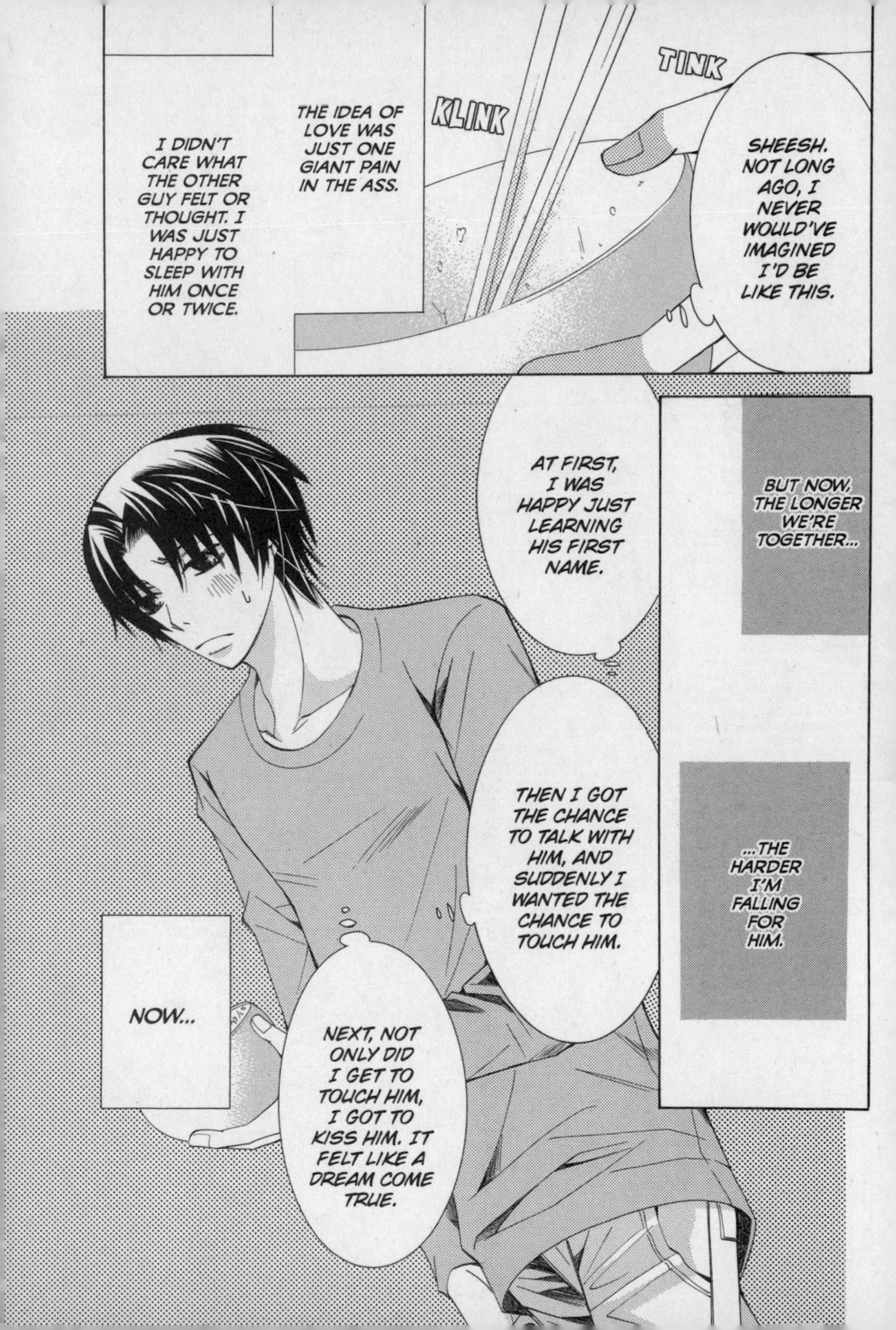
TINK
SHEESH. NOT LONG AGO, I NEVER WOULD'VE IMAGINED I'D BE LIKE THIS.
KLINK
THE IDEA OF LOVE WAS JUST ONE GIANT PAIN IN THE ASS.
I DIDN'T CARE WHAT THE OTHER GUY FELT OR THOUGHT. I WAS JUST HAPPY TO SLEEP WITH HIM ONCE OR TWICE.
BUT NOW, THE LONGER WE'RE TOGETHER...
...THE HARDER I'M FALLING FOR HIM.
AT FIRST, I WAS HAPPY JUST LEARNING HIS FIRST NAME.
THEN I GOT THE CHANCE TO TALK WITH HIM, AND SUDDENLY I WANTED THE CHANCE TO TOUCH HIM.
NEXT, NOT ONLY DID I GET TO TOUCH HIM, I GOT TO KISS HIM. IT FELT LIKE A DREAM COME TRUE.
NOW...

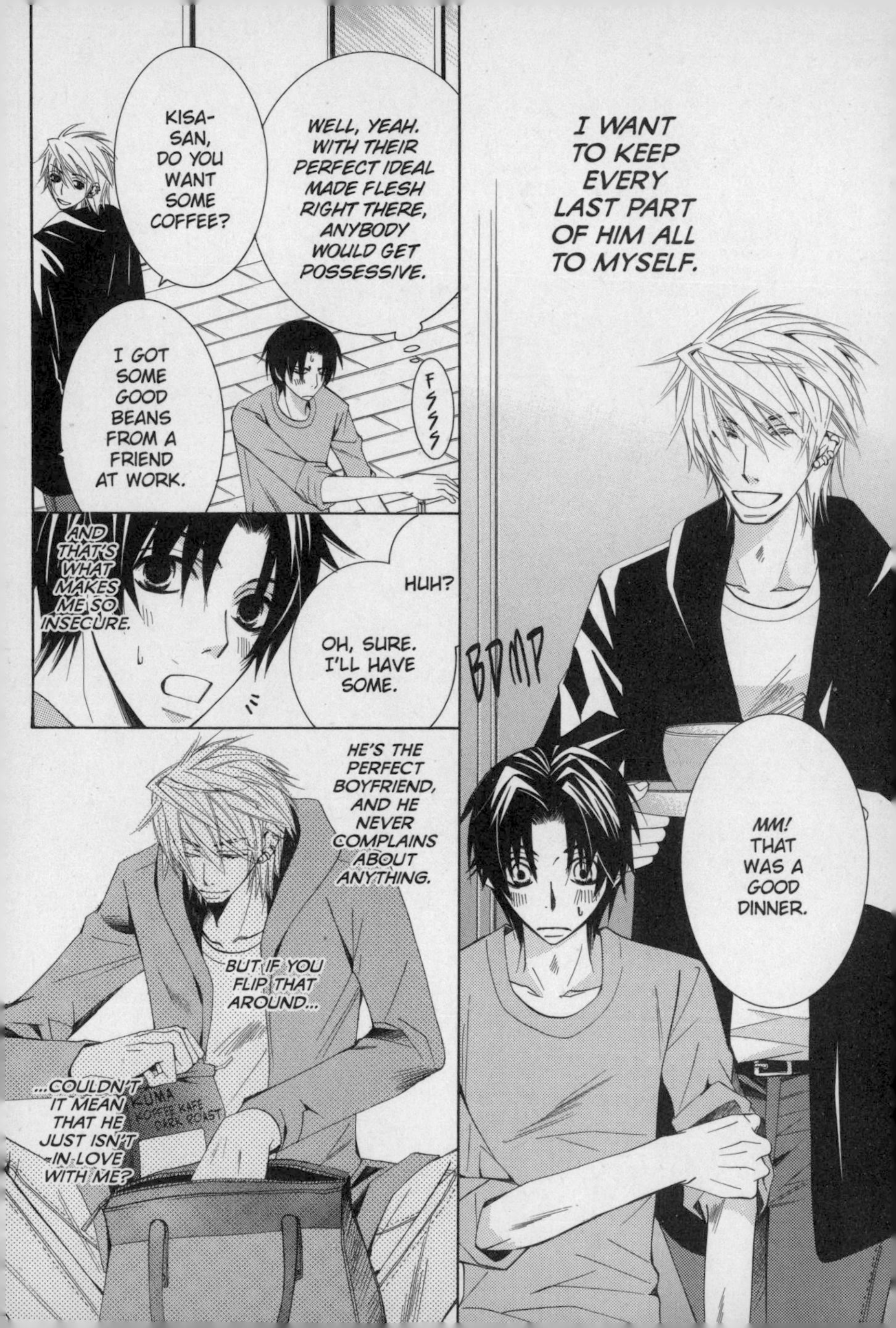
I WANT TO KEEP EVERY LAST PART OF HIM ALL TO MYSELF.
BDMP
MM! THAT WAS A GOOD DINNER.
WELL, YEAH. WITH THEIR PERFECT IDEAL MADE FLESH RIGHT THERE, ANYBODY WOULD GET POSSESSIVE.
KISA-SAN, DO YOU WANT SOME COFFEE?
I GOT SOME GOOD BEANS FROM A FRIEND AT WORK.
FSSS
HUH?
OH, SURE. I'LL HAVE SOME.
AND THAT'S WHAT MAKES ME SO INSECURE.
HE'S THE PERFECT BOYFRIEND, AND HE NEVER COMPLAINS ABOUT ANYTHING.
BUT IF YOU FLIP THAT AROUND...
...COULDN'T IT MEAN THAT HE JUST ISN'T IN LOVE WITH ME?
KUMA KOFFIE KAFE DARK ROAST

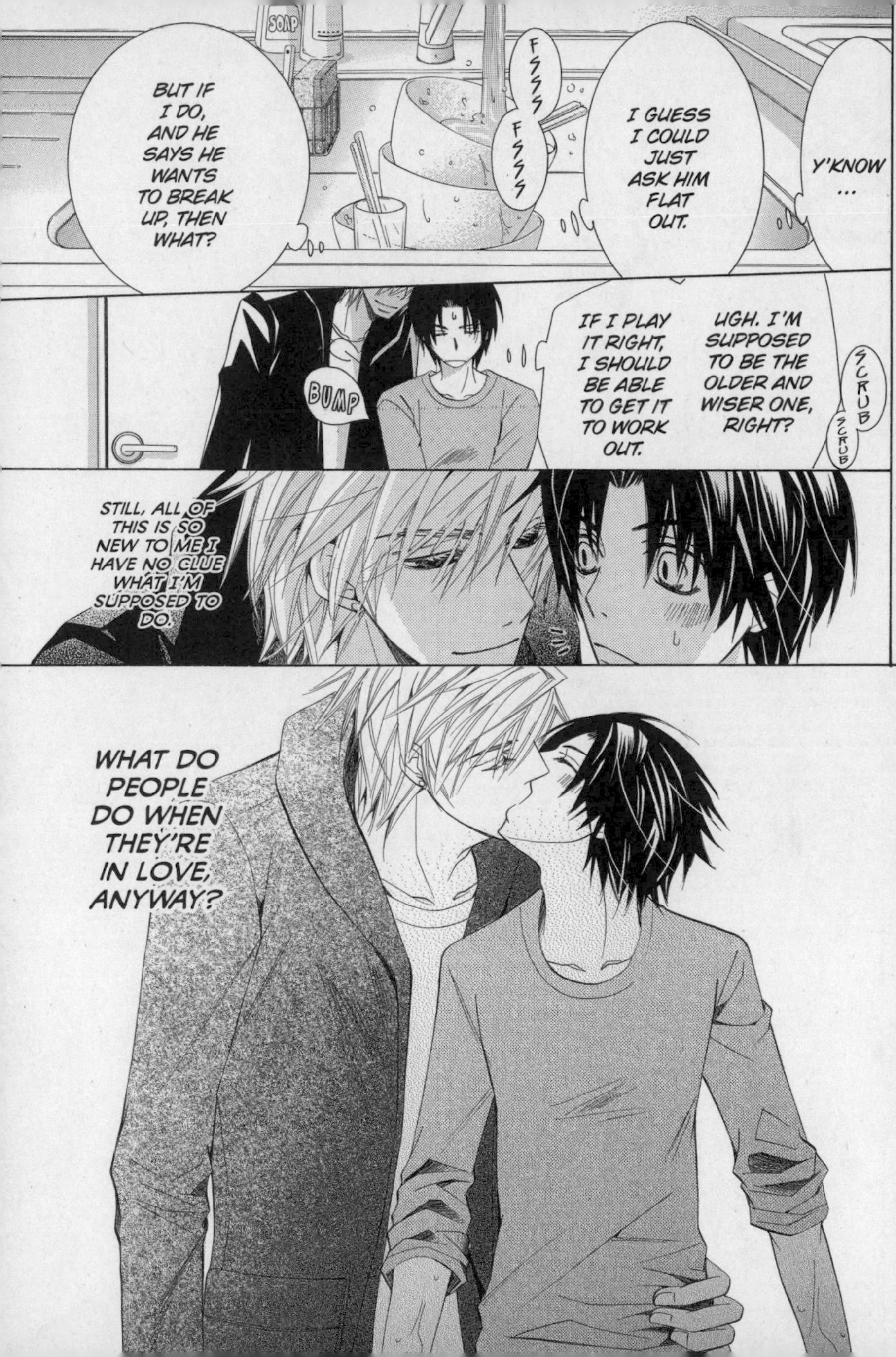
Y'KNOW ...
I GUESS I COULD JUST ASK HIM FLAT OUT.
FSSS
FSSS
BUT IF I DO, AND HE SAYS HE WANTS TO BREAK UP, THEN WHAT?
SCRUB
SCRUB
UGH. I'M SUPPOSED TO BE THE OLDER AND WISER ONE, RIGHT?
IF I PLAY IT RIGHT, I SHOULD BE ABLE TO GET IT TO WORK OUT.
BUMP
STILL, ALL OF THIS IS SO NEW TO ME I HAVE NO CLUE WHAT I'M SUPPOSED TO DO.
WHAT DO PEOPLE DO WHEN THEY'RE IN LOVE, ANYWAY?

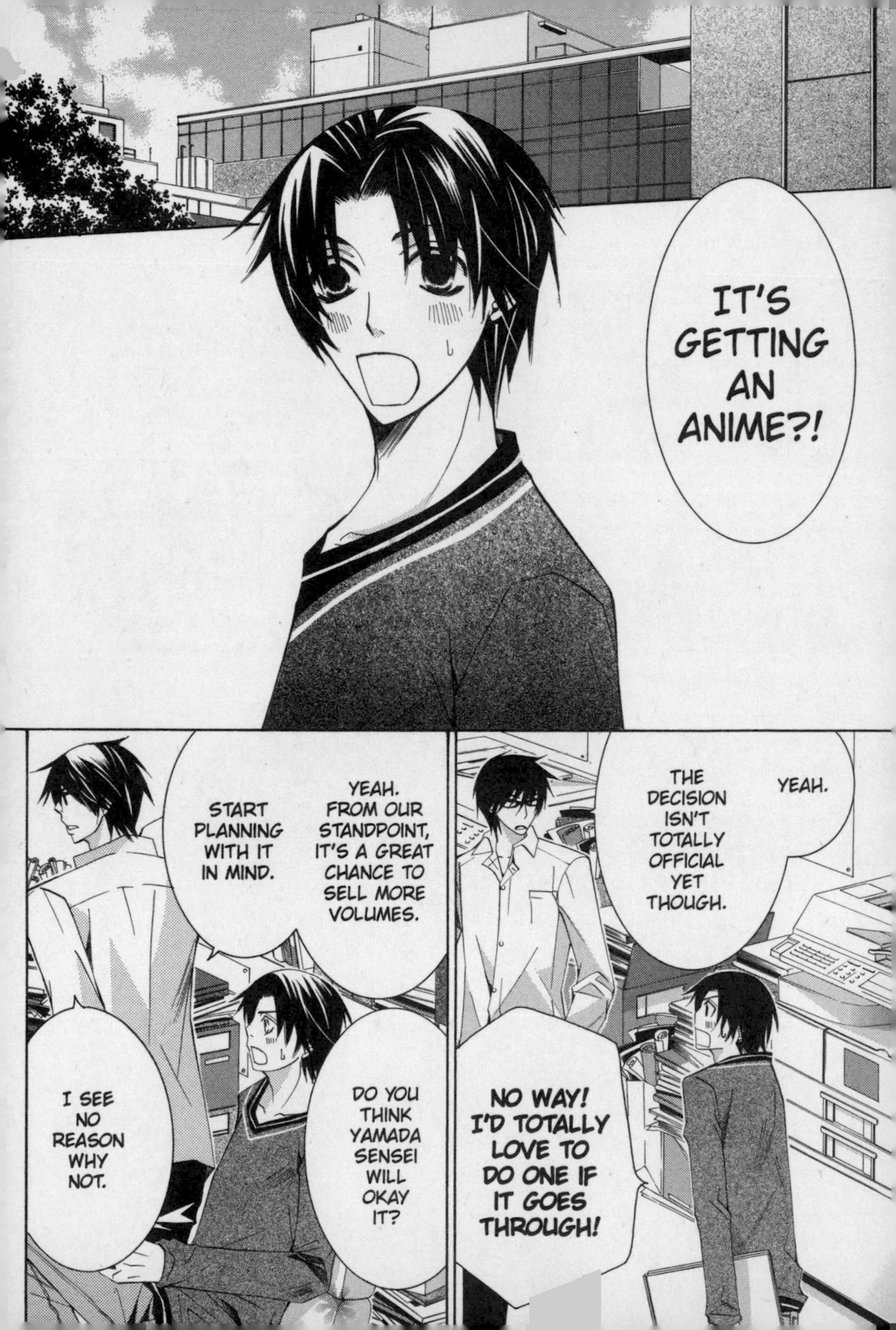
IT'S GETTING AN ANIME?!
YEAH.
THE DECISION ISN'T TOTALLY OFFICIAL YET THOUGH.
NO WAY! I'D TOTALLY LOVE TO DO ONE IF IT GOES THROUGH!
YEAH. FROM OUR STANDPOINT, IT'S A GREAT CHANCE TO SELL MORE VOLUMES.
START PLANNING WITH IT IN MIND.
DO YOU THINK YAMADA SENSEI WILL OKAY IT?
I SEE NO REASON WHY NOT.

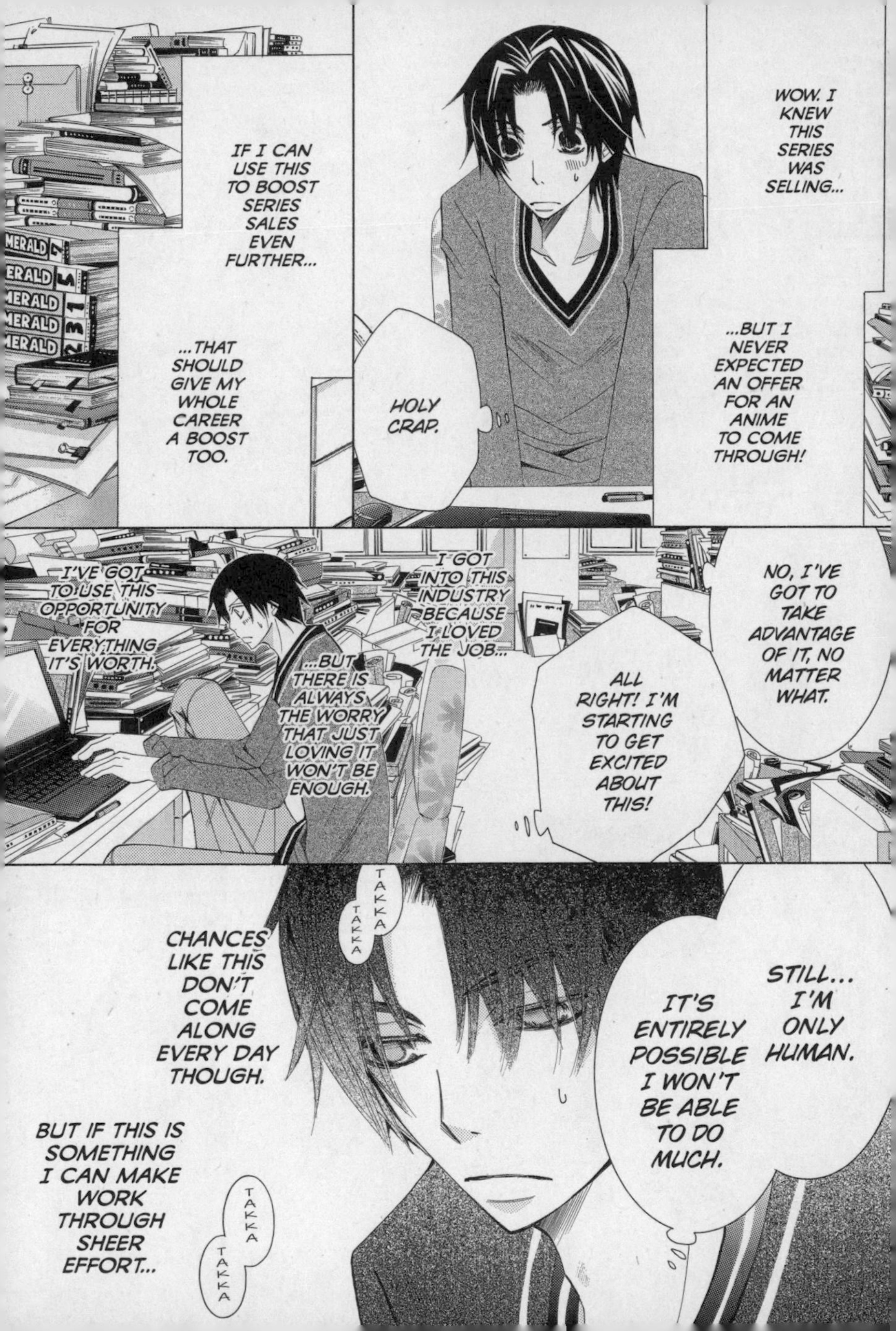
WOW. I KNEW THIS SERIES WAS SELLING...
...BUT I NEVER EXPECTED AN OFFER FOR AN ANIME TO COME THROUGH!
HOLY CRAP.
IF I CAN USE THIS TO BOOST SERIES SALES EVEN FURTHER...
...THAT SHOULD GIVE MY WHOLE CAREER A BOOST TOO.
NO, I'VE GOT TO TAKE ADVANTAGE OF IT, NO MATTER WHAT.
ALL RIGHT! I'M STARTING TO GET EXCITED ABOUT THIS!
I GOT INTO THIS INDUSTRY BECAUSE I LOVED THE JOB...
...BUT THERE IS ALWAYS THE WORRY THAT JUST LOVING IT WON'T BE ENOUGH.
I'VE GOT TO USE THIS OPPORTUNITY FOR EVERYTHING IT'S WORTH.
STILL... I'M ONLY HUMAN.
IT'S ENTIRELY POSSIBLE I WON'T BE ABLE TO DO MUCH.
TAKKA TAKKA
CHANCES LIKE THIS DON'T COME ALONG EVERY DAY THOUGH.
BUT IF THIS IS SOMETHING I CAN MAKE WORK THROUGH SHEER EFFORT...
TAKKA TAKKA

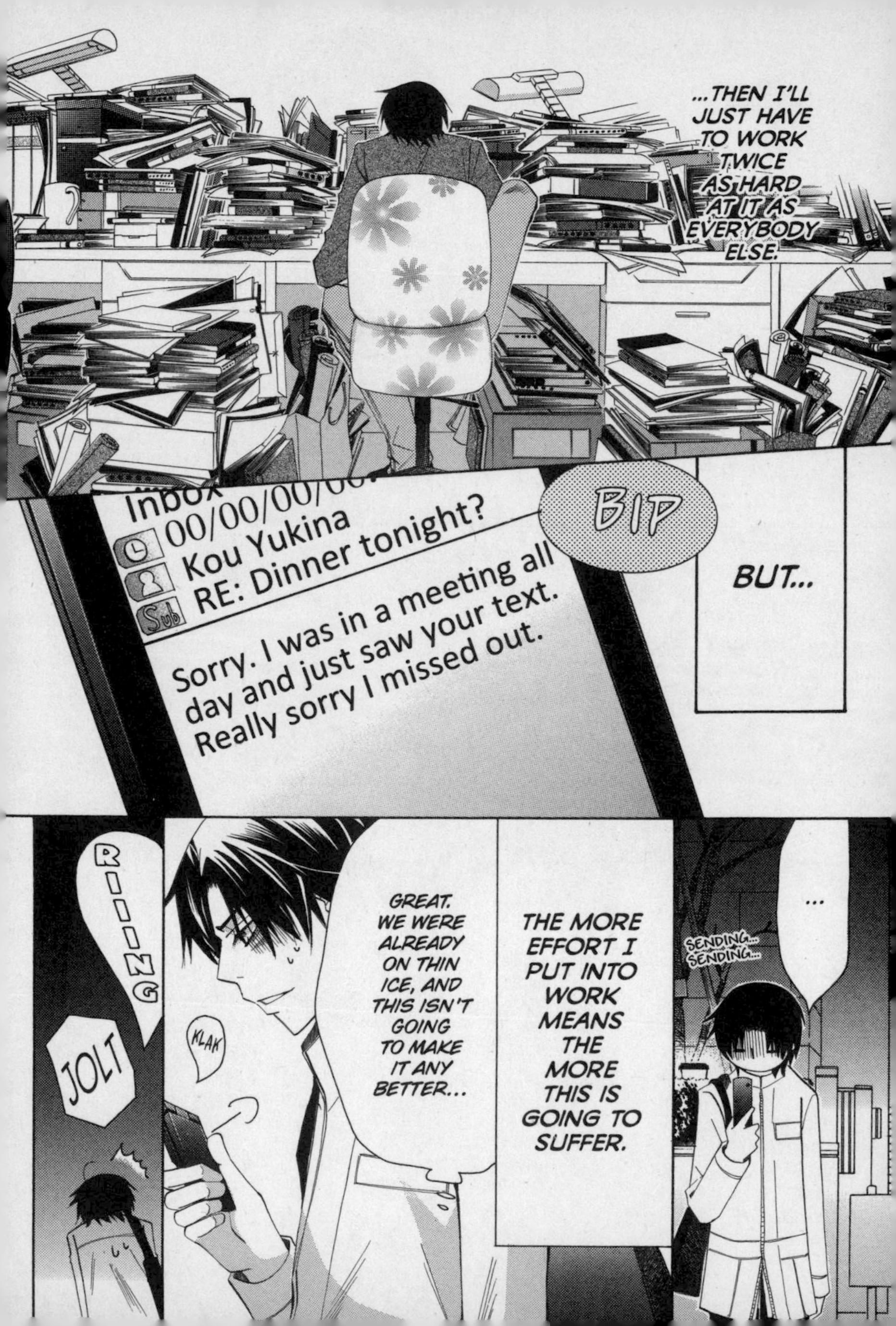
...THEN I'LL JUST HAVE TO WORK TWICE AS HARD AT IT AS EVERYBODY ELSE.
BUT...
BIP
Inbox
00/00/00/00
Kou Yukina
RE: Dinner tonight?
Sorry. I was in a meeting all day and just saw your text. Really sorry I missed out.
...
SENDING... SENDING...
THE MORE EFFORT I PUT INTO WORK MEANS THE MORE THIS IS GOING TO SUFFER.
GREAT. WE WERE ALREADY ON THIN ICE, AND THIS ISN'T GOING TO MAKE IT ANY BETTER...
KLAK
RIIIING
JOLT

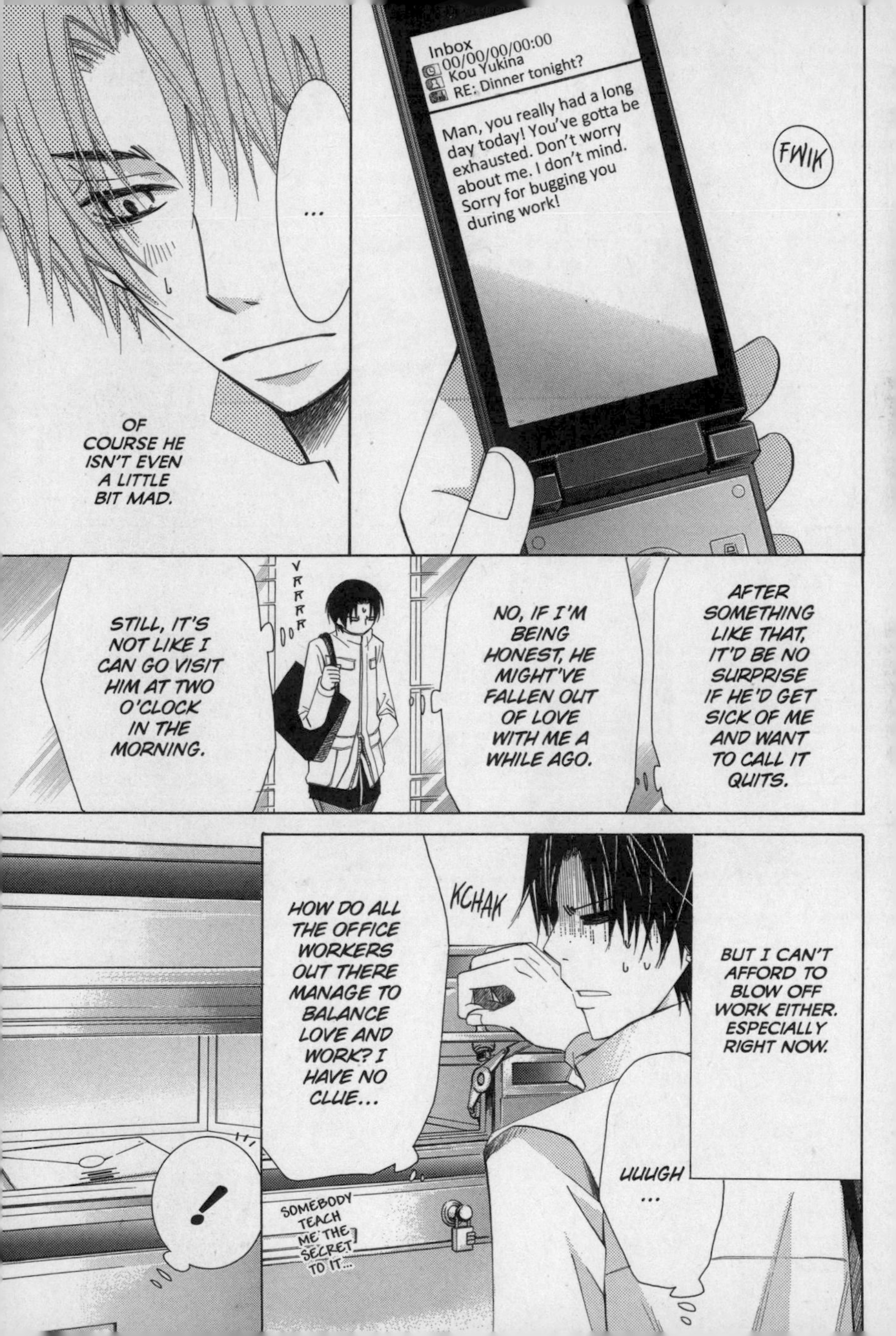
Inbox
00/00/00/00:00
Kou Yukina
RE: Dinner tonight?
Man, you really had a long day today! You've gotta be exhausted. Don't worry about me. I don't mind. Sorry for bugging you during work!
FWIK
...
OF COURSE HE ISN'T EVEN A LITTLE BIT MAD.
AFTER SOMETHING LIKE THAT, IT'D BE NO SURPRISE IF HE'D GET SICK OF ME AND WANT TO CALL IT QUITS.
NO, IF I'M BEING HONEST, HE MIGHT'VE FALLEN OUT OF LOVE WITH ME A WHILE AGO.
VRRRR
STILL, IT'S NOT LIKE I CAN GO VISIT HIM AT TWO O'CLOCK IN THE MORNING.
BUT I CAN'T AFFORD TO BLOW OFF WORK EITHER. ESPECIALLY RIGHT NOW.
KCHAK
HOW DO ALL THE OFFICE WORKERS OUT THERE MANAGE TO BALANCE LOVE AND WORK? I HAVE NO CLUE...
UUUGH...
SOMEBODY TEACH ME THE SECRET TO IT...
!

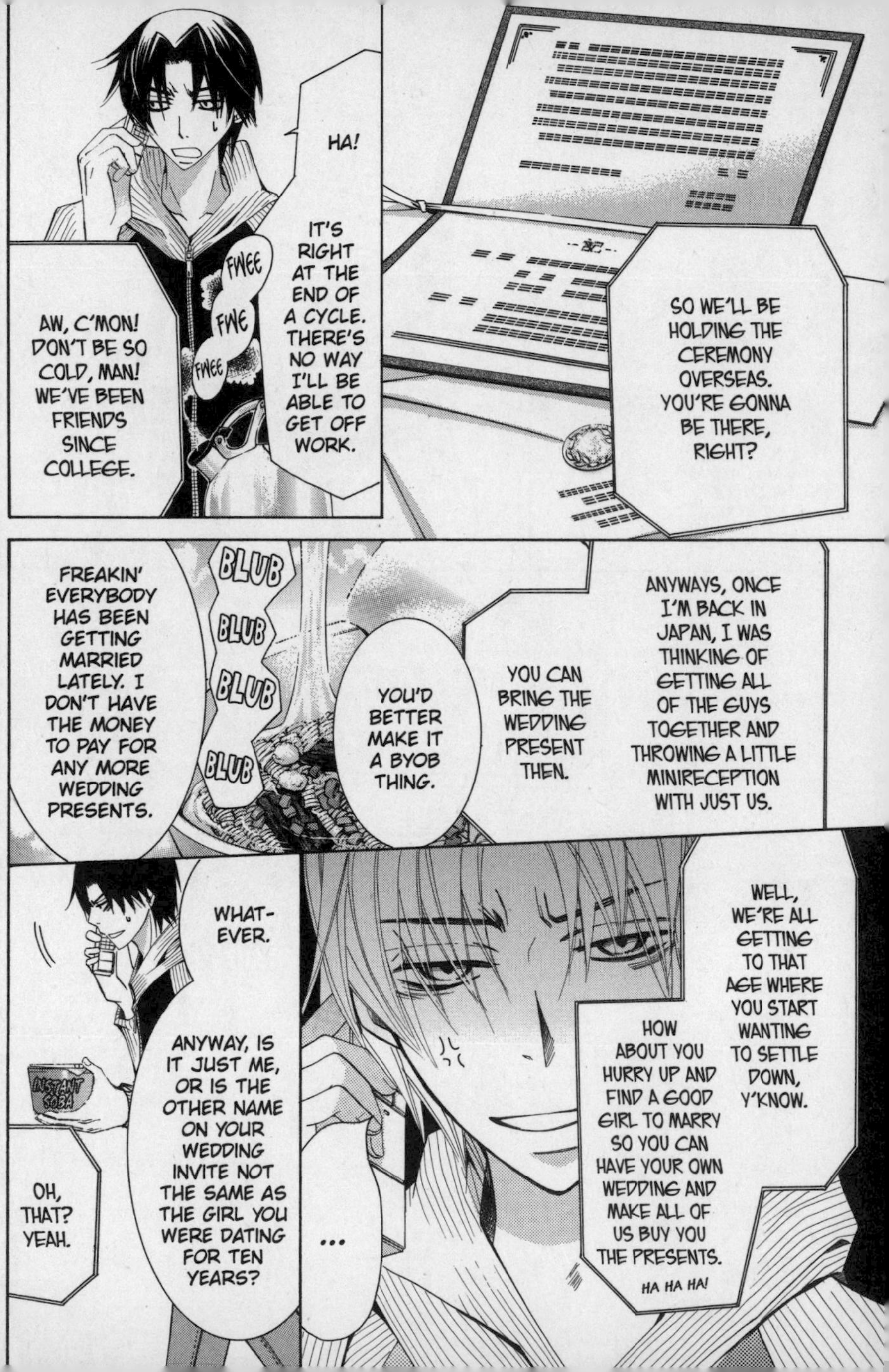
SO WE'LL BE HOLDING THE CEREMONY OVERSEAS. YOU'RE GONNA BE THERE, RIGHT?
HA!
IT'S RIGHT AT THE END OF A CYCLE. THERE'S NO WAY I'LL BE ABLE TO GET OFF WORK.
FWEE
FWE
FWEE
AW, C'MON! DON'T BE SO COLD, MAN! WE'VE BEEN FRIENDS SINCE COLLEGE.
ANYWAYS, ONCE I'M BACK IN JAPAN, I WAS THINKING OF GETTING ALL OF THE GUYS TOGETHER AND THROWING A LITTLE MINIRECEPTION WITH JUST US.
YOU CAN BRING THE WEDDING PRESENT THEN.
YOU'D BETTER MAKE IT A BYOB THING.
BLUB
BLUB
BLUB
BLUB
FREAKIN' EVERYBODY HAS BEEN GETTING MARRIED LATELY. I DON'T HAVE THE MONEY TO PAY FOR ANY MORE WEDDING PRESENTS.
WELL, WE'RE ALL GETTING TO THAT AGE WHERE YOU START WANTING TO SETTLE DOWN, Y'KNOW.
HOW ABOUT YOU HURRY UP AND FIND A GOOD GIRL TO MARRY SO YOU CAN HAVE YOUR OWN WEDDING AND MAKE ALL OF US BUY YOU THE PRESENTS.
HA HA HA!
...
WHAT-EVER.
ANYWAY, IS IT JUST ME, OR IS THE OTHER NAME ON YOUR WEDDING INVITE NOT THE SAME AS THE GIRL YOU WERE DATING FOR TEN YEARS?
OH, THAT? YEAH.
INSTANT SOBA

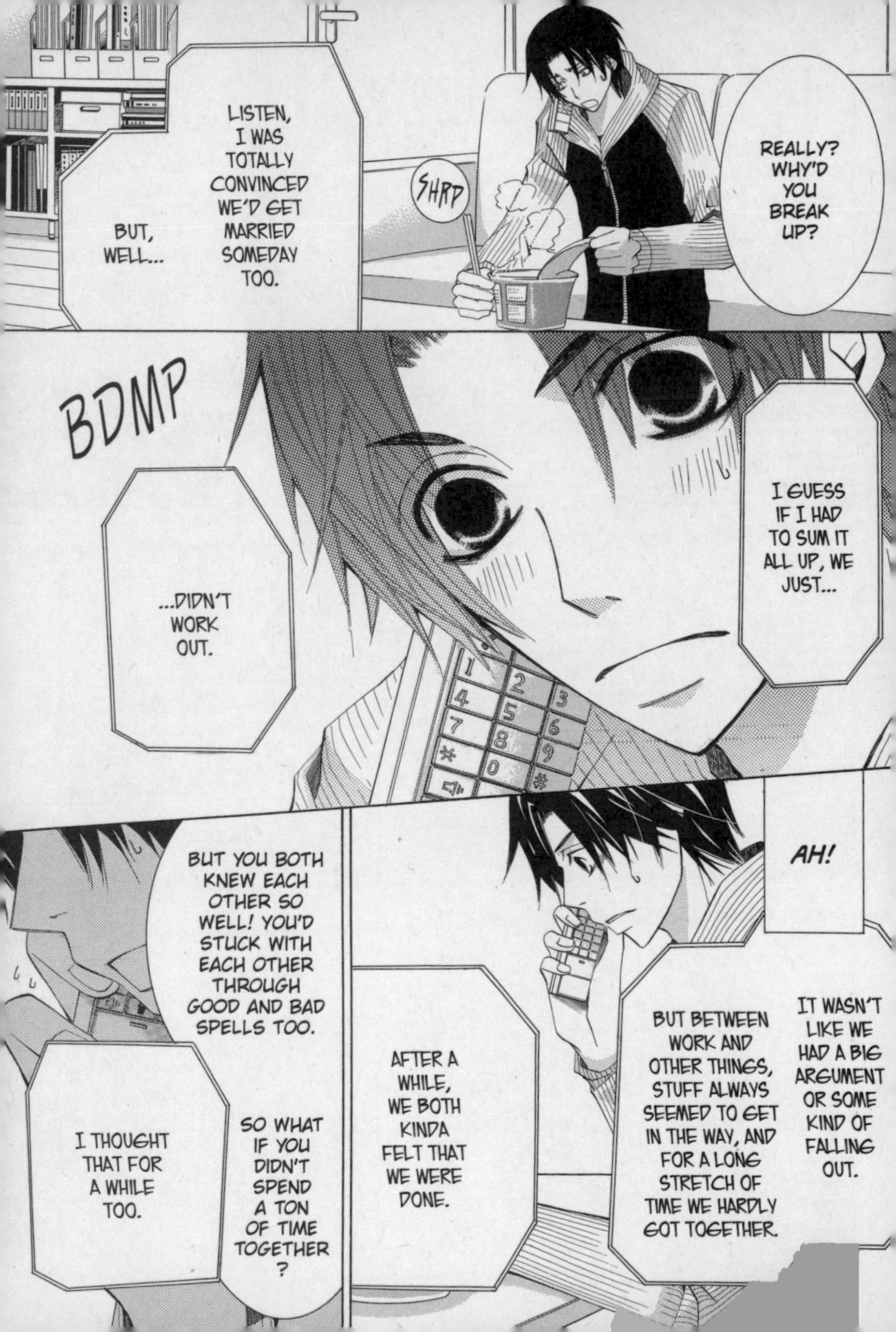
REALLY? WHY'D YOU BREAK UP?
SHRP
LISTEN, I WAS TOTALLY CONVINCED WE'D GET MARRIED SOMEDAY TOO.
BUT, WELL...
I GUESS IF I HAD TO SUM IT ALL UP, WE JUST...
BDMP
...DIDN'T WORK OUT.
AH!
IT WASN'T LIKE WE HAD A BIG ARGUMENT OR SOME KIND OF FALLING OUT.
BUT BETWEEN WORK AND OTHER THINGS, STUFF ALWAYS SEEMED TO GET IN THE WAY, AND FOR A LONG STRETCH OF TIME WE HARDLY GOT TOGETHER.
AFTER A WHILE, WE BOTH KINDA FELT THAT WE WERE DONE.
BUT YOU BOTH KNEW EACH OTHER SO WELL! YOU'D STUCK WITH EACH OTHER THROUGH GOOD AND BAD SPELLS TOO.
SO WHAT IF YOU DIDN'T SPEND A TON OF TIME TOGETHER?
I THOUGHT THAT FOR A WHILE TOO.

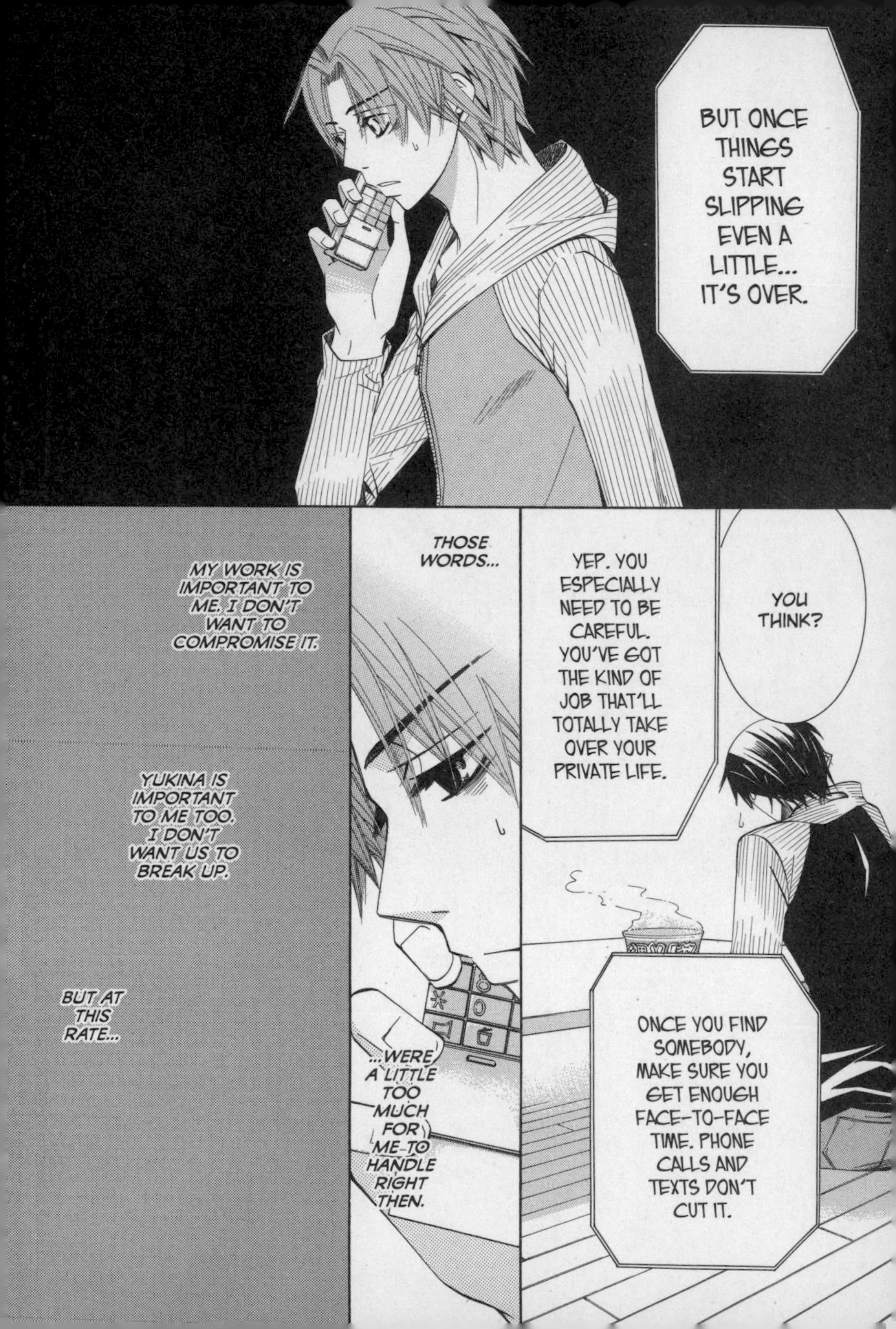
BUT ONCE THINGS START SLIPPING EVEN A LITTLE... IT'S OVER.
YOU THINK?
YEP. YOU ESPECIALLY NEED TO BE CAREFUL. YOU'VE GOT THE KIND OF JOB THAT'LL TOTALLY TAKE OVER YOUR PRIVATE LIFE.
ONCE YOU FIND SOMEBODY, MAKE SURE YOU GET ENOUGH FACE-TO-FACE TIME. PHONE CALLS AND TEXTS DON'T CUT IT.
THOSE WORDS...
...WERE A LITTLE TOO MUCH FOR ME TO HANDLE RIGHT THEN.
MY WORK IS IMPORTANT TO ME. I DON'T WANT TO COMPROMISE IT.
YUKINA IS IMPORTANT TO ME TOO. I DON'T WANT US TO BREAK UP.
BUT AT THIS RATE...

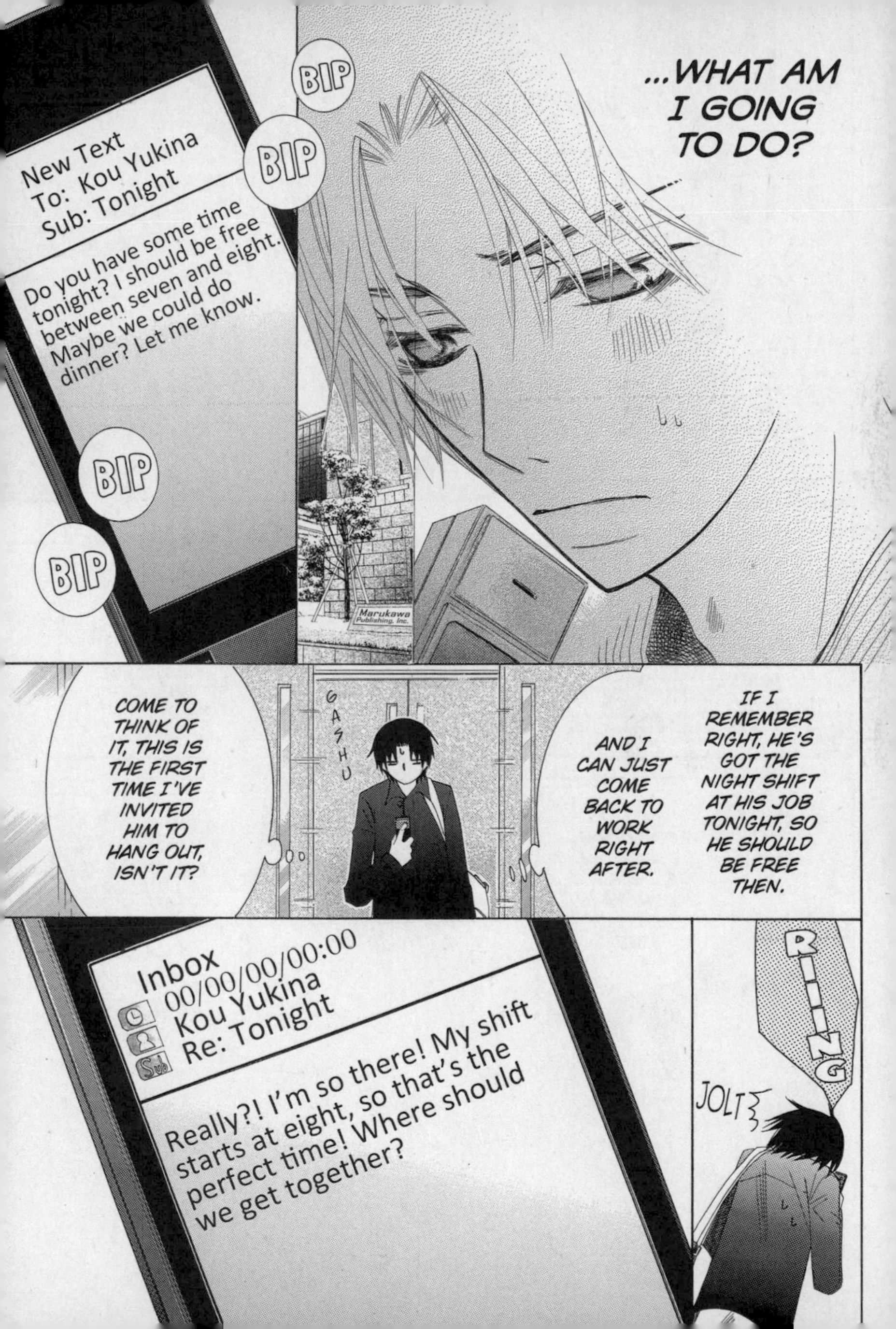
...WHAT AM I GOING TO DO?
BIP
BIP
BIP
BIP
New Text
To: Kou Yukina
Sub: Tonight
Do you have some time tonight? I should be free between seven and eight. Maybe we could do dinner? Let me know.
Marukawa Publishing, Inc.
IF I REMEMBER RIGHT, HE'S GOT THE NIGHT SHIFT AT HIS JOB TONIGHT, SO HE SHOULD BE FREE THEN.
AND I CAN JUST COME BACK TO WORK RIGHT AFTER.
GASHU
COME TO THINK OF IT, THIS IS THE FIRST TIME I'VE INVITED HIM TO HANG OUT, ISN'T IT?
RIIING
JOLT
Inbox
00/00/00/00:00
Kou Yukina
Re: Tonight
Really?! I'm so there! My shift starts at eight, so that's the perfect time! Where should we get together?

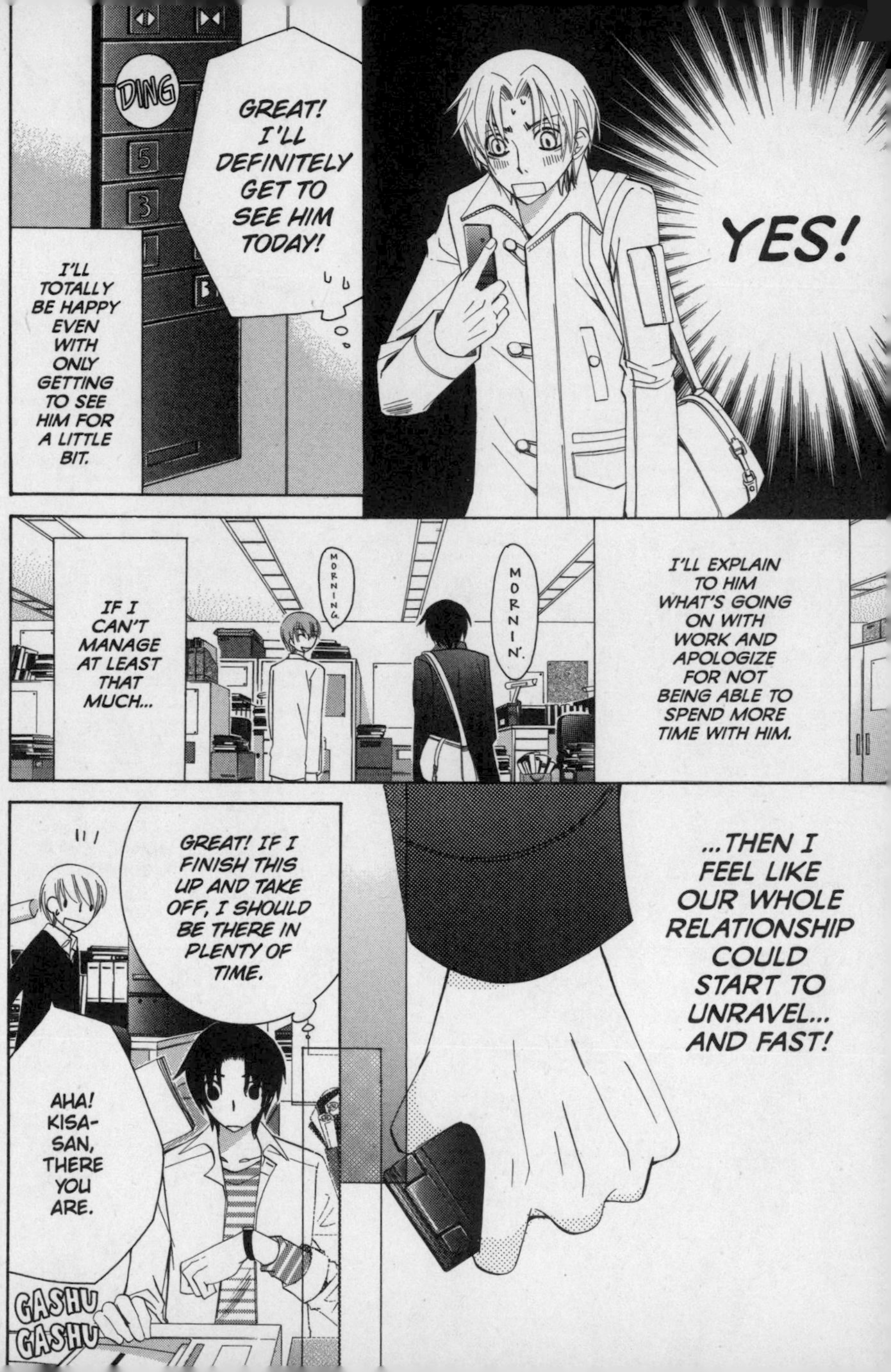

YES!
GREAT! I'LL DEFINITELY GET TO SEE HIM TODAY!
I'LL TOTALLY BE HAPPY EVEN WITH ONLY GETTING TO SEE HIM FOR A LITTLE BIT.
DING
I'LL EXPLAIN TO HIM WHAT'S GOING ON WITH WORK AND APOLOGIZE FOR NOT BEING ABLE TO SPEND MORE TIME WITH HIM.
MORNIN'.
MORNING.
IF I CAN'T MANAGE AT LEAST THAT MUCH...
...THEN I FEEL LIKE OUR WHOLE RELATIONSHIP COULD START TO UNRAVEL... AND FAST!
GREAT! IF I FINISH THIS UP AND TAKE OFF, I SHOULD BE THERE IN PLENTY OF TIME.
AHA! KISA-SAN, THERE YOU ARE.
GASHU GASHU

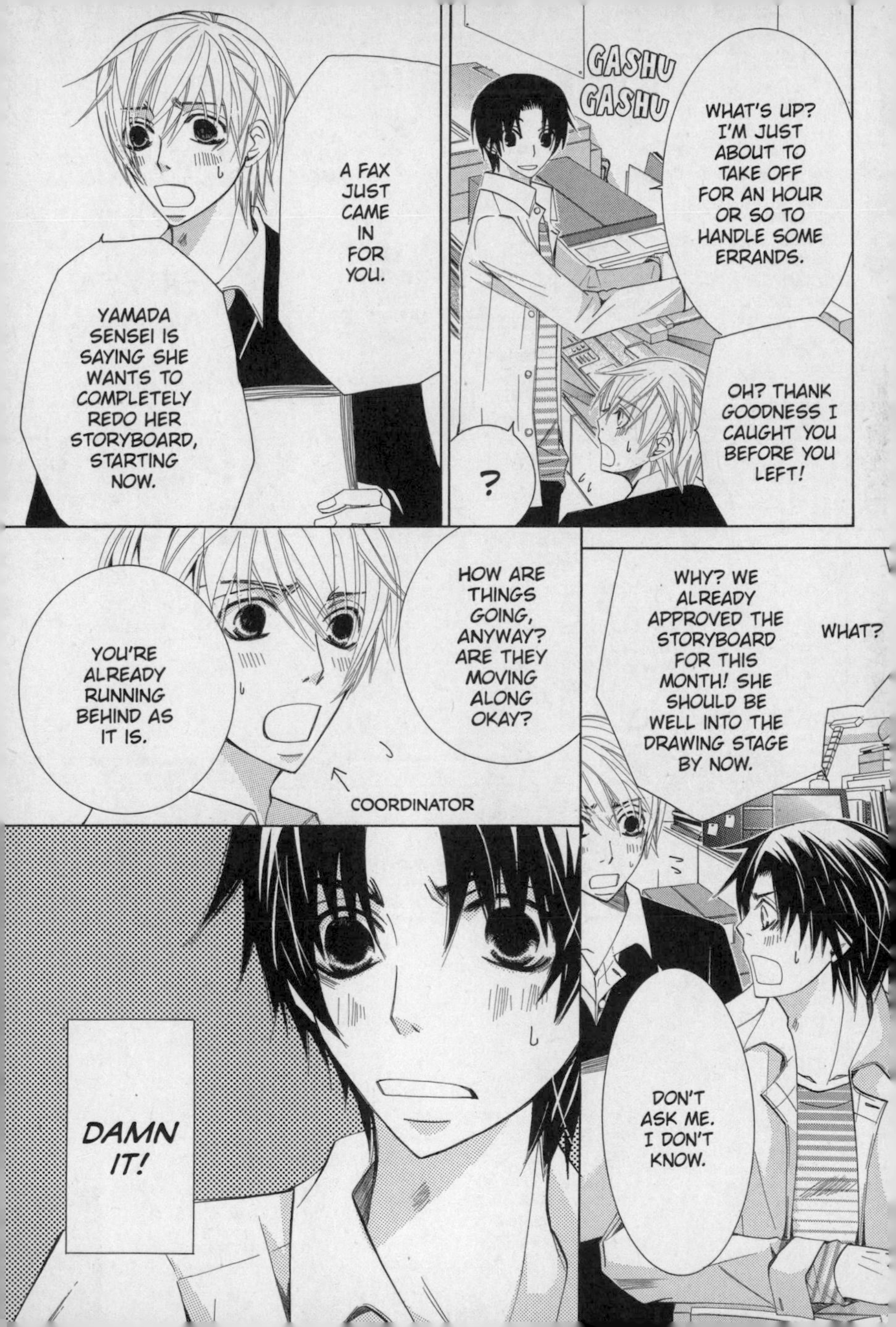
GASHU GASHU
WHAT'S UP? I'M JUST ABOUT TO TAKE OFF FOR AN HOUR OR SO TO HANDLE SOME ERRANDS.
OH? THANK GOODNESS I CAUGHT YOU BEFORE YOU LEFT!
?
A FAX JUST CAME IN FOR YOU.
YAMADA SENSEI IS SAYING SHE WANTS TO COMPLETELY REDO HER STORYBOARD, STARTING NOW.
WHAT?
WHY? WE ALREADY APPROVED THE STORYBOARD FOR THIS MONTH! SHE SHOULD BE WELL INTO THE DRAWING STAGE BY NOW.
DON'T ASK ME. I DON'T KNOW.
HOW ARE THINGS GOING, ANYWAY? ARE THEY MOVING ALONG OKAY?
YOU'RE ALREADY RUNNING BEHIND AS IT IS.
COORDINATOR
DAMN IT!

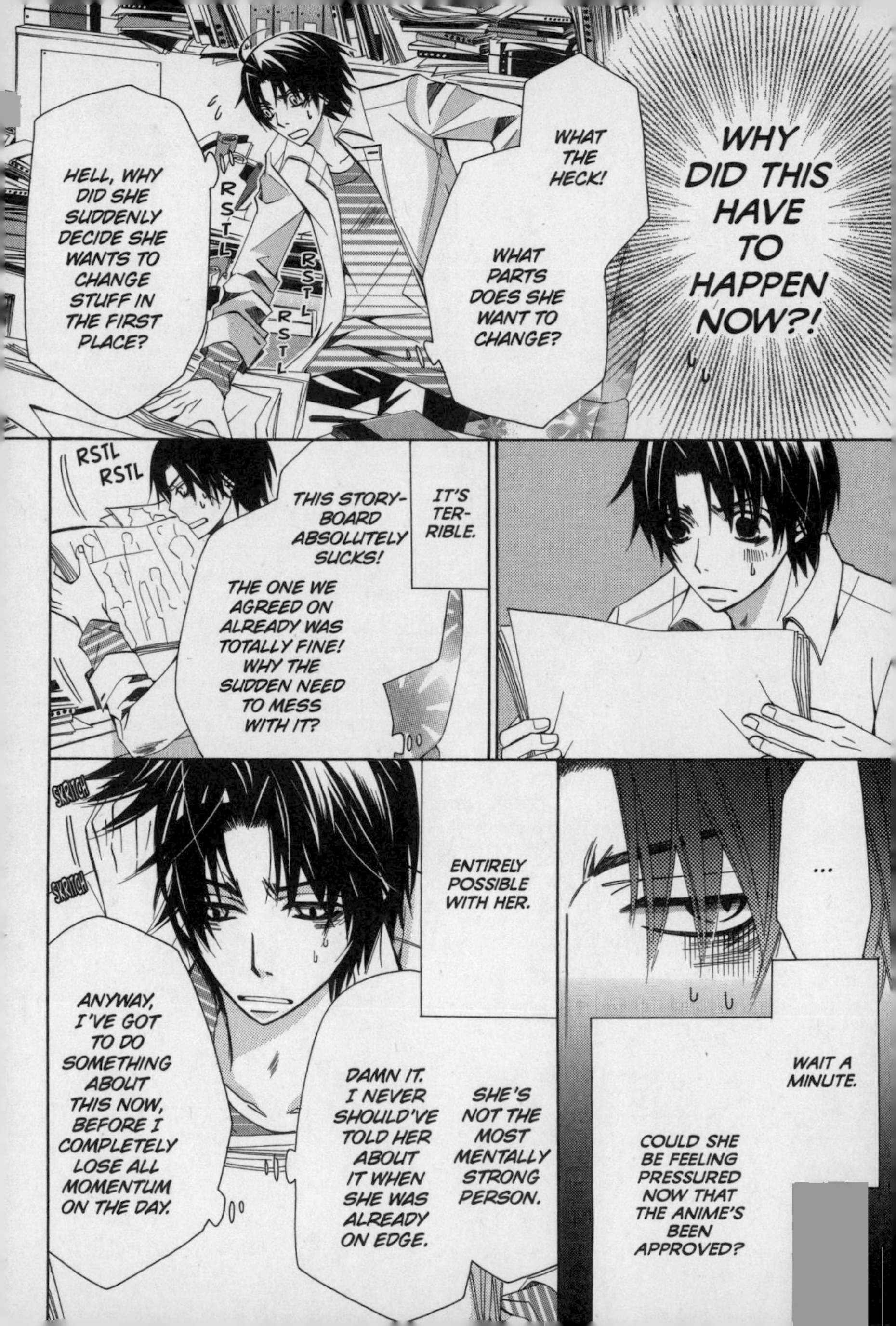
WHY DID THIS HAVE TO HAPPEN NOW?!
WHAT THE HECK!
WHAT PARTS DOES SHE WANT TO CHANGE?
RSTL RSTL RSTL
RSTL
HELL, WHY DID SHE SUDDENLY DECIDE SHE WANTS TO CHANGE STUFF IN THE FIRST PLACE?
IT'S TER-RIBLE.
THIS STORY-BOARD ABSOLUTELY SUCKS!
THE ONE WE AGREED ON ALREADY WAS TOTALLY FINE! WHY THE SUDDEN NEED TO MESS WITH IT?
RSTL RSTL
...
WAIT A MINUTE.
COULD SHE BE FEELING PRESSURED NOW THAT THE ANIME'S BEEN APPROVED?
ENTIRELY POSSIBLE WITH HER.
SHE'S NOT THE MOST MENTALLY STRONG PERSON.
DAMN IT. I NEVER SHOULD'VE TOLD HER ABOUT IT WHEN SHE WAS ALREADY ON EDGE.
ANYWAY, I'VE GOT TO DO SOMETHING ABOUT THIS NOW, BEFORE I COMPLETELY LOSE ALL MOMENTUM ON THE DAY.
SKRITCH
SKRITCH

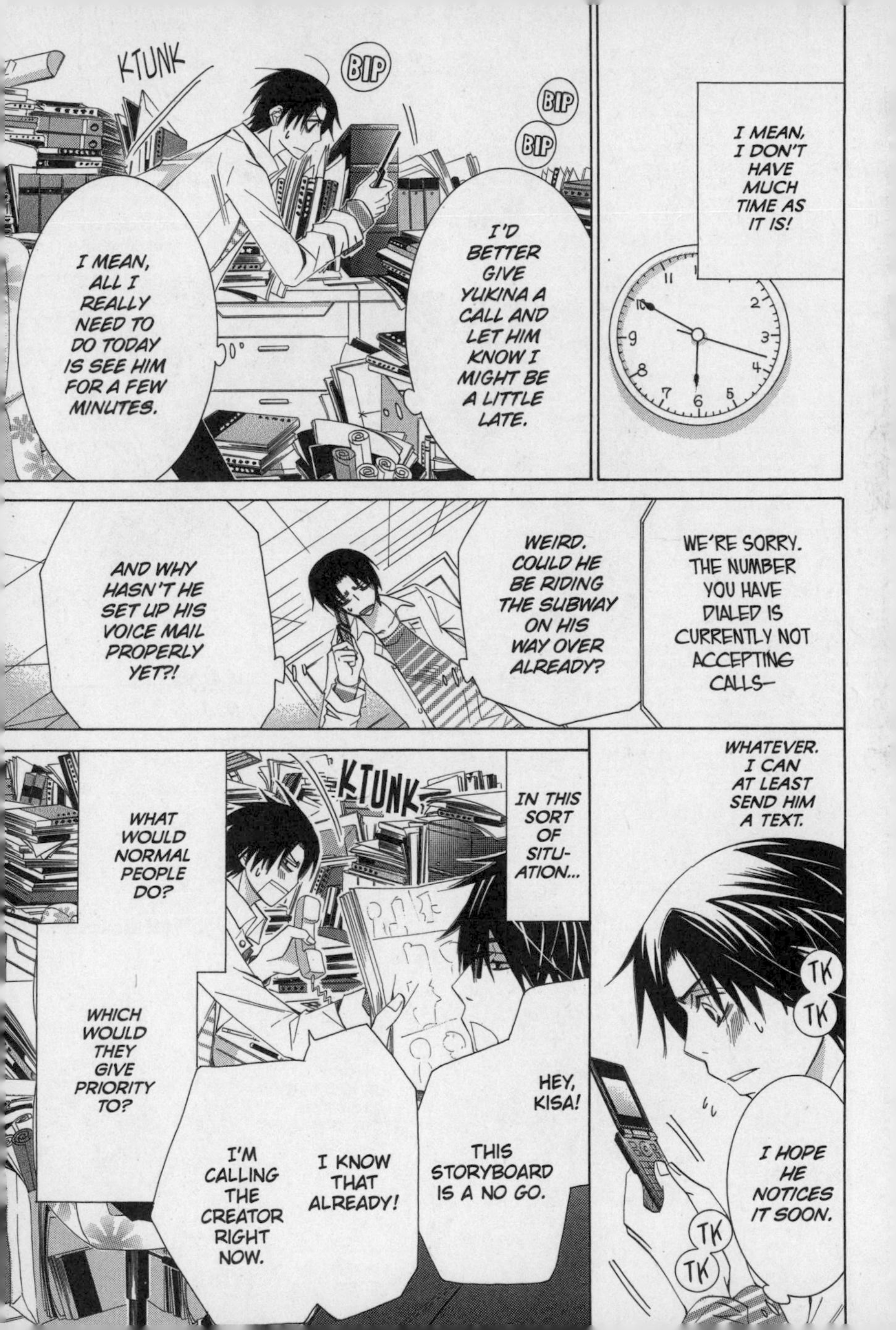
I MEAN, I DON'T HAVE MUCH TIME AS IT IS!
BIP
BIP
BIP
KTUNK
I'D BETTER GIVE YUKINA A CALL AND LET HIM KNOW I MIGHT BE A LITTLE LATE.
I MEAN, ALL I REALLY NEED TO DO TODAY IS SEE HIM FOR A FEW MINUTES.
WE'RE SORRY. THE NUMBER YOU HAVE DIALED IS CURRENTLY NOT ACCEPTING CALLS—
WEIRD. COULD HE BE RIDING THE SUBWAY ON HIS WAY OVER ALREADY?
AND WHY HASN'T HE SET UP HIS VOICE MAIL PROPERLY YET?!
WHATEVER. I CAN AT LEAST SEND HIM A TEXT.
TK
TK
I HOPE HE NOTICES IT SOON.
TK
TK
IN THIS SORT OF SITU-ATION...
KTUNK
WHAT WOULD NORMAL PEOPLE DO?
HEY, KISA!
THIS STORYBOARD IS A NO GO.
I KNOW THAT ALREADY!
I'M CALLING THE CREATOR RIGHT NOW.
WHICH WOULD THEY GIVE PRIORITY TO?

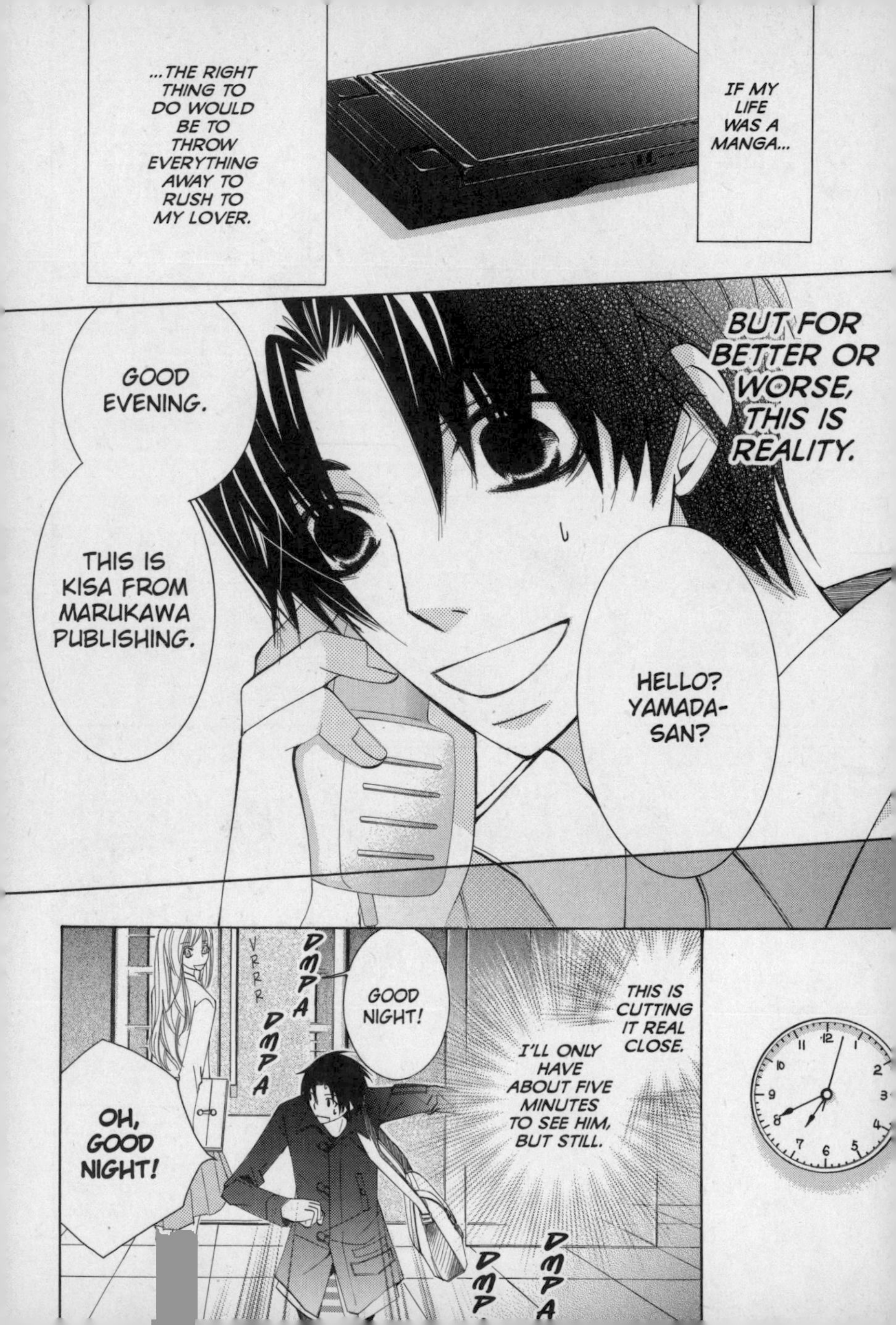
IF MY LIFE WAS A MANGA...
...THE RIGHT THING TO DO WOULD BE TO THROW EVERYTHING AWAY TO RUSH TO MY LOVER.
BUT FOR BETTER OR WORSE, THIS IS REALITY.
HELLO? YAMADA-SAN?
GOOD EVENING.
THIS IS KISA FROM MARUKAWA PUBLISHING.
THIS IS CUTTING IT REAL CLOSE.
I'LL ONLY HAVE ABOUT FIVE MINUTES TO SEE HIM, BUT STILL.
GOOD NIGHT!
DMPA
VRRR
DMPA
OH, GOOD NIGHT!
DMPA
DMPA
DMP

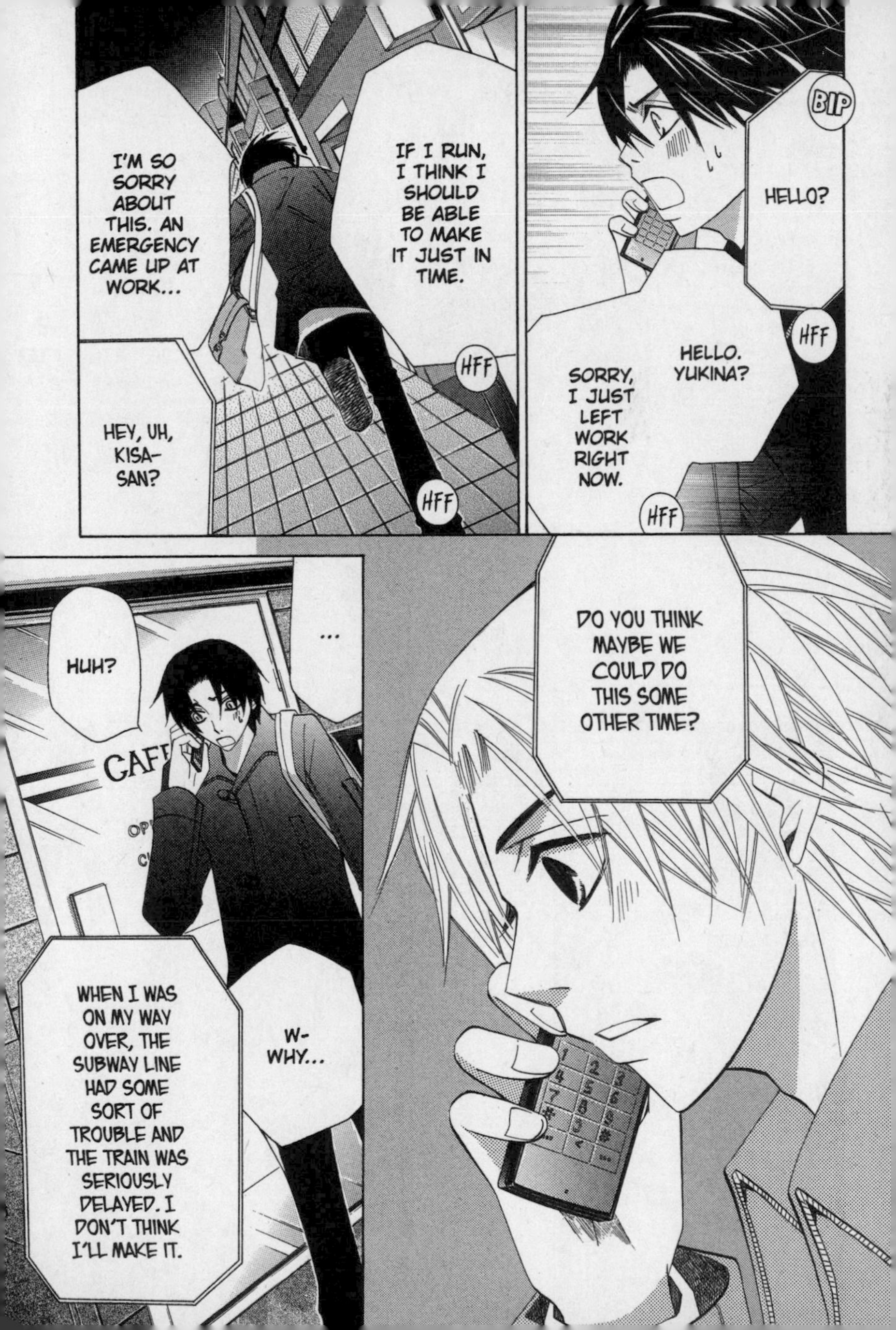
BIP
HELLO?
HFF
HELLO. YUKINA?
SORRY, I JUST LEFT WORK RIGHT NOW.
HFF
IF I RUN, I THINK I SHOULD BE ABLE TO MAKE IT JUST IN TIME.
I'M SO SORRY ABOUT THIS. AN EMERGENCY CAME UP AT WORK...
HFF
HEY, UH, KISA-SAN?
HFF
DO YOU THINK MAYBE WE COULD DO THIS SOME OTHER TIME?
...
HUH?
CAFE
W-WHY...
WHEN I WAS ON MY WAY OVER, THE SUBWAY LINE HAD SOME SORT OF TROUBLE AND THE TRAIN WAS SERIOUSLY DELAYED. I DON'T THINK I'LL MAKE IT.

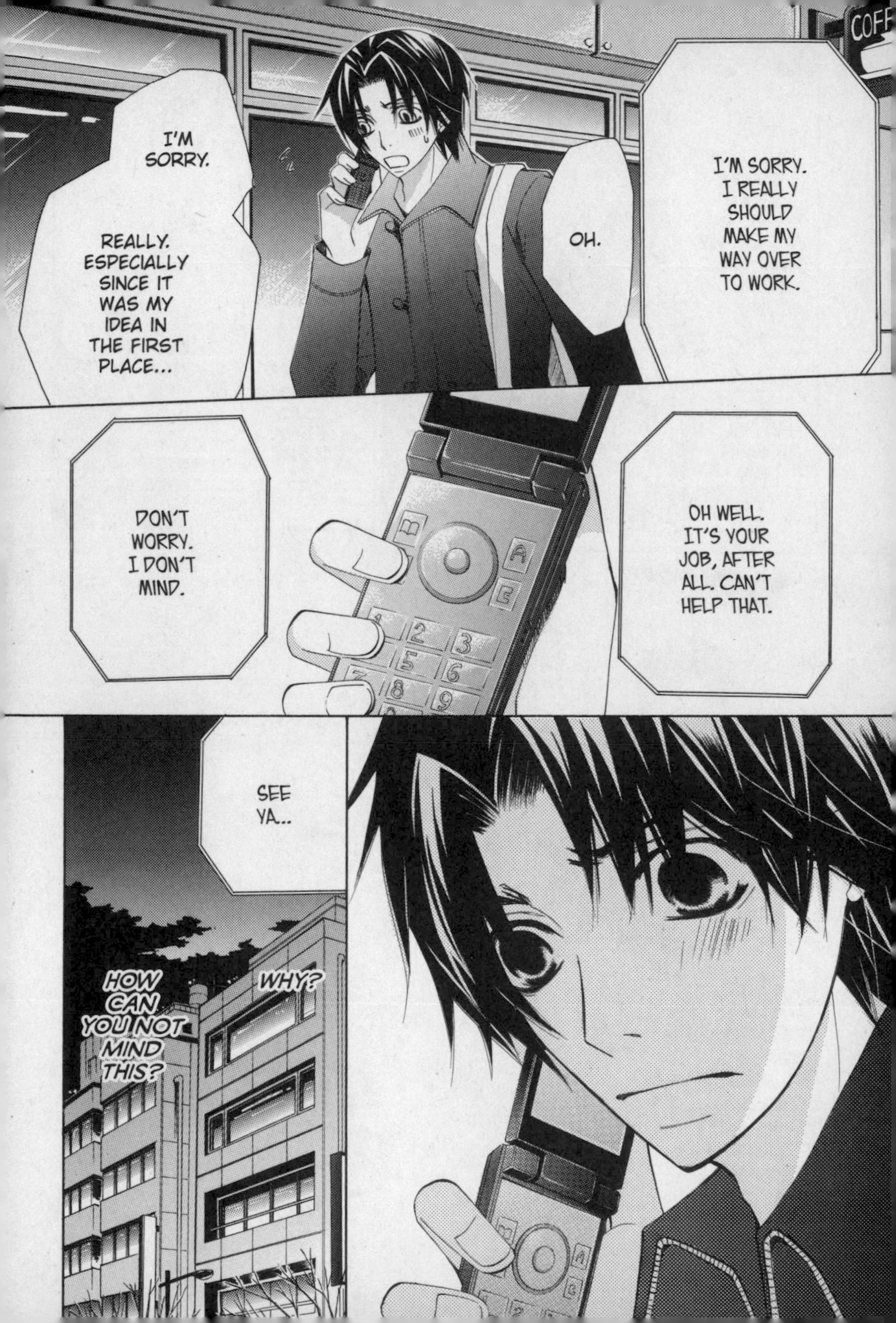
I'M SORRY. I REALLY SHOULD MAKE MY WAY OVER TO WORK.
OH.
I'M SORRY.
REALLY. ESPECIALLY SINCE IT WAS MY IDEA IN THE FIRST PLACE...
OH WELL. IT'S YOUR JOB, AFTER ALL. CAN'T HELP THAT.
DON'T WORRY. I DON'T MIND.
SEE YA...
WHY?
HOW CAN YOU NOT MIND THIS?

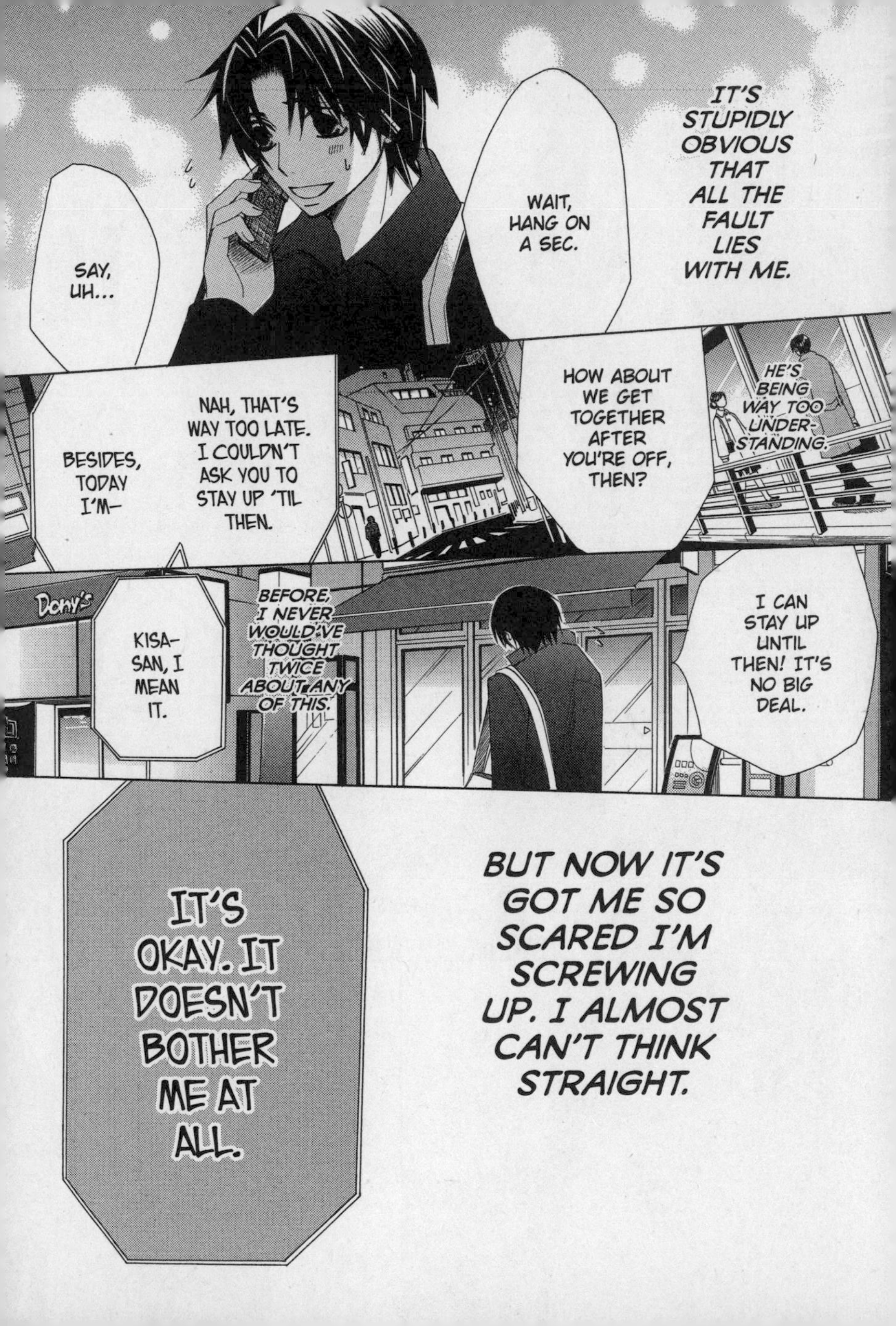

IT'S STUPIDLY OBVIOUS THAT ALL THE FAULT LIES WITH ME.
WAIT, HANG ON A SEC.
SAY, UH...
HE'S BEING WAY TOO UNDER-STANDING.
HOW ABOUT WE GET TOGETHER AFTER YOU'RE OFF, THEN?
NAH, THAT'S WAY TOO LATE. I COULDN'T ASK YOU TO STAY UP 'TIL THEN.
BESIDES, TODAY I'M—
I CAN STAY UP UNTIL THEN! IT'S NO BIG DEAL.
BEFORE, I NEVER WOULD'VE THOUGHT TWICE ABOUT ANY OF THIS.
KISA-SAN, I MEAN IT.
Dony's
BUT NOW IT'S GOT ME SO SCARED I'M SCREWING UP. I ALMOST CAN'T THINK STRAIGHT.
IT'S OKAY. IT DOESN'T BOTHER ME AT ALL.

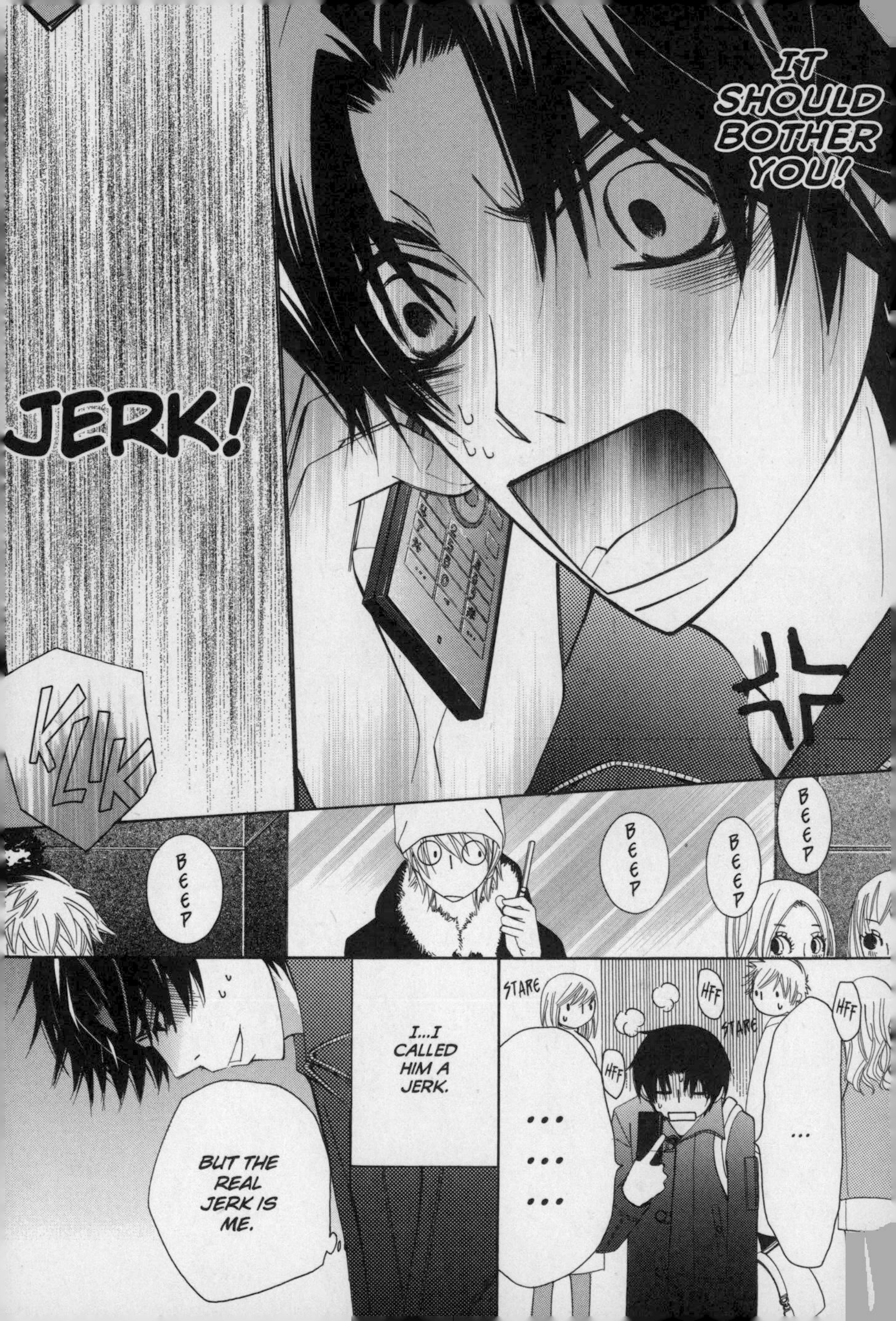
IT SHOULD BOTHER YOU!
JERK!
KLIK
BEEP
BEEP
BEEP
BEEP
HFF
...
STARE
HFF
STARE
HFF
...
...
...
I...I CALLED HIM A JERK.
BUT THE REAL JERK IS ME.

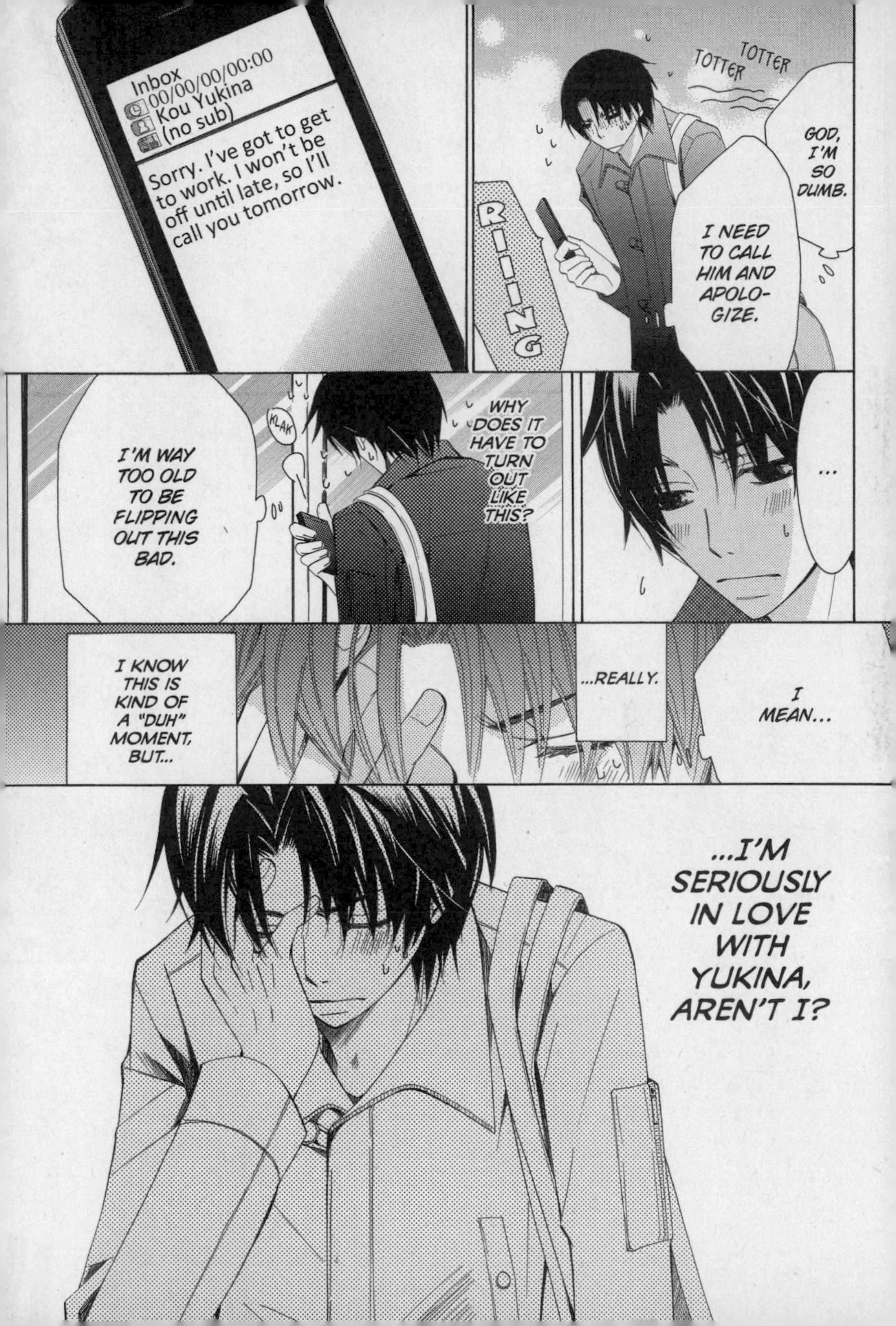
TOTTER TOTTER
GOD, I'M SO DUMB.
I NEED TO CALL HIM AND APOLOGIZE.
RIIIING
Inbox
00/00/00/00:00
Kou Yukina
(no sub)
Sorry. I've got to get to work. I won't be off until late, so I'll call you tomorrow.
...
WHY DOES IT HAVE TO TURN OUT LIKE THIS?
KLAK
I'M WAY TOO OLD TO BE FLIPPING OUT THIS BAD.
I MEAN...
...REALLY.
I KNOW THIS IS KIND OF A "DUH" MOMENT, BUT...
...I'M SERIOUSLY IN LOVE WITH YUKINA, AREN'T I?

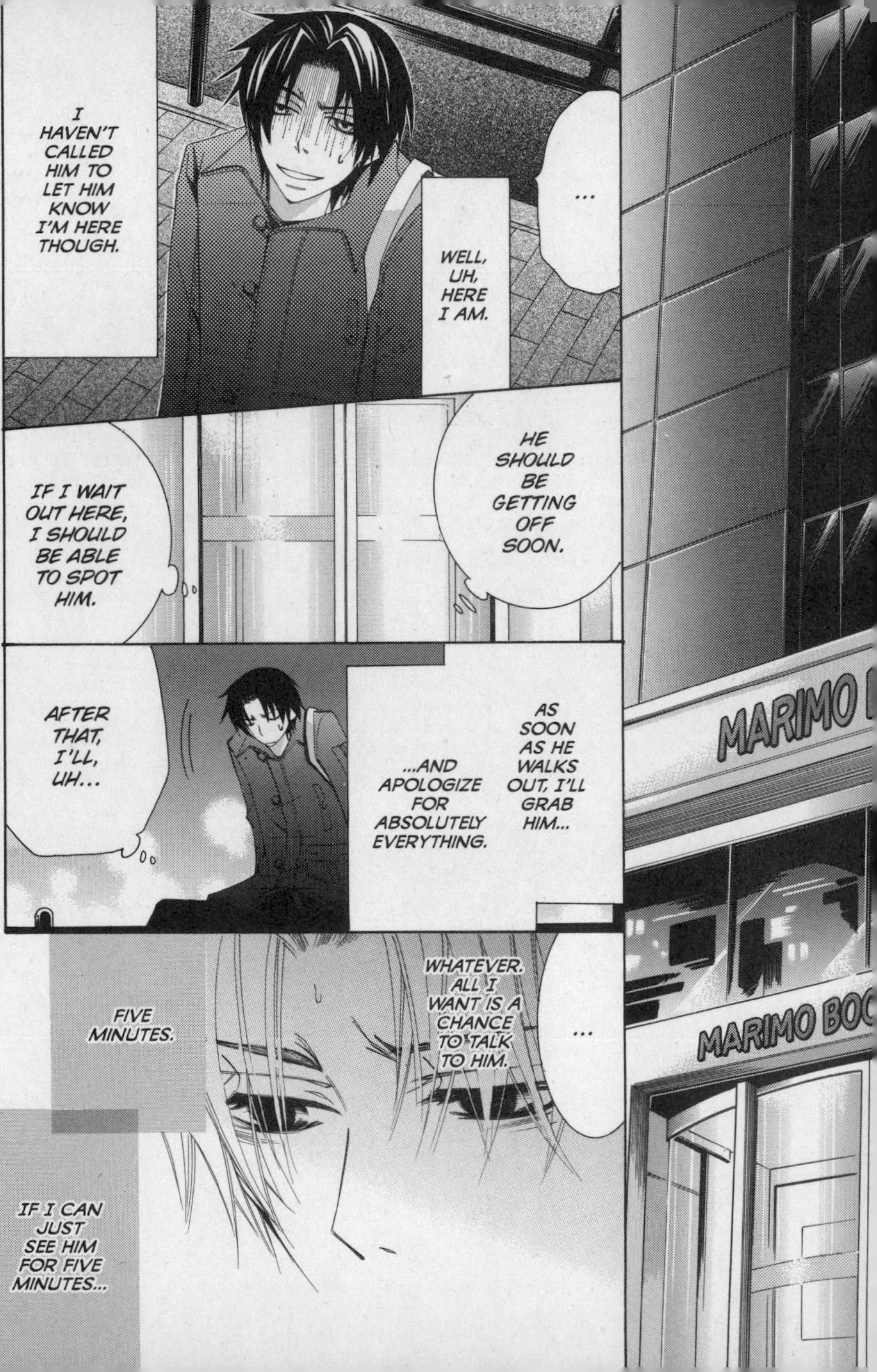
MARIMO
...
WELL, UH, HERE I AM.
I HAVEN'T CALLED HIM TO LET HIM KNOW I'M HERE THOUGH.
HE SHOULD BE GETTING OFF SOON.
IF I WAIT OUT HERE, I SHOULD BE ABLE TO SPOT HIM.
AS SOON AS HE WALKS OUT, I'LL GRAB HIM...
...AND APOLOGIZE FOR ABSOLUTELY EVERYTHING.
AFTER THAT, I'LL, UH...
...
WHATEVER. ALL I WANT IS A CHANCE TO TALK TO HIM.
FIVE MINUTES.
IF I CAN JUST SEE HIM FOR FIVE MINUTES...

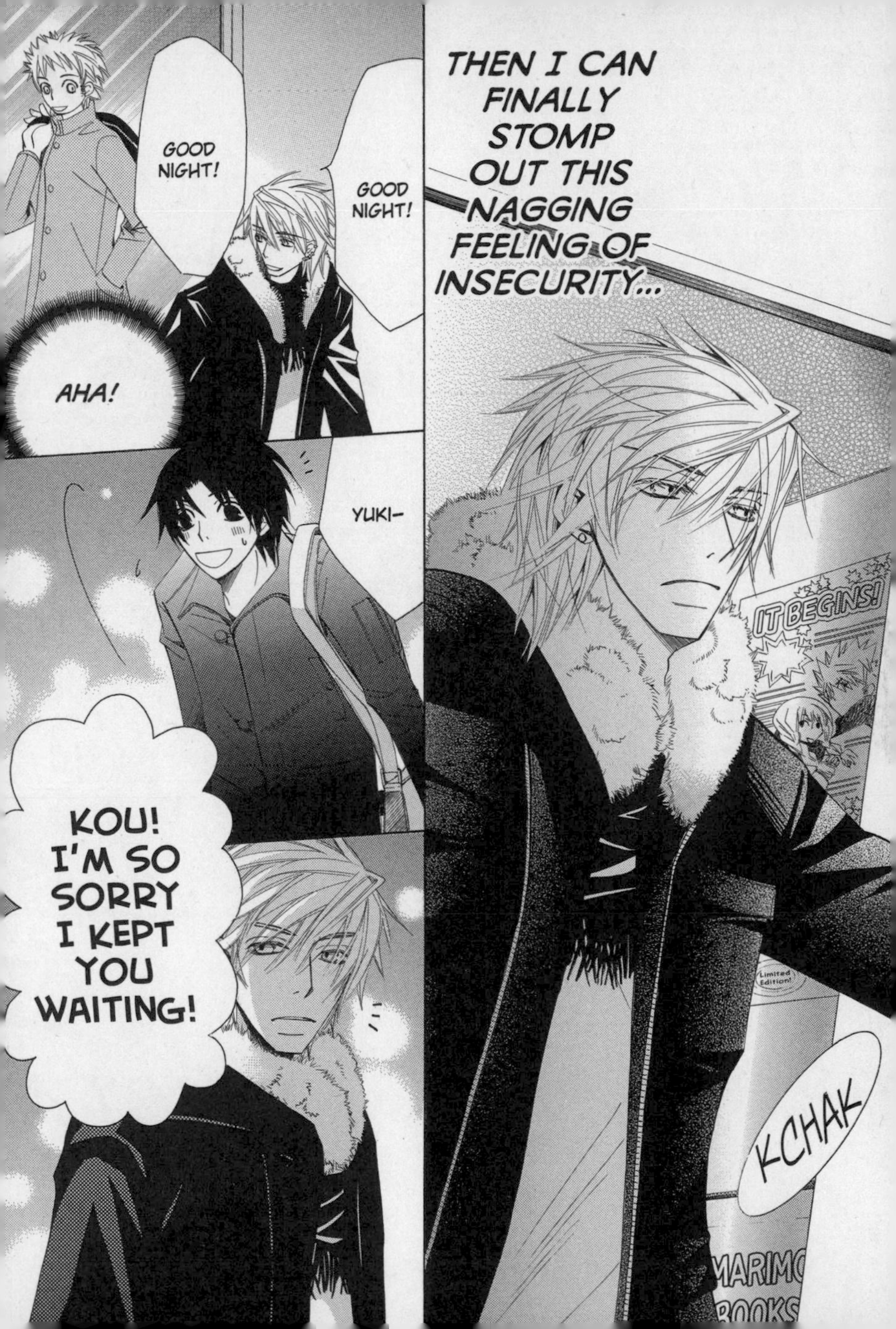
THEN I CAN FINALLY STOMP OUT THIS NAGGING FEELING OF INSECURITY...
IT BEGINS!
Limited Edition!
KCHAK
GOOD NIGHT!
GOOD NIGHT!
AHA!
YUKI-
KOU! I'M SO SORRY I KEPT YOU WAITING!

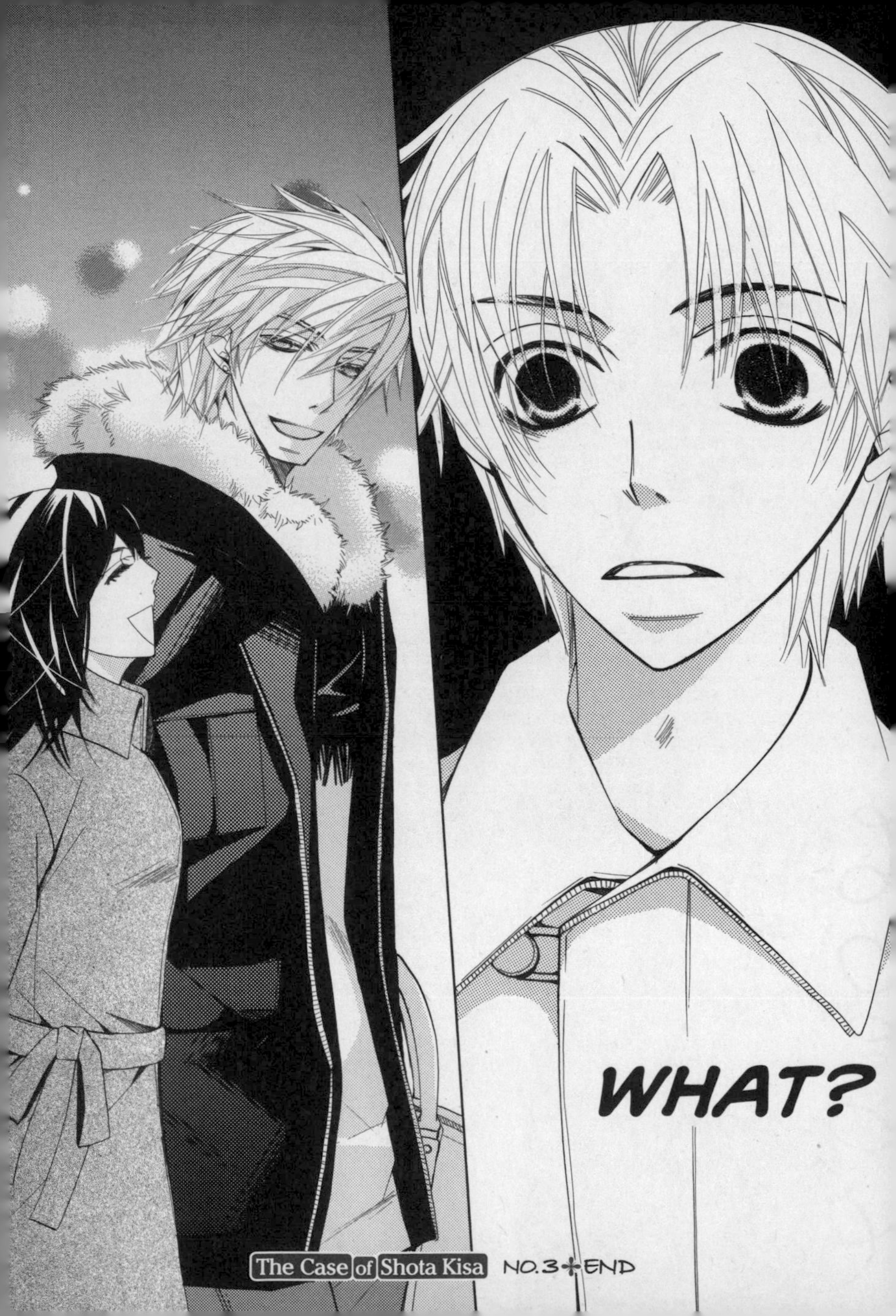
WHAT?
The Case of Shota Kisa NO.3 END

LOOK! THIS LITTLE MACHINE IS SUPPOSED TO RUN AROUND ON YOUR FLOOR AND CLEAN IT FOR YOU! IT'S ON SALE, SO THAT MEANS IT'S A GOOD BUY, RIGHT?
BEFORE YOU TURN IT ON, YOU'D FIRST HAVE TO PICK UP EVERYTHING OFF OF YOUR FLOOR. ARE YOU SURE YOU'D DO THAT?
...
Catalogue
ROOMBO!
CLEANS YOUR FLOORS FOR YOU!
BIG SALE!
ROBOTIC FLOOR SWEEPER

Hello. It's good to meet you! My name is Shungiku Nakamura. Thank you for buying volume 4 of *The World's Greatest First Love ~The Case of Ritsu Onodera~*! Thanks to everyone's kind and generous support, we've made it up to volume 4.

Also, there's going to be an anime! Details should soon be forthcoming from the anthology and other sources, so please keep an eye out.

Ruby Bunko is also releasing *The World's Greatest First Love ~The Case of Chiaki Yoshino~*.

If you are interested in that, please check it out! Then there's *Junjo Romantica*, which is also connected to Marukawa Publishing. Check that out too!

If you have any thoughts or comments, I would love to hear them. This story will keep chugging along for a bit yet, so I hope you'll keep reading. See you later!

2010 NAKAMURA

Current Situation:

I'm moving. I decided to do it because I was sick of the setting sun shining right in on me, but due to this, that, and the other thing, I'm stuck in a spot where it'll glare back in on me again...
Sigh. Ah well. Such is life.

GLARE

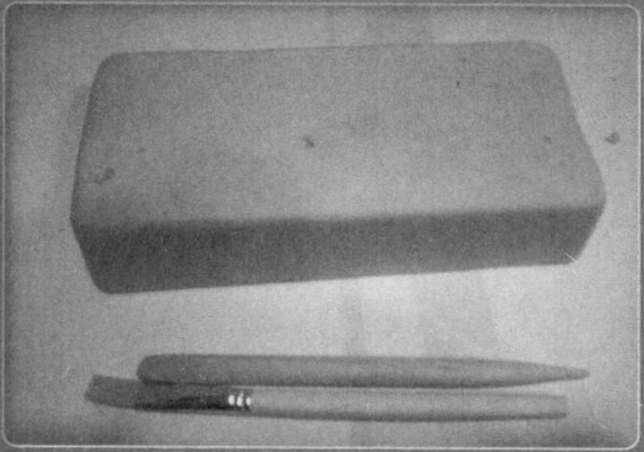

A friend got me this Egyptian excavation kit as a souvenir. I think I'm going to "dig in" right now! Pharaoh!

About the Author

Shungiku Nakamura
DOB December 13
Sagittarius
Blood Type O

The World's Greatest First Love:
The Case of Ritsu Onodera
Volume 4
SuBLime Manga Edition

Story and Art by **Shungiku Nakamura**

Translation—**Adrienne Beck**
Touch-up Art and Lettering—**NRP Studios**
Cover and Graphic Design—**Fawn Lau**
Editor—**Jennifer LeBlanc**

SEKAIICHI HATSUKOI ~ONODERA RITSU NO BAAI~ Volume 4
© Shungiku NAKAMURA 2010
First published in Japan in 2010 by KADOKAWA CORPORATION, Tokyo.
English translation rights arranged with KADOKAWA CORPORATION,
Tokyo.

ASUKA
COMICS
CL$_X^D$

Printed in the U.S.A.

Published by SuBLime Manga
P.O. Box 77010
San Francisco, CA 94107

10 9 8 7 6 5 4 3
First printing, March 2016
Third printing, April 2023

PARENTAL ADVISORY
THE WORLD'S GREATEST FIRST LOVE is rated M for Mature and is
recommended for mature readers. This volume contains graphic
MATURE   imagery and mature themes.

www.SuBLimeManga.com

For more information

on all our products, along with the most up-to-date news on releases, series announcements, and contests, please visit us at:

SuBLimeManga.com

twitter.com/**SuBLimeManga**

facebook.com/**SuBLimeManga**

SuBLimeManga.tumblr.com

SUBLIME
MANGA

A collection of masterful, sensual stories by Kou Yoneda!

NightS

Story & Art by Kou YONEDA

In the title story, Masato Karashima is a "transporter," a man paid to smuggle anything from guns to drugs to people. When he's hired by yakuza gang member Masaki Hozumi, he finds himself attracted to the older man, and what starts out as a business transaction quickly spirals into a cat-and-mouse game of lust and deception. In "Emotion Spectrum," a high-school student tries to be a good wingman for a classmate, with an unexpected result, while "Reply" is told from the alternating perspectives of an emotionally reserved salesman and the shy mechanic who's in love with him.

SUBLIME